Perilous Passage

WORLD SOCIAL CHANGE

Series Editor: Mark Selden

Perilous Passage: Mankind and the Global Ascendance of Capital
Amiya Kumar Bagchi

Water Frontier: Commerce and the Chinese in the Lower Mekong Region, 1750–1880
Edited by Nola Cooke and Li Tana

Empire to Nation: Historical Perspectives on the Making of the Modern World
Edited by Joseph W. Esherick, Hasan Kayali, and Eric Van Young

First Globalization: The Eurasian Exchange, 1500–1800
Geoffrey C. Gunn

Istanbul: Between the Global and the Local
Edited by Caglar Keyder

The Origins of the Modern World: A Global and Ecological Narrative
Robert B. Marks

The Politics of Greed: How Privatization Structured Politics in Central and Eastern Europe
Andrew Schwartz

Leaving China: Media, Mobility, and Transnational Imagination
Wanning Sun

Masters of Terror: Indonesia's Military and Violence in East Timor
Edited by Richard Tanter, Gerry van Klinken, and Desmond Ball

Through the Prism of Slavery: Labor, Capital, and World Economy
Dale W. Tomich

Politics and the Past: On Repairing Historical Injustices
Edited by John Torpey

Perilous Passage

Mankind and the Global Ascendancy of Capital

Amiya Kumar Bagchi

ROWMAN & LITTLEFIELD PUBLISHERS, INC.
Lanham • Boulder • New York • Toronto • Plymouth, UK

ROWMAN & LITTLEFIELD PUBLISHERS, INC.

Published in the United States of America
by Rowman & Littlefield Publishers, Inc.
A wholly owned subsidiary of The Rowman & Littlefield Publishing Group, Inc.
4501 Forbes Boulevard, Suite 200, Lanham, Maryland 20706
www.rowmanlittlefield.com

Estover Road, Plymouth PL6 7PY, UK

British Library Cataloguing in Publication Information Available

The hardback edition of this book was previously cataloged
by the Library of Congress as follows:

Bagchi, Amiya Kumar.
  Perilous passage : mankind and the global ascendancy of capital / Amiya Kumar
Bagchi
    p. cm. — (World social change)
    Includes bibliographical references and index.
    1. Capitalism—History. 2. Economic development—Social aspects. 3.
Eurocentrism—History. 4. Imperialism—History. 5. Equality—History. 6. Quality of
life—History. 7. Economic History. I. Title: Mankind and the global ascendancy of
capital. II. Title. III. Series.
  HB501.B224 2005
  306.3'42'091821—dc22
                                                                    2005016224
    ISBN-13: 978-0-7425-3920-4 (cloth : alk. paper)
    ISBN-10: 0-7425-3920-2 (cloth : alk. paper)
    ISBN-13: 978-0-7425-3921-1 (pbk : alk. paper)
    ISBN-10: 0-7425-3921-0 (pbk : alk. paper)

Printed in the United States of America

∞™ The paper used in this publication meets the minimum requirements of American
National Standard for Information Sciences—Permanence of Paper for Printed Library
Materials, ANSI/NISO Z39.48-1992.

Contents

List of Tables   ix

Preface   xi

Acknowledgments   xxiii

Abbreviations   xxv

**Part I: Conceptual Issues: Human Development and
Capitalist Growth**

1 History of Human Development as the Subject of History   3

2 Construction of the European Miracle   21

3 Profit Seeking under Actually Existing Capitalism and
       Human Development   35

**Part II: Capitalist Competition and
Human Development in Europe**

4 Race for Dominance among the Western European Countries
       since the Sixteenth Century   53

5 Population Growth and Mortality between the Sixteenth and
       Nineteenth Centuries: A First Look   77

6 The Netherlands: Rise and Fall of a Hegemonic Power   89

7 Delayed Transition to a Low-Mortality Regime in
       Europe and North America   101

8 Literacy in Western Europe since the Sixteenth Century   121

**Part III: The World beyond Europe in the Age of Emergence of
European Dominance**

9 China's Economic Development and Quality of Life between
       the Sixteenth and Eighteenth Centuries   135

10 India under Mughal Rule and After   145

11 Conducting Trade in Asia before and after the
        European Advent   167

12 Reconsidering Japanese Exceptionalism   179

13 Capitalist Competition, Colonialism, and the Physical
        Well-Being of Non-European Peoples   195

14 Civilizing Mission and Racialization: From
        Native Americans to Asians   209

15 Civilizing Mission in Lands Taken by European Settlers from
        the Original Inhabitants   221

16 Intercontinental Resource Flows Sustaining the
        Ascent of the European Powers   229

17 Colonial Tribute and Profits, 1870s Onward   239

18 Demographic Disasters in the Colonies and Semicolonies in
        the Heyday of European Colonialism   249

**Part IV: The Twentieth Century: Antisystemic Struggles, Wars,
and Challenges to Global Capital**

19 Setting the Stage for Megawars   267

20 Revolution, Nazism, Japanese Militarism, and World War II   279

21 Imperialism and Wars in the Late Twentieth Century 291

22 Capitalism and Uneven Development in the Twentieth Century 305

23 Destruction and Renewal in the Neoliberal Global Order 319

24 Contradictions, Challenges, and Resistance 327

References 339

Index 383

About the Author 395

List of Tables

4.1 Increase in Military Manpower in European Countries, 1470s–1700s (Figures in Thousands) — 73

5.1 Population of Selected Regions of the World, 1500–1900 (in Millions) — 78

5.2 Population, Crude Birth Rate (CBR), and Crude Death Rate (CDR) in France, 1740–1814 — 80

5.3 Crude Birth Rate (CBR) and Crude Death Rate (CDR) in Four Regions of Germany, 1750–1809 — 82

7.1 Total Intercontinental Emigration from Europe, 1846–1924 — 116

13.1 A Conservative Estimate of the Population of the Americas in 1492 (Figures in Thousands) — 197

13.2 Native Population in Central Mexico, 1518–1605 (in Millions) — 197

13.3 Slave Exports from Africa: The Atlantic Trade, 1450–1900 — 200

13.4 Numbers of Indentured Laborers Exported from China, India, and Elsewhere, 1831–1920 — 203

13.5 Average Mortality of Indian labor, 1871–1910 (Death Rate per Thousand per Year) — 203

13.6 Per Pupil Expenditures on Instruction, Selected Southern States (in 1950 U.S. dollars) — 206

13.7 Life Expectancy at Birth (in years) of Whites and African Americans in the United States, Selected Years, 1900–2001 — 207

16.1 Estimated Average Annual Production of American Silver and Movement of Silver Equivalent into and out of Europe, 1501–1800 (in Metric Tons) — 231

16.2   Estimates of Average Annual Exports of Silver and Silver
       Equivalent from Europe, 1600–1780 (in Metric tons)   232
17.1   Alternative Estimates of the Total Tribute Extracted and
       Profits Made by Europeans Connected with India and
       Burma, 1871–1916 (in Thousands of Pounds)   241
17.2   Accumulating Balances of Unrecompensed Indian Surpluses
       (Figures from Table 17.1) Compounded at 4 Percent
       (in Thousands of Pounds)   242
17.3   Estimated Export Surplus (Annual Averages) Generated by
       Indonesia after Taking European Profits into Account
       (in Million Guilders)   244
17.4   Figures of Annual Average Export Surplus Generated by
       Indonesia (in Million Guilders)   245
17.5   Burden of Interest Payments on the Egyptian Economy,
       1880–1919 (Currency in Egyptian Pounds)   247
18.1   Rates of Growth of Population and Expectation of Life in
       India as a Whole, 1891–1941   260
18.2   Expectation of Life at Birth (in Years) in Different Regions
       of India, 1881–1921   261

Preface

This book traverses the momentous period of history that witnessed the rise of the states on the North Atlantic seaboard to the position of the most prosperous and powerful nations in the world and their eventual domination over the rest of the world. It brings together the insights of the historians of war and those of Marxist and world-system theorists to characterize the emergence and operation of actually existing capitalism as a system that engages in unlimited combat, backed when necessary by arms, for the conquest of labor power, nonlabor resources, and markets rather than one that operates on the principle of free markets. But in tracing this history, it also charts what happened to the human beings who came under its sway during the last five centuries. It thus broadens the problem of the nature and history of capitalism and challenges the fetishism of commodities that still limits the perspective of most economic historians. The book also thereby challenges the Eurocentric view of the world that underlies the conceptual framework of many mainstream historians.

In attempting to write the history of human development or human fulfillment under capitalism, it joins earlier narratives that chronicle the history of human beings as living and struggling persons rather than as puppets serving the cause of economic growth in the abstract.

Our perspective differs radically from that of those who think that the rise of European nations to prosperity and dominance over the rest of the world is entirely due to the unfettered working of the market and who believe that the way forward for all the peoples of the world is to follow the Europeans and their descendants in North America along the path of unregulated free markets. As we know from recent developments in the architecture of international and national economic relations, the plea for "free markets" often turns out to be special pleading for removing all restraints on the operation of capital while imposing new fetters on the freedom of human beings. In contrast, we regard human development rather than accumulation of capital to be the central thrust of inquiry into the human condition. We also regard the process of victory of European-led capitalism as a far more complex and gory affair than free-market publicists would admit. We regard global capitalist competition as a process that almost always involved armed conflict and the manipulation of ideologies and institutions to obtain compliance with a compulsive drive for pelf at the cost of virtually all human values.

The contradictions between the ideology of free markets and human freedom that capitalism in Europe used to break the shackles of feudalism and hereditary absolutism and the actual working of the system are interwoven in my analysis. The rise and growth of capitalism with freedom on its public banner led to the birth of the largest slave trade in history and a system of slavery that denied all rights to the enslaved. That trade or system was not an aberration but contributed critically to the European merchants' ability to trade with Asia before they had acquired the military power to overthrow or subdue the major Asian empires. After the Spanish conquest of Mexico, the Caribbean islands, and Peru, those regions suffered a demographic disaster. The Portuguese had already been capturing slaves and using them in their colonies in the Atlantic and selling them in European markets. This trade was now extended by them and by other European maritime powers to supply slaves to the Spanish and Portuguese possessions in the Americas. The slave trade expanded vastly in the eighteenth century as the output of plantations in the British and French colonies in the Caribbean and North America grew. The slave-run mines in Mexico and Peru produced silver that was on demand in China, Indonesia, and India. Later on, Brazilian gold also could be used to settle Asian dues. The rum, tobacco, and sugar produced in the plantations could be traded for slaves in Africa and to settle the planters' dues to European bankers. The sugar produced in the slave-run plantations also added significantly to the calorie intake of a European population that was subject to crises of subsistence down to the end of the eighteenth century.

The contradictions between the promise of freedom and its actual realization did not stop at the frontiers of slave-trading ports or slave-run plantations. They came up in the racism that became part of the rationale for conquering the peoples of Latin America, Africa, and Asia and keeping them under colonial rule for centuries. In the heartland of European capitalism, a variety of racism was also a component of the ideology of control of labor.

The struggles between colonial usurpers and native peoples, between capitalists and workers, landlords and peasants, and between women and patriarchal men are central to my narrative. Correspondingly, transformations of different patterns of bondage, the forging of enslaving ideologies, and the quest of the oppressed for freedom are all elements of any real history of human beings. History is neither an endless tournament in which different countries vie for domination of the global market—rulers being given high or low marks for preparing their subjects for winning the competition—nor is it the outcome of the working of passive market forces.

A prominent group of historians and publicists regard human history as a tournament, and they have given the palm to Europe as the continent that prepared its people for victory in this global competition for markets and resources. This achievement has been styled by them as "the European miracle." The group includes, among others, Douglass North, R. P. Thomas, E. L. Jones, and David Landes. They would like to date the beginning of the European miracle to roughly the tenth century C.E.—from the rise of feudalism and the rediscovery of Roman law protecting private property rights. They view western European history as a seamless fabric stretching from Homeric and imperial Roman times to the triumphant crushing of the Soviet threat in 1989. I argue that this view is both proleptic and anachronistic. That perspective falsely pushes back the triumph of exclusionary private property rights in Europe by several centuries and it ignores the huge gaps in time and the political and social upheavals that separated the Greco-Roman civilization from, say, the Castile of Charles V, the Holy Roman emperor, or the England of Elizabeth I. The Eurocentric perspective not only essentializes the so-called cultural factors but also gives a purely internalist account of global history. The world outside Europe is portrayed as if the people there had no agency. Moreover, the influence of the extra-European world on Europe is almost entirely neglected. By contrast, I take account of material as well as cultural factors in the evolution of all societies, including those of western Europe. The agency and the fate of Europeans as well as non-Europeans in shaping human history is an essential part of my analysis. Slavery imposed on Africans had played an important role in strengthening European competition vis-à-vis Asians and sustaining nutrition in a Europe plagued by the deleterious effects of urbanization. In a later period, the non-white colonies of Europe played a similar role in transferring an enormous surplus to metropolitan countries and thereby enabling the massive flows of investment and migrants that helped build up the overseas settlements of the Europeans, including the leader of the contemporary capitalist world, namely, the United States. But the struggles of the European workers, the threat of socialism, and advances made by scientists and sanitary reformers were critical in enabling ordinary Europeans in peacetime to get out of nasty, brutish, and short lives.

In this book we explore the numerous ways the armed ascendancy of European capital has impacted the human development of not only the nonwhite dependencies of Europe but that of the Europeans themselves. It is important to remember that from the 1690s down to the beginning of the nineteenth century the Chinese empire, containing a population larger than that of the whole of western Europe, was a haven of peace compared with the war-torn heartland of Europe. Thus the so-called European miracle was not beneficial to the Europeans themselves before the last quarter of the nineteenth century. Indeed, arms and conquest at the service of capitalists and states controlled by them have destroyed human lives in their millions down to very recent times. The rise of fascism in Europe in the twentieth century and the misery caused by it is part of my story.

My argument in this book has several interrelated strands. First, I argue that economic growth in the sense of production of more goods and services can be said to be a good thing only if it leads to greater human development.

Second, I argue that very few large human groups had attained high levels of human fulfillment before the end of the nineteenth century. In particular, the dramatis personae of the miracle themselves were yet to enjoy a long life, reasonable health, or the power to decide their political destiny before the dawning of the twentieth century. The progress even for them was very uneven in both space and time: the majority of western Europeans did not enjoy a lot of civic freedom until the French Revolution and its aftermath had radically altered Europe's political landscape. For the people of Spain and Portugal, political liberty arrived only in the 1970s and for the people of Germany, Italy, and central Europe only after World War II.

Third, I argue that the rise of capitalism cannot be seen as simply the growth of free trade and free markets. Competition among capitalists and states supporting them has been an integral part of the rise of capitalism in Europe and its spread to the rest of the world. Labor-capital conflicts continually disrupted the smooth narrative of the rise of capital on the back of free markets. Competition between capitalist states involved the use of arms and force for capturing markets, sources of raw materials, territories, and human labor to be used in profit-making enterprises. The attempt to meet the challenge of labor was a prime factor behind the rise of fascism and has been a principal propellant of neoliberal policies that have swept the world since the 1970s.

The advantages reaped by the European ruling classes and, at some distance, by their fellow combatants in trade, territorial expansion, and accumulation were at the expense of the suffering of millions of people, in Europe, the Americas, Africa, and Asia. This suffering was imposed in the cause of mobilizing dispossessed and very often coerced and bonded labor for accu-

mulation and went hand in hand with the proletarianization of European labor to the same end. The tenants and cotters who were thrown off the land in
eighteenth-century England did not find equally gainful employment and so
their real wages and standards of living suffered in the process. During the beginning of the English Industrial Revolution, not only did vast numbers of
peasants lose their land and their access to common-property resources, but
as Michel Foucault and E. P. Thompson have documented, the common people of Britain and France alike were subjected to draconian forms of punishment on the slightest pretext. The soldiers and sailors who were expected to
die for king and country generally had a worse time than even the civilian
population.

Fourth, I argue that there is little evidence to support the view that the Europeans had gained a decisive advantage over China or India with respect to
most of the techniques of production or in their levels of consumption before
the maturing of the machine-based Industrial Revolution in England. I argue
further that in agriculture and civilian production, productivity growth in
western Europe was probably no faster than in China or India down to the beginning of the eighteenth century (in the case of China, probably down to the
eve of the Taiping Rebellion).

A number of historians of east Asia have argued that until the middle or the
end of the eighteenth century European products could not compete on equal
terms with the tradable commodities and especially manufactures produced
by China, India, and other major economies of Asia. This perspective has successfully challenged the Eurocentric, proleptic view of history that I referred
to earlier. My analysis supports this dissenting view. Some of these historians
have argued further that but for some conjunctural factors China, or more
broadly, the eastern and southeastern parts of the Eurasian continent might
have emerged as the dominant players in the world capitalist order.

I argue, however, that this extension of the dissenting argument underestimates the significance of the Industrial Revolution in altering the competitive
positions of the industrializing countries led by Britain vis-à-vis the rest of the
world. There is a crucial distinction between a state (such as Qing China) that
reins in the drive for unlimited accumulation and a social and political order
(as in Hanoverian England) that promotes the unchecked centralization of
economic power and thus facilitates the growth of factory-based industry.
Moreover, even if China or India had come out on top, but for the Industrial
Revolution in Europe or some other factor such as the "discovery" of the
Americas by the Europeans, under the capitalist rules of the game, ordinary
people would still have suffered the kind of misery documented in my story.
In the counterfactual account, China would have emerged as the supreme eco-
nomic and military power. This would have altered the global distribution of

income and standards of living; but the logic of armed capitalism would still have led to the marginalization and immiseration of vast numbers of people around the world.

Fifth, I argue that the business of the sovereign or the merchant counting his money in the chancery or the bank, getting into combat to make more money, and using that money again in peaceful competition or hot combat and the civilizing process within Europe and the civilizing mission abroad, with the aim of obtaining ever larger bases of docile labor to exploit, were all intimately connected facets of the same seething reality.

My analysis would lead to the inference that there was not one but two "axial ages" (to borrow a phrase used by Janet Hunter) separating the development of today's advanced capitalist countries from the rest of the world. The first was the Industrial Revolution, involving invention of new machines and processes that generated increasing returns to scale on an ever-widening circle. We can take this as roughly the period between ca. 1760, a widely accepted date for the beginning of the Industrial Revolution in England and the 1860s, when England reached the apogee of her economic dominance in industry.

The Industrial Revolution led to an increasing differential between the per capita incomes of industrializing countries and the lands that became dependencies of European powers. But it was not yet associated with a general improvement in the longevity or health of ordinary people in the pioneer industrializing economies. That had to wait for the second axial age, which I date from the last quarter of the nineteenth century. During this latter period, three developments helped lift the condition of the average worker in western Europe and in overseas white settlements of the United States, Canada, Australia, and New Zealand. The first was the development of the germ theory of disease and prophylactic measures resulting from that theory. The second was the migration of a large proportion of the European population to the United States, Canada, and other lands of settlement and the equipping of those migrants partly with outflows of investment from Britain and other western European countries. That flow in turn was balanced by the extraction of very large surpluses from colonies or informal dependencies such as India, Indonesia, Egypt, and China. Thus imperialism played a role in this period as it had done in the period of slave-run plantations to raise workers' standard of living in the industrializing societies. The third was that, as industrialization advanced, workers' struggles and democratic movements also became stronger. The bargaining power of European workers improved in the period of mass migration from Europe. These developments induced the governments of the advanced capitalist countries to take steps to improve public sanitation and health care and provide some security to the workers against the vagaries of the trade cycle. With interruptions caused by the rise of fascism, these steps were continued into the second half of the twentieth century.

The nonwhite colonies hardly shared in the sanitary and prophylactic revolution that radically improved the life chances of western Europeans and the people of their major overseas settlements. The cumulative results of the positive steps taken by the public authorities in the early industrializing lands from the late nineteenth century radically separated their literacy levels, their longevity, and their standard of living from those of the countries that came to be known as underdeveloped areas.

Many of the governments of the newly independent lands in Africa and Asia and some of the Latin American countries launched programs for developing their economies and their social sectors. The results up to the 1970s certainly exceeded their achievements under colonial rule. It would have seemed in, say, 1975, that the indexes of human development were going to converge worldwide. The faltering or failure of the developmental programs in most of these countries from the 1980s (with the exception of a block of countries in east Asia and a few isolated nations in other regions) has, however, fatally separated the haves from the have-nots of the world with respect to per capita incomes and the usual indexes of human development. This does not mean that the indexes of per capita income and human development move together over time or across countries, but there is a close concordance between the two sets of variables.

We may be currently witnessing the evolution of a third axial age. In this age the inequality of distribution of incomes and control over resources has increased to a historic high as between persons and countries. Both deliberate strategies pursued by the United States and its allies in the Organization for Economic Cooperation and Development (OECD) countries and the consequences of a new, entirely plutocratically oriented international economic order seem to ensure that no economy can emerge as a challenger to the top imperialist powers. Among the imperialist powers again, the United States has emerged as the superimperialist, and its government has claimed that no international law or organization can deter it from any military action it considers to be in the national interest (meaning, of course, the interest of big U.S. capital). At the same time that big capital, backed by the military might of the superimperialist, pursues its murderous course, the bargaining power of workers all over the world is pushed down to low levels through a combination of measures—totally deregulating finance, enfeebling the state, and depriving workers of all rights vis-à-vis capital through legislation.

In the book, I discuss in some detail how all this came about, but it might be useful to recapitulate the late twentieth-century story and its connection with the ideology and the politics of the earlier centuries of capitalism.

Several developments in the twentieth century have enabled the ruling classes of the rich nations to hone strategies of globalization in the interest of the rich. The first is the century-long growth of the United States as the most powerful capitalist economy and the leader of the advanced capitalist group of nations. Already before World War II, the United States had become the most powerful nation in the world, both economically and militarily. From 1945 it emerged as the most powerful military power on earth, with the Soviet Union as the only possible challenger. Second, the century witnessed the growth of powerful corporations straddling the global economy. Third, the Bretton Woods system that had been instituted effectively in 1946 for stabilizing exchange rates broke down between 1971 and 1973; the deregulation of financial markets and the proliferation of financial instruments from that time increased the instability of exchange and currency markets, the vulnerability of developing country economies, and the escalation of economic power of transnational corporations (TNCs), principally based in the G7 countries. The latter in turn came to shape international financial and other economic policies in their own interest. The Soviet Union, as the putative challenger of the United States, effectively collapsed in 1989. The final decade of the twentieth century witnessed the unleashing of the power of capital and that of the United States as the sole superpower against any country targeted by it as the enemy of "freedom," meaning the designs of U.S. capital for control of oil and other strategic resources worldwide. I briefly sketch the story of how this victory of capitalist imperialism came about.

The U.S. economy, which was already the richest in the world on the eve of World War I, became further enriched through the two world wars, while most of the other advanced capitalist economies suffered in the war. But after World War II, the Soviet Union along with Communist China posed a challenge to the dominance of global capital. Furthermore, the national liberation movements in the colonies acquired a new tempo and between 1946 and the early 1960s most of them gained their political independence. This clearly hurt the old empires; but the United States, with its technological, financial, and military prowess, established its presence in all the countries that had not undergone a communist revolution. The memories of the Nazi horror in Europe and their catastrophic results and the increased bargaining power of labor in a reconstructing Europe were among the factors that induced the governments of western Europe to adopt the policies of a welfare state. Paradoxically, these developments gave birth to what has been styled as the golden age of capitalism, stretching from 1945 to 1973.

However, that golden age, with its near-full employment conditions in major capitalist countries, eroded the profitability of capital. The quadrupling of the price of oil in 1973 also demonstrated the potential dangers to the hegemony of the Western bloc if further increases in the power of developing countries were not halted. The counterattack comprised the financial liberalization that simultaneously boosted the power of finance, badly damaged labor's bargaining power, and caused heightened instability of developing nations. Thus began the phase of what can be called finance-led capital. Other strategies included opposition to national liberation movements in most of southern Africa—led by parties openly professing socialism and opposition to the racist regime of South Africa—stoking the China-Soviet rivalry; fomenting terrorist attacks by the mujahideen against a liberal-communist regime in Afghanistan; and supporting Saddam Hussein, the dictator of Iraq, in his war against Iran, where a revolution led by Ayatollah Khomeini had overthrown the highly repressive but pro-Western regime of the Shah of Iran. In virtually all these conflicts, except in the case of the Iran-Iraq war (1980–1988), the Soviet Union was ranged on the side of the protagonists of national liberation. But those conflicts—especially the Soviet involvement in the war in Afghanistan—with an economically and militarily stronger capitalist bloc, exhausted the Soviet regime and led to the breakup of the Soviet Union and the collapse of the Soviet bloc.

However, it is in conformity with the general perspective of this book that the emergence of the United States as the sole superpower led neither to the ending of wars launched by the capitalist powers nor the quickening of the process of human development in poor countries under the heel of capital. The U.S. ascension as a superpower after World War II coincided with peace in the European core but with continued war in the periphery; in the epoch following collapse of the Soviet Union, that pattern has intensified. The decades of the 1980s and 1990s, when the major antisystemic challenger on the international plane was fatally weakened, have been decades of stagnation and regression in the majority of the developing countries.

Even before the terrorist attack on the World Trade Center in New York, on 11 September 2001, the U.S. establishment had evolved a doctrine under which it could attack any country or any person any time, if that country or person was considered to be inimical to U.S. interests, regardless of international law or the sanction of the United Nations. They applied this doctrine when pulverizing Afghanistan between October 2001 and March 2002 on the grounds that it had given shelter to Osama bin Laden, the alleged mastermind of the 9/11 attack. The United States attacked Iraq, with the old imperialist powers Britain, Portugal, and Spain among its allies, using the allegation that Saddam Hussein harbored weapons of mass destruction, although intensive searches by UN inspectors had failed to turn up a shred of evidence to back that charge. With the regime change in Iraq, the United States and its allies appeared poised to have a stranglehold on the supply of world oil and hence the commanding heights of the global economy.

This condition of total and permanent war deliberately created by the United States and the TNCs backing the aggression of President Bush and Prime Minister Blair is partly based on the overwhelming military superiority of the United States. But it is also necessitated by the fact that mere financial manipulation of currency, stock, and asset markets has not been sufficient to lift the U.S. economy out of a recession plaguing it since 2001. Capitalism has relied on markets so long as they have served its purpose. As in the past, big capital has not been squeamish in training big guns on innocent people when they appear as obstacles against its designs. As in the past, the propaganda of the civilizing mission was in full drive even as cluster bombs tore apart the bodies of the intended beneficiaries of that civilizing process or as two-thousand- or nine-thousand-pound bombs buried patients of a whole hospital under the debris. Operation Iraqi Freedom, the name for the savaging of Iraq, was only one of the million ways doublespeak was spread across all media channels by the shameless aggressors.

The system that promotes unlimited accumulation of capital and power is to be distinguished from peaceful and socially restrained exchange. The use of money for such peaceful exchange and the evolution of private property rights under suitable conditions of cooperation and social regulation long predate the march of unhindered capital accumulation guiding the destinies of nations. The new concern for environmental protection has brought to the fore the question of conserving our endowments against predatory and exhausting capitalist processes. The market-fundamentalist view of the evolution of human development has obscured from our gaze the proper role of markets working under socially acceptable norms. It has also obscured the distinction between life-enhancing innovations, such as the invention of penicillin, and life-destroying innovations, such as the nuclear bomb or the possibility of betting on financial derivatives such as the Nikkei index, which brought down the Barings Bank.

In this book, I have tried to interweave the ideologies governing the conquering career of capitalism. Two interlinked ideologies stand out in this history. One is the ideology of racism and the civilizing mission, under which whole groups of people, including entire populations of continents, were stereotyped as uncivilized and it was considered the duty of the civilized conquerors to make them civilized, even if it meant enslaving or slaughtering millions of the targeted population in the process. This ideology can be traced in an almost unbroken succession from the time of the Portuguese and the Spanish conquistadors to the influential neoconservatives in the Bush administration.

The second related ideology can be characterized as that of Malthusianism and social Darwinism, although most elements of that ideology predate the publication of the crucial texts by Malthus and Darwin. A major tenet of this ideology is that the resources of the world are limited and only the fittest are morally entitled to live in it. A vulgar form of Darwin's theory of natural selection is applied to suggest that whole populations are fated to be weeded out or made to serve the fitter aristocrats of humanity. This ideology not only justified colonial conquests but also the denial of basic civil and political rights to the working class on many occasions. Whether such ideologies actively inspired policy partly depended on the conditions of the supply and the social reproduction of labor. (I have given a more extended analysis of Malthusianism, social Darwinism, and their influence on ideology and policy making in appendix 1, available on the Rowman & Littlefield website at www.rowmanlittlefield.com/ ISBN/0742539202.)

One of the curious aspects of mainstream economics is its cavalier attitude to issues of human survival. In this book I have devoted special attention to the issues of reproduction of labor. Many analysts not only regard labor as a factor of production that should be disposable without cost but they also tend to value lives of human groups in accordance with their nearness or distance from the class, race, nation, or gender the analysts are affiliated to, without being conscious that they are doing so.

With economic growth powered by industrialization, workers and ordinary people in general began to enjoy better standards of living in the heartland of capitalism from the late nineteenth century. But these gains were continually interrupted by wars and changes in political regimes in the heartland. Moreover, these attainments were not shared by the vast majority of the people in the dependencies and ex-dependencies of Europe or the United States.

The tendency toward the centralization and concentration of capital was greatly accelerated as welfare states came under attack in Europe and elsewhere and the behavior of capital was increasingly freed from all restraint. We can now talk more firmly about the consolidation of the rule of monopoly capital than we could, say, in 1970. Capitalism, with the counterideology of socialism, was also associated with the growth of democracy and aspirations for democracy. However, as I argue in the last part of this book, the power of big money, especially super-rich TNCs, is subverting and obstructing the consolidation of democracy everywhere. In many cases, the most powerful governments in the world, namely, the G7 (G8 if we add Russia) governments seem to be acting as agents of these super-rich corporations.

In the beginning of the twenty-first century, we find a straight conflict between their agenda and the aspirations of ordinary people for democracy and equality. Even in formally democratic countries, the electoral process is often reduced to mockery through the power of money and the increasingly establishment-oriented media. In other countries, popular revolts are challenging the rule by governments that appear to owe greater allegiance to the rich and seem to be dependent for their survival on the favor of G7 govern-ments. As in the past, the promise of freedom and the rule of law premised on the theories of the pioneers of bourgeois civility have been largely be-lied by the actual performance of capitalism in its apparently unchallenge-able ascendancy. This book addresses the concerns of believers in genuine democracy all over the world.

Acknowledgments

This book originated in a paper I wrote in 1999 setting out some of the salient points in the history of human development and criticizing a dominant view of what really happened to the chances of human survival and improvement in the quality of life of ordinary people during the five centuries that have elapsed since the European "discovery" of the Americas by Columbus in 1492. The late Michael Sprinker happened to see that paper. He then suggested that I should write a book on the theme I had focused on in that paper.

Tragically, Michael passed away before I was able to finish the book. I dedicate this book to his memory with the consent of Modhumita Roy, his partner for a life dedicated to the cause of radical scholarship and the struggles of the oppressed everywhere.

Many friends have contributed to the building up of the argument, by reading various drafts, supplying references, and debating the argument with me. Himani Bannerji and Robin Blackburn commented extensively on the argument and helped sharpen it. Amartya Sen read through most of the book and helped in straightening out the analysis. My greatest debt is to Mark Selden, who has performed the labors of Hercules in cleaning up the whole text. I can only say that these friends tried their best, and if the book still has blemishes, it is not their fault. Michael Kuttner, Porus Olpadwala, Raj Chandavarkar, Simon Szreter, Salil Sarkar, Said Shah, Flavia Agnes, Sukumari Bhattacharji, Ranabir Chakravarti, Nirmal Chandra, Suchandra Ghosh, Martha Nussbaum, and Sumit and Tanika Sarkar helped in many ways that they may not be aware of. An invitation to Trent University, Peterborough, Ontario, in 1999 and to the Maison des Sciences de l'Homme, Paris, in 2000 allowed me to flesh out some of my arguments. I am very grateful to Peter Kulchyski, Maurice Aymard, and Jean Racine for arranging those visits.

The academic and nonacademic staff at the Centre for Studies in Social Sciences, Calcutta, and at the Institute of Development Studies Kolkata have helped with books, other reference materials, and with secretarial assistance. Sanchari Guha deserves special thanks for help in preparing the manuscript.

I also owe an immense debt of gratitude to Rowman and Littlefield and, in particular, to Susan McEachern, Jennifer Nemec, Becki Perna, and the copyeditor for the care they have taken at every stage of preparing the book for publication. I thank Barnita Bagchi and Subhanil Banerjee for help in checking the references and the latter also for help in preparing the index.

My immediate family, as usual, has provided a supportive home and companionship in this endeavor. Jasodhara's concern with issues of gender has continually acted as a corrective to my vision. Barnita's research on women writers of eighteenth-century Britain illuminated for me many aspects of women's and especially women workers' predicament during the British Industrial Revolution. Tista alerted me against the danger of getting trapped in a view of the human condition in terms of stereotypes. Aditya Bhattacharjea rallied with help in procuring critical references.

I owe an enormous debt of gratitude for the immense work done by scholars in the field of the human sciences straddling the whole world, and this book could not have been written if I could not quarry freely in the rich veins they have opened up. This debt will remain unpaid because it is part of the human heritage that should be preserved for posterity, and I can share in that heritage just because I belong to the human species.

None of the above persons, friends or relations, should be held responsible for the remaining deficiencies of the book.

Abbreviations

Some abbreviations frequently used in the text include the following:

EIC   British (English) East India Company
GDP   Gross domestic product
IMR   Infant mortality rate, that is, the number of children among 1,000
           live births dying within their first year
OECD   Organization for Economic Cooperation and Development
TNC   transnational corporation
TRIPs   trade-related intellectual property rights
VOC   Dutch East India Company
WTO   World Trade Organization
e_0 Expectation of life at birth
$ U.S. dollar, unless otherwise specified
£   British pound, unless otherwise specified

I

CONCEPTUAL ISSUES: HUMAN DEVELOPMENT AND CAPITALIST GROWTH

History of Human Development as the Subject of History

CONTOURS OF HUMAN DEVELOPMENT

Why are we interested in the history of humankind? The most significant facts in human history concern how human beings, and especially the mass of humankind, have fared in history. Yet, most of the large-canvas economic histories have been far more concerned with the artifacts created by wo(man) rather than the condition of the creators. This book addresses the question of human beings in the large during the period of the rise of capitalism in Europe since roughly the sixteenth century and its eventual domination of the rest of the world.

How do we decide the criteria by which the condition of people should be judged? A first answer would be that people should be able to live a good life. A good life, according to Aristotle's *Ethica Nicomachea* (Aristotle 1915/ 1975), Karl Marx and Frederick Engels (1845–1846/1976), Rabindranath Tagore (1914/1994, poem no. 35), and Hanna Arendt (1958), to take some eminent thinkers at random, or according to a Xhosa proverb (as quoted by Sparks 1991, p. 3) can be lived only by a free person living among other free human beings. They can, however, live freely only if they have access to such basic material wherewithal as food, clothing, shelter, peace, and community. Thinking along these lines is almost as old as human memory and certainly as old as decipherable human language. The Greeks of the pre-Christian era, the Indians of the Vedic and the Upanishadic periods, the Buddhists, the followers of Confucius, the Judeo-Christian thinkers, and the savants of the Arabo-Persian schools have preached most of the values embodied in the concept of human development. But old values have been interpreted in new ways as times and circumstances have changed (cf. Nussbaum 2000). Moreover, as

values have traveled from one country to another, they have frequently acquired new significance in the process.

History reveals that institutions or artifacts produced by human beings can
lead to the exploitation or the loss of freedom of other human beings. Thus
the celebration of the good life of an Athenian citizen in Plato's time can hide
the wretchedness of vast numbers of slaves whose labor made it possible for
the few free citizens to enjoy that good life. Our criteria then must apply to
all, or at least the vast majority of the human group concerned, if they are to
lay claim to universality.

Economic historians were until recently concerned mainly to find out the
causes and consequences of economic growth. Economic growth, however, is
only a means to an end; it is a necessary condition, but by no means a sufficient one, and certain kinds of economic growth may be positively harmful to
the people immediately affected by them. For example, the exploitation of
forest resources, especially by outsiders, may harm the people using forest resources for subsistence and farmers, the productivity of whose land is adversely affected by indiscriminate felling of trees in areas upstream of their
farms.

Why are we interested in measuring the rate of economic growth, finding
out why it accelerates or falls? It cannot be because twenty million tons of cement has any greater beauty than nineteen million tons. We cannot even say
that twenty million tons produces greater welfare than ten million tons unless
we know whether the extra cement is to be used for constructing concentration camps or for badly needed houses for ordinary people. Even in the last
case, we might want to know whether the houses will end up in the possession of a few or whether their ownership will be widely distributed. In other
words, whatever our scheme of valuation, the production or supply of more
goods can be interpreted as a better state of affairs only when we know that
those goods will be used for a purpose we can approve of. The only purpose
that is likely to elicit near-universal agreement is the use of the goods for the
good of human beings.

The values that Aristotle outlined in the *Ethica Nicomachaea* were set out
for the instruction of wealthy Athenians in his lyceum. Only a man of
leisure with land, slaves, and women dependants in the Athenian society of
Aristotle's day could think of leading the purely contemplative life of a
philosopher (Finley 1973/1985, 1980; Hutchinson 1995). These values were
extensively quoted in later ages. Even in societies without slaves a purely
contemplative life was possible—but only for people who did not have to
work for their living or for people who were paid by society to lead a
philosopher's life. Inspiring as these ethical discourses were to those with
leisure (and to our times, with our greater command over material re-

sources), they failed to address such issues as improving the nutrition and quality of physical well-being that were, inevitably, the daily preoccupation of the vast majority of wo(men) everywhere.

Aristotle's emphasis on the life of reason as the supreme goal of human endeavor has been echoed in various forms in the texts of world religions and in the sayings of many nonliterate peoples as well. The record of human history is also polluted throughout by the violation of the canons of good living laid down by the Greek or Indian philosophers or Confucius, Christ, or Muhammad. Organized violence, oppressive hierarchies, superstitions, and other social and political evils took tolls of human life and human well-being. But ordinary people fought against such oppression by taking up arms, creating dissenting religions, and building up new solidary communities. They also recognized, as the Xhosa people knew, that the realization of a good life by any individual requires the existence of other human beings living in society. Orientalist scholars (for example, Dumont 1970) have projected the fantasy that only Europeans had a notion of *Homo equalis*. For establishing that peculiar proposition, they have referred primarily to the classic texts of Rousseau and Tocqueville, forgetting all the movements for equality within Europe and in Asia long before Rousseau or Tocqueville lived. The Hussites, the followers of Wycliffe, the Diggers and the Levelers during the English civil war of the 1640s, the sixteenth-century miller from Friuli in Italy (Ginsburg 1980) were all fighting for greater equality among men and against the unreason preached by the established church in the name of religion. In India, Buddhism had risen as a protest against Brahmanical hierarchy. When Buddhism was replaced by a reinvented Brahmanical order, many religious sects arose preaching equality and brotherhood of men and, in some cases, even liberation for women. To cite some examples at random, Tukaram, Sena, and their followers in Maharashtra from the twelfth century; numerous groups of Vaishnavas in most regions of India; and the weaver-saint Kabir in the sixteenth century all preached brotherhood among men, and some preached equality between men and women as well (Tagore 1914/1994; Lele 1989; Bagchi 1995, "Introduction").

Rabindranath Tagore, the Indian poet, was deeply influenced by the Upanishads, by the dissident, egalitarian, and syncretic religious movements but also, of course, by the values of Western liberalism (Tagore 1901/1941, 1994a, 1994b).

An almost exact contemporary of Tagore, Kang Youwei, who grew up in the last days of the Qing empire and witnessed at firsthand both the disintegration of a social order and the imperialist onslaught on the body of his land, also formulated his vision of a good life in universalistic terms, notably in his *Datongshu*, or *Book of the Great Community* (Spence 1981, chapter 2). He called upon the heritage of ancient India, Greece, Persia, and Rome and that of "modern England, France, Germany, and America, as his own and linked his own fate to that of all other human beings. Acutely aware of the oppression that most human beings were undergoing, he singled out women's oppression by men as calling for special attention" (Spence 1981, p. 40).

Tagore also reacted to the gender oppression in India with mordant stories and pungent essays. And of course, many women writers of India, including Tagore's elder sister, Swarnakumari Debi, gave voice to women's protest in numerous essays and works of fiction.

With Karl Marx and Frederick Engels, writing sixty years before Tagore and Kang, we have a clear enunciation of the possibility of freedom for all human beings in organized societies without any class or gender distinctions or without the necessity of some wo(men) being unfree wage slaves and a few being the masters as controllers of means of production. According to them, capitalism, by developing the forces of production beyond what had been achieved under earlier modes of production, made it *possible* for everybody to be free individuals. But at the same time, capitalism, with its fundamental distinction between wage earners and capitalists, rendered it impossible for people to realize that potential.

If we now devote some space to the discussion of the elements that go into human development, it is because we have to recover the best thinking of the past from obloquy and deliberate neglect by apologists of capitalism and imperialism and not because what is said in the following is fundamentally new.

Most people would agree that preserving a human life is better than destroying it and, by extension, increasing the span of life of most human beings enjoying normal health is also a good thing.

A connected good most people would agree on is that people should live a healthy life and should be capable of doing the work that is needed to make a living or that makes life worth living. Yet another good that people should enjoy is the ability to communicate with other human beings and learn from them. The use of language enables most normally endowed people to speak to others and understand what they say. But with the invention of scripts, human beings can draw on the knowledge and the literary arts of past generations and exchange ideas with people at great distances. Thus we have come to regard literacy as a necessary good every wo(man) should possess.

With literacy as a desirable possession of every human being, we have moved from the characteristic of wo(men) as just another species of animal to their characteristic as a special kind of being. But the most important good valued by wo(men) as species being is freedom. There are huge debates about what freedom means, about what fosters it, about the most objectionable forms of restriction of freedom, about the relation of freedom to equality. But there is virtually no disagreement among serious philosophers and social theorists that more, rather than less, freedom makes for a better world.

The attainment of the various kinds of good we have sketched may be said to be the goal of development of human beings living in society or the development of a human form of life. But different groups do not have the same opportunities for human fulfillment. For example, in most countries women have a more restricted access than men to the substance of human development and the means for attaining it. And in general, in poor countries, the opportunities for human development are more restricted for most people than in rich countries.

In the *Human Development Reports*, published by the United Nations Development Program (UNDP) since 1990, an attempt has been made to capture some of these differences in the form of tables portraying the levels of literacy and education, longevity, rates of infant mortality, the literacy or expectation of life of women separately and so on, and indexes aggregating some of these aspects. While these documents and related writings have greatly advanced the general awareness of human development issues, they have also highlighted the complexity of the variables entering into the composition of human freedom and of the relation of human development to economic growth. Insofar as economic growth increases the availability of goods and services, it generates the potential for advancing human development and widening human freedom. However, whether that potential is realized depends on the composition of the basket of goods and services, on the state of knowledge regarding the impact of consumption of different kinds of goods, and on the distribution of what have been termed *entitlements* among different groups of people (Nozick 1974; Sen 1981). For example, before the discovery of the link between tobacco consumption and cancer, smoking of the weed would have been regarded as an innocent habit, adding to the well-being of the smoker.[1] Similarly, if additions to the stock of goods take the form mainly of armaments and equipment dedicated to war, then their contribution to human development becomes very questionable. Finally, if most people possess meager entitlements to food, clothing, education, and health services, then additions to the stock of goods and services enjoyed (and wasted) by a privileged few can hardly be said to contribute to human freedom or development.

Human beings live on earth and continually interact with nature as they themselves are the product of nature. An appropriate relationship between nature and human beings has been a necessary condition for sustained progress in human development. Awareness of this has been implicit in the conditions for survival of all human populations, and that awareness has been expressed in the writings of the ancient Greeks, Indians, and Chinese. Thus environmentalism has been embraced as a rubric for analysis and a movement in the twentieth century, but its roots are as ancient as thinking about other components of human development (Grove 1995, "Introduction"). Just as in other areas of human development, this awareness did not prevent environmental spoliation before the advent of capitalism—a social and political system that put the pursuit of profit by the few as the central motif of all goal-directed action. The Libyan granary of the Roman empire became a desert because of centuries of misuse of the environment. The dense forests of the foothills of Hindu Kush, which had supplied the elephants that King Puru mobilized to defend his kingdom against Alexander's invasion in 326 B.C.E., have long since disappeared. In contrast, over millennia, forests, grasslands, and river valleys have provided a livelihood to millions of people living in symbiotic peace or a shared recognition of one another's rights.

Large parts of the action of the two foremost Indian epics take place in forests. An arboreal existence remained an ideal of Indian ascetics down to the first millennium C.E. (Kosambi 1970; Erdosy 1998). Moreover, cultivators and hunter-gatherers lived side by side in many regions of India even after iron axes and plows were used to cut down forests and extend cultivation. Many communities depended on forests for medicinal plants, herbs, and fruits that did not form part of commercial horticulture. Erdosy (1998, p. 65) concluded that, in spite of a long history of colonization of the Gangetic valley by humankind, irreversible ecological decline came to the region only with the Industrial Revolution. The studies of Mark Elvin, Vaclav Smil, and others show that the destruction of Chinese forests, and more, has proceeded over the millennia. However, the rate of ecological disruption has been far more rapid in that region since the time of the Taiping revolt. As we shall see, this led to enormous losses of life, especially in the late nineteenth century.

The Industrial Revolution Erdosy is referring to occurred in England, not in the Gangetic valley. Capitalism posed a new kind of threat to the environment everywhere, but in colonial countries it posed an even greater threat. First of all, a private profit seeker does not—in fact, under conditions of unlimited competition, cannot—pay heed to the interests of other human beings, let alone dumb beasts and plants. Posterity also cannot figure in the profit seeker's calculation. Such concerns can play a decisive role only when, for some reason, capitalists can perceive a collective interest in enhancing aggregate profit through environmental concerns and collectively agree on a plan of action. Second, diversity of species as such plays no part in profit calculations. If teak comes to be valued as timber for shipbuilding, then all attention is devoted to finding new, cheaper sources of teak and, when necessary, to the conservation of teak forests, often to the detriment of the local users of forests in which teak grows. We will examine in more detail the ravages caused by aggressive capitalism to the environment in China, India, and

Africa, but this examination will be centered on the immediate physical welfare of the people concerned.[2]

Policies causing deforestation or usurpation of the commons were resisted by ordinary people—the uprooted peasants in England and millions of hunters and food gatherers in India or Africa. These opponents of dispossession were the true advocates of conservation in many cases (Rangarajan 1996; Saldanha 1998; Linebaugh and Rediker 2000). The construction of the modern capitalist state, celebrated by Jean Bodin and Thomas Hobbes, took place against the background of the disorderliness let loose by rampant capitalism. It is necessary to recount the story of that killing disorderliness to uncover the mask behind which that unjust social order still presents itself.

Capitalism and colonialism sundered the conditions of symbiosis and coexistence and, in many cases, led to a much faster environmental degradation than had been witnessed in the preceding millennia. In any social system, there is a problem of coordination failure. But under capitalism, this problem becomes extreme, as social and political constraints on private behavior are lifted. Ordinary people might resist some of these changes through collective struggles, but when their economic condition deteriorates, they might resort to the same free-riding behavior that predatory capitalism thrives on. We should remember this caveat when we sketch aspects of environmental destruction in part 3 of this book. Moreover, the adherence to a socialist ideology is no guarantee against ecological damage, especially when the professedly socialist state is wedded to the cause of industrialization at any cost and is caught in a competitive race against the dominant capitalist order. What we have tried to do is to pick out the most powerful forces causing the kind of environmental damage that can be directly linked to loss of human lives. The enormous decline in biodiversity and the rise of global warming and ozone depletion are some of the clearly recognizable effects of uncontrolled exploitation of natural resources by humankind, led by profit-seeking capital.

Capitalism and colonialism have almost certainly adversely affected the mental health of human beings. But we will have to leave that aspect out for lack of expertise and space (see, for example, Desjarlais et al. 1995). In this book, we will first examine the record of the biological or somatic well-being of human beings since the sixteenth century. But we will also look at certain other aspects of human development, such as literacy, and serious infringements of civil freedom.

This book aspires to get away from the fetishism of commodities and the Eurocentric view of the world that still limit the perspective of many economic historians and other social scientists. It is also in a long tradition of dissent from accounts of the journey of humankind that stress only the success of the rich and the powerful.

COMPETING PERSPECTIVES STRESSING MARKETS, ECONOMIC GROWTH, AND EUROPEAN EXCEPTIONALISM

We can distinguish four major perspectives on the history of humankind. The first is that of a purely Eurocentric, triumphalist view of the world. This has a long tradition in the historiography emanating from Europe and the imperialist powers that brought most of the globe under their dominion by the end of the nineteenth century. From this perspective, economic growth was only one aspect of the benefit supposedly brought by Europeans to conquered peoples. Much more important is the gift of civilization that they took to the Amerindian peoples of North and South America in the sixteenth century, to the Africans stretching over the five centuries from the sixteenth to the twentieth, to the Asians, and to the whole world from the nineteenth century. As the mantle of European hegemony has passed to the United States, so has this essentially imperialist perspective to the defenders of U.S. dominance.

A more restricted, but by no means less emphatic, version of this is presented by those economic historians who think that the rise of European peoples to prosperity and dominance over the rest of the world is primarily due to the unfettered working of the market and that the way forward for all peoples is to follow the Europeans along the same path.

A third perspective is offered by anti-imperialist writers, mainly using a Marxist framework, who view the history of the world as the outcome of the efforts of the first-mover nations under capitalism securing ever larger shares of markets, materials, and labor power in competition with one another. A fourth perspective is provided by the proponents of the world-system school. While members of this school may hold different views regarding the exact placing of hegemonic powers in time and space, all of them seem to agree that the capitalist system has given rise to a continual fight among states for hegemony; the system also creates and re-creates peripheral and semiperipheral regions, condemning vast numbers of people to dependence on the hegemonic core. In many ways, this view can be regarded as a cousin of the radical anti-imperialist school, and it is not surprising that many members of the school view the consequences of U.S. attempts to impose its rule over the rest of the world with deep misgivings.

Our perspective differs radically from the first two mentioned above. First, we regard human fulfillment rather than accumulation of commodities as the central quest of social policy and the central area of inquiry in the human sciences. We also regard the process of victory of European-led capitalism as a far more complex and gory affair than Eurocentric historians would admit. Finally, we refuse to regard the enormous cost paid by humankind in misery and death for the victory of capital as a negligible by-product of that history. We regard capitalist competition as a process that invariably involved armed conflict and the manipulation of ideologies and institutions to obtain compliance with the drive for pelf at the cost of virtually all other values.

There have been other critiques of the so-called European miracle by radical social scientists in recent years (Blaut 1993; Frank 1998; Pomeranz 2000a). I share their view that the difference between Europe and other continents before the eighteenth century with respect to levels of income, productivity, and technological advance has been exaggerated by the Eurocentric economic historians; if anything, China and, in many respects, India were in advance of virtually all European nations down to the middle of the eighteenth century. I also think that much of the advance of European capitalists and other members of the European ruling class was at the cost of misery of the colonized and enslaved peoples of Africa, Asia, and Latin America, and of course, of European workers. But my perspective differs in regarding changes in commodity production, trade, or income mainly as instruments for advancing human development rather than as the primary *quaesita* of analysis. Moreover, I emphasize that it does not matter whether, in a counterfactual narrative, China or India would have come out on top but for the Industrial Revolution in Europe. Even if that had happened, under the capitalist rules of the game, the majority of the people would have suffered the kind of misery I have documented in my story. I also have a more dialectical view of history than I come across in the books by Frank (1998) and Pomeranz (2000a) in the sense that the struggles between colonial usurpers and native peoples, struggles between capitalists and workers, and changes in the position of women are dynamic processes central to my narrative. Correspondingly, transformations of different patterns of bondage, search for freedom in its many dimensions on the part of oppressed people, and the forging of enslaving ideologies by profit-hungry marauders are all elements of any real history of human beings. We cannot regard human history as that of a tournament between different countries vying for the global market nor can we confine our attention only to the working of passive market forces.

Moreover, Frank and Pomeranz pay little attention to the ideological devices used by the European capitalist-conquerors to motivate their marauding missions and to consolidate their rule. To give a simple example, racism does not occur as a category of analysis in either Frank's or Pomeranz's account, whereas to my mind, it is a keystone of a hierarchical global capitalist order. Moreover, deliberate state action plays a critical role in the rise of the capitalist world order as I see it, and the quality of that action depends on the nature of the state and the classes dominating a particular state. This view rejects the myth that the rise of capitalism was powered by the working of an impersonal market and little else.[3]

Many Eurocentric historians trace the origins of the European miracle to the enthronement of private property rights as the guiding principle of asset distribution and the freedom of contract and the freeing of markets from state regulation as the mechanism for the allocation of resources. Leading proponents of this view, such as Douglass North, R. P. Thomas (North and Thomas 1973), E. L. Jones (1981/1987), and David Landes (1998) would like to date the beginning of the miracle in western Europe to roughly the tenth century C.E.—from the rise of feudalism and the rediscovery of Roman law protecting private property rights. They also view western European history as a seamless fabric stretching from the Homeric and imperial Roman times to the triumphant crushing of the Soviet threat in 1989. This is followed, among some of the devotees of free enterprise, by the even more self-righteous celebration of U.S. victory in the two Gulf Wars of 1991 and 2002–2005—which has led to so much suffering and death for the Iraqi people. This book seeks to challenge the proponents of the mainstream view on their own ground. But more importantly, it seeks to broaden the terms of the discourse by considering the real issues of human development, instead of confining it to economic growth narrowly conceived. In the next section we delineate in more detail some of the more quantifiable aspects of human development.

SOME MAJOR CONSTITUENTS OF HUMAN DEVELOPMENT

Although a few economic historians in the past tried to measure consumption levels of average citizens or even the poor or the working class, virtually no account was taken of their environment at work or in their homes. In this respect, Frederick Engels, one of the two founding fathers of Marxism, was ahead of his time and also of most mainstream social scientists following him. For in his *Condition of the Working Class in England* (Engels 1845/1962), he paid particular attention to the work and home environment of the workers. Following the economists' terminology, if we regard mental and somatic health as a product of the factors of production, nutrition, medicine, and environment, then they have a limitational relation to one another: if there was too little of one, then no amount of the other factors would render a person healthy or long-lived.

To take a single example, in the nineteenth century, before the bacillus for cholera had been identified, it could kill the overfed rich as indifferently as the ill-fed poor if they used the same polluted water. But if people were well nourished and lived in a clean environment with other well-nourished people, their resistance to the disease would be greater.

The history of physical aspects of well-being in western Europe and North America has been illuminated in recent years through the work of physical anthropologists, demographers, medical historians, nutrition specialists, and a few economists and historians (Drèze and Sen 1990a, 1991; Osmani 1992a; Dasgupta 1993; Tanner 1998).

Baldly stated, there is a strong relationship between the level of nutrition and the ability of human beings to resist infection and a strong relationship between a person's state of health and capacity to absorb nutrients. These capacities vary from person to person, but these intrapersonal variations, in nutrition intake and its absorption or resistance to disease, do not upset the generally positive relation between nutrition and the health enjoyed by human communities. This relationship is, however, affected by the disease environment of the population, which in turn is conditioned by the state of supply of clean water and air, arrangements for disposal of sewage and other harmful by-products of daily life, and agricultural and industrial activity (Gopalan 1992, 1995).

The need of a baby for adequate nutrients starts from the moment it is conceived. Mothers with inadequate or unbalanced nutritional intakes tend to give birth to underweight babies or babies with congenital health problems. The susceptibility of the baby to disease increases if it is deprived of essential nutrients in adequate quantities. If an underweight or otherwise malnourished baby survives its childhood but fails to make up for lost nutrients early enough, it grows into a stunted person with inadequate body weight. Particular individuals, though stunted and thin, may still lead a healthy life. But for large groups of individuals, life expectancy has been found to be strongly correlated with height (Fogel 1992, 1994).

Improvements in sanitation, nutrition, and prophylactic measures lead to improvements in physical capability, a good index of which has been found to be changes in stature. The discovery of height as a measure of human growth is credited to Carl Friedrich Jampert, whose thesis was submitted in Halle, Germany, in 1754 (Tanner 1998). Human biologists and physical anthropologists had long been aware of the relation between height and body mass as a measure of health (for example, Eveleth and Tanner 1990; Tanner 1981, 1998; Bogin 1999), but economic historians and students of human development have discovered it much more recently.

There is some controversy about whether height for age or weight for age is a better indicator for long-term health (Gopalan 1992). But the view propagated by Payne (1992) and Sukhatme (1978), that human communities can overcome nutritional deficiencies and live as "small but healthy" individuals, has no empirical basis (Krishnaji 1981; Gopalan 1992; Osmani 1992a). In particular, with low caloric intake, the risk of infection increases and the capacity for sustained work decreases.

Moreover, there may be individuals who in fact require the mean recommended amounts of nutrients *plus* twice the standard deviation of the requirements. If these individuals were given an intake of nutrients amounting to the mean intake minus twice the standard deviations, as recommended by Payne and Sukhatme, they would suffer severely from malnutrition and their probability of dying would increase dramatically. Both Payne and Sukhatme have been votaries of the doctrine of adaptation of the human organism to low nutrient and caloric intakes. But as Gopalan (1992, pp. 32–33) put it,

> Stunting is the outstanding feature of so-called "adaptation." It is the feature that ensures that not only this generation, but also the next, does not escape from the poverty trap. Stunted children with impaired learning abilities and schooling end up as stunted adults with low levels of productivity, educational attainment, and resourcefulness, earning low incomes and thus continuing to be enmeshed in the poverty trap, and so proving unable to feed their children adequately.[4]

The European experience of biological well-being is particularly instructive in this respect. As incomes and nutrient intakes improved for the general run of population since the last quarter of the nineteenth century and as infectious diseases could be controlled through measures of public health and sanitation and higher private spending on health, the longevity and heights of the general population also improved enormously (Fogel 1992, 1994; Steckel 1995). Equally impressive has been the Japanese gain in height and longevity after 1945. Such dramatic gains have not been observed in the underdeveloped countries even with all the advance in knowledge of disease control. One of the few exceptions to this generalization is Cuba, and its gains have been sustained by egalitarian social policies and an excellent public health service. The interactions between nutrition, proneness to disease, and control of such diseases are complex. A flavor of that complexity is captured in the following passage from Dasgupta:

> The complementary needs of nutrition and freedom from infections are . . . synergistic in a number of cases. This is so in the case of tuberculosis, measles, the diarrhoeas, cholera, and most respiratory diseases. It means that a person's nutrition requirements up to a point diminish as her environment improves.
>
> On the demand side, infections create an additional need for nutrition, by increasing a person's metabolic rate and the rate of breakdown of tissues. Indirectly they also reduce the supply of nutrients. This they do for a variety of reasons. First, infections often reduce a person's appetite. Second, they lower a person's ability to absorb nutrients, by affecting the functioning of the gastro-

intestinal tract. Third, there is increased loss of major macro-nutrients, vitamins and minerals through the faeces because of the increased speed of transit of the food that is eaten. And fourth, infections result in the direct loss of nutrients in the gut. Malnutrition is frequently precipitated by outbreaks of infectious diseases, such as gastroenteritis. (1993, pp. 406–7)

In the context of Europe and the United States, heights have been used as an important index of physical well-being. One reason is that data on heights were available but adequate information on consumption levels, income, mortality, or morbidity were not. Height data came from measurements for the army, for recruitment purposes, slave markets or plantations, information on convicts and deportees, and surveys or registration data for particular groups such as free African Americans in pre–Civil War United States. Apart from the question of availability of information,

> unlike conventional measures of living standards based on output, stature is a measure of consumption that incorporates or adjusts for individual nutritional needs; it is a net measure that captures not only the supply of inputs to health but demands on those inputs. . . . Because growth occurs largely in childhood, stature also provides valuable insights into resource allocation within the family, an interesting phenomenon obscured from household-level data on income or earnings, much less aggregative statistics on output or inequality. (Steckel 1995, pp. 1903–4)

Steckel (1995, p. 1906) has summarized the major determinants and consequences of attainment of adequate height or failure to do so for large human groups. He has classified the determinants into two groups, the socioeconomic and the proximate, and then he has listed the functional consequences of attainment of adequate stature or failure to do so. Under socioeconomic determinants he has listed income, inequality, public health, personal hygiene, disease environment, technology, labor organization, cultural values, and food prices. Under the proximate determinants he has grouped diet, disease, genetic factors, intensity of work, and maintenance inputs. Under functional consequences Steckel has put mortality levels distinguished by age, gender, and disease; morbidity, distinguished in a fashion similar to mortality; work intensity (that is, capacity for work); labor productivity; human capital formation; cognitive development; and personality development. Most of the factors listed as determinants and consequences are complex entities and interact with one another in even more complex patterns.

We will try to provide a very brief sketch of some of these complex interactions, mainly using the demographic experience of Europe since the eighteenth century as our empirical base. The principal reason for this choice is that the scholarly analysis and the data already gathered for the North Atlantic seaboard are far richer than for other countries of the world. But this evidence also demonstrates that neither in history nor in terms of our current understanding of causal links is there a simple relation between aggregate economic development or industrialization and achievements in the advance of human development. But later on we will take up the historical experience of other regions to establish the generality of our argument.

First of all, as we have already observed, an adequate level of nutrition is necessary to provide the basis for a healthy and long life. Nutrition is necessary to provide adequate energy for an organism to support life and metabolic functions at different levels of activity. The energy requirements vary according to the state of the activity. For example,

> pregnancy and breast-feeding require an additional supplement of energy, just as convalescence after an illness does. Energy requirements vary with age and sex, body weights, state of health, level of physical activity and environmental temperature. (Livi-Bacci 1991, p. 23)
>
> Inadequate nutrition of mothers can produce new-born babies with low birth weights. Given the same height, the lower the birth-weight, the higher is the chance of the baby dying before it has seen its first or fifth birth day. (Lunn 1991, pp. 131–33)

But adequate nutrition is not available to a child or an adult simply because she has received the minimum level of calorie requirements. Calories, vitamins, proteins, and certain minerals are required in proper proportions (which themselves vary according to the person's metabolic activity, climate, and disease environment), and at the same time the absolute quantities must be supplied at certain minimum levels. An extremely low intake of proteins and leafy vegetables, for example, cannot be made up by feeding on large quantities of starch and carbohydrates. The ingestion of these nutrients can be hampered by disease, and malnutrition itself allows diseases to get a grip on the human organism. A study of Gambian children found that they were born with abnormally low body weight. But just as they were beginning to catch up, they became subject to illnesses such as gastroenteric diseases, which were themselves precipitated by the rainy season, and poverty that precluded the provision of proper nutrition, prophylactics, and medicine. This weight loss could never be made up by most of the children, and a great proportion of them perished by age five (Lunn 1991, pp. 132–35). Prolonged malnutrition renders people of all ages especially susceptible to infectious diseases, which may have a viral, bacterial, parasitic, fungal, or any other cause.

Direct evidence on the state of nutrition of populations in history is rare, and patchy where it exists. The body-mass index (BMI), which is the ratio of a person's weight in kilograms to height squared in meters, gives a good measure of a person's health.[5] But this information is more scarce than that on heights, which is why I have mainly depended on indexes other than BMI for my analysis. I shall, then, use available indexes of infant mortality rates (IMRs), that is, of the number of deaths within one year of a thousand babies born; overall mortality rates; projected lifetime at birth; and heights as indicators of demographic well-being.

It is obvious that not only aggregate incomes or total nutrients available to a population but distribution of incomes and nutrients will affect the well-being of a population group. So will differences in disease environment. For example, before the advent of modern sanitation and public health facilities, by and large, villages were more salubrious for humans than cities. On the other hand, paupers and the poor in general were unlikely to obtain much benefit from that salubrity if they did not have enough to eat.

Similarly, women of working-class families and working mothers who did not have enough to eat themselves and could not take adequate care of their children would suffer greater morbidity and earlier deaths and would see more of their children die in their early infancy. So class, location, and gender mattered in determining the demographic trajectory of a population. But the evolution of disease environments, and the absence or presence of knowledge of pathogens and how to prevent or ameliorate their ill effects, also mattered a great deal (cf. Bagchi 1982, chapter 8; Guha 1993, 1994).

That a greater supply of nutrients, beyond a point, could not produce better health before the advent of better control of the disease environment is well illustrated by the fact that in England, between 1550 and 1750, the life expectancy of the members of the peerage was roughly the same as that for the rest of the population (if anything, between 1575 and 1675, it tended to be lower); for peers it oscillated from a minimum of 32 years in 1650–1675 to a maximum of 38.1 years in 1725–1750; for the rest of the population, from a minimum of 32 years in 1650–1675 to a maximum of 38.0 years in 1575–1600. It was during the course of the eighteenth century that peers finally gained the advantage by 1.1 years in the first quarter of the century, 4.3 in the second, and 9.1 in the third (Hollingsworth 1957). It is possible that in the earlier period a bloody civil war, frequent military service on the European continent, and addiction to sport and excesses of eating and drinking took their toll on the life of the nobility.

Even with the limited information at our disposal, we can say that most human beings in practically every corner of the world led nasty, brutish, and short lives, at least until the last quarter of the nineteenth century. Only then did people in some of the western European countries and in the United States and Canada forge ahead of people in other continents. Yet Eurocentric historians want to propagate the view that Europe was always (or at least since the ninth century) exceptional in culture and that Europeans and their cousins in other continents have reaped the benefits of that superior culture. If other people cannot follow them, it is their fault in not emulating the superior culture of the white man and the sooner they recognize it, the better it is for everybody.

This apologia is part of a wider apologia of the unequally controlled market and for justifying the havoc that abolition of social regulation of markets and the use of naked power to support that deregulation has caused over most of the world population.

The *Human Development Report 1999* (HDR 1999) lists some of the major ills currently afflicting the majority of women and men. In many senses many men, women, and children not only remain insecure, in numerous cases their insecurity has increased. With the use of existing technologies, the earth is capable of supporting the livelihood of a much larger number of people than are alive today (Smil 1994). But millions in Sub-Saharan Africa and South Asia remain undernourished and in fear of facing starvation every year. Many hundreds of thousands, if not millions, have died of starvation in Africa since the 1970s and continue to die today (see discussion of the U.S. empire in chapter 21). By 1997 the average expectation of life had gone up to 80 years in Japan and 79 years in Canada and medical experts were talking about 100 years as the normal span of human life in the future. But in a great number of countries, for example, Zambia, Sierra Leone, Rwanda, Burundi, and Ethiopia, it remained less than 45 years (Smil 1994, pp. 170–71). In several countries, such as Zambia, Malawi, Uganda, Rwanda, and Burundi, the longevity of people was lower in 1997 than it had been in 1970. In post-Soviet Russia, between 1988 and 1994, the length of life of males had gone down by 7 years (from 65 to 57.5 years) and that of females had shrunk by 3 years (from 74.4 to 71.3 years; Andreev, Scherbov, and Willekens 1998). In a country with a far higher level of manufacturing and military technology, people were dying sooner than in Sri Lanka and Vietnam. Declared and undeclared wars and civil wars were raging not only in Africa but also in several regions of Asia and eastern and southeastern Europe, even after NATO and the Russian Federation had carried out savage pacification campaigns in the territories of former Yugoslavia and Chechnya, respectively.

Inequality of income and wealth had reached a historic high in practically all the rich members of the Organization for Economic Cooperation and Development (OECD), and it was reaching new heights in most of the less developed countries, where income distribution had been extremely uneven to start with (UNCTAD 1997, part 2). Yet the financial press, most of the media, and a very large proportion of economists and economic historians were rapturous about the wonderful results of the final victory of the market over the state and more generally of other collective bodies and of the ongoing process of globalization of the rich, by the rich, and most importantly, for the rich. The downside of this style of globalization is generally ignored by these protagonists of the market. When they recognize it, they use two different strategies for keeping these uncomfortable facts out of real public debate. The first one is to recommend palliatives, which have repeatedly failed in remedying the real evils. In many cases, they have worsened the situation, often by strengthening the hands and extending the reach of the persons and institutions responsible for the damage caused to the welfare and capabilities of the majority. The second ploy is to provide an apologia for the poor performance of the less developed countries, if not of the poor everywhere—an apologia that smacks of attributing an original sin, from which the western European countries alone were able to free themselves. This book addresses this second stratagem of the upholders of inequalizing and dehumanizing globalization and exposes the falsity of much of the mainstream, Eurocentric economic and social history.

CONCLUSION

Human beings have cared about the welfare and freedom of other human beings from the beginning of history. No culture can make an exclusive claim to the heritage of thinking about human beings as capable of reasoning and feeling sympathy for others. However, the scientific and technological means of providing adequate health care to everybody and rendering them fully capable of sharing in the heritage of human knowledge were perfected only in the nineteenth century. There is a Eurocentric perspective on global history that considers Europe and the free market to be almost the sole architects of the advances made in the *possibility* of high levels of standards of living by promoting economic growth. This book challenges that perspective by pointing out that there is more to human fulfillment than achieving a high rate of economic growth and that Europe was not the sole repository of values or methods of organization that advance human development. It also refuses to ignore the enormous price paid by humanity in the course of the spread of the free market (which was rarely free in reality) under capitalist auspices. Capitalism was always associated with the escalation of armed conflict and had led to the enslavement of enormous numbers of people, especially in Africa. I demonstrate that capitalism has continued to exact a high price in terms of human deprivation and deaths. The potential of attaining high levels of human development is yet to be realized by the majority of human beings. I argue that the strategies used by the major capitalist powers are largely responsible for depriving *Homo sapiens* of their birthright as free and fulfilled creatures. Our perspective thus broadens the field of inquiry to include the advance of the majority of humankind and concerns itself with a more complex problematic than an accounting exercise in the domain of economic growth.

NOTES

1. It is, of course, ironical that even now in national income accounting the output of tobacco and tobacco manufactures is taken as an addition to national income instead of being deducted as a nuisance or a cost item.

2. European colonialists reenacted in India, Africa, or other ravaged lands what their fellow members of the governing classes had already been practicing in Europe: policies of enclosing the land by big landowners and depriving the peasants of the right to the use of the commons had been systematically implemented in England from the sixteenth century. The reservation of the game for the gentry to hunt had also been a standard policy (Thompson 1977, 1991; Linebaugh and Rediker 2000). For a colonial valorization of hunting in reserved forests as being peculiarly fitted to the calling of the British rulers, see Pandian 1998.

3. Frank and Pomeranz both use primarily tools of neoclassical and monetarist economics in their exposition. The mode of production does not appear as a category in their account and the dialectics of history or systemic change can find little place in their analysis. In this connection, see Amin 1999; Arrighi 1999; and Wallerstein 1999.

4. Curiously enough, as the concentration of economic power has reached a historic high in the beginning of the twenty-first century, the rich have become victim to rampant obesity, most notably in the United States but also in Japan, many European countries, and beyond.

5. The optimal value of BMI has been found to be about twenty-one for males older than forty, in the sense that the risk of mortality is the lowest for that value. The BMI for two samples of Norwegian and U.S. adult males has been found to lie between twenty-two and twenty-eight. Moreover, given the same BMI, taller persons have a lower mortality risk. For women the risk of mortality is lower with relatively high values of BMI (Fogel 1992, pp. 271–79; Dasgupta 1993, pp. 413–16). The probability of dying at different ages increases steeply as we move outside optimal ranges. That is, it is bad to be either too thin or too fat, although for women the tolerance levels of BMI are higher.

2

Construction of the European Miracle

INVENTING THE IDEA OF EUROPE AND
ITS EXCEPTIONAL CHARACTER

It has been suggested that the idea that Europe was somehow exceptional goes as far back as the ancient Greeks. However, when the Greek writers referred to Europe and Asia, they had in mind only the distinction between themselves and the expanding Persian empire that threatened them and had only the vaguest notions of how far Europe extended, let alone of the geographic, demographic, or civilizational dimension of Asia. If ancient European writers seemed to be convinced of their exceptional society, polity, speech, or culture, so were Chinese or Indian writers of the uniqueness of their situation. Jambudvipa for the Indians and the Middle Kingdom for the Chinese were centers of the known world, and the achievement of everyone else was to be measured by the Indian or the Chinese measuring rod. Territorial chauvinism unfortunately is not a peculiarly European possession, though that particular chauvinism pervades much of the current literature on history and culture.

Finally, the witnesses presented as protagonists of superior European culture are very selective in several ways. You could select other passages, very often from the same writers, to support the most humane attitudes to all living creatures, including human beings, and passages to vindicate some of the most oppressive institutions ever devised. In the very first book of his *Politics*, Aristotle divided humankind into natural slaves and natural masters. But his ideas have been used by later philosophers to espouse universalistic values.[1] Again, Karl Popper excoriated Plato as the most ancient and redoubtable enemy of what he styled the "open society." But Plato's *Dialogues* have served for centuries as models of philosophical reasoning and the Socratic method of teaching and learning (Nussbaum 1997). Thus every generation and every participant in the discourse about human values have interpreted the writings of great thinkers in their own way, and a claim that a designated group of people (such as Europeans) are the only fount of wisdom is hardly sustainable.

There are two other difficulties yet in the way of viewing the European tradition as unbroken through the last two millennia. The first is that at about the beginning of the second millennium much of the Greek learning, including the Aristotelian corpus, was recovered by the Europeans through Arabic translations and textual reconstructions by scholars working in countries ruled by Muslim sultans. The second irony is that the homelands of Greco-Roman culture remained shrouded for centuries in obscurantist ideologies and could be brought back into prosperity and democratic living only through association with parts of Europe, which had been regarded as the frontiers of barbarism within Greco-Roman civilization. The invocation of European exceptionalism in a modern sense gained new force from the final struggle of Christian Spaniards to throw out the Moorish rulers and the Portuguese voyages and raids on the western coast of Africa in search of gold, slaves, and Christian allies (such as the mythical Prester John; Boxer 1973a). The targets of enslavement were racialized and dehumanized, and sanctions of Christian scripture and Aristotelian texts were sought for them (Blackburn 1997; Pagden 1986).

A new twist to the arguments portraying peoples of non-European origin and states ruled by non-European rulers as inferior to Europeans was provided from the seventeenth century. It was alleged by Bernier and Tavernier, French traders in seventeenth-century India, for example, that the Mughal empire, for all its wealth and prosperity, lacked the kind of military technology that was being developed and tried out in the European wars of the century. When these empires were defeated and conquered and colonized by the Europeans, the disdain for their culture changed to utter contempt. For many of the European observers, superiority in the brute power to kill and the ability to subjugate others were the final proofs of superiority of European culture. James Mill wrote one of the most ill-informed histories of British India ever penned and gained the most powerful and lucrative post in the bureaucracy of the British East India Company (EIC). Despite the severe criticism of Mill's book by his editor, the great Sanskritist scholar and former master of the Calcutta mint, Horace Hayman Wilson, it became the standard reference for the colonialist history of India.

Mill's contemporary Hegel, even while he was pioneering a method for analyzing the dialectics of historical change, saw the non-Europeans as peoples without history. The Eurocentric view of history has depended on stereotypes to escape the duty of subjecting all types of human history to the scrutiny of logical and evidential analysis. For example, when absolutist states are discussed in the European context, they are often lauded as necessary precursors of states with bourgeois hegemony. But in the context of non-European societies, they are demonized as universal enemies of human freedom and the spread of the market.

In the eighteenth century, the initial accounts written by European travelers had led the leading European savants to characterize China, India, and Turkey[2] as varieties of despotism. This characterization gained more currency through the writings of Hegel, James Mill, and a large number of writers following them in the nineteenth century. However, the crudest enunciation of this characterization was made at the height of the Cold War by Wittfogel (1957), who resurrected the formulation that virtually all societies outside western Europe before European contact or conquest had been under some form of Oriental despotism. He also provided a plausible explanation for the emergence and durability of such societies. The latter, according to Wittfogel, required large-scale irrigation and water control, and only a centralized and despotic state apparatus could ensure the necessary mobilization of vast numbers of workers for carrying out the task. The findings of most scholars before and after Wittfogel have pretty thoroughly exposed the empirical invalidity of his hypotheses for every civilization from pre-Colombian Central and South America to the river valleys of western Asia, India, and China. But the proponents of the European miracle generally refer to Wittfogel respectfully and implicitly adopt his general perspective on non-European counties (Jones 1981/1987, chapters 1 and 11; Landes 1998, chapter 1).

European-miracle adherents claim to be not just the inheritors but almost the lineal descendants of both the Greco-Roman and the Judeo-Christian civilizations. In a sense, every human being can claim to be the inheritor of whatever has been left as a legacy by all her human predecessors. The Eurocentric historians would deny that claim to a universal legacy. Ironically, however, the Judeo-Christian civilization originated in Asia, the final flowering of Greek science and mathematics took place in Egypt, and the Europeans lost much Greco-Roman philosophy, technology, and law in the centuries between the fall of the Roman empire and the rise of feudalism in Europe. A large fraction of all that knowledge was recovered from Arab sources because the scholars of west Asia, North Africa, and southern Europe paid special attention to the Greek philosophers during the period when the Arabo-Persian civilization spread from the banks of the Indus to the banks of the Danube, the Tagus, and beyond. Much of the so-called peculiarly European inheritance is the result of reconstruction, some of which involved deliberate distortion and erasure as well (Said 1978; Bernal 1987). Considering these interchanges between different parts of Eurasia, it is possible to talk about a common Eurasian civilization rather than an exclusively European one, as favored by Jones and Landes. But that concept will have to include a large part of Africa as well. So if we do talk of differences in civilizational heritage, then we will have to talk about a common Old World civilization as against a New World civilization or an antipodean civilization (comprising Australia, New Zealand, and the more isolated islands of the Pacific).

As we have seen, the Eurocentric historians portray the record of Europe's internal ascent and its outdistancing of the rest of the world as a much more ancient history than it actually is. There is little evidence that European records of human survival, health, consumption, or incomes were in advance of major Asian countries before the nineteenth century. Most of the advances in the crude indicators of human development were registered in Europe only from the late eighteenth century. Even in England, the homeland of the first industrial revolution, the changeover to factory methods was not attended immediately with an improvement in consumption and nutrition of the ordinary people. The grandiose invocation of a "consumer revolution" in eighteenth-century England by McKendrick (1982) has not stood up to serious empirical scrutiny (Weatherill 1988, 1993; Shammas 1993). As far as ordinary men, women, and children working in the fields, factories, and mines were concerned, the Industrial Revolution turned out to be an "industrious revolution" (to use a characterization of De Vries 1993, pp. 117–18). The industriousness was induced by poverty as well as the prospect of making a living by producing goods for the expanding market. The greater industriousness of workers was in many instances associated with worse states of nutrition, poorer physique, and shorter lives. In the phase of domination of merchant capital and so-called protoindustrialization, this also involved more work by women and children working under a putting-out system.

The Eurocentric historians have mystified the growth of private property rights in Europe itself. Common property rights held sway over a very large part of the cultivated land and forests in most countries of Europe until the final triumph of capitalism in the nineteenth century. Private property in land and goods had been recognized in most of the older settled civilizations of Eurasia. In India private property rights were recognized in the times of Gautama Buddha, that is, fifth century B.C. and probably earlier. Moreover, the victory of Europe over the rest of the world owed much more to intra-European military conflict and the resultant advance in the arts of war than to the protection of property rights as such. It is the marriage between the pursuit of profit and the arts of warfare, rather than firm protection of private property rights, that has to be credited with European conquests. Furthermore, the protection of property rights at home very often went hand in hand with trampling rights to property, liberty, and lives of conquered peoples. But as in Europe, also in settled Asian lands such as India, common property rights and overlapping—very often hierarchical—property rights coexisted with exclusive property rights of individuals, communities, and corporations. This generated a mosaic rather than a map of lands clearly demarcated as exclusively common property or unmistakably private property of designated individuals (Perlin 1978; Bagchi 1981; Kumar 1985).

Those who idealize the working of the market tend to underestimate the role of preexisting bastions of privilege in facilitating the concentration of wealth and power under capitalist rules of the game. It is well-known, for example, that through the Protestant Reformation in the sixteenth century and the civil wars of the seventeenth century, a class of landlords came to power in Britain that increased its wealth and power further in the eighteenth century (Habakkuk 1940; Stone and Stone 1984). By various devices such as primogeniture, strict settlement at the time of marriage, and entail, this class tried to prevent subdivision of their property and would impede the working of the land market when it threatened their hold on landed property. One of the weirdest devices used by them to retain their stranglehold on large properties was that of the so-called equity of redemption (Sugarman and Warrington 1996). Under this legal doctrine, which gathered strength between the seventeenth and eighteenth centuries, even after a landlord had mortgaged his property, was unable to repay his debt to the mortgagee, and his property was foreclosed, he retained the right to reclaim his property at some future date. Hence the land market remained heavily biased in favor of incumbent landlords. On the other side of the coin, in nonwhite colonies such as India, in which private property rights already existed, the British conquerors generally subverted the rights of native proprietors and replaced them with much more insecure tenures, contingent on a regular payment of tribute to the new rulers (Bagchi 1992). In countries in which private property in land had not yet appeared, the British colonizers in the seventeenth and eighteenth centuries at first transplanted many features of a feudal tenure, seeking to create a land-based white aristocracy (Craton 1996). When freehold tenure was introduced in any nonwhite dependency, it was restricted almost exclusively to ownership by Europeans (Bagchi 1992; Craton 1996). So the much-vaunted institution of private property rights was racially tinted whenever European conquerors had a free hand. For all these reasons and for the cultural associations that went with them (such as the value placed on ancestry, hunting and sport, going to the right school, and a paradoxical disdain for the trade that fueled capitalist colonialism), British capitalism has been styled "gentlemanly capitalism" by Cain and Hopkins (1986). This story or the story of how the health, education, and purchasing power of the British working people could be ultimately improved only through struggles for democracy, the suspension of the freedom of contract, and extensive state or municipal action (Atiyah 1979; Justman and Gradstein 1999) is generally overlooked in Eurocentric historiography.

That historiography also minimizes the destructive impact that much of European enterprise had on the rest of the world and also the contribution made by the forced extraction of resources from other continents to the development of human capabilities in Europe. Genocide has an old history among humankind (Diamond 1992, 1998). But it is not to be excused just because it has an old history. In many lands, genocide was a systemic outcome of the spread of actually existing capitalism, and some of it was deliberately engineered by the advancing troops of capital. Some of the destruction enhanced the power of the conquistadores and merchants. However, some of the destruction of life, social cohesion, or ecology was a deadweight loss that benefited nobody but could not be stopped because of the very logic of profit-seeking capital and power-seeking ruling classes. The destruction of so-called natural economies did not always or even in the majority of cases lead to the growth of new economic structures that made people richer, longer-lived, or freer. The changes wrought by the onslaught of European capital also left legacies that rendered productivity-raising or freedom-enhancing transformations that much harder for vast numbers of people. Racism, for example, has remained as a permanent legacy of chattel slavery inflicted on Africans by European capital. The caste system in India acquired a new rigidity under the kind of law and order without prosperity or freedom that became a hallmark of British rule in India. Landlordism in India and Latin America inherited from the nineteenth century or earlier has continued to hinder the freedom and development of hundreds of millions of people (Bagchi 1976b, 1982; Morris 1992; Banerjee and Iyer 2002). The ideology of capitalism in its pure form was all the time mocked by the actual developments under the hegemony of European, North American (and Japanese) capital.

This book addresses issues primarily in the domains of the economy and the state and the questions of mortality and survival, literacy, and education. But I also note the pattern and variety of moments in the history of the civilizing mission as conceived by the European conquerors.

Not only the Eurocentric historians but some of the nativist critics of Orientalism tend to ignore these uglier aspects of the civilizing mission. Certainly, religion and science have been extensively used for achieving ideological hegemony and securing legitimacy over non-European peoples. But material and coercive correlatives and their resultant evils have undergirded such discursive manifestations of the civilizing mission. Moreover, similar iniquities were inflicted on their own peoples by European property owners and power holders.

Edward Said's ringing denunciation of Orientalism is also a rebuttal of the Eurocentric view of human affairs (Said 1978). Orientalism and the construction of the West or the essence of being, say, English shaped the way Europeans wrote the history of their own peoples. These constructions were in turn intertwined with theories that justified colonial conquests or opposed them, often by invoking the principles of free trade or liberalism (Said 1993; Semmel 1993; Lindeborg 1994). These theorists were often involved in contradictions, because they were examining a contradictory and complex phenomenon going on through centuries. For example, the great novelist Joseph Conrad wrote of the cruelty and barbarity in Belgian Congo, which King Leopold held as his personal domain, in *The Heart of Darkness*. In *Nostromo* the theme was the sordidness and romance of prospecting for precious metals in South America. But he also wanted the civilization of the West to be purged of the kind of cloak-and-dagger politics portrayed in *The Secret Agent* (GoGwilt 1993). By implication, the lands of Europe populated by Slavs, including Poland, Conrad's country of origin, would be outside the West, as constructed by him. But the countries settled by Europeans outside Europe would be included. Thus the Western civilization in his account is not synonymous with European civilization but a construct limited to a certain style of functioning of states and societies. Perhaps he had only England and its overseas offshoots in mind?

The economic historians and publicists who have come forward as the new champions of the glory of European culture have adopted Conrad's construction of the West. But they would not acknowledge the depredations of the likes of Kurtz as part of the same legacy of the Europe they have embraced. The new phase of Eurocentrism seems to have been inspired, on the one hand, by the experience of the so-called golden age of capitalism (roughly 1950–1973) and more recently and paradoxically, by the patent failure of the Eurocentric, free-market project in most countries outside the North Atlantic seaboard. The dogmatic believers in the virtues of an unrestrained market are trying to explain away these failures by invoking the myth of a unique European culture that the non-European peoples are unable to emulate.

SOME RECENT VARIATIONS ON THE THEME OF THE EUROPEAN MIRACLE

I will take three major works of the European-miracle school, viz., North and Thomas (1973), Jones (1981/1987) and Landes (1998), and try to lay out the

basic architecture of their construct. The most fundamental construct was provided by North and Thomas (1973), as a historical illustration of the validity
of the institutional approach to economics. But unfortunately, they restricted
their view of institutions to the question of property rights and valorized what
they considered to be the strongest attribute of Western societies in the past, a
strong protection for exclusive private property rights. Their analysis closely
mirrored that of Posner, who applied Chicago-style economics to the analysis
of legal rules and institutions (Posner 1973). Later, North seems to have recognized the complexity of Western institutions (North 1989, 1990). He also
admitted that basic political changes were necessary to put private property
rights on a firm foundation and that that did not happen before the close of the
seventeenth century, even in England (North and Weingast 1989).

The most sophisticated analysis of this genre has perhaps been penned by
Eric Jones, since he seems to be more aware of the conflict-ridden and conjunctural nature of the alleged European miracle (Jones 1996, pp. 83–99). In
between lies Landes (1998), who makes a great display of scholarly objec-
tivity and ends up as a less analytically gifted acolyte of his predecessors.

North and Thomas argue, first, that the rise of the Western world to the top
of the tree was almost exclusively due to the fashioning of market-friendly institutions. As they put it, quite baldly (North and Thomas 1973, p. 1),

> Efficient economic organization is the key to growth, the development of an ef-
> ficient economic organization in Western Europe accounts for the rise of the
> West.
>
> Efficient organization entails the establishment of institutional arrangements
> and property rights that create an incentive to channel individual economic ef-
> fort into activities that bring the private rate of return close to the social return.

The North-Thomas (N-T) model is a variation on the neoclassical model of
general equilibrium. In this model, prices and quantities of commodities and
agents or factors of production are determined by initial endowments of land,
the technology available, and demands for goods and services, which in turn
depend on preferences. The principal dynamic of the N-T model is provided
by population growth in Europe between 900 and 1200 C.E. Demographic
growth led to the growth of markets and market exchanges and to rules protecting property rights and better allocation of resources for sustaining larger
populations. Feudal institutions were efficient because serfdom and the
manorial system minimized enforcement costs and provided better protection
to peasants against marauding knights and other invaders.

The notion of efficiency that crops up repeatedly in the market-centered
European-miracle literature is itself problematic, in the absence of freely
working factor or product markets. Under feudalism or systems of coerced la-

bor, which were the norm for most of the period of maturing European miracle, there could be no free factor markets. Hence it is difficult to know whether what was produced was efficiently produced. Moreover, the further question, Efficient for whom? is never even asked. Was it efficient for the serfs to spend their lives working on the manor or trying to pay the rent in commutation for corvée?

The N-T model has further problems. As Field (1981, p. 190) put it, "If population is the key parameter driving the system, how is it that the weakening of feudal bonds is explained first as the result of increasing population (11th–13th centuries), and then as the result of decreasing population (14th–15th centuries)?" The contradiction of the N-T construct with the historical record is accentuated by the re-enserfment and tightening of feudal bonds in eastern Europe, which coincided with the demise of feudal bonds in western Europe. In both regions during this period, population declined and participation in international markets increased (Blum 1961). The typical Eurocentric view deals cavalierly with the dating of the historical changes that are critical for their narrative. Moreover, that view is totally inadequate for analytically tackling issues of interregional interactions—especially those involving unequal power relations between states or population groups.

Eric Jones's story of the European miracle can be regarded as a variety of environmental determinism. If one believed in the pristine continuity of European culture, one could trace this line of thinking back to the Greek physician Hippocrates, who wrote around 400 B.C.,

> We have now discussed the organic and structural differences between the populations of Asia and Europe but we have still to consider the problem why the Asiatics are of a less warlike and a more tame disposition than the Europeans. The deficiency of spirit and courage observable in the human inhabitants of Asia has for its principal cause the low margin of seasonal variability in that continent, which is approximately stable throughout the year. Such a climate does not provide those mental shocks and violent bodily dislocations which would naturally render the temperament ferocious and would introduce a stronger current of irrationality and passion than would be the case under stable conditions. It is invariably changes that stimulate the human mind and that prevent it from remaining passive. (Hippocrates 1924)

When interpreting this passage, we should remember that for Hippocrates Asia could have meant only lands immediately east of Greece and in particular western Asia. He could have had little idea, let alone knowledge, of the peoples of China or India. When he is interpreted today as a precursor of European attitudes to Asia, he must be seen as a person placed in a particular place (which is an extremity of Europe) and particular epoch in relation to a very small part of Asia. (There is yet a further problem: we do not know exactly which books were authored by Hippocrates and which are later compositions foisted on him.)

For Hippocrates, it was the variability of the European seasons that rendered the Europeans more valiant than the Asians (meaning the Greeks compared with the Persians). For Jones, the geographical and topographical variety of Europe, its relative immunity to barbarian invasions from the states of central Asia, and the paradoxical difficulty of setting up centralized empires made Europe politically, militarily, and economically the most dynamic region in the world. I will not quibble here about some of the details of this account, such as whether Marco Polo could have traveled from Italy to China and back without the peace established by the barbarian empire of Kublai Khan or whether the Germanic tribes or the Vikings were less barbarous only because they ultimately merged in the general European population. (The conquest of a large part of Europe by the Mongol emperors and later by the Ottoman Turks also refutes Jones's claim that Europe was immune to foreign conquest.) I will comment only on the absence of any real sense of temporal change in Jones's account and a completely baseless assertion of European superiority, an assertion that is grounded on sheer prejudice derived from old colonialist accounts.

Take at random a number of assertions from Jones's concluding chapter. "European society always contained a number of individuals whose creative talents were directed to improving the methods of production" (Jones 1981/1987, p. 228). Always? And the other societies, never? Why is it then that some of the most important inventions of the world such as paper, silk, gunpowder, or printing were Chinese,[3] that the Arabs had better navigational skills and techniques than the Europeans down to the fifteenth century, or that until the very end of the eighteenth century Europeans were unable to compete with India and China in most areas of agriculture or craft production?

Take another assertion from the same chapter:

Income per capita was higher in Europe than Asia partly because natural disasters were fewer. There was less of the compulsion that Asians felt to breed as many sons as possible in order to ensure family labour for the phases of recovery. (Jones 1981/1987, p. 226)

This is really unadulterated imperialist propaganda. One of the standard arguments of imperialist historiography on colonial India used to be Why is India poor? Because India is overpopulated. Why is India overpopulated? Because Indians breed too much.

Jones seems to be unaware of any demographic work done on Asia or Europe, for that matter, since Kingsley Davis's book on the population of India and Pakistan (Davis 1951). In Germany, for example, birth rates were systematically higher than 40 per thousand and often more than 50 per thousand down to the middle of the nineteenth century, and these were not lower than rates of birth in colonial India and other parts of benighted Asia (R. Lee 1979). Even in 1877, the birth rate in Germany was 40.6, in Hungary it declined below 40 per thousand only after 1897 (Mitchell 1998a). Moreover, Europeans, like other human beings, experienced higher rates of nuptiality and birth after natural disasters and epidemics had caused normal rates of population growth to decline (Van de Valle 1979; Henry 1987/1989; Fogel 1991).

In addition, available evidence indicates that the Chinese were practicing various means of population control from at least the seventeenth century (Li 1998a, p. 20; Zhao 1997b). Finally, there is no evidence that before the end of the eighteenth century Chinese or Indian per capita incomes were lower than the income of an average western European (Bairoch 1981; Parthasarathi 1998). It is symptomatic of the spotty nature of Jones's scholarship that in his bibliographical guide to "India and the Mughal Empire," there is not a single reference to the enormous volume of work accomplished by Indian scholars.

When we come to Landes (1998), the bibliographical references are rather better but the conceptual framework is set in no less a culturalist and ahistorical mold than in the case of Jones. All the stereotypes are there: a full chapter (chapter 3) is devoted to "European exceptionalism," and the view of the author is stated with bluntness, reiterated throughout the book, and summarized again with elegiac satisfaction in the concluding chapter. Landes asserts, rather than proves, that "for the last thousand years, Europe (the West) has been the prime mover of development and modernity" (Landes 1998, p. xxi). He regards Europeans as exceptional because they had democracy and private property from the time of the Greeks as against the Orientals, who were oppressed by despotism and ownership of all property by the monarch (Landes 1998, p. 31). His tome concludes with a culturalist view of global history: "If we learn anything from the history of economic development, it is that culture makes all the difference. (Here Max Weber was right on.)" (Landes 1998, p. 516).

Like the mythical devotee of Krishna, who succeeded in circumnavigating the earth by simply going around the living god, Landes has completed his *pradakshina* of world history by going around Weber and stopping to do his obeisance. Landes's satisfaction with his narrative of the eternal damnation of the non-Europeans reminds me of the story of the walrus, the carpenter, and the oysters in Lewis Carroll's *Through the Looking Glass* (Carroll 1872/ 1965, pp. 153–54), where, you may recall, the walrus expressed his grief over the prospect of eating the oysters after having tricked them into accompanying him.

One reason for the durability of the European-miracle myth is that it has become part of the naturalized common sense of the educated white man in the countries of the Atlantic seaboard. This is what allows serious economic historians to assert, without any methodical inquiry, that Europe was already economically better developed than China or India in the seventeenth century or that allows serious demographers to assert, on the basis of very doubtful evidence, that the expectation of life in Europe was already higher in the eighteenth century than in the rest of the world, or the "present-day primitive societies," or in the "Middle Ages" (Livi-Bacci 1991, p. 20; Hill 1998).

The European miracle, its protagonists would affirm, can be generalized all over the world: all that the learners have to do is to draw the right lessons from the European experience. In its simplest form, the catechism would run as follows: Free all factors of production, including labor and capital, from legal restrictions on their mobility and their use, encourage competition and money-making by profit-seeking entrepreneurs, make private property rights the dominant mode of control of assets, and provide legal protection for those rights. The state should act only as an umpire that from time to time redraws the rules of the game and helps in resolving disputes. Such an environment will lead to economic growth benefiting everybody and that will lead to better nutrition, a stronger demand for education and other goods, and make for better human development all around. An initially favorable endowment of human capital can, of course, speed up economic growth and accelerate the process of further human development. This book rejects this false and fetishized view of human history and the correlated view that human welfare can be left to the mercies of an unregulated market, which is continually manipulated by the most powerful capitalist enterprises and is supported by the power of the best-practice technologies of war.

The construction of the European-miracle story relies on a selective use of European history, on the elision of a large chunk of the history of the majority of humankind, and on a false account of how so-called free markets energized the European civilization and allowed it to conquer the rest of the world. It ignores the role of armed conquest in allowing western European countries and their overseas offshoots to become the dominant economic and political powers in the world. My analysis seeks not only to rescue the history of humankind from the contumely of Eurocentric historians but also to render a truer account of what free markets and private rights meant in different phases of the history of capitalism and of the world under its domination. It is hoped that this will also help us to address the issue of the nature and optimal scope of property rights in the contemporary world.

NOTES

1. See, for example, Martha Nussbaum, "Non-Relative Virtues: An Aristotelian Approach," in Nussbaum and Sen 1993, pp. 242–69.

2. The Europeans were perhaps better informed about Turkey but had a more prejudiced view of it because of the long history of conflict between the European kingdoms or empires and the Ottoman Empire.

3. For accounts of Chinese technical inventions see Ho (1975); and the multivolume work of Joseph Needham and his collaborators *Science and Civilisation in China*, 1954–).

3

Profit Seeking under Actually Existing Capitalism and Human Development

LOGIC OF LIMITLESS PROFIT SEEKING AND COMPETITION

From the late nineteenth century, with the arrival of what has been styled neoclassical economics, economists constructed a polite fiction of competition under capitalism. It was styled as pure competition or, in an even more rarefied version, as perfect competition. Under this conceptualization, a seller or producer operating in the market was supposed to take the price as given and then produce the quantity that maximized the difference between current sale value and current costs. Under this kind of assumption, the passively reacting capitalists end up with zero profit, because anyone can enter the market and competitively price goods so that whatever profit the earlier producers or sellers were making before the entry of new competitors is lost. There are markets or areas of production that have such passive, small capitalists adapting to a given market situation, but capitalism did not conquer the world through such passive adaptation. Capitalism always had as its leading forces aggressive competitors who went out to poach other people's markets, exercised monopoly control over sources of raw materials or acquired powerful holds on them, and ruthlessly exploited the labor of others, without caring much for their welfare.

The nature of the competitive struggle under capitalism was well captured by Daniel Defoe, the great English novelist and an indefatigable reporter on British business from the early part of the eighteenth century. In his account of travels through the length and breadth of England, Defoe described the town of Halifax in Yorkshire, a town that specialized in the manufacture and sale of woolen cloth (Defoe 1724–1726/1971, pp. 491–99). According to

Defoe, the clothing manufacture in the town went back to the reign of Henry
VII, who,

> by giving encouragement to foreigners to settle in England, and to set up
> woollen manufactures, caused an Act to pass prohibiting the exportation of wool
> to foreign parts unwrought, and to encourage foreign manufacturers to come and
> settle here, of whom several coming over settled the manufactures of cloths in
> several parts of the kingdom. (p. 497)

The town grew up as a settlement of scattered dwellings and was a convenient
location for clothing manufacture because "the bounty of nature" in that "otherwise frightful country" provided "coals and running water upon the tops of
the highest hills" (pp. 491–499), two inputs essential for woolen manufacture
in Defoe's day. To prevent the theft of cloth hung on tenters (frames to dry the
cloth) all night, a law was passed directed against stealing, which gave the
power of life and death over thieves into the hands of magistrates of Halifax.
According to Defoe, executions were so frequent under this law that people
became quite inured to them and a proverb grew up among the people of
Yorkshire, "From Hell, Hull, Hallifax, Good Lord, deliver us" (p. 498).

     State policy encouraged the immigration of skilled foreigners and the pro-
tection of property even at the cost of human lives: there was little evidence
of a passive adaptation to given prices in the rising industries portrayed in Defoe's numerous accounts. The notion of competition implicit in classical political economy is that of an active process. Searching for the highest rates of
return, capitalists and protagonists of the capitalist order use political and economic instruments to break down barriers against the mobility of capital and
the agent that it uses, namely, labor (Clifton 1977; D'Agata 1998).

     Writers on issues of political economy were aware of the myriad ways cap-
italist competition used political power to augment profits. This can be illustrated by the writings of some eminent commentators from the seventeenth to
nineteenth centuries. For example, Sir James Steuart in his magnum opus
(Steuart 1767/1966) devoted more than two hundred pages to trade and
industry—but mostly to trade and how to win more trade and more income
from foreign trade and export of manufactures to foreign countries or from
manufactures established abroad by the members of a nation (Steuart 1767/
1966). Steuart has a chapter in his book on the "Consequences of the introduction of a passive foreign trade among a people who live in simplicity and
idleness." He defines *passive trade* as the trade in goods for which the buyers already have a demand and *active trade* as that driven by demand that has
been deliberately fostered or whose supply base has been established in a foreign country. Suppose the traders arrive in a country whose inhabitants have

"great simplicity of manners," who are "abundantly provided by nature with great advantages for commerce," and who are "capable of adopting a taste for luxuries" (Steuart 1767/1966, p. 166). What is and should be the policy of the foreign traders? The answer is "Destroy the simplicity of manners of the natives." If the natives have skins of wild beasts or furs for exchange, offer them brandy in return.

> So soon as all the furs are disposed of, and a taste for superfluity introduced, both the traders and the natives will be equally interested in the advantages of industry in this country. Many new objects of profit for the first will be discovered, which the proper employment of the inhabitants, in reaping the natural advantages of their soil and climate, will make effectual. The traders will therefore endeavour to set on foot many branches of industry among the savages, and the allurements of brandy, arms and clothing, will animate them in the pursuit of them. . . .
>
>   If we suppose slavery to be established in this country, then all the slaves will be set to work, in order to provide furs and other things demanded by the traders, that the masters may thereby be enabled to indulge in the superfluities brought to them by the merchants. When liberty is the system, everyone, according to his disposition, becomes industrious, in order to procure such enjoyments for himself. (Steuart 1767/1966, p. 168)

Steuart here encapsulates the system that grew up around the fur trade and its successors in North America, so long as Amerindians remained major players. But his assumption that Amerindians had an extensive system of slavery among themselves is gratuitous. Hirschman (1977, 1982) has analyzed with insight arguments for capitalism that relied on its potential for bringing about a civilizing and pacifying influence on a world that was racked by conflicts or wars between groups that were ruled by unregulated passions. The basic argument was that calculating capitalists would not give way to irrational conflicts because they would see their profit endangered by mindless passions. But as Hirschman (1982, p. 1483) pointed out, Montesquieu, in the eighteenth century, had already realized that capitalists would use reason instrumentally and, hence, in the pursuit of profit, the welfare of other people or the cause of a peaceful society could be easily sacrificed.

In the middle of the nineteenth century, three powerful thinkers incisively analyzed the possibility of conflict under capitalism. Alexis de Tocqueville, the conservative theorist of the ancien régime in France, hypothesized that when men are radically individualized and their ties of caste, family, and even class are loosened under a system that measures individuals' worth by victory in competition, society may take on the aspect of a collection of isolated individuals ruthlessly pursuing their own goals. "In societies of this stamp, in which there are no fixed landmarks, every man is constantly spurred on by a desire to rise and a fear of falling." (Tocqueville 1856/1988, preface, p. xxvi). The winner-take-all society is only the extreme manifestation of this tendency.

Marx and Engels, the younger contemporaries of Tocqueville, from an opposing ideological viewpoint, eloquently portrayed the reach of competition under capitalism and the armory of weapons wielded by capitalists in search of profit. In their early, but posthumously published work, *German Ideology,* they examined the way capitalist competition pits man against man and transforms social relations. *The Condition of the Working Class in England* by Engels extensively analyzes how worker is forced to compete against worker and how that competition can take the hue of ethnic conflict (such as Irish versus English workers). The *Communist Manifesto* puts the consequences of capitalist competition as prophetic axioms of history. In his magnum opus, *Capital*, vol. 1, Marx covered virtually the gamut of instruments used by European capitalists for advancing their position. They included conversion of free people into slaves, establishing dependent colonies in foreign lands, the forcible expropriation of producers and their conversion into the proletariat, and so on.

A century earlier, Adam Smith had devoted considerable attention to the analysis of monopolies, some of which were legally established (such as the Dutch and English East India companies). In *Capital*, vol. 3, Marx, however, demonstrated that, through the working of the twin processes of centralization and concentration of capital, monopoly arises out of competition (Marx 1894/1966, especially chapter 15). When a capitalist firm makes so much profit that it captures a larger and larger share of the market and drives out many competitors the concentration of capital rises. The centralization of capital occurs when a firm grows in wealth and market share by acquiring one or more firms or by merging with other firms. The twin processes have worked throughout the history of capitalism, but they have waxed and waned with changes in economic circumstances and in regulatory regimes. In the last quarter of the twentieth century, for example, the process of centralization of capital has been much more powerful than that of its concentration, but both processes have contributed to an enormous increase in the concentration of economic power among a handful of TNCs.

Marx was also the originator of what has come to be known as the Schumpeterian theory of innovation. In his *Theory of Economic Development,* Schumpeter (1911/1934, p. 66) defined *economic development* as the emergence of new combinations and proceeded to provide a list of cases covered by the concept:

(1) The appearance of a new good—that is[,] one with which consumers are not yet familiar—or of a new quality of a good. (2) The introduction of a new method of production. . . . (3) The opening of a new market. . . . (4) The conquest of a new source of supply of raw materials or half-manufactured goods. . . . (5) The carrying out of the new organization of any industry, like the creation of a monopoly position (for example through trustification) or the breaking up of a monopoly position.

In his *Theories of Surplus Value*, which was posthumously published in German around 1908, Marx summarized his account of the way capitalism expands (Marx 1971, pp. 280–90). The list comprises practically all the items Schumpeter listed. But Marx goes beyond his predecessors in the school of classical political economy in conceptualizing technical change and the industrialization of research and development as an essential aspect of industrial capitalism and regarding innovation as a major weapon in the competitive struggle. He also went far beyond Schumpeter in visualizing social change as both a consequence and an instrument of the competitive game.[1] For example, Marx theorized that the ability of landlords to realize ground rent because of the concentration of land in a few hands was a positive hindrance to the development of capitalism. Hence his advocacy of abolition of landlordism and feudal remnants in Europe and elsewhere was motivated as much by his perception that capitalist development expands the civil freedom of workers as by his vision of an egalitarian land distribution as a stage in the ascent toward socialism.

We must recognize the use of innovations in the instruments of war and their use in the competition of capitalists of different nation-states in their struggles for markets, labor, and materials (cf. McNeill 1983, pp. 103–316). Early proponents of the spread of the market economy recognized the importance of innovations in the technologies of war as well as production for winning in competitive struggles. For example, Francis Bacon, in his *New Atlantis*, published posthumously in 1627, provided a powerful project of conquering nature by means of scientific research to extract wonderful riches from it, producing new products and new methods of production. But Bacon's amazing list of new methods and products to be created by scientific research, given in the words of his fictional character of a "Father of Salomon's House," also included engines of war that could be wielded to give faster speeds to projectiles and greater destructive power and boats that could navigate under water (Bacon 1627/1986, pp. 77–78).

Daniel Defoe's writings a century later are full of projects of colonization and conquest. The pirates who roamed the seas in the sixteenth century and later or the invaders of the Americas or of Asia by the sea route around Africa did not lack imagination or the spirit of adventure. In a film on early industrial capitalism in Poland, called *The Promised Land,* Andrez Wajda portrays how adventure as well as the search for more profit motivated many pioneering capitalists. But capital has required workers to exploit, and the conquerors have always required victims for their glory. And competition has required humane considerations to be sacrificed at the altar of profit—and extensions of markets or sources of cheaper materials. Thus glory and grime, prosperity and destitution have marched in tandem in the history of capitalism.

But as capitalism transformed the world, it also changed from a system centered in Europe to one straddling the rest of the world, from one in which merchant capital played the dominant role to one in which industrial capital became dominant. As capitalism changed, governing ideologies also changed. Marx and Engels had seen this clearly and had shown how most social institutions are both used and simultaneously subverted by forces of capitalist competition. Values of freedom and unfreedom, scientific advance and its misuse are all the time intertwined under capitalism. Marx, for example, was a great admirer of Darwin's theory of evolution. But he also thought that Darwin was applying the laws of the conflict-ridden civil society that had emerged under capitalism to the kingdom of all living creatures (Marx 1862). Darwin's theory was extended to a theory of social Darwinism, according to which competition sorts out not only individual human beings but whole groups and races into the fit and the (losing) unfit, who are classed as advanced and backward, respectively, the inference being that it is scientifically ordained that the fit are to dispose of, or lord it over, the losers in the competitive struggle (see appendix 1, available on the Rowman & Littlefield website at www.rowmanlittlefield.com/ISBN/0742539202).

Paradoxically, concurrent with stereotyping whole peoples as superior or inferior, capitalist ideology also propagates the fallacy that the behavior of societies can be portrayed as that of a simple aggregate of atomized individuals. In fact, human beings, men, women, and children, almost from the time they are born become socialized individuals. Capitalism socializes individuals in particular ways. Even as it endows a small group with control over means of production and, through the "culture industry" (in the phrase coined by Theodor Adorno [Adorno and Horkheimer 1944/1979, 120–67]), over the means of acculturation, it converts large numbers of people into propertyless workers who can survive only by selling their labor power and who become objects of manipulation by the culture industry (Marx 1857–1858/1973, pp. 485–582). As capitalism advances, individuals also become institutionalized: some are workers in particular companies with their own work rules and authority patterns, others become owners and managers of those companies, yet others become stockbrokers; bankers; or performers in the entertainment industry, print and electronic media, theater, ballet, opera, or vaudeville. In advanced market economies, these socialized and institutionalized individuals enjoy civil freedom. Many different kinds of freedom from restraint have been regarded as civil freedom. I shall generally mean by this the freedom of a person to earn a living, profess a faith or religion, move from one place to another, and engage in ordinary exchange activities so long as these activities do not harm other people or do not violate the laws essential for the continuance of the existing constitution of the state. This last qualification indicates that civil freedom may not be conjoined with political freedom under all circumstances. Civil freedom became universal in western European countries only after World War II. In colonies and dependencies, not only political but also civil freedom was denied to the vast majority of people. Workers were enslaved in Africa and many parts of Asia and Latin America; millions were indentured under conditions amounting to slavery; pass laws and other restrictions kept them confined to particular locations, virtually as prisoners in large compounds. Capital used the male-dominated family, women's labor for family subsistence, and caste or clan networks to secure its ends. Of course, workers waged long and sometimes revolutionary struggles to free themselves from bondage. But the liberatory potential of the market, envisaged by Adam Smith and other Enlightenment theorists remained a cruel fantasy for most of the centuries since capitalism was born.

There is an enduring dialectic under capitalism of freedom and unfreedom, equality and inequality, homogenization and segmentation, as well as of so-called modernity and tradition—a complex interplay of contradictions, which have provided it with its dynamics and its survival through many crises and have aroused protests and resistance of the victims throughout history (Bagchi 1999).

Aristotle had been a dominating influence on the European Scholastic and Renaissance thinkers at the time of birth of capitalism. His major writings are universalistic in their message, as I have already noted. However, as capitalists began to search for cheap labor to appropriate land from the native people in the Atlantic islands and enslave the native people or bring in slaves from Africa to run them, one Aristotelian distinction that came in very handy was that between "natural slaves" and "natural masters" (Aristotle 1988, p. 2). After the conquest of Mexico and Peru, a controversy erupted about whether the Amerindians could be formally enslaved (Gerbi 1955/1973; Pagden 1986) but not about whether any human being could be enslaved by another. That issue surfaced in influential European thought only with the major figures of the French Enlightenment in the eighteenth century, such as Jean Jacques Rousseau, and with the advocates of democracy and egalitarianism such as Tom Paine, Marquis de Condorcet, William Godwin, and Mary Wollstonecraft.

In actual practice, chattel slavery assumed its most extensive and murderous form under the dominance of the market and the sanctification of private property à la North and Thomas, Jones and Landes. Although William Wilberforce and his followers are celebrated in the conventional histories as the great abolitionists, their agitation succeeded only in getting British trade in slaves banned in 1807, that is, leaving intact slavery throughout the empire. The first measure of formal abolition of slavery was carried out by the slaves themselves, soon after the French Revolution, under the leadership of Toussaint-Louverture and his comrades on the island of St. Domingue (Haiti today)— then the richest French colony in the Caribbean (Blackburn 1988; James 1989).

The formal abolition of slavery in the British empire took place only in 1834, after a series of revolts and simmering discontent convinced parliament that it might be dangerous for plantation owners and for British rule itself to keep the system alive (Craton 1982, 1987). But almost immediately the system of indentured labor took its place, which reintroduced severe limitations on the civil liberties of the laborers. By definition, all nonwhite inhabitants of colonies were subjects without any political rights. Moreover, over large parts of the British and French empires in Africa and Asia, only the legal recognition of slavery was withdrawn and no attempt was made until the eve of the independence of those colonies to actively suppress slavery and hereditary bondage (Lovejoy and Hogendorn 1993). It has been estimated, on the basis of data gathered by the League of Nations, that as late as 1936 there were forty thousand slaves and children of slaves in northern Nigeria alone (Lovejoy and Hogendorn 1993, pp. 278–280). Even after the suppression of formal slavery, casual bondage has remained endemic in many of the ex-colonial countries of Asia, Africa, and Latin America.

In the metropolitan countries themselves and the white-dominated countries overseas, the market used preexisting structures of bondage and created new patterns of bondage when competitive pressures made such utilization profitable. In Scotland, for example, down to the end of the eighteenth century, a form of serfdom was used to work the mines.[2] Women's subordination assumed new forms as industrialization spread to new areas. In the so-called protoindustrialization phase, women and children were used in cottages and workshops, and the familial pattern of work and living remained virtually intact even as it became subject to the dictates of the market (Kriedte, Medick, and Schlumbohm 1981). But the coming of the factories destroyed this work pattern, converting many kinds of women's work into men's by mechanizing them and putting men in charge of the machines. In Chinese and Japanese factories in the early twentieth century, especially textile factories, much of the labor was performed by women and girls. Faster population growth in

England increased labor supply and burdens on families. This situation led, under the logic of competitiveness and search for higher profits, to extensive employment of low-paid women and children in mines and other hazardous and murderous occupations (for some illustrations of the conditions of such work, see, for example, the photographs facing p. 181 in Himmelfarb 1984). It took long years of struggle by workers and the more democratic or far-sighted forces to correct the worst abuses of this kind and get the children transferred from the mines and factories into schools. These changes in the pattern of employment in turn affected fertility, longevity, and the position of women in the family, the workplace, and the political sphere (Thompson 1984; Clark 1995; Szreter 1996).

I have used the evidence of changes in health conditions in Europe to argue that the increase in productivity resulting from the spread and intensification of capitalism did not actually improve the physical well-being of human beings until long after the Industrial Revolution had matured in Britain, western Europe, and the United States. Thus the Industrial Revolution as such cannot be credited with the upward movement of this component of human development, although it may have been a necessary precondition (Fogel 1991; Steckel and Floud 1997).

The rise of capitalism was intertwined with the ideology of nationalism. However, armed conflict between city-states in Italy, controlled mainly by powerful merchants and their aristocratic associates, predates the growth of nationalism and the formation of nation-states there and elsewhere. Although the wars in Europe in the sixteenth century were largely centered on dynastic issues, nationalism was already becoming a powerful force in the struggles of England and the Netherlands against the Spanish-Hapsburg empire. Nationalism really came into full play as an ideology only with the French Revolution and the havoc the citizen army of France caused the dynastic monarchies and princedoms in continental Europe. But nationalism was almost always associated with adherence to a particular branch of Christianity, and bourgeois nationalism shared with racialism the tendency to exclude certain groups from full participation in civic and political life.[3]

CAPITALIST COLONIALISM AND THE
ELABORATION OF THE CIVILIZING IDEOLOGY

Merchants have traveled from country to country, from Asia to Africa, from Africa to Europe, and from Europe to Asia for at least twenty-five hundred years, if not from more ancient times. They have accompanied marauding hordes and shared the spoils of conquest in military adventures all over the world. Kings and emperors have also used the wealth of merchants to finance their campaigns. What, however, seems to distinguish European merchants and capitalists since the late fifteenth century is the systematic use of state power to further the interests of merchants, partly to benefit the public or monarchical exchequer, and the habitual use of arms by merchants to boost their profit-earning potential. The use of state power by Prince Henry the Navigator of Portugal and his supporters from the early fifteenth century to conquer ports in western and North Africa, to capture slaves from Africa, to enslave the Guanches, and to get part of the gold travelling from southwest Africa across the Sahara is an early illustration of this process (Boxer 1973a).

European powers could never conquer and subjugate other peoples by using only naked force. The conquerors needed an ideology for justifying conquest in terms of their habitual moral universe; further, to keep the subjugated people under their rule, the rulers required an ideology of superiority with which to indoctrinate the ruled. We witness in these cases exercises in the extensive use of what has been termed "the civilizing mission" by Norbert Elias in his explanation of the growth of politeness of manners among the European ruling classes. Elias is here referring to the *Mission Civilisatrice*, which concerns the preparation of the European gentleman for rule in an ordered society. In the phase of European colonialism, that gentleman would be expected to shoulder the "white man's burden" and try to civilize the benighted natives of the periphery. As we shall see later, the civilizing mission of the European rulers and their ruling apparatus has played a major role in the paradigms of colonial governance.

Elias's work (Elias 1939/1978, 1939/1982) gave currency to the idea that a civilizing process among the ruling class underlay the building up of the architecture of modern European states. The concept is used here to comprehend several other processes as well. One is the fact of the conquest itself and the justification of that conquest. Just as in orthodox Christian theology, it might be better for the heathen to die than to go on living when a Christian has brought the message of the Lord to him but he refuses to accept it, it is also better that an ignoble savage should die rather than go on living after successfully resisting conquest by the civilized white man. Then we have to bring in the ideology of the colonial ruling class, a class that consciously or unconsciously used the ideology of racism to segregate themselves from the people they ruled. Thus racialization of the conquered and enslaved peoples has been a component of this extended exercise of the civilizing mission. The civilizing mission, especially in a nonwhite colony, also comprised a continual enterprise of softening up of the natives and inculcating them with a belief that they *were* inferior to the whites. The civilizing mission comprised the training of the conquerors in the art of rule and the creation of a hegemonic ideology for securing the compliance of the conquered to the rule of the alien conqueror.

The Christianizing justification for aggression of the European merchant-adventurers against the Guanches and the Africans who were targeted for enslavement are early illustrations of one form of the civilizing mission. It came into full play when the Treaty of Tordesillas (1494) between Portugal and Spain, sanctioned by the pope, divided the whole world outside Christian Europe between the two Crowns for future exploration and colonization or conquest. Just before this treaty was signed, Christopher Columbus, a Genoese naval commander employed by the Christian monarchs of Castile and Aragon, had come back with the news, mistaken as it turned out, that he had discovered a new route to the fabled Indies.

The Christianizing justification remained for a long time in the saga of conquest of, and rule over, other peoples. But as secular ideals came to play a bigger role in European ruling circles, it was increasingly conjoined with the conviction that non-Europeans needed to be conquered because they lacked civilization, and it was the duty and the historic burden of the white man to bring the light of reason, science, and civility to these unfortunate people. This idea became, ironically enough, linked to a particular view of progress in human history when Hegel pronounced that non-Europeans lacked history because there was no meaningful change in their histories (Wolf 1982).

A major qualification of a ruler would be a demonstrably masculine quality in outward bearing and daily habits. A certain degree of martial valor would be associated with an ideal member of the ruling class. The first fully capitalist nation, the United Provinces of the northern Netherlands, chose its martial leaders from the Stadholder family of the House of Orange and in moments of crisis would sacrifice mere commoners like Oldenbarnveldt and the De Witt brothers. In England the other emerging capitalist country, early in the era of Tudor absolutism, in 1531, Sir Thomas Elyot declared that the "governors" should engage in manly exercises and that, in his opinion,

> the most honourable exercise . . . and that beseemeth the estate of every noble person, is to ride surely and clean on a great horse and a rough, which undoubtedly . . . importeth a majesty and dread to inferior persons. (Elyot 1531/1966, as quoted by Lahiri-Choudhury 1999a, p. xxvi)

When this ethic of the ruler as the gentleman-warrior was transported to a dependent colony such as India, it acquired other associations as well. Higher officials had to distinguish themselves from mere shopkeepers among other Europeans. This was a snobbery the British took to their colonies from home. Joseph Schumpeter (1943/1950, pp. 134–39) thought that the capitalist order always needed a precapitalist ruling class for putting some discipline into the disorderly working of capital and the cult of the ruler as the educated but martial gentleman provided the ideology for these strata. Gentlemanly capitalism, as christened by Cain and Hopkins (1986, 1987), was born not in 1688, with the final triumph of the gentry-dominated parliament over the king, James II, but much earlier, at the very dawn of capitalism in England.[4] As Elyot and Castiglione make clear, the gentleman was also to be a warrior. In the fight for colonies and resources, he was to be the commander of armies, navies, or the bureaucracy: the qualifications of the rulers must match the needs of the nation-state at the service of capital.

When the gentleman as ruler or the conqueror turned ruler turned gentleman operated in a dependent colony, he evolved a code to distinguish himself from the natives, especially the mere native as opposed to one of the upper classes who might be useful for the sustenance of colonial rule. In 1821 Sir John Malcolm, for example, in his instructions to officers serving under him in the newly conquered territories of western and central India, laid down that, while they must not "sink the rank of the European superior in the estimation of those subject to his control," the new rulers must also accord symbolic deference to the insignia of the status of the superior class of natives (Bagchi 1996a). The British put on oriental robes and manners to conform to their idea of Indian love for pomp. For example, the discipline of the orderly room in many army barracks was styled a *durbar*, that is, at the court of a ruler; Indian noncommissioned officers (NCOs) or other ranks were not to sit down in the presence of their British superiors (Lahiri-Choudhury 1999b).

Masculinity was one of the most complicated tropes used by colonial rulers to legitimate their rule over natives. Quite early in the nineteenth century, Abbé Dubois, a Roman Catholic missionary, characterized the Hindus as timid and attributed their alleged vices of "untrustworthiness, deceit and double-dealing" to their ill-treatment at the hands of their erstwhile Muslim rulers (Sangari 1991, p. 53). The EIC ideologues eagerly seized upon this formulation, for it damned the Hindus as unfit for rule and also became a springboard for maligning those Indian rulers who were adherents of Islam and who were supposed to treat women badly. However, in their own homeland, for a long time, European women were assigned to the private sphere. Moreover, under English law, a woman suffered a civil death on marriage and could not own property or enter into any contract without her husband's permission. In contrast, under Islamic law, women could own property on their own, even after marriage, and did not suffer additional civil disability after marriage. Englishwomen had to conduct a long struggle to acquire even approximately equal rights with men in the civil, let alone political, arena. Because of their own inclination, and out of a desire to minimize the risk of disturbance to their rule, the British rulers assigned Indian women also to the private sphere that orthodox Muslims or upper-caste Hindus considered to be the proper habitat of women. In fact, some Europeans admired the secluded lifestyle of upper-class Indian women (Jyotsna Singh 1996).

On the other hand, there was also the image of the hot-blooded, lascivious native who was out to prey on any woman, especially the pure, innocent white woman. Hence she had to be specially guarded when she lived in India or other tropical or semitropical colonies. Many imperial officials rightly thought that something ought to be done to improve the condition of Indian women, to rescue them from burning on a dead husband's funeral pyre and stop their sexual molestation by the wedded husband, sometimes even before puberty, and getting pregnant in the early teens.

Many social reformers in India, who took to heart the lessons of European Enlightenment or the rationality encoded in many Indian and Arabo-Persian texts, seriously supported the rulers in these endeavors and prodded them to take appropriate measures to eradicate these social evils. However, many of the reformers and the conservatives were early proponents of Indian nationalism. Both groups tended to idealize women as the repository of all domestic virtues, and the private sphere of women was regarded as an altar that must not be polluted by an alien gaze (Bagchi 1990; Sangari 1991). Many Indian women in turn refused to consider themselves consigned to only the private sphere and fought for their rights to education, civil freedom, and a healthy life (see, for example, the writings of Pandita Ramabai [1858–1922] in Ramabai 2000; Bagchi 1990; and Bannerji 2000).

Some Englishwomen, who were themselves victims of class and gender oppression, internalized the image of the typical Indian male as an effeminate libertine. For example, during the agitation over the so-called Ilbert Bill, which sought to bring European residents under the jurisdiction of Indian judges, many Englishwomen were as vociferous as men in denouncing the bill because, according to them, it would endanger the lives and the honor of all European residents and particularly of European women. For good measure, they also doubted whether Indians could be relied on to guard the honor of women of their own race (Burton 1994; Sinha 1995). But on the other side, of course, quite a number of British women were attracted by various strands of Indian religions and sympathized and took an active part in nationalist struggles in South Asia (Jayawardena 1995).

The cult of the masculine European as the natural ruler, because he could hunt dangerous animals, led to the slaughter of vast numbers of wildlife, including elephants and peacocks, which had earlier been taboo to hunt in many parts of India (Lahiri-Choudhury 1999b). For state visits of governors or royal princes, the killing of big (i.e., noble) game was often staged in ways that made a mockery of the valor supposed to be required for such sport (Pandian 1998). That slaughter was somewhat abated by laws passed in the 1860s protecting forests and game and, increasingly, by the greater scarcity of game.

That the civilizing mission could produce many contradictions and effects that had not been intended by the colonizers may also be illustrated by the history of English studies or of scientific research in colonial India. The members of the English ruling class brought with them Western-style theater and a public display of their love for English literature. Many of them also wanted to introduce Indians to the study of Western-style science and medicine. The Education Act of 1835 partly embodied these intentions of the new rulers. But even before that act was promulgated, a number of Indians had taken the initiative to found the Hindu College, in 1817, and the study of English literature was a major component of the curriculum of that college (Bagchi 1991; Singh 1996). British doctors and natural scientists broadened their knowledge of the flora, fauna, topography, and geology of India. Indians had little share in that imperial enterprise until some Indians such as Jagadis Chandra Bose began their own investigations and research centers were set up on the initiative of Indians such as Mahendralal Sarkar and Ashutosh Mukherjee. It was at the Indian Association for the Cultivation of Science, founded by Sarkar, for example, that C. V. Raman carried out the experiments that led to his being awarded the Nobel Prize for physics. Throughout the history of colonialism, there was a dialectical relationship between the civilizing mission of the colonizers and the absorption of the learning of the Europeans; many of the new perspectives and knowledge were used by the colonized for resisting oppression and cultural imperialism. Resistance was also mounted by the colonized by using and reinventing their tradition. Thus the duality between tradition and modernity or between the culture of the colonizers and the colonized became blurred among many groups and in many phases of history.

In this book I hope to dispel the mistaken belief that the so-called European miracle was beneficial to large masses of population before the last quarter of the nineteenth century. I will also document how arms and conquest at the service of capitalists, and states controlled by them, have destroyed human lives in their millions down to the present.

In the above analysis, I have tried to bring out the relationship of the rise of capitalism to the waging of war. In particular, nationalism became associated with winning in competition for markets and resources, and hence war became a tool in the business strategy of states and capitalists. For waging wars, an ideology was needed as a tool for training the rulers and conversely as a rationale for subjugating the workers and the colonized subjects of the conquering powers. "Civilizing mission" in its various transformations provided this essential ideological complement to the conquering mission of capital.

ARRANGEMENT OF THE BOOK

It would be useful to provide a rough idea of the menu of the rest of the book. Part 2 sketches the conflicts among the major European countries between the sixteenth and eighteenth centuries, because this is the period when the leaders among them came to dominate the rest of the world, excluding China and Japan, militarily and politically. This history itself has been broken up into several sections to focus on the competition unleashed by emerging capitalist classes in the marketplace and outside it. I have also sketched some of the major aspects of the state of human development in western and northern Europe during those centuries. I have documented the lateness of the improvements of these basic aspects of human development in the countries of the North Atlantic seaboard. In the process, I have also sought to extricate the analysis of demographic change from the straitjacket of neo-Malthusian ideology.

Part 3 offers an account of the travails of human development in major non-European regions under the sway of capitalist hegemony. To supply a perspective against which to assess the nature of those travails, I have also sketched the history of human survival and economic and human development in China and India between the sixteenth and nineteenth centuries. I hope that this account will demolish the notion that, even before the era of the Industrial Revolution in England, Europe was far ahead of all other regions of the world. I next turn to assessing the cost imposed on other peoples by the competitive drive of the European rulers for grabbing the lands, labor power, and markets of others. (Some of the costs imposed on the European peoples themselves have been covered in earlier chapters.) Finally, I assess how the extraction of surplus from other continents contributed to populating the Americas and Australasia with migrants from Europe and refute the idea that investment by European countries was the prime mover behind the development of non-European countries.

Unfortunately, the damage to human lives, human freedom, and human rights caused by unregulated capitalist competition and myths about the exclusiveness of European heritage to the basic values of human development are not just past history. The whole of the twentieth century was full of conflicts that cost human lives in hundreds of millions and violated the human rights of even larger numbers of people. The danger of wars and violation of basic human rights in the interest of imperialist aggrandizement is even greater today than before. Hence in Part 4 I end with a rapid sketch of the dangers looming before humankind.

NOTES

1. Schumpeter was aware of Marx's priority in both including innovation as an essential aspect of capitalist development and the much broader nature of the Marxian problematic. This is demonstrated, inter alia, in a footnote in the central chapter of his *Theory of Economic Development* (Schumpeter 1911/1934, p. 60n).

2. Scottish colliers were bound to a particular colliery for life. It was only in 1799 that their serfdom was abolished by law (Campbell 1985, p. 142).

3. For a short discussion of the historiography of nationalism in Europe and India, and references to the literature, see Bagchi 2002a.

4. The justification for Schumpeter's view might be found in the books written to advise princes and their advisors and courtiers in the sixteenth century (Skinner 1978a, chapters 5 and 8), Castiglione's *Book of the Courtier* (1528/1959) being the most famous of this genre.

II

CAPITALIST COMPETITION AND
HUMAN DEVELOPMENT IN EUROPE

4

Race for Dominance among the Western European Countries since the Sixteenth Century

ITALIAN PRECEDENTS AND SPAIN'S DRIVE TO ACQUIRE EUROPEAN HEGEMONY

The five centuries that have elapsed since Columbus's landing on the island of Hispaniola have been captured in history, myths, social theory, epics, novels, plays, poetry, and art known throughout the entire world. Much of this history is replete with the celebration of advances in statecraft, political theory, and technologies of production, transport, exchange, and the slaughter of other human beings. We are primarily interested in the fate of living human beings and their records of survival, welfare, and freedom. To investigate this, we need to gain a perspective on the major forces working through the momentous transformations in Europe. How did ordinary people around the world experience the activities of Europeans? European assaults on non-Europeans arose out of a background of intra-European competition for territory and resources and ideologies associated with that competition. It is in the crucible of Europe, with ordinary Europeans as the experimental subjects, that the intertwined techniques of capitalism and war were perfected. Hence it is necessary to sketch, however briefly, the European background to the beginning of exploration and conquest of the peoples of other regions. This exercise will take us over the histories of struggle for European hegemony, singly or in alliance with other powers, between Spain and other powers in the sixteenth century; between France, the Austro-Hungarian empire, the Netherlands, Sweden, and England in the seventeenth century; and finally between France and England in the eighteenth century. But first I have to say something about Renaissance Italy because that is where the culture of belligerence between states for profit (and secondarily, for territory) flowered first.

Between the twelfth and the beginning of the fifteenth century, the Italian city-states of Venice, Genoa, Florence, and several other states of Tuscany led other regions of Europe with respect to technology, social organization, state formation, and major branches of arts, philosophy, and science. Jacob Burckhardt's great work on the *Civilization of the Renaissance in Italy* (Burckhardt 1860/1950) celebrated those achievements. But Burckhardt's work also details the sanguinary nature of the conflicts that accompanied the achievements. If the state became a work of art in Renaissance Italy, as Burckhardt claimed (1860/1950, p. 2) and others have confirmed (Skinner 1978a), under the government of aristocrats, merchant princes, and plain military adventurers, it could also be an instrument of tyranny over ordinary people such as small traders, artisans, and the peasants living in the countryside ruled by the city-states. Moreover, competition for power and territorial expansion kept the multitude of states almost continually in a state of war or preparedness for war. The advances in civilian technology and science also fed into the military machine in many ways (McNeill 1983, chapter 3; Hale 1985, chapters 2 and 8). The condition of the civilians in these states under the quadruple onslaught of excessive taxation, war, pestilence, and famine was as bad as has been witnessed anywhere else in the world (Hale 1985, chapters 7–9).

During the period of feudalism's rise in Europe, it remained a land periodically ravaged by war in one part of the subcontinent or other. Hordes of professional soldiers and knights, many of them unattached to any lord, except for particular campaigns, depended on marauding raids and war for their living (Bloch 1965; Hale 1971, pp. 259–63; McNeill 1983, pp. 65–79). Italy, for various reasons, became a hotbed of conflict (Procacci 1973, chapters 1–5). First of all, Italian city-states were frequently in conflict with one another over questions of trade, dynastic claims, and as willing or unwilling allies of Continental powers such as the Holy Roman Empire, France, Spain, or the papacy. The pope himself was a temporal power in Italy. Then there were civil wars within most city-states between different factions of the ruling elite, often allied with the underprivileged part of the populace. Italy was the first European country to have given rise to rulers whose only claim to power was that they had acquired it. That is, their rule was not based on dynastic claims or their election or choice by a legal body of electors or by some other body claiming to represent the people (Burckhardt 1860/1950).

In the struggle between the Hohenstaufen emperors and the pope, the Italian communes managed to shake off most of their feudal obligations (Procacci 1973, chapters 1–3). The city gained control of the countryside: the city was run by merchants and heads of craft guilds. It relied both on citizen militia and mercenaries for retaining and expanding its power at the expense of other cities.

the great conflict between Pope and Emperor left behind more than a tradition of internecine war. It unleashed chaos; an anarchy of power in which the strong devoured the weak. . . . From 1350 to 1450 Italy scarcely knew a month, let alone a year, of peace. (Plumb 1964, p. 33)

Continual warfare required a steady supply of soldiers. Feudal lords would have retainers who fought on the side of their liege lord when war broke out. But when peace reigned these men would be unemployed. Their livelihood, almost as much as that of knights, depended on there being frequent wars. Thus the increase in the supply of fighting men looking for a master or warlord to serve became a pressure and a temptation to an expansionist prince or an ambitious condottiere.

By the end of the fifteenth century, virtually all the states of Italy had passed under the control of some signor or the pope, become part of the Holy Roman Empire, or were under the Bourbon kings of Naples and Sicily. The only major exceptions were Florence and Venice, which continued to be ruled by a closed oligarchy (Procacci 1973, chapter 4)

While Italian city-states were being overwhelmed by the onslaught of the king of France (Charles VIII led his army into Italy in 1494) and later by the monarchs of Spain contending over suzerainty over the Italian peninsula, Portugal and Spain on the Atlantic seaboard were seeking new routes to Asia, which was seen as the source of untold wealth to be won by the hardy adventurer. They wanted to circumvent the old routes through the Levant and the Mediterranean, which were dominated by Venice and an expanding Ottoman empire, which had taken over Constantinople, the capital of the derelict Byzantine empire, in 1453. The search for Christian allies against the Muslim kingdoms ringing the southern and eastern shores of the Mediterranean also provided a strong stimulus for this search (Parry 1973, chapter 1). They expected to find Christian allies in Ethiopia, the land ruled by the mythical Prester John. The marriage between the counting house and combat, united against non-European heathen and other monarchies, whether they professed Christianity of a Catholic or Protestant denomination, was solemnized, as I have noted previously, by the rhetoric of the civilizing mission.[1]

The history of Europe was greatly influenced by four events that occurred in the 1490s, namely, the final victory of Ferdinand and Isabella over the Moorish kingdom of Grenada, the voyage of Columbus to the Caribbean in 1492, the invasion of Italy by Charles VIII of France in 1494, and the voyage of Vasco da Gama in 1498 to the western coast of India by circumnavigating Africa. By the time Charles invaded Italy, his kingdom had probably become the most populous country of western Europe. But through inheritance and dynastic alliances, Charles V, the Holy Roman emperor, became also the king of Castile, Aragon, and the kingdom of Naples and emerged as the most powerful monarch of Europe (Elliott 1963a, chapter 3).

Why did Spain ultimately fail to emerge as the supreme capitalist power in Europe, instead becoming increasingly mired in economic and fiscal stagnation? First, the Spanish monarchs could never solve the problem of raising enough money to afford their military and territorial ambitions. Second, the social and political structures became more rigid as a result of the compromises the Spanish monarchs had to adopt and stifled the growth of capitalist classes and institutions backing them. I will pick out only some of the more salient examples of these contradictions before moving on to the story of the other challengers for European hegemony.

Even at the conclusion of the reign of the intensely anti-Muslim Catholic monarchs, the fiscal balance of Spain had been in the red (Rich 1971, p. 449). They often borrowed money from the Mesta, the immensely wealthy Honourable Consejo de los Pastores de estos Reinos, the guild of Castilian sheep owners. They also raised money on the security of the pasture grounds owned by the Crown (Batista i Roca 1971, pp. 317–19). As the financial needs of the Spanish monarchs increased in the sixteenth century, so did the power of the Mesta and the concessions exacted by it. This harmed not only the exchequer but also the growth of field crops, especially wheat, because the Crown forbade cultivation in larger and larger areas so that sheep could be pastured. The transhumant pasturing of sheep in Spain tended to increase the risk of soil exhaustion.

During the reigns of Charles V and his son, Philip II, the immense access of riches and liquid capital resulting from the conquest of Mexico and Peru led to fiscal profligacy: this was the inevitable result of continual warfare and the entrenchment of feudal lords who escaped most forms of taxation but fattened on lucrative positions in the royal administration. The inflow of silver into Spain from the mines of Mexico and Peru led to price inflation. This caused a gap between prices and wages and increased the share of profits of capitalists in countries such as England and France that had an emerging capitalist class. This stimulated the growth of production in those countries. But in Spain itself, because of the dominance of feudal lords and other feudal elements, prices rose without inducing a corresponding supply response. Inflation in Spain induced formulation of the monetarist theories of Jean Bodin and some of his Spanish contemporaries. Earl Hamilton, and following him Keynes, put forward the hypothesis that the influx of American silver raised prices while wages lagged behind. This led to profit inflation and hence stimulated economic growth (Hamilton 1929; Keynes 1930, vol. 2, chapter 30). That thesis had been anticipated by Richard Cantillon in the eighteenth century and Karl Marx in the nineteenth (Marx 1849/1969, p. 164). There is, however, grave doubt about the validity of the thesis in this form for Spain, or even for England. The former experienced economic stagnation, and in the latter the growth of capitalism was facilitated by the abolition of feudal tenures and a significant growth of population between the sixteenth and the middle of the seventeenth century (Felix 1956; Vilar 1956)

In Spain, price rise with its deleterious effect on the standard of living of ordinary people began even before the influx of American silver. Taking the price index of wheat in Castile as 100 in 1511, it increased to 273 by 1531, long before the flood of silver inflow from the Americas. The poorer peasantry, along with herders and craftsmen in villages and towns, were net buyers of grain and they all suffered from the inflation (Batista i Roca 1971, p. 317). The Spanish rulers tried to centralize administration and put the absolutist state above society. But while the monarchs acquired a degree of control over the administrative apparatus, a large part of the political reality on the ground escaped their grasp, even with the institution of *corregidores* as the eyes and arms of the royalty in Castilian domains. Another paradox of the Spanish state was that the formal union of various patrimonial realms of the monarchs under the same ruler never really united those realms either politically or economically (Elliott 1963a, 1963b; Anderson 1974, pp. 60–84; TePaske and Klein 1981). As Elliott (1963b, p. 2) put it, the union of Castile and Aragon was "not a union of equal partners, and, . . . as union, it was no more than dynastic." The laws and customs remained different, and the currency remained different. There were also enormous differences in the demographic and economic weight of the different constituents of the Spanish kingdom: while Catalonia (a part of the kingdom of Aragon), for example, was the most developed province in terms of commerce and trade, the population of the kingdom of Aragon was less than a sixth of that of Castile-Leon (Elliott 1963b, chapter 1; Mauro and Parker 1980, table 2.1).

The conquest of the Americas was financed by Castile and, therefore, the kingdom of Aragon and other domains of the Spanish monarch were kept out of the monopoly of trade with the Americas that Castilian citizens were granted. Other aspects of Castilian rule also tended to keep the ruling stratum of the far-flung dominions of the Spanish empire alienated from the ruling apparatus located in Castile. Most of the lucrative posts of the administration were taken by Castilian grandees. Moreover, in their zeal for attaining centralization and bureaucratic rationality, the top officials tried to bypass and override the liberties of estates in non-Castilian domains. This created resentment and sometimes active revolt, as in the Netherlands and Portugal and even in Catalonia (between 1640 and 1652).

Catalonia and Valencia had been the commercially advanced part of Spain at least from the thirteenth to the fifteenth centuries (Batista i Roca 1971,

p. 317). Catalonia suffered from the general depression of European trade in the fourteenth century and was badly battered by the revolt of 1462–1472 against the rule of John II, the father of Ferdinand. Catalonia emerged exhausted from the revolt but retained its traditional liberties (*fueros*). If Castile had allowed the Barcelona merchants to participate in its transatlantic trade, both Spain and Aragon would have benefited but the sclerotic structure of Spanish rule and its dynamics would not allow this to happen.

The Spanish monarchs created councils for different parts of the realm and viceroys who were supposed to report to the councils and ultimately the king. But the different parts of the realm had very different political structures. In Castile municipal governments were handmaidens of the central government. But Aragon, especially Catalonia and Barcelona, enjoyed a very high degree of autonomy, typified by the oath of allegiance to the king sworn by its nobility: "We who are as good as you swear to you who are no better than we to accept you as our king and sovereign lord, provided you observe all our liberties and laws; but, if not, not" (quoted by Anderson 1974, p. 65n).

From the union of the two Crowns, the final victory against the Moorish kingdom of Granada, and the conquest of Mexico and Peru, Spain emerged as the strongest military power in Europe. The ideological backing provided by the papacy in its fight against Protestantism also was a powerful instrument in Spain's armed confrontation against England, the Netherlands, and the Protestant princes of the Holy Roman Empire in Germany.

As I have noted, despite the inflow of apparently limitless supplies of treasure from its American colonies, the ordinary people of Spain did not gain economically from the imperial splendor. Prices rose in Castile, then in other regions in Spain and other countries of Europe (Davis 1973; Spooner 1968). Price rise and the expansion of expenditures in Castile by the government and private individuals benefiting from the American trade and plunder at first attracted immigrants into Castile and parts of Aragon, which had more cultivable land. But the expansionary impulses of the real economy were soon exhausted. The artisanal manufactures became too expensive compared with the produce of its competitors, and imports of foreign products flooded the Castilian territories. Moreover, the restrictions on the expansion of the arable land, noted earlier, necessitated the import of grain from abroad. These developments were compounded by the almost continual state of war in which Charles V and Philip II plunged the Spanish state.

Hapsburg imperialism eventually placed an insupportable burden on the resources of Castile. Because the country was so effectively tamed and so efficiently governed after the *comuneros* rising of 1520–1521, it proved possible to levy far higher taxes on the Castilians than in any other European state. By the 1590s some farmers were obliged to pay half their income in taxes, tithes, and seigneurial dues. The level of taxation doubled between 1556 and 1584, rising faster than even the level of prices (Mauro and Parker 1980, p. 49).

Despite the uncertainty surrounding the data, most authorities agree that the population of Castile actually declined from the last quarter of the sixteenth century (Elliott 1970, pp. 438–39; Mauro and Parker 1980, pp. 37–41). At the same time the population of Catalonia probably continued to increase until the 1630s. However, the kingdom of Aragon was a very reluctant participant in the war effort of the Hapsburg monarchs. From the 1630s the principality of Barcelona began to suffer from the recession that affected most sectors of European trade. Then the Duke of Olivares, who guided the fortunes of Spain at the time, pushed Spain into war with France over dynastic claims to the kingdoms of Navarre and Catalonia and had imperial soldiers billeted on Catalonian soil. Because soldiers lived off the region they were billeted on, the people experienced heightened oppression. The social and political distance of the Catalonians from effective central rule also produced increased disorder and the rebellious peasantry often turned into bandits (Elliott 1963b, chapter 3; 1970, pp. 466–69; Parry 1973, chapter 12). The revolt of the Catalans started on 7 June 1640 with riots in Barcelona culminating in the murder of the viceroy (Elliott 1970, p. 469). It took twelve years for the revolt to be put down. By then the Catalonian economy was in ruins and Spanish power was exhausted.

In military technology, Spain had led the rest of Europe in the sixteenth century. But then the Netherlands, Sweden, and France caught up with and surpassed the Catholic kingdom. The weaknesses resulting from excessive centralization and the financial problems of the state multiplied as Spain got more and more enmeshed in expansionist projects. Charles V and Philip II were bankrupts and had ruined some of the biggest financiers of Europe, such as the Fuggers of Augsburg.

The American possessions of Spain were critical in allowing Philip II to pursue imperialist aims well beyond the real resources of the Spanish economy. In spite of repeated bankruptcies, the bankers were willing to lend money to the Spanish monarch on the expectation, and often the security, of treasure-laden Spanish galleons (Koenigsberger 1968). Silver acted as the hegemonic currency and provided Spain with the power to dispose of real resources, that could not be matched by any one of Philip's enemies acting alone. But ultimately this resource could not save Spain from debility. When Philip II died in 1598, interest payments on the public debt of Spain amounted to two-thirds of all revenues (p. 312). Connected with the parlous state of the public fisc was the increasing inability of Spain as a country to afford the imports forced by the ruin of its manufacture and arable agriculture. These deficits were met by inflows of silver from the Americas. But official or semiofficial pirates from

England, France, and the Netherlands often captured the treasure galleons on the high seas, even when there was no active war with those countries. More importantly, the silver was already mortgaged for servicing Spain's debt: many of Spain's creditors were foreign financiers and many belonged to enemy countries such as the Netherlands.

Stemming from the predominance of feudal institutions in Castile was its great dependence on royal and administrative initiatives in many areas in which private enterprise in countries such as England, France, and the Netherlands proved to be far more efficient. This was particularly true of seaborne trade, naval warfare, and shipping. In 1620, for example, the year in which war again broke out between the Netherlands and Spain, out of 105 voyages made directly from the Iberian peninsula to the Baltic, 91 were made by Dutch vessels. In 1670 the value of goods shipped to Cadiz from the Netherlands came to six million *livres tournois* and correspondingly, the value of silver remitted to the Netherlands from Cadiz came to two million pesos (Israel 1989, pp. 29, 232). In 1670 France was the biggest exporter to Spain and the biggest recipient of silver from that country. From 1716 down to the end of the eighteenth century, Spain had a continual trade deficit with other European countries and its deficit with France was particularly large (Mauro and Parker 1980, pp. 46–48}. The exploitation of the Amerindians and the imported slaves from Africa, however, allowed the Spanish ruling classes to maintain a social and political structure that contrasted with the ordinary Spaniards' poverty, squalor, and illiteracy (Elliott 1963a, 1963b; Spooner 1968, pp. 67–78; Williams 1972, chapters 3 and 4).

LA GLOIRE OF FRANCE AND THE CONDITION OF THE FRENCH PEOPLE

The country that disputed the attempt of the Catholic kings and the Hapsburgs to dominate European affairs was France. In the sixteenth century it emerged as the most populous realm of western Europe and the French king controlled larger domestic resources than the Spanish monarch. Effective French challenge to the Hapsburgs of Spain and Austria for European hegemony had to wait until the beginning of the seventeenth century because it was riven by civil war between the Protestant Huguenots and the Catholics. That conflict was compounded by the challenge to royal authority posed by the great Catholic and Huguenot nobles alike (Koenigsberger 1968, pp. 291–318).

It is no accident that the theory of sovereignty to rationalize the consolidation of the absolutist state should have been given a canonical formulation by Jean Bodin, who lived through the civil war in France (Mousnier 1970a;

Skinner 1978b, pp. 284–301). Henry of Navarre renounced Protestantism and became King of France and managed for the time being to douse the fires of civil war.

Unlike most parts of Spain, France had a large population of peasants who had freed themselves from feudal bondage and thriving merchants trading from the western and southern ports (Mousnier 1970b; Anderson 1974, chapter 4). The real foundations of the absolutist state in France were laid under Louis XIII who effectively vested the chief executive power in Cardinal Richelieu. The cardinal proceeded to destroy the armies and independent power bases of regional grandees such as duc de Rohan, who had emerged as the leader of the Huguenots (Mousnier 1970b, pp. 484–89). During the minority of Louis XIV the regional nobles led the revolt of the Fronde (1648–1653), and the French state was once more threatened with disintegration. However, with the suppression of the Fronde, under Louis XIV French absolutism reached its apogee.

The absolutist state of France, however, was also highly corrupt, with offices being sold to the highest bidders and becoming heritable. Richelieu, who merely imitated the usual practices of his time, "made his relations marshals of France, generals of galleys, governors, dukes and peers. He made one of his nieces duchesse d'Aiguillon; another married the duc d'Enghien and became a princess of the blood. He owned fortresses which he left to his heirs, at Brouage and Le Havre" (Mousnier 1970b, p. 493). The society this state presided over remained poor and subject to periodic famines and what were dubbed periods of mortalities (Mousnier 1970b; Spooner 1968).

When poor harvests were accompanied by epidemics—the time of mortalities—the workers were the worst hit, especially in 1630–1632, 1648–1653, and 1660–1662. "In the poorest quarters of Beauvais the expectation of life was eighteen years. . . . In the country 'mortalities' might carry off a third of the population. Day labourers were the main victims, and with the death of many craftsmen there were long economic crises . . . . Bands of vagabonds descended on the towns and there were peasant risings" (Mousnier 1970b, p. 480).

Cardinal Mazarin took Richelieu's place after the death of the latter and became the chief advisor of Louis XIV during his minority. After his death, Louis XIV became both the monarch and the chief executive of France. He may or may not have said, "L'etat c'est moi," "but that was the position ascribed to him by his extreme admirers and his extreme opponents" (Clark 1961, p. 181). The principal purpose for which he and his ministers used the absolutist institutions was internal pacification and glory through conquest. Colbert, the finance minister of Louis, rationalized internal customs, tolls, and trade restrictions and protected French manufactures and other produce against foreign competition. But his reforms fell short of a really developmental effort. In any case, most of his policies were aimed at furthering power rather than plenty, although as Viner (1948/1969) argued, the contrast between the two can be exaggerated. Furthermore, under the prevailing tax system of France, the peasantry and artisans bore most of the burden. The chief sources of revenue were the *gabelle*, the salt tax, and the *taille*, the direct tax that impinged very unequally on different regions and on town and country. Townsmen paid less than country people, and nobles and other people who could buy an official position or a title of nobility were exempted. Everybody with a social standing tried to use influence and overt or covert bribes to reduce the assessments. The *taille* and the *gabelle*, then, bore heavily upon the poor, and especially the peasants (Lough 1961; De Vries 1976, pp. 200–4). France, of course, was not alone in imposing a crushing fiscal burden on an overburdened and often unfree peasantry. But the contrast between the public grandeur of the Sun King (*le roi soleil*) and the squalor behind the effulgence was more stark than in most other countries of western Europe of the time.

The size of the army under Louis XIV reached a new high, with 350,000 or more men under arms. But despite the heavy taxation the French people were subjected to and despite large loans raised by the government, the troops were often paid by booty, sometimes exacted from the subjects of the Sun King, but more often from the enemy population. Apart from plunder, contributions were extracted from the residents of an area in which the army operated. These were

> levied over a sizeable area to be paid in a regular fashion, usually during an extended period of time. On his own initiative, the local army commander set and apportioned the amount demanded and backed his demands with the threat of violence, essentially burning. While part might be paid in kind, Wallenstein's [a general in the imperial army] contributions were a money payment. The Thirty Years' War [1618–1648] was primarily funded through contributions. (Lynn 1993, p. 296)

In the case of the French state, contributions from people in foreign lands where the army might operate came to play a regular part under the rule of Louis XIV. "Contributions for major areas were set by formal agreements, *traites*, hammered out by French officials and local authorities. These *traites* laid out the financial obligations and promised protection to those who paid regularly" (Lynn 1993, p. 297).

At the end of the long reign of Louis XIV, France was exhausted. It is doubtful whether, with all the famines and excess deaths caused by wars and the deprivation civilians underwent because of the wars, the population of France had expanded over the fifty years of his absolutist rule (Goubert 1970, chapters 1 and 15; 1991, chapter 9). Inequality between commoners and nobles almost certainly increased during his reign, in spite of expansion in certain pockets of manufactures. In 1694 Archbishop Fénelon wrote that "France had become 'nothing more than a great hospital, devastated and without provisions'" (Le Roy Ladurie 1996, p. 210). In short, in France, as earlier in Spain, the grandeur at the height of European and world empire inflicted heavy and debilitating punishment on the domestic population as well as the targets of conquest.

IMPERIAL VENTURES OF SWEDEN AND THE NETHERLANDS

From the beginning of the eighteenth century, the major struggle for ascendancy in Europe was fought out by Britain and France, and it ended only with the final defeat of Napoleon in the battle of Waterloo. But two small countries played the role of big powers in the seventeenth century. These two were Sweden and the northern provinces of the Netherlands, which revolted against Spanish rule in the sixteenth century and became the most powerful maritime power in western Europe, until superseded in that role by Britain. At this point, I shall briefly recall the history of Sweden. It illustrates the roles of absolutism and the army and armaments industry in the rise of a state otherwise poor and suffering natural disadvantages, as well as the contradictory and changeable impact of that absolutism on the human development of the people governed by it.[2] The evolution of the absolutist state and its impact on the lives of the ordinary people also depended on developments in the wider European and global economy. For example, the stagnation of agriculture in Europe in the latter half of the seventeenth century and fall or stagnation in population induced many landlords and nobles to increase the burdens on the peasantry. These included in some cases a greater burden of labor services on even nominally free tenants and greater restrictions on the mobility of peasants and laborers.

With the successful intervention by its king, Gustavus Adolphus, in the Thirty Years' War on the Protestant side, Sweden's career as a great power was recognized by other European belligerents. Gustavus Adolphus was killed in the battle of Lützen, but the Swedish came out victorious, and the war was continued by his successors. Along with France, Sweden was a guarantor of the Peace of Westphalia (1648) that ended the Thirty Years' War. Under that treaty Sweden gained enormous possessions in Germany, and the great rivers of north Germany and the port of Stettin came under Swedish control. But the Swedish peasantry paid a heavy price, as did most peasantries of the belligerent countries, for this martial glory.

Sweden's nobility formed a small fraction of the population, but it controlled most of the nation's wealth. Over the first half of the seventeenth century, because of incessant wars and the taxes paid by the ordinary people to defray the cost, the share of the high nobility in the landed property increased steeply. The nobility enjoyed exemption from direct taxation and the taxable capacity of the common people, who were the main taxpayers, declined over time. Crown lands as well as taxes from the landowning peasants passed into the hands of the nobility, especially the high nobility, as payment for recruiting of regiments or in lieu of unpaid salaries. This applied especially to the newly conquered provinces; but even in Sweden and Finland the loss of Crown land reached such proportions that in 1655 "two-thirds of all farms were reckoned to be in the hands of the nobility. Since the nobility enjoyed tax-exemption, taxes were paid from every third farm only, and the resulting deficit had to be covered by extraordinary contributions formally voted by the Estates during a session of the Diet" (Rosen 1961, p. 520). All this caused enormous dissatisfaction among the landowning peasantry and the smaller nobility, but the situation did not change until the beginning of the absolute rule of Charles XI in 1680.

Sweden was able to mobilize resources other than domestic taxes on land for defraying war expenditure. Gustavus Adolphus succeeded in attracting Flemish and Dutch entrepreneurs to come and invest in Swedish mining and industry. Sweden had rich copper and iron mines, and it became the major source of metal for the extensive copper coinage of the times and the base of a profitable armament industry for making guns and artillery. The state exercised a monopoly over the sale of copper. After its defeat of Denmark and capture of large parts of north Germany, it issued licenses for a fee to ships plying the Baltic or using the ports controlled by it. These practices were resented by its allies, particularly the Dutch. But they were fully congruent with the practice of providing protection for a fee wherever any European power could get away with such exactions.

The power of the high nobility declined after the war of 1675–1679, in which Sweden sided with France and fought against Denmark and the Holy Roman emperor of Germany. Initially, the war went badly for Sweden when its affairs were managed by a regency of high nobles that had been formed during the minority of Charles XI. When the latter took charge, he proved his generalship, overcame the reverses suffered under the regency, and thoroughly defeated the Danes. Sweden enjoyed relative peace during the period 1680–1699, partly because its potential enemies, such as Denmark, Poland, and Russia, were distracted by other conflicts. Charles also tried to decrease Sweden's dependence on contributions from subsidiary territories by raising funds from internal resources (Black 1990, pp. 17–18).

During Sweden's peaceful period, Charles XI took a number of steps to punish those considered to be particularly culpable for the regency policy. By the beginning of the 1690s he made himself an absolute monarch, accountable only to God. His policies included the resumption (*reduktion*) of Crown lands from the high nobles and fresh grants made on the principle of service tenure, or *indelningsverk* in Swedish.

> The income from certain farms was earmarked for certain officials, officers were assigned farms to live on, etc. . . . About 80 per cent of all the farms alienated to the nobility returned to the Crown or to peasants who paid taxes to the Crown. . . . While the nobility in 1655 possessed two-thirds of the total number of farms inside Sweden-Finland, the proportion at the end of the seventeenth century inside the new borders (that is, inside the provinces conquered from Denmark-Norway) was: 33 per cent of the farms was owned by the nobility, 36 per cent by the Crown, and the final 31 per cent by the tax-paying peasants. (Rosen 1961, pp. 534–35)

The peasants became dependent on the Crown officials rather than the nobles but their condition was little better than before.

Did the ordinary people enjoy greater freedom under the royal absolutism of Charles XI than under conjoint absolutism of the king and the nobility in the earlier epoch? Sweden had effective conscription much earlier than other European states, and it took a heavy toll of Swedish lives during the Thirty Years' War. Charles XI's reforms increased the rigors of conscription and servitude to the emergent hard state (which very probably provided the contrasting model for the "soft state" that Gunnar Myrdal [1968] blamed for the ineffectiveness of the incipient developmentalism in most Asian underdeveloped lands, especially the countries of South Asia). He introduced a labor law restricting the movement of peasants and artisans. By the Church Law of 1686, he decreed that every Swede must be able to read the Bible to receive communion and without communion nobody could marry. This measure was taken partly because it was thought that literate males would make better soldiers. This apparently made literacy, in terms of reading but not writing, universal in Sweden by the latter half of the eighteenth century, that is, earlier than in any other country in the world. This singular achievement did not increase the political freedom of the ordinary people. The civil freedom of propertyless (wo)men was restricted in the interest of the landowning peasantry and nobility; moreover, the liability for serving the army constrained the civil freedom of everybody except the privileged nobility. The Swedish state also followed a policy of making Swedish the only language of instruction for all the provinces conquered from Denmark and German princes. This policy succeeded remarkably in spreading the Swedish language in the case of Scania

and other former Danish possessions now within Sweden but not for other territories such as Livonia and Estonia. But the successful cases must have involved a considerable degree of official (including church) tyranny. Thus a reforming hard state adversely affected several aspects of human development
even as it promoted it in other directions.

The expansionist policies of the next ruler of Sweden, Charles XII, nearly
ended in a disaster for the country, and the situation was saved only by the
death of Peter the Great of Russia, and the conciliatory policies pursued by
Catherine II, his successor. After the death of Charles XII in 1718, a new
constitution, promulgated in 1720, pared the powers of the king and established the representatives of the four estates, namely, the nobility, clergy,
burghers, and landowning peasants as the supreme legislative and executive
authority (Hatton 1957, pp. 351–64). It is likely that in this period of rule by
the property-holders, which ended with the absolutist coup of Gustavus III
in 1772, the landowning peasantry gained more rights. Such gains were reflected in an improvement of the crude indexes of standards of living but
with a lag. It has been estimated that the infant mortality rate (IMR; newborns per thousand who die in the first year of life) was 205 in the decade
1751–1760, rose to 216 in the next decade, and then began to fall—steadily,
but slowly—from the next decade (Imhof 1979, p. 360). This improvement
was achieved earlier than elsewhere in Europe. The drastic fall in real wages,
however, may have slowed the advance in survival rates. For both agricultural laborers in all of Sweden and hodmen (who can be taken to represent
unskilled labor) in Stockholm, real wages fell from a little less than about an
index of 150 in 1730 to a low of 50 before recovering to about 100 but
showed little change thereafter until 1850 (Soderberg 1987).

This brief sketch of the experience of Sweden shows that this precocious
country used policies of absolutist states to promote human development, but
the policies also restricted civil freedom in important ways and had an adverse impact on the survival rates of citizens. Moreover, the actions of the
Swedish state demonstrated little concern for the rights of private property,
especially for the most important productive asset of the time, namely, land.

The story of the rise of the northern Netherlands, which became the Dutch
republic after its successful revolt against Spanish rule, to a position of supremacy in European and transoceanic navigation, with a disproportionate
share of the world trade in the seventeenth century, has been recounted by
many major historians of the twentieth century (Braudel 1984, chapter 3;
Wallerstein 1980; Israel 1989, 1995; Van Zanden 1993; De Vries and Van der
Woude 1997). The story of its decline has also been recounted many times. A
singular lack of feudal institutions, an enterprising class of businessmen
turned rulers who literally built much of the country by reclaiming land from

the sea, a tradition of seafaring that was enriched in the desperate struggle of the small nation against a mighty empire, and trade borne on skills of navigation, shipbuilding, craft production, and merchandising — all contributed to its rise.

In the long years of struggle (from the 1570s to 1648) to gain recognition of its independence from Spain, the Dutch also became an imperial power on a global scale. Because Portugal was under Spanish rule from 1580 to 1640, the Dutch treated all Portuguese overseas possessions as enemy property and systematically targeted them. They rapidly wrested practically all their possessions from the Portuguese in Indonesia and, by pursuing ruthless methods, established more or less a monopoly over the trade in spices from the archipelago (Boxer 1973a, chapter 5; 1973b, chapter 4). Even after the Portuguese gained independence from Spain, proclaiming the Duke of Braganza as their king, and signed a truce with the Dutch, the latter refused to give up their conquests. The officers of the Dutch East India Company (VOC) and the West India Company ignored the remonstrances of the States General, the supreme governing body of the Netherlands, and refused to hand over territories conquered from the Portuguese (Boxer 1973b, chapter 4). The Portuguese in Brazil succeeded in expelling the Dutch from Bahia and Pernambuco. But the Dutch retained the parts of Ceylon they had conquered from the Portuguese and also expelled the Portuguese from Malabar Coast ports in India.

After reaching the zenith of their power between 1648, when a peace treaty was finally signed with Spain, and 1672, the Netherlands became embroiled in simultaneous wars with two of its greatest rivals, England and France. Eventually, an alliance with England and the accession of the Dutch Stadholder, William of Orange, to the English throne after the so-called Glorious Revolution of 1688 in England saved the Netherlands from becoming a dependency of France. However, in the eighteenth century, the Netherlands went into a phase of rapid decline of both its political and economic power.

The reasons for its downfall and eventual subjugation by France, to be rescued as an independent state only after the collapse of the Napoleonic empire, are even more complex than the factors favoring its rise to dominance. Competition against much bigger countries such as France and England, which, partly learning from the Dutch republic, were able to organize and mobilize much vaster resources of men-at-arms and finances to field them, the conversion of its ruling class into financiers who sometimes lent money to the enemy, and the decline of some of its major staples in the face of foreign competition combined to bring about its decline. I focus on one particular aspect of the ills of the republic, which is the failure of social reproduction of labor to keep up with the needs of the Dutch economy from the end of the seventeenth century, and discuss the issues surrounding the problem in chapter 6.

In this phase of the conflict between European powers, we mostly witness a clash of different absolutist regimes, except in the cases of the Dutch republic from its inception and England from the time of the so-called Glorious Revolution of 1688. The absolutist regimes themselves worked on different social bases. Spain worked mainly with feudal institutions and the monarch had to negotiate between several entrenched interests. England's monarchs, from the time of Henry VIII, depended on a nobility that derived its wealth and most of its power from royal sources. This nobility did not enjoy many legal privileges that were denied to commoners. So there was a broad corridor of mobility between that class and the bankers and merchant princes who benefited from expanding trade at home and abroad. But there were conflicts of interest between magnates who derived much of their power from their connection with the court and other landlords and merchants who saw their political ambitions and profit-making enterprises constricted by the arbitrary use of royal prerogatives. The clash between two different groups of magnates and the entrenched nobility on one side, and the broad class of landed proprietors who felt oppressed by the fiscal exactions of an intransigent monarch on the other, served as a torch to ignite the English civil war of the 1640s.

In France royal absolutism reached a new height under Louis XIV. In Sweden the monarchy subdued the nobility to its will under Charles XI and XII, losing control for a time but subduing them again by the end of the eighteenth century. Spain in the sixteenth century and France under Louis XIV became noted for intolerant Catholicism espoused by the court and the established Church. England under the Tudors from Henry VII to James I was fiercely anti-Catholic. Anti-Catholicism gained a new momentum under William of Orange. In Sweden the only religion tolerated was Lutheran Protestantism. Thus this period can hardly be characterized as one of expanding liberties for the general population except in the two cases of the Netherlands and England. Even in those two cases, the liberties of religious minorities or dissenters were severely circumscribed in law (Le Roy Ladurie 1996, chapter 5; Porter 1990, pp. 174–84). If Sir William Temple in the seventeenth century admired the religious tolerance of the Dutch and Voltaire admired English tolerance of minorities (Porter 1990, pp. 171–72), it was only in contrast with the horrors of the Spanish Inquisition and the intolerant regime of Louis XIV foisted on an increasingly anticlerical upper class. But certainly religious tolerance was good for commerce, and the Netherlands in its heyday and Britain from the eighteenth century benefited greatly from the immigration of merchants and skilled craftsmen fleeing religious persecution.

A state that enjoyed the confidence of the propertied sections of the population, especially its bankers, enjoyed another advantage over absolutist states in which monarchs reneged on their debts, namely, it could create a system of public credit it could draw on in emergencies, especially in times of war. England and the Netherlands were far more successful than France or the Hapsburg emperors in creating such a system of credit.[3]

We have looked primarily at the way the European state system evolved through armed competition for territory, trade, markets, and colonial tribute. That story is told in terms of the strategies of rulers. The latter wielded not only military and political power but also the powers of imposing hegemonic ideologies of conformity and obedience and the fostering of a culture of inequality, even as many of the insignia of inequality of status characteristic of feudalism were being battered down by the advance of capitalism. However, the common people, who formed the increasingly dispossessed army of the working class and literally served as cannon fodder in the wars of the European powers, continued to fight for a world that would deliver evenhanded justice to every human being, even when most of these struggles ended in defeat.

In the 1640s, for example, during the English civil war, there was a vast outpouring of political literature claiming equality for all men (Hill 1955, 1975). While the Diggers and the Levelers were defeated by the Cromwellian gentry and the civil war led to the consolidation of landowners as the rulers of England, that struggle struck the final death blow of feudalism. Furthermore, the thought of men like Henry Ireton or Gerrard Winstanley remained in folk memory and continued to reverberate until the time when William Blake or Tom Paine would give a fresh voice to workingmen's demand for freedom and equality. Seamen and others on sailing voyages and slaves on plantations of the age of merchant capital often revolted against their oppressors (Rediker 1987; Linebaugh and Rediker 2000). Thus much of the soil for the first black republic in St. Domingue and the explosion of the French Revolution was prepared in the maritime ventures of merchant capital. So confining our attention to only the apparent summits of power would blind us to the subterranean nature of the causes of many of the changes even at those exalted regions. The Eurocentric historians almost never refer to these factors. I have occasionally referred to some of them, but a fuller account must give far more prominence to them than the limits of this study allow.

CIVILIZING MISSION AND EUROPE'S WAR MACHINE IN THE AGE OF MERCHANT CAPITAL

I have already referred to Elias's theory of the civilizing mission accompanying the process of state formation in Europe in the era of absolutism and the growth of rational bureaucracies. His work has a special poignancy in that he wrote his volumes on the *Civilizing Process* (Elias 1939/1978 and 1939/1982) in the shadow of the Nazi terror in Germany and central Europe. In his book he showed that state formation involves strengthening the combative power of the state and the upper classes against the external enemy and a simultaneous softening of private aggression of feudal lords or landed magnates and their retainers against cocitizens. The second part of the civilizing process involved the adoption of courtly manners by the politicians, the bureaucrats, and upwardly mobile or aspiring members of the middle classes. Elias also hypothesized that the spread of the money economy and the decline of a subsistence mode of living concentrated wealth in a few hands and threw not only landless peasants but also many traditional knights, without much inherited wealth, into the growing market for mercenary soldiers (Elias 1939/1982, pp. 8–12). There is little doubt that the lag of wages behind prices and the growth of landlessness rendered lives cheap to the marauding powers in the sixteenth and the early part of the seventeenth centuries.

Elias has concentrated primarily on the softening of manners among the bureaucracy and the politicians from the seventeenth century. However, Castiglione, Della Casa, and other writers of the sixteenth century were already producing books of etiquette and behavior for actual and would-be courtiers. Castiglione emphasized the close connection between the humanist aims of education and the correct behavior of courtiers and princes. According to him, "although 'the principal and true profession of the courtier must be that of arms', he should also be a man of high cultural attainments, 'conversant not only with the Latin language but with the Greek as well,' and 'more than passably learned' in 'those studies which we call the humanities'" (Skinner 1978b, p. 122). In England and the British colonies of North America, later the United States, John Locke provided an ideology of education as the proper means of socializing a human being (J. Dunn 1969; Yolton 1985; Milton 1994). In his *Thoughts on Education* (1693) and his *Two Treatises of Government,* he disputed the right of the father to treat his children as his slaves and imposed on him the duty to educate his children in the proper ways of civility, until the end of their apprenticeship. Locke's language is universalistic; however, most of the detailed instructions were suitable for sons of gentlemen and men of property: women and propertyless men had little place in his scheme of education. Confirming Elias's view of how manners were being reformed during these centuries, Locke also stressed the necessity of proper toilet training, since it seems to have been lacking even in the aristocratic circles in his time (J. Dunn 1969, p. 203n).

The absolutist states provided a wider arena for the practice of civilized behavior at home as the counterpart to unbridled savagery abroad (cf. "The etiquette of atrocity" as illustrated in the English booklet *The Lamentations of Germany* (1638) and referred to in Parker 1993, p. 161).

We have to distinguish between the kind of civilizing ruling classes underwent and the kind of civilizing or softening up that the ruled—especially in the colonies populated by nonwhites—were subjected to. The former were taught how to rule (Symonds 1986). The ruled were coerced with arms and then the rulers sedulously propagated an ideology, stressing their unfitness to rule themselves. Of course, the ideological conditioning of the (male) rulers included preparing for war and possible death.

In eighteenth-century England (and neighboring France), when common people refused to obey privatization by the civilized few of what had been considered to be the common inheritance, the state responded by passing draconian laws and criminalizing petty theft and casual trespass (Thompson 1977; Foucault 1977).

War at the service of a centralizing and aggrandizing state and a thrusting, marauding bourgeoisie was the constant accompaniment of the civilizing process. War, military expenditures, taxation to defray those expenditures, and the ravages caused by military movements were among the major causes of demographic stagnation in Europe in the seventeenth century. Moreover, the shadow of war was ever present in the fiscal expedients of the government, in the draft of manpower for the army and navy, and in the fall in nutrition levels and greater threat of succumbing to diseases in the presence of harvest failures or an epidemic (De Vries 1976; Parker 1988). When grain reserves were depleted by harvest failure, fiscal exactions, or military movements, nutrition levels fell and epidemics struck, causing excess mortality.

The epidemic diseases included bubonic plague, smallpox, typhus, and influenza. In France

> the French province of Anjou witnessed severe plague epidemics in 1583, 1605, and 1625, and dysentery in 1639 and 1707. Seville, the focal point of Spain's imperial economy, was struck in 1599–1600, 1616, and 1648–49. From the last of these epidemics it never recovered. In northern Italy, the plagues of 1576–77 and 1630 created labour shortages and caused the flight of the well-to-do from the cities, thus compounding the problems of Italy's already vulnerable industries. (De Vries 1976, pp. 7–8)

As capitalism has done always, it created new demands through wasteful, in particular, military, expenditures as well as through productive investment. This was true of the seventeenth as well as the twentieth century.

> Two categories account[ed] for the great bulk of government expenditure in this period: military expenses and the costs of court and bureaucracy. Of these, the first was by far the most important: in years of peace it claimed over half the

French budgets, while the public debts of most states were entirely the result of military operations. (De Vries 1976, p. 203)

These enormous military expenditures were due to both the frequent wars of the period and the new standards of armed preparedness. Until about 1600, armies of more than 30,000 men were rarely put in the field. Moreover, armies consisted chiefly of mercenary soldiers and recruits temporarily brought together by a military contractor. Innovations in the Spanish and French armies forced a gradual decrease in mercenary use and the maintenance of much larger standing armies. France, which maintained the largest standing forces, attained peacetime levels of 150,000 men by the late seventeenth century; her wartime military strength (and war years were nearly half of all years) could reach 400,000 troops. Such armies exceeded 5 percent of the male population between ages sixteen and forty, but several smaller states outdid populous France in this regard. The peak strength of the Swedish army numbered 110,000 men, while the normal strength of the Prussian army rose from 29,000 under Frederick William, the Great Elector, to more than 83,000 under King Frederick William I in 1739 (De Vries 1976, pp. 203–4).

The terrible cost incurred by Sweden for Gustavus Adolphus's intervention in the Thirty Years' War is illustrated by the following data on the parish of Bygdea cited by Parker (1988, p. 54):

In 1620 the parish provided 36 soldiers for the wars; in 1639, 36.; But in the years between, 230 men were conscripted, of whom all but 15 died in service (and 5 of these were discharged as too crippled to serve further). At the same time, the number of adult males available for service but not yet drafted fell until it was scarcely enough to keep the village's economy going.

The advance of capitalism in Europe may thus have been powered as much by the rise of multilateral war and its commercialization as by the growth of multilateral trade and its militarization. Table 4.1 gives an idea of the escalation in the number of soldiers maintained by various western European states between the 1470s and 1700s.

Not only did the size of each of the European powers' armies and navies increase, but the cost of putting a soldier or sailor into battle also increased dramatically. By 1630 it cost five times as much to put a soldier in the field as it had a century before (Parker 1988, p. 61). Continual preparedness for war and actual wars in these countries meant heavy casualties at a time when hygiene was unknown and antibiotics undiscovered. If earlier estimates regarding the demographic disaster caused by the Thirty Years' War in Germany (which often put the loss at half or two-thirds of the population) now appear exaggerated, conservative estimates still put the net population loss in

Table 4.1.   Increase in Military Manpower in European Countries, 1470s–1700s (Figures in Thousands)

Decade	Spanish Monarchy	Dutch Republic	France	England	Sweden
1470s	20	n.a.	40	25	n.a.
1550s	150	n.a.	50	20	n.a.
1590s	200	20	80	30	15
1630s	300	50	150	n.a.	45
1650s	100	n.a.	100	70	70
1670s	70	110	120	n.a.	63
1700s	50	100	400	87	100

Source: Parker and Smith 1978a, p. 14.
Note: n.a. = not available

the Holy Roman Empire at about 15–20 percent, "from some 20 million before the war to about 16 or 17 million after it" (estimate by Freiderichs, in Parker 1997, p. 188). There were few signs of improved agricultural productivity in seventeenth-century western Europe (Bairoch 1988, pp. 130–33). Most indicators, including prices and yield-to-seed ratios, point to a stagnant agriculture that up to 85 percent of the population depended on for their subsistence. As Steensgaard (1978, p. 41) puts it, we should not look for the explanation of the seventeenth-century crisis of falling yields and falling prices "solely in poorer climatic conditions or in population pressure—for in that case the prices would have been rising—but in the inability of the population to buy corn and their inability to survive. Finally, if we take a look at the public sector and reckon protection to be a service, in the economic-theoretical meaning of the word, the whole question of a seventeenth-century crisis falls to the ground. Never before was Spain so thoroughly protected as under Philip IV; never before was Germany so thoroughly protected as during the Thirty Years' War; and never before was France so thoroughly protected as under the cardinals and Louis XIV. The production of protection was the seventeenth century's 'leading sector.'"

As we have seen already, even in the Netherlands, which by the 1640s became the leading maritime power and the most prosperous economy of western Europe, the population stagnated in the late seventeenth century and declined in the first half of the eighteenth century (De Vries and Van der Woude 1997; Van Zanden 1993). Even in England, which was a partial exception to the western European demographic pattern, the population level of 1651 was not reached again until 1731 (Wrigley and Schofield 1981/1989, pp. 208–9).

The constant state of military preparedness took a toll of human lives even when there was no actual war. The quartering of troops on the civilian population, the pillaging by soldiers of ordinary people on their march to another locale for war or rest increased insecurity and the risk of death. Moreover, even in peacetime, soldiers were dying due to overcrowded and unsanitary barracks at greater rates than members of the civilian population. Houdaille (1977, p. 485) estimated that the rate of mortality of soldiers in the regiment posted in Isle de France between 1766 and 1796 was, in most years, higher by more than a factor of 2 and ranged up to a factor of 4.68 for every age group from 15 to 64 compared with the general male population of France in the same age groups.

I have not gone into the detailed history of the conflicts in Europe between the Treaty of Utrecht (1713) and the end of the Franco-British wars in 1815, which established the military and political supremacy of Britain in Europe. That the wars had major adverse effects on the condition of ordinary people does not need to be stated again. The nineteenth century witnessed the conquest of most of Asia and Africa by European powers and setting up of direct dependencies or client states in those continents. The nineteenth century also saw the emergence of the military-bureaucratic state of Prussia as suzerain over Germany. That state was to play a leading part in the two world wars of the twentieth century and the apotheosis of a fascist regime.

EUROPEAN ECONOMIC GROWTH
IN THE AGE OF MERCHANT CAPITAL

War, pestilence, and famine were the common lot of Europeans in the sixteenth to eighteenth centuries. England appears to have escaped major famines from the eighteenth century. The English Poor Law provided even destitutes rudimentary protection against death from starvation. But even in England scarcity or a spurt in prices caused riots: in 1766–1767 three thousand troops were sent to quell food riots in Somerset and Wiltshire (Porter 1990, p. 100). Yet economic progress was occurring through a process of commercialization, monetization, and specialization in England, France, and several other smaller regions of western Europe. This process has sometimes been styled as Smithian dynamics (Wong 1997) because of Adam Smith's canonical exposition in *Wealth of Nations* (Smith 1791/1910, book 1). But many writers before Smith had extensively analyzed the processes involved (for example, Defoe 1724–1726/1971; Hume 1752/1987; Tucker 1774). The processes led to extensive division of labor between enterprises, industries, and their subsectors; between regions; between town and country; and between different countries. Specialization of operations within a single enterprise led to the development of skills of operatives; specialization between enterprises led to reduction of cost and improvement of products; specialization between regions created external economies of agglomeration; and specialization between countries led to enormous savings as different countries enjoyed advantages in supplies of different kinds of raw materials, inherited or cultivated skills of labor in different lines of production, and so on.

The specialization was supported by institutions such as credit and marketing networks; emergence of joint-stock companies to gain the advantage of large capital to negotiate the inevitable uncertainty of business; and, in some cases, the economies of scale resulting from further specialization within an enterprise. The drive toward specialization was helped by expanding international trade and the flow of precious metals from the Americas, Japan, and some areas of Europe and Africa. Bankers and financiers used these flows to build their credit networks. In periods of population growth the trade and production flows were energized by expanding demand. Supplies of a much greater diversity of articles for consumption from other regions of the world and of commodities produced by slave-run plantations in the Caribbean and other parts of the Americas stimulated the consumption of ordinary people. The affluent and the aspiring middle classes also went in for innovations in their housing, furnishings, and articles of consumption.

However, before the development of internal waterways and all-weather roads, social changes, and countrywide and international credit networks, exchanges typically intensified within "circuits of exchange," to use a phrase that seems to have been coined by Jean Meuvret (Grantham 1989). These circuits were connected at the borders by long-distance traders and their financiers but were liable to be seriously impaired by crises of subsistence from time to time. Moreover, the processes of market exchange were often interrupted and slowed by wars, demographic disasters, and shortages of precious metals. The last could be mitigated by innovations in credit instruments such as bank notes, local tokens issued by large employers, and the truck system (Pressnell 1956; Mann 1971) but precious metals remained the final means of settlement in international trade, and their shortage could create severe problems.

The much larger population of France might have provided a better base for Smithian dynamics. But England pioneered the installation of large factories, increasingly powered by coal and steam rather than water, wind, or muscle power of men and animals, and this made for a decisive break in the patterns of specialization as between England and France or, for that matter, England and China. Many economic historians (Nef 1943; Roehl 1976; O'Brien and Keyder 1978) have expressed skepticism about the allegedly superior economic performance of England compared with France in the eighteenth century. Some estimates by Rostow (1975) showed that if the index of income per capita in France was 127 in 1780, compared with 100 in 1700, in England the income per capita was 129 in 1780, with the same base year. I shall argue in some detail later that before the factory- and exhaustible-resource-based Industrial

Revolution, the different countries of western Europe and the two most populous countries of the world, India and China, all shared more similarities than
such historians as Jones (1981/1987) or Landes (1998) would admit.

NOTES

1. The idea of what civilization meant changed over time. The idea that a civilized
man was simply a good man gave way to the idea that he must be a man who fitted
into the kind of life lived in a European city. Accordingly, the civilized were almost
automatically transformed into people who must belong to Europe. The civilized
world was changed from being all of Christiandom into Christian Europe alone, and
both classical and biblical justifications were found for this construct. As Samuel Pur-
chas put it in 1625, "Jesus Christ is their way, their truth, their life; who hath given a
Bill of divorce to ingratefull Asia where he was borne, and Africa the place of his
flight . . . and is become almost wholly and onely [*sic*] European" (Cooper 1970b,
p. 5). The ideology of the civilizing process and the civilizing mission was needed for
cementing the modes of governance in a world shaped by money, markets, and competition, often in the form of active warfare.

2. My account is based on Hatton 1957, 1970; Rosen 1961; Beller 1970; Roberts
1970; Bromley 1970a; Anderson 1974; Black 1990; Doyle 1992.

3. On the usefulness of public credit, backed initially by the bonds of large joint-
stock companies such as the Bank of England, the East India Company and South Sea
Company, see Defoe 1724–1726/1971; Hume 1752/1987, pp. 349–65; Clark 1947;
O'Brien 1988b.

5

Population Growth and Mortality between the Sixteenth and Nineteenth Centuries: A First Look

POPULATION GROWTH, INFANT MORTALITY, AND LONGEVITY

In the nineteenth century, populations in Europe and colonies of European settlement are known to have increased faster than in other regions of the world. However, there is no solid ground for projecting this differential to the centuries when European countries are supposed to have forged ahead of other continents. Such a supposition has been often based on prejudices of European observers and, following them, of other Eurocentric scholars. For example, W. H. Moreland, a British official and educationist, with a firm belief that Indians were better off under British rule than under Mughal rule, had put the Indian population figure at the low value of 100 million in 1600 (Moreland 1920). Kingsley Davis (1951), then taking an unrealistically low figure for the Indian population in 1800, arrived at respectable figures of population growth under British rule. He ignored the evidence of widespread famines and deserted villages in India in the period before the first full-scale census of 1872. Similarly, the U.S. anthropologist Alfred Kroeber grossly underestimated the size of the native American population in the sixteenth century (Denevan 1976a, 1976b).

These preliminary remarks are necessary to put the growth of European population in a proper global and temporal perspective. Table 5.1 gives the figures of population of six countries of western and southern Europe between 1500 and 1900. I also include the ranges of reasonable estimates of the populations of China and the Indian subcontinent (i.e., India, Pakistan, and Bangladesh). Fuller accounts of their demographic history will be presented later.

Table 5.1. Population of Selected Regions of the World, 1500–1900 (in Millions)

Region or Country	1500	1600	1750	1850	1900
China[a]	100–150		190–225	420(?)	400–450
India-Pakistan-Bangladesh	75–150		160–200		285–295
England		4.1	5.7	16.5	
Holland		1.5	1.9	3.1	
Germany		12.0	15.0	27.0	
France		19.0	25.0	35.8	
Italy		12.0	15.7	24.8	
Spain		6.8	8.4	14.5	
Total of six European countries		55.4	71.7	121.7	

Sources: Durand 1977, table 2; Chesnaux, Bastid, and Bergère 1976, chapter 1; Livi- Bacci 1991, table 2).
[a] The latest estimates for Chinese population in different periods as given in Lee, Campbell, and Wang (2002, p. 600) are 125 million in 1600, 200 million in 1600, 200 million in 1700, 350 million in 1800, and 500 million in 1900.

Most of the European estimates for the period before 1750 are highly conjectural and were based on the pioneering work of William Willcox, an American demographer, and Alexander Carr-Saunders, a British demographer following in his footsteps. Many of the estimates themselves were influenced by a Eurocentric bias (Caldwell and Schindlmayr 2002). For example, Willcox wrote in 1906: "There is nothing in the history of the last few centuries more notable than the increase in the population of the world and the degree to which that increase has been a result, direct or indirect, of the expansion of Europe" (Willcox 1906/1985, p. 745, as quoted by Caldwell and Schindlmayr 2002, p. 187). This attitude led generally to the underestimation of the size of both the initial population of most non-European regions and the rate of growth of that population before European contact. Moreover, the adverse impact of European contact and colonization was generally ignored. A very similar bias continues to affect the estimates of per capita incomes of non-European peoples before the twentieth century made by even such recognized authorities as Angus Maddison (1995, 2001).[1] Perhaps the best estimate of the population of India (including Pakistan and Bangladesh) in 1600 is the 125 million given by Kingsley Davis (1951, as quoted by Visaria and Visaria 1983, p. 466). This figure lies between the 140 million given by Habib (1982a) and the 116 million arrived at by Guha (2001). For 1750 we have an estimate of 190 million by Bhattacharya (1967) and a medium estimate of the same value by Durand (1967). The implicit rate of growth of Indian population at 52 percent is almost double that for the population of the six European countries between the 1600s and the 1750s (see table 5.1). Lee, Campbell, and Wang (2002, table 1) estimate China's population as 100 million in 1500, 150 million in 1600, only 151 million in 1700 because of stagnation in the seventeenth century caused by disturbances associated with the conquest of China by the Manchus, and 322 million in 1800; even the alternative estimate of 275 million Chinese in 1700 and 360–400 million in 1800 favored by Mote (1999), would put the Chinese demographic growth above that of Europe during the relevant period.

The increase in population in the six European countries, which include three of the most dynamic economies of Europe—England, Holland, and France—between 1600 and 1750 was quite mediocre, by less than a third in 150 years. By the sixteenth century, European populations had recovered from the ravages of the Black Death; population grew in most parts of western Europe and even at a fast clip in some regions. However, European countries were repeatedly visited by famine, disease, and excess mortality.[2] The seventeenth century was particularly disastrous: the religious wars in northern Europe, known as the Thirty Years' War, took a severe toll of lives in Germany and neighboring lands. Their effects were compounded by the recurrence of famines and disease. Plague visited Europe again in the 1630s and made repeat visits in Chester and other English towns in 1646–1648, "parts of Spain in 1648–50, Munich in 1649–50, Copenhagen in 1654, Amsterdam and Leiden in 1655" (Coleman 1961, p. 20). In the Italian plague of 1656–1657, 50 percent of the people of Naples died. The London plague of 1665–1666 killed an estimated 100,000. Plague continued to strike other parts of Europe down to the 1680s (Coleman 1961).

Almost certainly far fewer people fell to the soldiery than to the conditions that the soldiery helped to create. Warfare conducted in the manner of the Thirty Years' War had three main sorts of impact on population. First, it stimulated emigration from the war zones to more happily placed towns. Second, by placing a heavy burden on food supplies and at the same time disrupting agriculture, it could readily turn a harvest failure into a local famine. And third, by thus increasing population movement and helping to lower already low standards of nutrition, it provided ready channels for the growth and spread of infectious diseases (Coleman 1961, p. 20).

The English demographic experience will figure prominently in my account for several reasons. It was one of the first countries in Europe to be rid of feudal constraints on civil freedom. It was the first country to experience the victory of factories over handicraft production, emerging as the globally dominant economic and military power in the nineteenth century. Thanks also to the work of a group of historians we know a good deal about the mortality and fertility patterns in that country, going back to the 1540s (Wrigley and Schofield 1981/1989; Goldstone 1986; Fogel 1991).

The rate of growth of the English population during 1600–1750 was the highest among the six European countries listed in table 5.1. This growth was uneven over time. In 1541–1651, England had crude death rates ranging from the low 30s to 40 per thousand (with some years of abnormally high mortality) but birth rates were often above 40 (Wrigley and Schofield 1981/1989, pp. 313–20). The English population grew from 2.77 million in 1541 to 5.23 million in 1651. But between 1651 and 1751 the population increased by only 10 percent, to 5.77 million. The really strong surge in English population growth occurred during the next century, when birth rates went from the low 30s to more than 40, before declining to a steady rate around the middle 30s.

We now look at the aggregate growth patterns of two other European countries that were transformed into capitalist societies relatively early, viz., the Netherlands and France. The Dutch population increased by a little more than 25 percent between 1600 and 1750; the increase occurred only up to the middle or third quarter of the seventeenth century, then growth stopped and declined in the first half of the eighteenth century before starting to increase again (De Vries and Van der Woude 1997; Van Zanden 1993). As we shall see later, this demographic crisis was connected with the characteristics of a mercantile capitalism that first rendered the Dutch supreme in the trading and naval world of Europe but then contributed to its decline.

We now turn to France, a land that had set the standards of civilized behavior among the upper classes of European countries from the seventeenth to eighteenth centuries. Table 5.2 reproduces the crude birth rates (CBRs) and crude death rates (CDRs) of France from 1740 to 1814.

Table 5.2. Population, Crude Birth Rate (CBR), and Crude Death Rate (CDR) in France, 1740–1814

Period	Midperiod Population (in Thousands)	CBR	CDR
1740–1744	24,600	39.9	40.1
1745–1749	24,560	39.6	40.1
1750–1754	25,770	39.8	35.8
1755–1759	25,370	41.0	35.5
1760–1764	26,900	39.1	36.3
1765–1769	26,320	39.0	35.3
1770–1774	27,770	37.2	34.1
1775–1779	27,260	37.7	33.6
1780–1784	27,600	37.8	37.1
1785–1789	27,880	38.8	35.5
1790–1794	28,100	37.1 (38.5)[a]	37.1 (38.5)[a]
1795–1799	28,610	36.6 (40.0)[a]	29.5 (32.9)[a]
1800–1804	29,290	32.9	30.6
1805–1809	29,730	32.4	28.7
1810–1814	30,150	32.6	30.7

Source: Dupaquier 1979, p.98.
[a] Numbers in parentheses are alternative estimates from another source.

We do not have comprehensive data for the death and birth rates in France for the seventeenth century. But an analysis of the data on population and burials in 1695 shows that in that year the CDRs and CBRs were 54.7 and 47.0, respectively, in Aix-en-Provence (Ostroot 1997).

Much of the celebration of the European miracle is based on the art of forgetting. The debate on the trend of the standard of living during the English Industrial Revolution, which was rekindled by Hobsbawm's work in the 1950s (Hobsbawm 1957, 1968; Hobsbawm and Hartwell 1963) has just been revived. Hobsbawm realized the significance of the so-called demographic indicators for the standard of living debate. He pointed out that up to the 1870s CDRs and infant mortality rates (IMRs) did not fall significantly in England and may have gone up in urban areas in the "golden decades" of the early Victorian age (Hobsbawm 1968, p. 133; 1957). He saw a working class in England

> stunted and debilitated by a century of industrialism. In the 1870s eleven- to twelve-year old boys from the upper class public schools were on average *five inches taller* than boys from industrial schools, and at all teen-ages three inches taller than the sons of artisans. When the British people was [*sic*] for the first time medically examined *en masse* for medical service in 1917, it included ten per cent of young men totally unfit for service, 41.5 percent (in London forty-eight to forty-nine per cent) with "marked disabilities", twenty-two per cent with "partial disabilities" and only a little more than a third in satisfactory shape. Ours was a country filled with a stoic mass of those destined to live all their lives on a bare and uncertain subsistence until old age threw them on the scrap heap of the Poor Law, underfed, badly housed, badly clothed (Hobsbawm 1968, p. 137).

What happened to the population of Germany after the Thirty Years' War (1618–1648)? It recovered from the terrible losses of that war and began to grow quickly in the eighteenth century. However, the death and birth rates remained typical of what has been characterized by demographers as the ancien régime. In table 5.3, I have reproduced figures for four regions of Germany for 1750–1809.

There were obvious differences between different regions. But plenty of other evidence indicates that the quickening of population growth in Germany in the latter part of the nineteenth century was due as much to a high fertility as to a decline in death rates. As late as 1900, the birth rate in Germany was 35.6 per thousand and the death rate was 22.1 per thousand. Austria also had very similar birth and death rates (Mitchell 1998a).

We now turn to two other indicators of the biological well-being of a population, IMRs and life expectancy. Unregulated urbanization under capitalism

Table 5.3. Crude Birth Rate (CBR) and Crude Death Rate (CDR) in Four Regions of Germany, 1750–1809

	CBR				CDR			
	Böhringen	Durlach	Mulsun	Hochdorf, Besenfeld and Göttelfingen	Böhringen	Durlach	Mulsun	Hochdorf, Besenfeld and Göttelfingen
1750–1759	52.4	24.8	38.3	43.5	35.6	35.9	39.7	27.6
1760–1769	47.2	25.5	41.3	40.9	36.4	28.8	38.0	29.2
1770–1779	43.8	25.8	30.0	35.3	32.7	32.0	33.3	26.9
1780–1789	50.7	26.8	26.3	38.7	36.1	30.8	32.6	21.2
1790–1799	50.9	29.7	32.0	41.5	49.7	31.9	22.3	25.3
1800–1809	55.5	30.5	31.3	40.3	40.5	40.1	30.7	26.9

Source: Robert Lee 1979, in W. R. Lee 1979.

in Europe adversely affected both these indicators until almost the last decade of the nineteenth century.

During the years 1750–1759, the IMR, the number of newborns per thousand dying within the first year of life, was as high as 273 in France and as low as 165 in England. Over roughly the same period IMRs in Sweden and Denmark were 200 and 191, respectively (Livi-Bacci 1991, table 14). It is suspected that the IMR in England has been underestimated because many infant deaths were not reported and, therefore, not recorded in the parish registers (Razzell 1993).[3] In France the IMR declined dramatically to stabilize at a middling value, fluctuating between 148 and 180 from 1881 to 1900. Over the same twenty-year period, the IMR in England and Wales varied between 130 and 161, and in Prussia, industrially the most vibrant economy of Europe, the IMR varied between 193 and 225 (Woods, Watterson, and Woodward 1988).

The trend of IMRs in major European countries showed no significant decline until the first decade of the twentieth century. After World War II the difference between the best-performing developing countries and the countries of the North Atlantic seaboard rapidly narrowed. For example, in Costa Rica, the IMR was 58 in 1970 and 12 in 1997; in Cuba, 34 in 1970 and 7 in 1997, the same level as in the United States; in South Korea, 43 in 1970 and 6 in 1997 (UNDP 1999, pp. 168–169; see also chapter 22 in this volume).

The benefits of medical advances have not reached the common people in developing countries that have not undergone social transformation abolishing the power of landlords or have suffered badly from wars, as we shall see in chapter 21. The thinly populated Scandinavian countries were the only ones to have experienced an improvement in overall survival rates before the last quarter of the nineteenth century. The realization and sustenance of high levels of human development in Sweden, Denmark, and Norway were as much the result of external circumstances deeply connected with European imperialism as of their domestic policies, as we shall see later.

The expectation of life at birth (life expectancy, e_0) is widely used to judge the overall prospects of survival of a newborn baby through infancy to adulthood and old age. Since mortality may be very different for different cohorts, this can be supplemented with measures of life expectancy at later ages. However, if the IMR is very high for a given population, it is unlikely that the mortality rates for surviving cohorts will be very low at later ages, unless some dramatic improvement takes place in disease environment, nutrition, and medical technology.

Over the period covered by the Wrigley-Schofield study, i.e., 1541–1871, life expectancy in England varied from a low of 27.77 years in 1561 to a high of 41.68 in 1581, a high of 40.82 years in 1606, Shakespeare's time, to a low of 28.41 in 1681, and from a low of 27.88 years in 1731 to a high of 38.17 in the late eighteenth century. In 1871 the value was 41.31 years, little higher than the life expectancy of a younger contemporary of Shakespeare (Wrigley and Schofield 1981/1989). The reasons for this stagnation in life expectancy, even when population growth rates were reaching record heights and England had become the top industrial nation in the world, have to do with the characteristic problems of social reproduction of labor under early capitalism. With minimal social security and underdevelopment of both medical science and prophylactic technology in Europe and the world until the last quarter of the nineteenth century, stagnation is the expected outcome. On the mainland of Europe, wars also contributed to the high death rates.

The records of survival during the centuries down to the nineteenth show that prospects were no better for other European lands. For France or Germany, time series of life expectancy are available for a shorter period than for England. In the case of France, life expectancy has been estimated as 24.8 years in 1740–1749, as 27.9 in 1750–1759, and as 27.7 in 1760–1769. French life expectancy began to rise during 1790–1799 but was still only 39.8 years in 1850–1859 (Livi-Bacci 1991, table 12). In countries that experienced rapid commercialization or industrialization and accompanying urbanization, rural areas were on the whole less unhealthy than urban areas. But high rates of agricultural growth could also be associated with high rates of mortality and low life expectancy. This is well illustrated by many regions of Germany, including Prussia, where acceleration of agricultural growth was often accompanied by higher mortality and lower life expectancy: the latter figure went down to 35.0 years in the 1830–1839 decade (Robert Lee 1979, p. 153).[4]

I will end this section by looking at the life expectancy and IMRs in Belgium, a small country that was the first to follow England in industrializing. The population of Belgium quickly increased from 1784 to 1876, growing from 2.4 million to 5.3 million, before entering a phase of slower growth, in common with most other western European populations (Deprez 1979). But life expectancy in Belgium in urban areas was 22.4 years in 1827 and only 20.6 years for males in 1832, 25.0 years for the whole population in 1832, and 24.9 years overall in 1841–1847 (Deprez 1979). These shocking records were being set exactly when the country was industrializing fast. By 1881–1890 life expectancy rose to 43.6 years for males and 46.7 years for females and kept improving thereafter. But the initial improvement in life expectancy was primarily due to a fall in adult mortality, because the IMR remained above 150 practically through the nineteenth century (Deprez 1979, tables 6.32 and 6.34).

Thus there was little improvement in the chances of human survival in Europe before the last quarter of the nineteenth century. Moreover, the gains from improvement in public sanitation, prophylactic measures, and medical technology were reaped fully only after World War II.

NON-EUROPEAN CONTRIBUTIONS TO EUROPEAN GAINS
IN PHYSICAL WELL-BEING

For many purposes it is useful to divide European history into the phases of development dominated by merchant capital, sometimes in collaboration with absolutist states and sometimes in opposition to it, and a phase dominated by industrial capital. The northern part of the Spanish Netherlands, after its liberation from the Hapsburg empire as the United Provinces of the Netherlands, or the Dutch Republic, set the pace for intra-European political and economic developments and commercial, naval, and military competition overseas between 1600 and 1700. But combat between England and France came to play an increasingly important role in the later part of the period. From 1815, England set the pace in economic, technological, and ideological apparatuses of capitalism and the world polity and economy. I turn now to the record of human development in Europe in the age of merchant capital.

In many of the standard histories of population and demography in Europe, it is claimed that survival chances of the European population were already improving in the eighteenth century because of a decline in the virulence of epidemics and better control over food production and distribution, leading to a smaller degree and frequency of incidence of subsistence crises (see, for example, Schofield and Reher 1991). However, the historical evidence falsifies this claim. Subsistence crises became less frequent in England but not in other European countries. Indeed, the most murderous subsistence crisis in the British Isles occurred in Ireland in 1846–1850. Many countries of continental Europe experienced localized or even nationwide famines well into the nineteenth century. The data on CDRs in England, France, and the Scandinavian countries between 1740 and 1920 plotted by Vallin (1991, pp. 40–41) display no discernible variation in trend for England, France, or Sweden down to 1800 and for Finland even down to 1840.

In England and several other regions of Europe, mortality increased again with industrialization and it is not until the 1870s that we can begin to discern a definite improvement in the chances of survival of the population of western Europe.

Non-European lands made a substantial contribution to the improvement of nutrition and the disease environment in Europe. The first element of this contribution was the introduction of new crops from the Americas. Among these, the potato played a crucial role in raising the levels of nutrition in areas where soil was not suitable for grain crops, as in many parts of the hilly districts of Scotland, or where the agrarian system consisted of a handful of landlords exploiting a mass of cotters, landless laborers, and small peasants, as in Ireland (Lenman 1977, pp. 112–13; Ó Grada 1994, pp. 80–89). A second major contribution was made by cane sugar produced in slave-run plantations. Bairoch (1988) has estimated that imported sugar accounted for 11 percent of the energy consumption of the urban areas of northwestern Europe. In England and Wales, the value (1850 prices) of total national consumption of grains such as wheat and barley may have stagnated or even declined between 1700 and 1800 but that of sugar rose from two hundred thousand pounds sterling in 1700 to four hundred thousand pounds sterling in 1850 (Lindert 1994, p. 367). By 1900 sugar composed almost a sixth of the total calorie consumption in England (Mintz 1985). Sugar and tea (obtained from China) may have made its contribution in making life literally supportable for the English worker when unregulated industrialism pushed the standard of living down:

> As milk and the malt used to make beer became too expensive for the working class, sweetened tea emerged as the substitute with which to eat the basic meal of white bread and potatoes. This nexus between the consumption of tea and sugar noted by Mintz, is further explained by John Burnett. . . . "White bread and tea were no longer luxuries, but the irreducible minimum below which there was only starvation." (Mazumdar 1998, p. 51; the quote is from Burnett 1966, pp. 37–38)

Not only the West Indies colonies but also Ireland contributed to the metropolitan country's growth in consumption through its increasing grain exports and exports of butter and meat, even as the Irish peasant subsisted on potatoes and milk.

Inoculation against smallpox, a major killer in Europe up to the middle of the nineteenth century, was a practice imported from Ottoman Turkey. Lady Mary Wortley Montagu described the procedure for inoculation in England in a 1717 letter (Porter 1995). Inoculation was thereafter widely introduced in many parts of northern and western Europe and, as Jennerian vaccination, became part of the public health system by the end of the eighteenth century and the beginning of the nineteenth. This practice substantially reduced infant mortality, especially in the Scandinavian countries.

NOTES

1. See the review of Maddison (2001) by Caldwell (2002).
2. War, famine, disease, and mortality produced apocalyptic visions, especially between 1500 and 1648, and led to the outpouring of an apocalyptic iconography in Protestant lands (Cunningham and Grell 2000).

3. Razzell has suggested an adjustment to England's IMR, which would bring down English expectancy of life at birth in the precensus decades by three to five years.

4. It would be instructive to find out whether the greater insecurity the peasants faced and the self-exploitation they had to practice under a scheme of abolition of serfdom, which made the freed peasants pay dearly for whatever land they managed to acquire, played any part in this decrease in life expectancy.

6

The Netherlands:
Rise and Fall of a Hegemonic Power

SMITHIAN DYNAMICS IN A CAPITALIST SOCIETY:
THE NETHERLANDS IN THE AGE OF MERCHANT CAPITAL

In chapter 4 I sketched the process of economic growth in an economy undergoing commercialization, with both peasants and artisans being involved in the production of commodities in an expanding market. We can distinguish at least two different types among such economies. One is an economy in which almost every person enjoys secure rights in the products they produce and in the use of the means of production needed for such activities. But the right to transfer or inherit land was restricted because it was the most important asset in agrarian economies.

Under feudalism, peasants had few rights independent of the authority of the lord of the manor. With the dissolution of feudalism, peasants came to acquire rights to land, but very often these rights were circumscribed. In some countries, however, landlords were given almost unlimited power to get rid of peasants when it suited them. In England after the civil war of the 1640s, the ruling oligarchy used the private and public enclosure acts to get rid of their tenants and deprive poorer peasants of their rights to common property resources.

In China under Qing rule or in India under the Mughals and the pre-British successor regimes, land could be bought and sold freely. But peasants enjoyed a degree of security against eviction by landlords or moneylenders for default on debt (Fukazawa 1982a, 1991; Bagchi 1992; Mazumdar 1998, chapter 4). As a policy to curb power of the Ming elite who had resisted the Manchu conquest for decades and also increase the base for the land tax, the Qing emperors gave security of tenure to the peasants, freed them of the legal burden of slavery or serfdom, and encouraged them to open up new lands by granting tax exemptions on newly settled lands. Tenant rights and land rights were alienable, but landlords could not accumulate any amounts of land and throw out tenants according to their convenience. Very similar measures for the protection of peasants were adopted by the Mughal rulers and their successors. Thus private property in land was recognized, but it was subject to regulatory measures and monitoring by the state. This is the kind of property rights that prevailed in most countries of Europe before the spread of capitalism.[1] A second type of private property rights develops when powerful men with private property rights, through purchase or legal instruments of dispossession, take over the assets of others. Such a society came up in Europe for perhaps the first time in the Dutch republic but assumed a far more aggressive form in England after the civil war. In the latter kind of society, nationalism became the main organizing ideology for cohesion, because the earlier devices of social cohesion were eroded by unlimited competition for profit, markets, and assets.

Both noncapitalist commercializing societies and capitalist societies require expanding supplies of labor for sustaining economic growth. However, the demographic requirements of capitalist growth have certain peculiarities of their own. Any society needs to reproduce the workforce required to carry on production with the existing techniques. It also needs to nurture and socialize the new generation so as to fit it into the ways of living in that society. The household has almost universally been the site for reproduction and nurturing of children, and women's labor in its multiple senses is involved throughout this process. Socialization, however, takes place through the conscious or unstated intervention of a society's dominant forces, with various kinds of rituals playing a part. In a noncapitalist society with little net immigration or migration, the workforce must increase in size if the total output of the society has to increase, because in precapitalist societies, with a slow pace of technical progress, land or labor productivity grows slowly.

A capitalist society, to reproduce itself and expand, requires not only that the workforce grow but that the labor dependent on employment provided by the controllers of the means of production also expand. A capitalist society is polarized between the owners or controllers of the means of production and the proletariat, who must sell their labor power in order to make a living. This polarization is generally a slow process and is virtually never completed. Nevertheless, until the onset of jobless growth in many operations of large-scale industry and in office work, expanding production under capitalism required an expanding supply of wage labor.

The size of the proletariat can increase through (1) separation of increasing proportions of the existing producers from the means of production, (2) growth in numbers and power of the potential employers of the proletariat, and (3) increase in the population of the already dispossessed members of the proletariat.[2] In an open economy, capitalists can import free or bonded labor, and capitalism can use mechanisms of reproduction outside its core theater of operations for augmenting the supply of labor power. My argument is that this is precisely what capitalism has done for the major part of its career since its appearance on the global scene. According to eminent students of the system (Dobb 1946; Wallerstein 1974), the capitalist world-system originated in the sixteenth century. How did the nascent capitalist order secure and maintain the necessary wage labor to build and sustain itself? In particular, what relationship did the colonies bear to the development of the metropolitan economies?

The history of the Netherlands, the archetypal capitalist economy before the arrival of the Industrial Revolution, provides some important answers to these questions. J. L. Van Zanden (1993) has analyzed the rise and fall of the Dutch economy between the late sixteenth century and the eighteenth century. He focused on two aspects of that history, namely, the problem of mobilizing labor power and the role played by the Dutch colonies.

Van Zanden (1997) presents a more or less complete list of the ways (other than the natural increase and proletarianization of the home population) labor power of the center, or metropolitan, enterprises can be augmented: through (1) permanent immigration; (2) seasonal immigration according to the needs of the employers; (3) subsidized reproduction of labor by households engaged in subsistence activities or other gainful work in the periphery, when the employers in the center fail to pay a full subsistence wage to workers moving from the periphery; (4) use of precapitalist methods of exploitation such as the advent of the second serfdom in eastern Europe, more or less coinciding with the ascent of merchant capital in pockets of western Europe; and (5) imposition of chattel slavery in areas of scarce labor in tropical and subtropical lands.

Van Zanden's list of strategies for filling up the deficiencies of social reproduction of labor would also apply to the nonwhite dependencies of Europe in the age of global colonialism and imperialism. In settler colonies with people of European stock in the majority, immigration and, until the nineteenth century, slave labor made up shortages of labor. In settler colonies such as South Africa, Zimbabwe, and Kenya, in which European immigrants remained a minority, a mass of dependent peasantry or landless labor was created by dispossessing the native inhabitants (Bagchi 1982).

The Dutch economy in its golden age dominated Europe in the age of merchant capital (Van der Linden 1997). Merchant capital takes principally three forms: trade in commodities, trade in money and credit, and craft production under merchant control. There has long been a controversy regarding whether the northern Netherlands (i.e., the Dutch republic) can be regarded as a full-fledged capitalist power or a feudal-bourgeois economy in which the feudal element ultimately caused its downfall (for opposing views on the question, see Hobsbawm 1954; Wallerstein 1974, 1980).[3]

By 1500 certain natural and social factors had already marked the whole territory known as the Low Countries, comprising today's Netherlands, Luxembourg, and Belgium, as a region with enormous potential for trade, shipping, and mercantile dominance. Then the political factor of revolt separated the northern and southern provinces of the Netherlands. The southern Netherlands, where the revolt was suppressed, remained under the Spanish yoke, and the successful north formed the Dutch Republic. For almost a century (1580–1670) that republic claimed European supremacy in oceanic trade, shipping, and naval warfare.

Most of the Netherlands, including the southern part with Antwerp as its chief city and port, had become a major center of internal and international trade by the middle of the sixteenth century (Israel 1995, part 1; De Vries and Van der Woude 1997, chapter 2). Demands on peasant labor for land reclamation and navigation in a country of rivers, inland lakes, swamps, and backwaters; the position of Antwerp and, later, Amsterdam as a major entrepôt between southern European lands and the Baltic; and the difficulty of enforcing feudal control in such a sea-fragmented country had virtually ended feudalism in most of the coastal areas and their immediate hinterland (Israel 1995; De Vries and Van der Woude 1997). The land of the Netherlands has rightly been styled a "landscape in movement" (De Vries and Van der Woude 1997, p. 27).

The governance structure of the Netherlands was highly decentralized in the sixteenth century. In the Netherlands, especially in the northern part, economic and social power of the great nobles was more circumscribed than elsewhere in western Europe. Peasants and the smaller nobility and merchants in the nearby towns or cities held most of the land. Moreover, by 1580 the Netherlands was easily the most urbanized region of Europe: the proportion of people living in towns of 2,500 inhabitants and above to the total population was around 27–30 percent, a proportion that would perhaps reach 45 percent at the peak of Dutch prosperity in the middle of the seventeenth century (Schama 1987, chapter 1; De Vries and Van der Woude 1997, pp. 57–71). The status and power of functionaries such as dike reeves, who looked after the embankments, or city councils and burgomasters were not equaled in most other parts of Europe (Schama 1987). Intensive involvement of the people in trade and commerce and the innovations that were called forth by struggles against an inclement nature made the Netherlands's agriculture and animal husbandry the most productive in western Europe and provided the basis for the highly urbanized society in which, already by the beginning of the seventeenth century, a majority of the people drew their sustenance from a variety of nonagricultural pursuits, including shipping, shipbuilding, textiles, and of course, transportation and trade—both internal and external (De Vries 1976; Israel 1995; De Vries and Van der Woude 1997).

The revolt of the Netherlands against Spanish suzerainty was triggered by the attempt of Philip II to impose a centralized administration and to outlaw all varieties of religion except Roman Catholicism (Koenigsberger 1968, especially pp. 264–80). In the 1560s the southern Netherlands was ahead of the northern provinces in trade and manufacture, with Antwerp as the fulcrum of trade and finance. The artisans of the southern Netherlands had increasingly been converted to the newly emerging Calvinism. Goaded both by a cyclical fall in their real earnings and the threat of heavy taxation, those artisans began openly opposing Spanish rule. The nobles were at first divided in their loyalties. However, in the northern Netherlands the burghers were already prepared to revolt, and a large fraction of the nobles led by William, Prince of Orange (known in history as William the Silent), joined them. The revolt then became a struggle for national independence from Spanish rule. The southern part of the Netherlands was reconquered by the Spaniards and remained under their rule until the nineteenth century, when it gained independence as the modern state of Belgium. That reconquest and the sacking of Antwerp by Spanish troops, who had not been paid for months, changed the economic balance between the independent northern Netherlands and the southern part. After the Spanish reconquest, huge numbers of Calvinist preachers, artisans, and merchants migrated from the southern to the northern Netherlands and further tilted the demographic, political, and economic balance in favor of the independent United Provinces. (From now on, *the Netherlands* refers to the northern provinces, or the modern territory of the Netherlands, rather than all of the Low Countries, including Belgium.)

Writing within a few years of each other, and treating roughly the same period, Ralph Davis (1973) and Jan de Vries (1976) gave apparently contradictory titles to their books, namely, *The Rise of the Atlantic Economies* and *The Economy of Europe in the Age of Crisis, 1600–1750*, respectively. But the contradictions are essential parts of the story. The problems the Dutch eventually faced because of the small size of the country's population, the archaic structure of its politics in an age of increasingly centralized decision making and exercise of power, and its being locked in the pursuit of carrying trade have been widely discussed (Wilson 1939). I will now analyze how Dutch achievements in human and economic development came to be reversed.

DEMOGRAPHIC VICISSITUDES OF THE DUTCH REPUBLIC

The population of Holland and Friesland, which together accounted for a majority of the population of the Netherlands, is estimated to have tripled between 1500 and 1650, from 350,000 to a million—a rate of growth unequalled anywhere else in Europe during the period (De Vries and Van der Woude 1997, p. 51). Most of this growth was endogenous, but immigration also contributed substantially. The total number of immigrants in the Dutch republic over the seventeenth and eighteenth centuries has been estimated as 500,000 (p. 72). The immigrants, mostly adult men and women, formed 4 to 5 percent of the child-rearing population (p. 73). This flow of immigrants became critical from the latter half of the seventeenth century, because in the cities of Holland death rates exceeded birth rates. Moreover, the surplus of births over deaths in the rural areas of Holland was not enough to fill the urban deficits. The population of the Dutch republic became stagnant, or actually declined, from the second half of the seventeenth century: the population of Holland, the most important province of the republic, declined from 883,000 in ca. 1680 to 783,000 in 1795; this decline in the major cities and the western part of the republic was partly compensated by growth in the east and the north (De Vries and Van der Woude 1997, chapter 3).

The Dutch cities had become famous because of their cleanliness, their orderliness, and the apparent freedom of Dutch women. The latter had better property rights than their English or French counterparts, and they often managed shops and other businesses on their own or in their husbands' absence (Schama 1987; Israel 1995; De Vries and Van der Woude 1997). But all this could not save the cities from the scourges of bubonic plague, smallpox, malaria, and other epidemic diseases.

How did this happen? The short answer is that this outcome is characteristic of every highly urbanized population before the advent of Jennerian vaccination, the technology for the supply of clean water to a concentrated population, and the advent of the germ theory of disease and requisite prophylactic measures. The modernity of the economy did not ensure the availability of modern sanitation and health care systems. Overcrowding in the Dutch cities caused high mortality rates. Moreover, the famed livestock industry of Holland, by putting pigs and other animals in close touch with human beings, exposed them to diseases caused by bacteria parasitic on animals (Diamond 1998, chapter 11; cf. also Crosby 1986, chapter 9). In addition, a growing imbalance in the proportions of men and women of marriageable age resulted from excess male deaths, many of them from wars and sailing expeditions (cf. Rediker 1987). The incidence of nuptials also declined from the latter part of the eighteenth century owing to economic distress. Hence the effective fertility of Dutch women also fell to below-replacement levels.

The sailing boats of the VOC, the Dutch East India Company, killed off sailors in very large numbers. Men were coerced both by economic necessity and often by the authorities to join the boats as sailors, cooks, or other functionaries. We are back to the mordant irony of early capitalism: the golden age of Holland almost inexorably led to misery and death for a very large fraction, if not the majority, of working people. It has been estimated that, during the entire existence of VOC (1602–1795), of nearly 975,000 persons who boarded its ships to sail for Asia, only about 485,000 eventually returned to the Netherlands,

> which means that some 490,000 men settled somewhere in Asia or Africa or more likely, died. Now, of those 975,000 who set sail, only half a million were men born in the Netherlands. The rest had come to the Republic's port cities from abroad, and of those 475,000 immigrants, 255,000 never returned. Hence the German adage that "Holland is the graveyard of Germany." (De Vries and Van der Woude 1997, p. 75)

Ordinary sailors died of disease but also of almost deliberate starvation because captains wanted to add to their and the company's profits by skimping on food. Extreme physical cruelty inflicted on the sailors in the name of discipline also killed them. Vast numbers of seamen were simply murdered by their captains or other superior officers (Rediker 1987, chapter 5). As a late eighteenth-century sailor explained to a green hand about the reality of life on a sailing boat, "There is no justice or injustice on board ship, my lad. There are only two things: duty and mutiny—mind that. All that you are ordered to do is duty. All that you refuse to do is mutiny" (quoted by Rediker 1987, p. 211). Although Rediker's account is primarily based on the records of British mariners, the experience of their Dutch brethren could not have been very different.

The high rate of participation of Dutch women in paid work as wage earners or in self-employment did not provide them with earnings on a par with men. From the late seventeenth century, the Dutch cities had an excess of women over men, so that their position in the marriage market worsened. A large fraction of the women workers in cities, as in early industrial England, were domestic servants (Folbre 1994; De Vries and Van der Woude 1997). As I have already noted, large numbers of women remained unmarried or married late, so that there was a decline in fertility. This was caused by distress rather than voluntary choice, just as happened on the other side of the world, in late Tokugawa Japan, as we shall see. Gender equity and the overall standard of living of all (including children) suffered even as the Dutch golden age proceeded toward twilight.

Under a capitalist dispensation, the Dutch economy, in its golden age and after, was also subject to the vicissitudes of fluctuations in effective demand. As a result, even with a stagnant population, the republic could not find employment for adult men in the period of economic stagnation that coincided with demographic stagnation. The demographic stagnation may in fact have aggravated the problem of deficiency of effective demand.

The Dutch golden age was characterized by a high degree of inequality of assets and incomes, and this inequality further increased as that age unfolded (De Vries and Van der Woude 1997, chapter 11; Van Zanden 1998). This increased inequality was caused originally by the power of the merchants and burghers who controlled the administration and regulated the main channels of trade, finance, and manufacture. The cost of running the government was borne by all classes, mainly through regressive taxation. Moreover, the financiers earned the interest and capital gains on the public debt. The Bank of Amsterdam, founded in 1809, was a chief support of that public credit.

The economic stagnation from the late seventeenth century accentuated the inequality. In rural areas landownership became more concentrated and the dependence of the rural poor on capitalist farmers and landlords increased. In urban areas, nominal wages increased substantially in the first seventy years or so of the republic. Even when urban industry and trade ceased to grow, or even declined, the real wages of those who were employed in officially registered professions or enjoyed the protection of guilds held up, because of a fall in agricultural prices. However, in the eighteenth century real wages of most workers declined precipitously (De Vries and Van der Woude 1997, section 12.5).

As the Dutch republic entered the so-called periwig age—its period of decline—it continued to be ruled by the entrenched burgher-oligarchs. During this period, the Dutch bankers emerged as chief financiers of the governments of other western European nations. Because many of the big loans originated in the wars fought between those countries, the Dutch became the financiers of other monarchs' wars, including, ironically enough, wars fought by the English against the Dutch republic (Dickson and Sperling 1970; Neal 1990; Bagchi 2000).

The colonial ventures of the Dutch republic played a crucial role in first quickening its maturity to the golden age, later shoring up a faltering economy, and finally, helping it to rejoin the ranks of the advanced European economies in the nineteenth century after it had stagnated for a century. The failure to reproduce the inhabitants of the republic in sufficient numbers, however, brought it to its knees by the end of the eighteenth century. This happened despite it having notched up better records than its rivals, Britain and France, with respect to literacy and the status of women in society.

The Dutch colonies played a multiplicity of roles in sustaining golden-age growth. The Dutch pioneered large, slave-run sugarcane plantations. Sugar became a staple of European trade and a major provider of calories to urban Europe. They also thereby showed that one way of overcoming the problem of social reproduction of labor was to mine labor nurtured in non-European societies and treat it as costlessly disposable (Van Zanden 1993). The non-European colonies helped the Dutch to amass the bullion and other media of exchange that were critical for their financing activities.

Finally, the colony of Indonesia was critical for Dutch external finances in the nineteenth century. In chapter 16 I give figures of the amount of tribute and profits the Europeans, mainly the Dutch, realized from Indonesia. It is not perhaps accidental that the Dutch economy, including its agriculture, began to grow again only from the second half of the nineteenth century. This was the time when the so-called cultivation system, based on the forced labor of Indonesian villagers, introduced by Governor van den Bosch, began to yield large revenues and demonstrated the potential profitability of privately owned Dutch sugar plantations based on the same labor regime (Bagchi 1982, chapter 4; Van Zanden 1994). The Dutch had led the rest of Europe in agricultural innovations. But between 1810 and 1850, while labor input into Dutch agriculture increased by more than a third, production per person-year fell by almost 9 percent (Van Zanden 1994, p. 20). Thus for the Dutch the late seventeenth-century crisis became an affair spanning two centuries; it required the "gift" of return of the Indonesian colony by the British as part of the European settlement in the post-Napoleonic period and the industrialization of other parts of Europe for them to get back to the path leading to affluence. Colonialism and external factors gave a new push to an achievement that had turned into a disaster.

A large part of the story of the world affected by European enterprise can be told in terms of the brutal search for exploitable labor when Europe failed to ensure the expanded reproduction of labor matching the drive for accumulation. Van Zanden (1993) has claimed that, in contrast to industrial capitalism, the phase of merchant capitalism is an open system in the following sense: under industrial capitalism, "Labour power reproduces itself because the wages it receives—which are equal to the reproduction costs of labour—are adequate to purchase the commodities necessary for subsistence." By contrast, "The reproduction of labour power occurs largely outside of the sphere of merchant capitalism, namely, in the pre-capitalist modes of production" (Van Zanden 1993, section 1.3). Even under industrial capitalism, some workers might have other work outside the factory, but as factory work becomes routine, this becomes more and more difficult, so expanded reproduction of labor has to take place internally.

This view certainly goes well with Marx's fragmentary remarks on the nature and limitations of merchant capitalism. But it also reproduces Marx's judgment that industrial capitalism, through rise in the productivity of labor that accompanies it, succeeds in effecting expanded reproduction of labor. In fact, however, accelerated economic growth and industrialization between the 1750s and 1850s in England were accompanied by a horrendous rise in urban mortality rates. As a result, social reproduction of labor was often jeopardized (Bairoch 1988; Szreter 1988, 1996). Moreover, industrial capitalism remained geared to the exploitation, breakup, and transformation of precapitalist formations into new structures mediated by both market power and nonmarket coercion, especially in Latin America, Africa, and Asia. The clear-cut contrast posited by Van Zanden (1993) and Marx and Engels between the ages of merchant capital and industrial capital with regard to processes of social reproduction of labor would not be validated worldwide until perhaps the end of World War II.

The problem of the expanded social reproduction of labor power under capitalism is, of course, not synonymous with the problem of sustaining a higher rate of growth of any given population. It has to be ensured that the amount of labor power *at the service of capital* is expanded. The term *proletariat* was borrowed from Roman history but entered the English language in the seventeenth century as a pejorative description of groups whose function was just to produce children (Linebaugh and Rediker 2000, p. 93). This at once ideologically devalued women's function of biological reproduction and the status of the vast masses of dispossessed workers. The rise of merchant capital coincided with continual expropriation of the lands of the peasants and the incumbent occupiers of the soil—be they hunter-gatherers, pastoralists, fishers, practitioners of swidden cultivation, or settled cultivators in England, Ireland, the Americas, the African coast, or Asia. When mere dispossession did not produce enough profit, the capitalist powers resorted to enslaving the people, trying to turn them into animate machines for producing profit. During this phase, as I have argued, in the heartland of Europe, the process of social reproduction of labor was too feeble to guarantee the supply necessary to carry on the extensive system of exploitation with basically artisanal techniques. European capital could as yet claim little superiority in production methods over the two largest economies of the world, China and India. It is only after the advent of the Industrial Revolution in England that Europeans could defeat the older manufacturing nations in the markets for manufactures.

One suggested solution to the problem of creating demand for manufactures was to create markets by getting Europeans to move overseas and equipping them with the capital they needed. This was essentially the course recommended by John Stuart Mill, following E. G. Wakefield (Mill 1848;

Wakefield 1849; Fieldhouse 1967). But as Marx (1867/1886) pointed out in his magnum opus, capital needs wage labor before it can be invested or it can form a market by means of which to realize its profit. Hence even in the nineteenth century, when European workers migrated overseas in ever-increasing numbers, property rights in the territories they settled in were regulated in such a way that they had either a new supply of non-Europeans to exploit or they themselves became differentiated and formed part of the proletariat.

The story of the rise and decline of the Netherlands in the golden age is important for several reasons. First, it shows how intercapitalist competition brought down an economy that had dominated the trade of Europe with the world in the seventeenth century. Second, it points up the difficulties of social reproduction of labor power in the age of merchant capital. Third, it vividly demonstrates the role of dependent colonies in sustaining accumulation in the core capitalist economies in the age of merchant capital and beyond. Fourth, it exemplifies how capitalist accumulation or its faltering can give rise to increasing inequality of income and wealth and become a barrier to further growth and advancement of human development.

NOTES

1. My shorthand guidepost is not meant as a true characterization of the modes of production or social formations of all societies in which commercial production is expanding but private property rights are restricted. The social formations may be those that prevailed in western Europe between the eleventh and thirteenth centuries, China during the Qing rule, India under the Mughals, or even Venice under the doges. Each of these formations has been analyzed in hundreds of monographs, but the common elements have perhaps not been sufficiently emphasized.

2. Seccombe (1983) rightly criticized Marxist scholars for neglecting the issue of social reproduction and the role of women in the process of reproduction and nurturing of human beings. That lacuna has been filled only partially as yet.

3. On Dutch supremacy in that part of the world trading system that was centered in Europe, see Braudel (1982, 1984) and Israel (1989).

Delayed Transition to a Low-Mortality Regime in Europe and North America

ADVANCES IN MEDICINE, PUBLIC HEALTH, AND WORKERS' STRUGGLES AND IMPROVED CHANCES OF SURVIVAL

We have seen how population growth suffered in most parts of western Europe in the seventeenth century because of wars, epidemics, and famines. Eighteenth-century Europe was still subjected to periodic food crises, leading in some cases to famines. Subsistence crises and faminelike situations ended in England earlier than in most other European countries. In France subsistence crises (for example, in Le Maine, in 1739, 1752, 1770, and 1785) continued till the last quarter of the eighteenth century (Braudel 1973, p. 39). According to Olwen Hufton, general famines had become rare in the France of that time. But with positive population growth, there was a "proliferation of people who experienced increasing difficulties in providing themselves with the bare necessities of subsistence" (Hufton 1974, p. 15).

The French population increased from about 18–20 million in 1720 to about 27 million by the end of the eighteenth century (Hufton 1974, p. 14) and 36 million in 1850 (Livi-Bacci 1991, p. 6). But high and, in many periods, increased levels of poverty continued not only in the isolated Massif Central region but in Paris itself. For example, in 1790, the proportion of the population dependent on, or belonging to, the category of so-called passive citizens, who were unable to support a family of 4–5 persons, was estimated at 30–40 percent of the population (Hufton 1974, p. 23). The French IMR has been estimated as 270 in the 1770s, falling to 200 in 1800 (Bairoch 1988, p. 229), but it remained as high as 165 down to the early 1880s (Woods, Watterson, and Woodward 1988).

Controversies have surrounded the proposed causes for the undoubted increase in the rate of population growth in England after 1750. Thomas Mc-
Keown (1976) argued that the acceleration in English population growth was
primarily due to a decline in mortality caused by improvement in levels of nutrition. McKeown's thesis in its simplest form of a monotonic relation between
increase in nutritional inputs and a decline in mortality has been largely con-
tradicted by the experience of European countries. First, in several European
countries besides England, population growth rates rose but there was little improvement in nutritional standards (Livi-Bacci 1991, chapter 1). Second, in
England itself a fall in the marriage age and a rise in the incidence of nuptiality as well as some increase in marital fertility were major contributors to the
acceleration of population growth (Wrigley and Schofield 1981/1989).

The English experience between the last quarter of the eighteenth century
and the 1860s has been sufficiently complex to provoke a considerable
amount of controversy (Szreter 1988; Fogel 1994; Guha 1994; Szreter 1994,
1997; Szreter and Mooney 1998; Mokyr and Ó Grada 1996). New researches
by medical experts, demographers, and social scientists have led to much
more complex formulations regarding the components of well-being in terms
of mortality at different ages, morbidity, and longevity than can be compre-
hended by a balancing of crude death and birth rates. I have earlier discussed
how nutrition, absorption, disease, and disease environment interacted to influence survival, growth, life chances at different ages, and heights or other
indices of health.

An adequate level of nutrition is necessary to provide the basis for a
healthy and long life. Nutrition is necessary first of all to provide adequate energy for an organism to support life and metabolic functions at different levels of activity. The energy requirements vary according to the state of the activity. For example, as I noted in chapter 1, pregnancy, breast-feeding, and
convalescence after illness would all require additional calories. The required
calories would also vary with age, sex, level of physical activity, and so on.

But nutrition is not simply a matter of caloric intake. Calories, vitamins.
proteins, and certain minerals are required in proper proportions and at the
same time minimum levels of the absolute quantities must be supplied. An extremely low intake of proteins and leafy vegetables, for example, cannot be
made up by feeding on large quantities of starch and carbohydrates. But on
the other hand, with suboptimal intake of calories, the body requires a larger-
than-normal protein supplement (Gopalan 1992). The ingestion of these inputs can be hampered by disease, and malnutrition itself allows diseases to
get a hold on the human organism.

Hence not only aggregate incomes or total nutrients available to a population but their distribution also will affect its well-being. So will differences in

disease environment. For example, before the advent of modern sanitation and public health facilities, by and large, villages were more salubrious for humans than cities. On the other hand, paupers and the hungry poor in general were unlikely to obtain much benefit from that salubrity. Similarly, women of working class families and working mothers without enough food and unable to properly nourish their children would suffer greater morbidity and earlier deaths, and their children would die in early infancy. So class, location, and gender influence the demographic trajectory of a population. But the disease environments and the knowledge of pathogens and ways of guarding against their effects also matter in health affairs. Hence the state of nutrition by itself cannot be a decisive influence on the health or mortality of a population.

Thus, for example, in England, between 1550 and 1750 the life expectancy of the members of the peerage (a well-nourished group) was roughly the same as that for the rest of the population (if anything, between 1575 and 1675 it tended to be lower); for peers it oscillated from a minimum of 32 years in 1650–1675 to a maximum of 38.1 in 1725–1750; for the rest of the population, from a minimum of 32 years in 1650–1675 to a maximum of 38.0 in 1575–1600. It was during the course of the eighteenth century that peers finally gained the advantage by 1.1 years in the first quarter of the century, 4.3 in the second, and 9.1 in the third (Livi-Bacci 1991, p. 64). These data also underscore the demographic disasters of the seventeenth century. The downward trend in life expectancy for the general English population continued into the next century: life expectancy declined to a low of 27.88 years in 1731 before beginning a slow and halting upward movement to 40.80 years in 1836, and it remained more or less at that level until 1871, when it grew to 41.31 years (Wrigley and Schofield 1989, table A3.1).

Life expectancy levels for the English population were subject to a number of factors, such as differential IMRs between town and country, differential IMRs between industrial towns and resort towns for the rich and the middle class, such as Bath or Tunbridge Wells, and differential adult mortality rates between different classes and people in different localities. Rapid urbanization, especially urbanization associated with smoke-belching, water- and air-polluting factories, and exploitation of cheap labor housed in congested quarters could be a great killer of babies and adults alike (Bairoch 1988; Szreter 1996; Szreter and Mooney 1998). English urbanization was greatly speeded up in the eighteenth century. In 1700 the total urban population (that is, of centers with population of 5,000 and above) of England was 880,000, of which London alone accounted for 550,000, in a total population of about 5 million (Bairoch 1988, p. 254; Wrigley and Schofield 1989, table A3.1). By 1800 London had grown to a city of 860,000 and by 1850 to one of 2,320,000.

The total urban population of England had grown to 2.1 million in 1800 and 8 million in 1850. Taking the total populations of those dates into account, the number of urban residents as a percentage of total population had grown from about 17.6 percent in 1700 to about 24.2 percent in 1800 and to about 48 percent in 1850. Most of this growth in urban population was contributed by new industrial towns such as Birmingham, Liverpool, Manchester, and Leeds (Bairoch 1988, p. 255). London grew more slowly than these towns, but it remained the chief city of Britain and became by far the largest city in western Europe.

Until about 1750, London was a net killer of its residents, but from a little before 1800 it experienced a net increase in population, as crude deaths per thousand went down from 520 in 1728–1757 to 500 in 1771–1780 and 292 in 1801–1810 (Wrigley and Schofield 1981, table 6.5; Guha 1994, table 1). From the end of the seventeenth century, the congested quarters of London began to be made more spacious and healthier through the laying out of squares, the demolition of rickety structures to build new thoroughfares, the paving of streets, the laying down of drains and drainpipes, the supply of piped water, and the lighting of streets. Gradually the built environment became friendlier to human life (Langford 1989, pp. 424–32). Some of the other towns also followed London with improvement acts of their own. But the furious growth of new industrial towns and the profit-making drive of mill owners and tradesmen created new centers of unsanitary urban congestion. While some of the southern market towns may have followed London in improving their sanitation, unregulated industrialization in many industrial towns of the north of England and Scotland such as Carlisle, Manchester, Liverpool, and Glasgow pushed mortality levels to a new high in the three or four decades following the 1820s: life expectancy in those towns went down to as low as twenty-five to thirty years (Szreter 1997; Szreter and Mooney 1998).

Moreover, this unprecedented urban and industrial growth led to an unequal distribution of the good things of life, including life itself, among the general population. For occupations in demand in London and industrial districts and in urban areas, real wages increased during the last quarter of the eighteenth century and the first half of the nineteenth. But many occupations declined, and by and large, real wages of agricultural labor, especially in the south of England, lagged badly behind and declined especially from the 1790s to 1815, the end of the Napoleonic Wars. Both push and pull factors propelled labor from the villages to the towns but not fast enough to raise real wages in the rural areas (Williamson 1989).

Standards of living are not fully captured by movements in real wages or real earnings. Taking consumption levels as the index, Mokyr (1988) found no improvement in English living standards between 1790 and 1850. As I have noted, the acceleration of population growth during the onset of the English Industrial Revolution was more the result of a higher birth rate than a decline in mortality. The standard of living of many sections of the population declined in the period 1780–1815; with some recovery in the early 1820s, it again declined and did not really get on to a trajectory of steady growth until the 1860s (Johnson and Nicholas 1997; Feinstein 1998). Many sections of the population, such as agricultural laborers, were hard hit by price rises in the late eighteenth and early nineteenth centuries and the failure of wages to keep up with that rise. Working women were particularly badly hit, as they lost many of their earlier occupations. The inclusive family wage of the whole family working for a merchant, or on their own in their homes, or working in manufactories was increasingly replaced by a factory or mine wage for individuals, which took no account of the needs of the family (cf., Tilly and Scott 1978, chapter 4). In the tumultuous 1790s such radical women as Mary Hays (1798/1994) and Mary Anne Radcliffe complained bitterly about the displacement of women from their traditional modes of gainful employment. "There are very few trades for women, the men have usurped two-thirds of those that used to belong to them; the remainder are over-stocked, and there are few resources for them" (Radcliffe 1799/1994, pp. 119–20).

Later research has confirmed that these complaints were justified. Market opportunities for women shrank, and in the gender-biased allocation of commodities, including nutrients, women suffered. Burnette (1997) found that the proportion of women's wages to those of men declined from 0.46 in the decades immediately preceding 1800 to 0.42 after 1800; the explanation was not an increased gender discrimination but a decline in the demand for skills peculiar to women's professions.

It is difficult to calculate the absorption of nutrients by people, but as I noted earlier, heights of adults can serve as an index of such absorption in the years of body growth. In a study of the heights of women convicts transported from England and Ireland to the penal colony of New South Wales between 1800 and 1815, Nicholas and Oxley (1993) found that the average heights of rural-born English women fell 1.9 centimeters (0.75 inch) over those years, and that the heights of rural-born women fell more than those of urban-born women and also more than those of rural-born men. But to complicate matters, the heights of rural-born Irish women rose, though very slightly. A later study by Nicholas and Oxley (1996) of the heights of 16,573 women prisoners of Newgate between 1785 and 1815, confirmed their earlier finding of a decline in stature. Summarizing the findings of other studies, Johnson and Nicholas (1997) found that after gaining a little up to 1825, rural-born English women lost height again around 1830 and, with some further fluctuations, both rural and urban-born English women lost stature down to the

1850s: they were between 2 and 2.5 centimeters shorter in the 1850s than they had been around 1820.

Deterioration in the biological well-being of English women in these years was also associated with deterioration in other respects. The incidence of illiteracy among the women convicts, the population under study, increased between 1795 and 1815 (Nicholas and Oxley 1993). In his pioneering study of measurement of changes in literacy in England, on the basis of a large sample of marriage registers preserved in the parish churches, Schofield (1973) had claimed that while male illiteracy in England had remained stagnant for fifty years between 1750 and 1800 at around 40 percent of the adult population, it began to fall after that date; however, adult female illiteracy almost continuously declined from a level of above 60 percent in 1750 to 50 percent in 1839. But his figure 2, plotting the illiteracy data, shows a distinct upward kink for both males and females around the years 1795–1805.

Both men and women suffered a decline in their biological well-being and their standard of living during the meridian years of the English Industrial Revolution. During this period, all industrial action of workers was considered to be illegal, and political power was concentrated in the hands of a small group of property owners. This regime pitted workers in all occupations, but especially the losers in the process of structural change, one against another without restraint and naturally depressed their real wages. But the inflation of food prices during the Anglo-French wars of the 1790s to 1815 also affected the living conditions of the average English working man.

Fogel (1994, p. 371) pointed out that, for many European nations before the middle of the nineteenth century, the national production was at such low levels that the poorer classes were bound to have been malnourished under any conceivable circumstance and that the high disease rates of the period were not merely a cause of malnutrition but undoubtedly, to a considerable degree, a consequence of exceedingly poor diets.

Fogel's generalization covered Great Britain also, the land of the so-called agricultural revolution accompanying the Industrial Revolution. In a study of EIC recruits in the United Kingdom between 1815 and 1860, Mokyr and Ó Grada (1996) found no evidence of a rise in their heights and hence no evidence of improvement in nutritional standards. The average final heights of British men who reached maturity in the third quarter of the eighteenth century were more than 9 centimeters shorter than of those who reached maturity in the third quarter of the twentieth century. Moreover, while an average British male grew a little taller in the last quarter of the eighteenth century, he lost in height again in the third quarter of the nineteenth century (Fogel 1994; Floud and Harris 1997).

Using the mean heights of the EIC recruits as their sample, Mokyr and Ó Grada (1994, quoted by Ó Grada 1994) estimated that between ca. 1800 and 1815 the average Irishman, though coming from a desperately poor and agrarian economy, was 1.25 centimeters (half an inch) taller than an average adult male of England and Wales. Fogel (1994) hypothesizes that the vast numbers of paupers and vagrants in England and France owed their ill-repute as ne'er-do-wells to their low level of nutrition, which left them too feeble to work for more than a few hours a day.

Efforts to tackle the effects of congestion, pollution, and bad housing on mortality rates, and hence life expectancy, noticeably lagged the requirements in the burgeoning industrial cities of the north and the Midlands of England. In 1779–1787, people in the northern town of Carlisle had a life expectancy of 38.7 years compared with the national average of 36 to 37 years calculated by Schofield and Wrigley. In the last two decades of the eighteenth century, Carlisle also experienced a decline in mortality, partly because of the introduction of vaccination against smallpox. However, thereafter the mortality rates of Carlisle increased among infants and adults, the crude death rate reaching a level of forty per thousand. Life expectancy went down to 33 years in 1838–1853, substantially below the national average of about 40 years (Armstrong 1981; Wrigley and Schofield 1981/1989, table A3.1; Szreter and Mooney 1998).

Carlisle's experience was by no means unique. Contemporary calculations put life expectancy at 25.3 years and 25.7 years in 1841 for Manchester and Liverpool, respectively, and 29 years for Bristol in 1825 (Szreter and Mooney 1998, p. 93). A time series for life expectancy in Glasgow from 1821 to 1861 shows a decline from 35.0 years in 1821–1825 to 27.3 years in 1837–1841, and even after a slow recovery it was only 32.1 years in 1861 (p. 96). This deterioration in living standards in the industrial towns, and especially in the areas where workers' quarters and factories were concentrated, is confirmed by Huck (1995). In a study of nine parishes in the industrial north of England over 1813–1836, he found the IMR rising from 160 in 1813–1818 to 180 in 1831–1836.

For much of the period survival rates in rural areas in western Europe were better than in urban areas. For example, although in Sweden IMRs in 1811–1820 and 1831–1840 were 243 and 229, respectively, in urban areas, the corresponding rates in rural areas were 177 and 161, respectively. In Amsterdam, the IMR was 228 in 1851–1860 but 197 in the country as a whole (Bairoch 1988, table 14.1). When life expectancy was less than 30 years in 1841 in most northern industrial towns of England and in Glasgow, it was 45.1 years in rural Surrey (Szreter and Mooney 1998, tables 3 and 5).

Nonetheless, with unequal development of different occupations, many workers, especially women, in rural areas and traditional market towns found their job opportunities shrinking, and the results were pretty grim for rural as well as urban women in different parts of England.

Summarizing the record of English population growth since the seventeenth century, we can say that it went through three distinct phases. After a reasonable growth down to the 1640s, population stagnated for the latter half of the seventeenth century and, from the middle of the eighteenth century, its growth rate increased steeply. The stagnation in population growth may be linked to the general crisis in agriculture and other areas of economic activity in Europe, including England, as suggested by Hobsbawm (1954) and as reiterated by students of agricultural history such as Allen (1992). In the eighteenth century, however, farm output grew at a reasonable rate (from forty million pounds sterling to fifty-nine million pounds in constant 1815 prices, according to the direct measure of farm output, as given in Allen 1994, p. 102).

The influence of Malthusianism is present even in the analysis of such eminent demographers as Wrigley and Schofield. In the first edition of their book, Wrigley and Schofield (1981) tried to explain the change in the rate of population growth by relating rates of nuptiality to changes in real wages with a lag: a rise in real wages led to a fall in the age of marriage and a higher incidence of marriage among women of reproductive age groups, perhaps a generation later. The lags involved turned out to be implausibly high. Real wages in England as measured by the Phelps Brown and Hopkins (1981) series declined precipitously from the 1570s to the 1640s but rose in the latter part of the century; this rise was sustained till the 1730s and then stagnated in the later part of the seventeenth century. In the second edition of their book, Wrigley and Schofield (1989, pp. xx–xxi; see also Schofield 1994, pp. 80–81) tried to tackle the problem by splicing the Phelps Brown–Hopkins series with a series of agricultural wages constructed by Elizabeth Gilboy (1936) but the fit between the crude marriage rate and the real-wage series remains distinctly problematic. Goldstone (1986) suggested that because the enclosure movement and other aspects of commercialization led to greater proletarianization and because in the earlier part of the eighteenth century employment opportunities expanded faster than the labor force, the perceived constraints on starting a family declined and nuptiality among that section of the population went up. Thus the fall or stagnation in real wages in the later part of the century could have been due to the expanding labor force failing to be matched by an equal expansion of demand for labor.

The experience of other European nations and of Canada and the United States with respect to mortality levels from the late eighteenth century was basically similar to that of England. I noted earlier the high levels of mortality in major regions of Germany. Belgium, one of the first continental European countries to industrialize, had very high levels of infant and child mortality down to the third quarter of the nineteenth century, levels that were higher than in the northern Netherlands. This may have had something to do with the consolidation of magnate and landlord power after the reconquest of the southern Netherlands by the Spaniards in the 1580s.

For even a country like France, which experienced a lower degree of urbanization than Britain or Belgium, the crude death rate was 27.4 as late as 1849 (Mitchell 1998a). Mortality rates for children declined rather slowly during the nineteenth century, and the decline accelerated from the late nineteenth century. For older people real progress in reducing mortality took place only after World War II. As in England, the mortality rates were much higher in the cities and, in particular Paris, than in the rural areas. The limited improvement in mortality rates between 1800 and 1880 was primarily the effect of a mortality decline in the cities to the levels in rural areas. The diffusion of Enlightenment thinking improved child-rearing practices such as more breast-feeding of children by mothers rather than by wet nurses. From the latter part of the nineteenth century, Pasteur's discoveries helped improve public health and hygiene. Unlike the declines and fluctuations displayed by British data on heights during the corresponding period, French data show a slow but steady increase in heights of army conscripts throughout the nineteenth century (Weir 1997). This may have been partly due to the slower rate of industrial transformation and urbanization in France compared with England.

Sweden seems to have been one of the earliest countries to have experienced a fall in IMRs and crude death rates (Imhof 1979). But even in Sweden, the crude death rate climbed to 40 per thousand in 1809 and came down below 20 only from the 1850s (Mitchell 1998a). Even for Sweden the IMR was still as high as 146 in 1850; in that year it was down to 102 in Norway, a very thinly populated country. Although Sandberg and Steckel (1997) confidently assert that (capitalist) industrialization did not harm health in Sweden, the fact is that neither life expectancy nor heights display a decisive upward shift until after 1865 (Hill 1996; Sandberg and Steckel 1997).

The long delay between the attainment of reading literacy and improvement of the biological well-being of the people in Sweden was not accidental. The science and technology of disease control and sanitation remained in a primitive stage until the latter half of the nineteenth century. Sweden, in spite of its mineral resources, was a very poor country until the 1850s. Moreover, real wages in Stockholm, along with those in other major cities in western Europe, were on a downward trend in the second half of the eighteenth century, and they did not move upward until the second half of the nineteenth century (Soderberg 1987). As I argue elsewhere, migration of a large fraction of the European population overseas, especially from the 1870s, improved the bargaining power of the working class in Europe. In Sweden, this factor, in combination with public action induced by the needs of elderly people remaining behind and the politics of social democracy played a decisive role in improving the well-being of the ordinary people (Sommestad 1998). The IMR went down below 100 in Norway in the late 1870s and in Sweden twenty years later (Mitchell 1998a).

What was happening to the migrants from Europe in the lands across the Atlantic? The natural rate of growth of those populations was generally higher than those of the people they left behind. But their longevity, height, or other indicators of biological well-being did not improve much until the last quarter of the nineteenth century and in most cases not until the early 1900s.

The United States and Canada were not yet industrialized nations in the first half of the nineteenth century. But apart from the southern United States, where African Americans were treated as chattel, these two lands were mostly free of major restrictions on capitalist competition in the domestic market, and markets decided allocation and investment of resources. Until the last quarter of the nineteenth century, many regions in the United States and Canada were empty of people or peopled with Amerindians and Inuits who were being systematically hunted down, killed, or corralled into native reserves. Yet these lands of ideal capitalist competition were not free of the urban and other crises created by capitalist competition.

In a study of West Point cadets in the United States, Komlos (1987) found that their heights and weights declined between the 1820s and 1870s. "The decline was geographically widespread and affected farmers and blue-collar workers the most." Middle-class cadets were not affected. The decline occurred because labor productivity in agriculture did not keep pace with growth in the demand for food, and especially food grains, caused by growth of population and the nonagricultural work force. Costa and Steckel (1997) found that, while cohorts of U.S. army recruits born in 1830 were taller than earlier generations, the cohorts born thereafter lost height; the cohorts born around the 1880s were almost four centimeters shorter than those born half a century earlier. In a study of rural-urban mortality differentials in nineteenth-century Quebec (Canada), Pelletier, Legare, and Bourbeau (1997) found urban mortality to be distinctly higher; the two mortality rates declined and converged only toward the end of the century. Thus even with plenty of land and resources, much of it taken from dispossessed Amerindians, the European migrants to the Americas did not enjoy improved health until the last two decades of the nineteenth century. Advances in sanitation and an increase in the pace of economic growth were needed before the plenitude of natural resources could be translated into improved physical health.

On the other side of the Atlantic also, improved health had to wait for advances in medical and sanitary practices—much of it effected under public auspices—a tightening of the labor market, and workers' struggles for better deals, which were helped by massive migration of Europeans across the Atlantic. This migration and European investment in the Americas and Australia in turn had as its counterpart the extraction of enormous surpluses from the dependent colonies peopled by Asians and Africans. The reality of that intercontinental resource flow itself has been hidden in the mainstream literature. In part 3 of this book I shall turn to the mechanisms of the extraction and transfer of resources from the nonwhite dependencies of the European powers.

The actions of the state and society in major European countries in pushing forward schemes for educating the public, providing them with relief in times of distress through poor laws and other rudimentary social insurance schemes, and creating new public health facilities—all contributed to the upturn in human development in Europe, especially since the 1870s. The governments of Scandinavian countries, in particular, have been cited as pioneers in these respects (Sandberg 1979; Senghaas 1985). By the 1850s, in terms of human capital and death rates, the Scandinavian nations were doing almost as well as, if not better than richer countries such as England or France. These countries were rich in human capital, agricultural land, and in the case of Sweden and Norway, other natural resources as well. But they were poor in terms of industrial capital and production. Two external factors helped them finally to make the transition to industrial nations. One was the access to the fast-growing British markets for many of their agricultural, forest, and mineral products. The expansion of British markets was itself helped by the surpluses transferred from the colonies and by returns on British investment overseas, factors that cannot be overlooked in this context. Another principal factor helping the final transition of the Scandinavian lands to a state of high human development was, as I have previously noted, the emigration of vast numbers to the overseas settlements of the Europeans, especially the United States The investment needed to feed and equip the migrants in the new lands was massively supplemented by fund flows from Europe, especially Britain. However, that massive foreign investment flow from Europe to the temperate lands to which Europeans emigrated was supported by the surplus extracted from the nonwhite dependencies of European powers. While the role of overseas migration in raising living standards is recognized in the literature (Massey 1988; Hatton and Williamson 1994), the links of that migration with British investment overseas and, even more importantly, with the transfer of surpluses from the nonwhite colonies to the metropolitan heartland are almost totally ignored in the Eurocentric literature.

A large proportion, if not the majority, of migrants from European countries consisted of agricultural laborers, tenants and poor farmers, general laborers, and domestic servants. This is strikingly true of Ireland and the Scandinavian countries, but this is also true of England, Wales, and Scotland (Pounds 1985, chapter 3; Ó Grada 1994, chapter 9). These waves of emigration raised wages in rural areas and declining occupations in general and eased the urban crisis—especially in Britain. At the same time, they accelerated the rate of urbanization of the remaining population and left the European countries with a proportionately larger fraction of skilled labor force. The mass migrations were in turn driven largely by the increase in population growth rates in most European countries and by the prospect of earning higher incomes in the United States (Hatton and Williamson 1994; Ó Grada 1994, chapter 9). Thus along with improvements in nutrition, medical technology, and public policy, overseas migration played a vital role in improving human development in western Europe between the 1850s and the 1920s.

The dependent colonies of Britain or other European powers—mainly populated with nonwhites—received only a fraction of British or other European investment, even in gross terms (Nurkse 1961; Simon 1968; Edelstein 1982). According to Simon (1968), the continents of Asia and Africa accounted for only 25 percent of the new British portfolio investment between 1865 and 1914. By contrast, North America and Australia—recipients of the major stream of white emigration—took 45 percent of the total new British portfolio investment. In a detailed study of the patterns of British emigration to the United States, and trade cycles in Britain and the United States, Thomas (1954, 1968) found that British domestic investment troughs coincided with peaks of British investment going to the United States but that overseas migration peaks and troughs coincided pretty closely with the peaks and troughs of British net income available for foreign investment.

Not everybody benefited substantially from the emergence of the United States as the industrial leader of the world. Slavery and incomplete emancipation in 1865 left a permanent imprint on the life chances of African Americans in that country (see chapter 13). A process of emancipation that deprived the African Americans of all political rights and proletarianized them without providing equal access to education, public health facilities, and employment may have worsened their health compared with the pre–Civil War situation. An examination of the skeletal remains of 80 African Americans between 1890 and 1927 by Rose (1989) showed evidence of deterioration in health over that period. This would appear to be a small sample on which to base any generalization, but this is consistent with other evidence we have of the worsening conditions of African Americans' access to health care and public education in the period in which Jim Crow legislation was used to deprive them of their civil and political rights.

The discrimination against African Americans in health care and education was severe in the period before the U.S. Civil Rights Act of 1964 and had the expected effects in depressing longevity and other indicators of well-being.

If this was the situation as regards the reproduction and demographic health of the ordinary people and workers in the most favored lands of the Industrial Revolution, the condition of the workers in the not-so-favored areas can be well imagined. To take an example at random almost, on the basis of slave registration data collected in Trinidad (then a colony of Britain), John (1988) found life expectancy for a plantation slave to be 17 years. The IMR was somewhere between 255 and 485 for girls and 287 and 443 for boys. Fewer than half of all slave children survived to their fifth birthday.

The evidence available for England, France, and Prussia or Germany suggests that a major breakthrough in human survival rates was made only from the last quarter of the nineteenth century. Some of the rural areas in England showed a decline in their IMRs (which were lower than in the neighboring towns) from the 1860s (Williams and Galley 1995). However, these declines were not enough to counteract the stubbornly high IMRs in urban areas. The IMR series given in Woods, Watterson, and Woodward (1988) covering 1881–1913 or 1881–1912 for several western European countries display no statistically significant trend for England and Wales, France, and Prussia up to 1900 (if anything, there is a slightly upward trend in the case of England and Wales) but a sharp structural break in the year 1900. Life expectancy at birth in England and Wales increased by about 24 years between 1901 and 1960. In Austria, for example, the IMR came down from 231 in 1900 to 75 in 1949. In Denmark the IMR came down from 128 in 1900 to 34 in 1949, in England and Wales the IMR declined from 154 in 1900 to 32 in 1949 (Mitchell 1998a).

The largest improvements in health indexes took place during the two world wars. This appears to be paradoxical since we would expect living conditions to deteriorate during those wars. The paradox disappears and the efficacy of a free market in delivering health care is brought into question when we know that during those wars, in the interest of the conservation of resources and improving the health and morale of the combatants and their families, the state had to introduce rationing and public provisioning (Sen 1999, pp. 49–51, 96–98).

Interestingly enough, in comparing the health experience of British and Indian soldiers in the British Indian army and their families, Guha (1993) found that in 1880–1900, the advantage in nutritional status British soldiers and their families enjoyed made for rather small differences in their health status—with IMRs of 224.3 and 214.7 for Indian boys and for British children (of both sexes), respectively. But by 1910–1914, the IMRs for the children of the British soldiers had come down to 88, and the crude death rates for British troops and Indian troops had changed from 16.13 and 15.23, respectively, in the earlier period, to 4.5 for British soldiers and 5.6 for Indian soldiers, respectively, during the later period.

Even before 1900, nutrition, sanitation, education, and measures of public health did make a contribution to human health. After all, IMRs were already declining fast in Sweden and Norway in the 1880s, if not earlier. These countries are known to have been better endowed with human capital and less plagued by unplanned industrialization. The appropriate public health measures took time to be diffused throughout the industrial towns, and education also produced results only tardily, especially because women, who were already in a disadvantageous position, were disfranchised even in formally democratic countries. It was not so much a desire to advance human development as concern for keeping abreast in industrial and military competitiveness or stealing the thunder of the socialists that produced legislation and public action. In Germany the measures of social insurance introduced by Bismarck were accompanied by repressive, antisocialist legislation. Under the Liberal administration of Campbell-Bannerman in England, the early measures of social insurance were meant to correct the infirmity displayed by the British soldiers fighting the Boers in the Anglo-Boer war at the turn of the twentieth century. But however it happened, public health measures and rudimentary health insurance both contributed, along with improved nutrition, to the process of the social reproduction of the proletariat in the core areas of capitalism (Szreter 1997; Szreter and Mooney 1998; Winegarden and Murray 1998).

The European miracle, then, was not obvious in the health and longevity enjoyed by the average European until the very end of the nineteenth century, that is, until almost a century and a half had elapsed after the first cohort of modern machine-run factories had appeared on British soil. This in turn required the discovery of the bacterial origins of disease, the technology for delivering safe drinking water and sanitary disposal of urban sewage, and the rousing of the awareness of urban bourgeoisie to the dangers of keeping their workers and potential soldiers unhealthy and short-lived. The implementation of that new knowledge was in turn quickened by the threat of workers' struggles turning into demands for the overthrow of capitalism, especially on the mainland of Europe, only a promontory of Eurasia.

The delivery of the new private and public health system was not simply a function of internal developments. The unequal interdependence into which the first-mover capitalism of Europe had entangled the rest of the world in turn permitted the resources generated by the labor of the nonwhite populations of other continents to be sucked into the project of further accumulation in Europe and the overseas lands settled by Europeans.

EUROPEAN MIGRATION, FOREIGN INVESTMENT, AND EXTRACTION OF SURPLUS FROM THE COLONIES

We have seen that in Europe an aggressive, belligerent, and urbanizing capitalism with merchants to the fore was unable to solve the problem of the expanded reproduction of capital and labor. Increases in productivity were rather sporadic and the accumulation process could proceed only by subjecting more and more people to the sway of the merchant capitalists. The subjection of the people of the Americas did not fully answer this need, because as we will see later, the native Americans died off too fast. The enormous expansion of the Atlantic slave trade between the sixteenth and eighteenth centuries was one answer to this problem of expanding the labor base of exploitation. By the end of the nineteenth century, within European countries, the problem of expanded reproduction of labor was nearing solution. However, such a solution in Europe was accompanied in the nineteenth century by a significant deterioration of conditions of social reproduction of labor in the two most populous counties of the world, India and China, and this deterioration was directly connected with the onslaught of the European powers on their freedom, leading to the establishment of British rule over India and a conjoint form of European dominion over the prostrate and decadent Qing empire. The connection of these conquests and damages with the European ascent is not accidental: that was established through a pattern of overseas migration of European workers accompanied by massive investments in these colonies of European settlement and the offsetting extraction of enormous surpluses from the formal and informal dependencies of the European powers in Asia, Africa, and Latin America.

By the end of the nineteenth century, all of Africa (barring Ethiopia) was finally brought under European dominion. Excepting Japan, a few nominally independent states, and the mainland of China, all of Asia was reduced to a vassal status by the major European powers. In Latin America, formal Spanish and Portuguese rule was ended but the regimes that followed were controlled by Creoles claiming European descent and were dependent for most of their ventures into modern industry and communications on British or other European capital (Bagchi 1982).

As table 7.1 indicates, there was a massive migration of Europeans, to the New World and Australasia, during what has been styled as the long nineteenth century. Massey (1988, p. 384) has argued that "overseas migration played a

Table 7.1.   Total Intercontinental Emigration from Europe, 1846–1924

Country or Region	Number of Emigrants (in Thousands)	Emigrants as a Percentage of Total Intercontinental Emigration	Emigrants as a Percentage Country's Population in 1900
Austria-Hungary	4,878	10.0	10.4
Belgium	172	0.3	2.6
British Isles	16,974	34.9	40.9
Denmark	349	0.7	14.2
Finland	342	0.7	12.9
France	497	1.0	1.3
Germany	4,533	9.3	8.0
Italy	9,474	19.5	29.2
Netherlands	201	0.4	3.9
Norway	804	1.7	35.9
Portugal	1,633	3.4	30.1
Russia-Poland	2,551	5.3	2.0
Spain	4,314	8.9	23.2
Sweden	1,145	2.4	22.3
Switzerland	307	0.6	13.3
Total Europe	48,174	99.2	12.3

vital and generally unrecognized role in the process of European economic development" and was a major factor in facilitating the transformation of European countries "from rural peasant societies to modern industrial powers." As population growth accelerated in Europe, and increasing use of nonlabor inputs raised per capita productivity in agriculture, peasants migrated to manufacturing towns and cities, "which expanded to produce a widening array of goods for consumption. Higher wages and more people earning those wages increased aggregate demand, leading to more employment and additional demand" (p. 385).

But from the last thirty years of the nineteenth century, these manufacturing towns receiving European emigrants would be located not only within Europe but in the United States, Canada, Australia, New Zealand, Argentina, Uruguay, and South Africa. Moreover, as new immigrants came into the eastern United States, old immigrants moved farther west, and many of the new immigrants with some capital at their command would also be encouraged to become farmers, through the Homestead Act and other governmental measures encouraging settlement of the land by working farmers. Thus along with improvements in nutrition, medical technology, and public policy, overseas migration played a vital role in improving human development in western Europe between the 1850s and the 1920s.

British investment in the United States had as its counterpart large trade deficits of Britain with the latter. In the balancing acts that supported the British empire, before World War I, Indian exports generated large surpluses with the United States even as India had a nominal and increasing deficit with the United Kingdom (Saul 1960).

I have argued (Bagchi 1982) that in the dependent nonwhite colonies most of the so-called invisible earnings of the metropolitan country contained vary-ing elements of (1) a political tribute (often self-ransom such as repayment of the British Indian government debt contracted for quelling the so-called mutiny of 1857–1858 or the debt contracted by the Netherlands East Indies government for fighting numerous counterinsurgency wars in Indonesia) and (2) monopoly rents on business that natives were formally or informally ex-cluded from and competition was minimized. In view of this, the export sur-plus of a dependent colony gives a minimal measure of the transfer of surplus from a colonial country. In the case of British India, the annual export surplus was mostly absorbed by Home Charges and by the profits remitted by Euro-pean residents in India principally as part of the proceeds of exports and re-mittances made by British officials.

I have made new estimates of the surplus transferred from India and In-donesia to metropolitan countries and present the basis for them in chapter 17. If we compare my figures with those of British foreign investment, estimated by Imlah (1958, pp. 70–75), we find that they formed more than half of such investment flows (in fact, they exceeded them in some years) up to the 1890s and a very substantial fraction still of British foreign investment in the peak years before World War I.

The export surpluses of Indonesia, a Dutch colony since the seventeenth century, played a very important role in supporting Dutch public finances, Dutch investment and Dutch external balances (Bagchi 1978, 1982; CEI 1976, 1979, 1987). In the 1830s the Dutch introduced a cultivation system that reduced peasants to the status of government serfs on the land they oc-cupied and extracted most of their profit. This was a substantial addition to Dutch resources when the Netherlands was trying to catch up with other Eu-ropean nations that had left it far behind after the Napoleonic Wars.

Over time, the number of Europeans (predominantly Dutch citizens) work-ing in Indonesia increased at a high rate (because the Dutch were much slower than the British in India to promote natives to higher ranks or accept them as business associates) and so did the earnings of those Europeans. Hence the export surplus figures are perhaps less useful as an indication of in-comes earned by the Dutch in Indonesia (but in my estimates I have tried to take account of the profits made by European traders). However, from 1921 to 1939 we have a series of national income calculations, differentiated by origin or citizenship of earners (CEI, 1979). They show that in 1925 almost a fifth of the national income was earned by non-Indonesians.

There are other ways also in which the same chain of unequal interdependence helped improve standards of living in Europe. The period from the 1870s to the end of the 1890s has been characterized as the Great Depression, primarily because of a fall in prices, which was led by the fall in gold prices of agricultural commodities (Saul 1969; Mitchell and Deane 1976, pp. 471–73). This in turn was precipitated by the outflow of grain and other agricultural products from the United States, Canada, Argentina, and Australia but also from India and other nonwhite dependencies. The export stream from the white-settled colonies was generated by extension of transport and acreage of lands emptied of Amerindians or other native peoples. But much of the grain or other agricultural products exported from India was pushed out by poverty-stricken peasants having to find money for taxes and necessities in an increasingly commercialized economy. There were other mechanisms such as the enforced absorption of silver—a rapidly depreciating metal—by India and other eastern lands—when most of the European economies adopted the gold standard, following the British and German examples (Bagchi 1979). This fall in agricultural prices and availability of cheaper grain made a significant contribution to improved nutrition and reduction of mortality rates in Europe, even as they deepened the problems of undernutrition and starvation in countries such as India.

Until the end of World War II, the benefits of advances in the knowledge of pathogens and the technology of prophylaxis and public sanitation remained largely confined to lands settled by whites, and even in those lands the benefits were differentially distributed along lines of class, gender, and race, thus belying the claims of universalism proclaimed by the primary ideologies of capitalism (see in this connection, "Capitalist Civilization" in Wallerstein 1995, pp. 113–63). As I have recorded above, even in the United States, which had emerged as the top capitalist power by the beginning of the twentieth century, the severe discrimination practiced against the newly freed African Americans in the postbellum era in the fields of public education, health, and employment had set them back badly compared with the whites. Even today, the expectation of life in many of the U.S. slums and ghettoes populated by African Americans is no higher than in developing countries. Such an outcome is the result of the public neglect of the health care needs of the average, working-class, African American as well as the working of market forces, condemning them to low-paid jobs and long stretches of unemployment, interspersed with prison terms, especially in the case of young male African Americans (Beardsley 1987; McBride 1989).

Before the promise of improved health, better control of environmental hazards, and education for all could be realized even in the heartland of capitalism, World War I burst upon Europe and the rest of the world was dragged into that interimperialist conflict. The years between 1916 and 1939 were marked mostly by an uneasy calm, to be shattered by the rise of fascism, first in Italy and then in a more terrible form in Hitler's Germany, in Spain, and in other countries of central and northern Europe with the help of Germany and Italy and the connivance of the rulers of Britain and France. For the world as a whole, though not for Britain and France, this war proved to be an even greater holocaust than World War I. The final ascent of the European peoples to their current standards of health, longevity, and education was made possible through state action to provide a minimum standard of literacy, nutrition, and health care to all citizens. In most of the democratic countries that had escaped Nazi occupation, such action predated the victory of the Allied powers. But the continuation of these programs in most countries owed as much to the fear of the attraction and challenge posed by the Soviet regime for the loyalty of the working classes as to the memory of the devastation caused by the Nazi dictatorship at the service of racist capitalism. It is not accidental that the fall of the Soviet regime has been associated with further onslaughts on the living conditions of workers in almost every country.

8

Literacy in Western Europe since the Sixteenth Century

REFORMATION, COUNTER-REFORMATION, AND LITERACY

In all the societies in which a written language has evolved, high value was placed on learning, which meant generally to read and, in most cases, to write. If we turn to the European tradition, much of which also entered into learned discourse through translations from Arabo-Persian texts, we can start from Aristotle. In his *Nicomachean Ethics*, Aristotle considered the reasoning power of human beings to be the essential character distinguishing them from other animals (for a comparison between the Aristotelian and Chinese traditions, see Needham and Wang Ling 1956, chapter 9). The reasoning power is expressed through language, which is also a distinguishing mark of human beings. The complicated system of signs and symbols that make up human language seems to be specifically a human possession (Chomsky 1968). Once language began to be written down, the reach of human communication was extended formidably, conquering differences in time, place, and persons.

To use Sen's classification, literacy is both a constitutive and an instrumental aspect of human freedom. The possession of literacy itself is part of the freedom of a human being: he is free to exercise certain kinds of choice which would be otherwise unavailable to him irrespective of whether he chooses to use that freedom (Sen 1999, pp. 6–9). The uneven distribution of literacy in a society that has begun using writing can have serious consequences: the illiterate may suffer deprivation *and* subjection to the literate few.

Before the institutionalization of education at the elementary level, it was difficult to judge what proportion of the population was literate (Schofield

1968; Houston 1988, chapter 1). In Europe since the sixteenth century, especially in Protestant countries, ability to read the Bible was often considered
the mark of a true Christian. Moreover, after the invention of movable type
by Gutenberg (who was preceded in this respect by the Chinese and Koreans),
the production and circulation of printed books increased phenomenally.
From these developments, it has been too widely inferred that European populations must also have become substantially literate from the sixteenth century. Protestantism in most countries, however, was largely an urban and elite
phenomenon until the rise of Pietism in Germany and Wesleyan Methodism
in England (Gawthrop and Straus 1984; Parker 1992).

In spite of an initial enthusiasm for Bible reading in the vernacular, many
Protestant theologians opposed the idea that reading the Bible was a condition of grace and salvation. As remarkable a man as

> Thomas More, for example, denied that 'the having of the scripture in English
> be a thing so requisite of precise necessity that the people's souls should needs
> perish but if they have it translated into their own tongue,' since the illiterate
> multitude would not be able to benefit from it. In any case religious literacy is
> beside the point. 'Many . . . shall with God's grace, though they never read word
> of scripture, come as well to heaven.' (Cressy 1980, p. 2; the quotes within are
> from Thomas More, *The Apologye*, 1533, pp. 20–20v; see also Gawthrop and
> Straus 1984)

It has been claimed that there was an enormous increase in demand for education and printed means of communication in England between the sixteenth
century and the period of the civil war (Wrightson 1982, pp. 184–85). But in
peasant families and among children of the poor, the demand on the child's
labor was too great and the rewards of book learning were judged to be too
slender for most of them to acquire a basic education, even when they had access to a school (Cressy 1980; Wrightson 1982).

In the secular world of competitiveness and social control, many ideologues of the existing order considered literacy of ordinary people not only
unnecessary but a positive hindrance to prosperity. Mandeville in his famous
Fable of the Bees (1732) argued that Great Britain had too many "knowing
men," and he urged the necessity of preserving "a certain Portion of Ignorance in a well-order'd Society" (quoted by Mitch 1993, p. 289). In Germany
and many other parts of western Europe, "confronting an increasingly plural-
istic and unstable religious scene, Lutheran [and other Protestant—A. B.] religious authorities were too frightened of heterodoxy to encourage people to
meet the Bible on their own terms" (Gawthrop and Straus 1984, p. 42). The
competition between different sects of Protestantism and between the Protestants and the Roman Catholics for the command of souls may have stimulated

the attempt to diffuse biblical knowledge. But visitations by prelates of both faiths revealed that many of their flock were only nominally Christian, with little knowledge of the Book or Christian doctrines. Catholicism, in particular, survived by adjusting to what were considered to be practices tinged by superstition and idolatry. Ordinary people in those areas had little to do with literacy for the good of their worldly existence or their spiritual welfare (Parker 1992).

I have noted how in Sweden the power of the state was put behind the church to promote the reading of the Bible. It has been claimed that after the 1620s, the number of ordained priests in Sweden rose dramatically until by 1700 "most parishes had two fully trained ministers—one for religious instruction and the other for teaching in the school" (Parker 1992, p. 77). Much of the growth in reading ability took place through instruction at home rather than in formal schools. At the end of the seventeenth century, reading ability in Sweden had still not gone far above 50 percent (Johansson 1977). But it increased steeply after that, very largely as a result of the draconian measures adopted under Charles XI (Britannica 1887; Rosen 1961). In 1686 he passed a law under which the Lutheran church was recognized as the national church, and the ability to read the Swedish translation of Luther's Little Catechism was made compulsory for every citizen (Graff 1981/1987, 1986/ 1987). Ability to read was made a necessary requirement for somebody to marry. The goals were conservative: "piety, civility, orderliness, and military preparedness" (Graff 1981/1987, p. 34). Reading ability increased fast under this program so that, in this sense, Sweden achieved universal literacy by 1750 and became the most literate country in Europe (Johansson 1977/1981; Houston 1988). Remarkably, and in contrast with other countries at the time, female literacy rates attained levels that were as high as, or even higher than, male literacy—an exceptional achievement in the history of transition to mass literacy (Graff 1986/1987, p. 250). But literacy in the sense of ability to read *and* write was still at only 20 percent until 1800, rose to 50 percent by 1850, and reached nearly 100 percent by 1900. To put this aspect of expansion of human capabilities in context, we should remember that the Swedish population was still very small by European and global standards, and that Swedish imperialism and the continued conflict between the so-called great powers in Europe took a toll of the potentialities of Swedish development. *Pace* Sandberg (1979) the "impoverished sophisticate" that Sweden was needed the external stimuli of the growth of overseas demand for its products and mass migration overseas to make the final transition to high human development levels (cf. Senghaas 1985).

In other countries of Europe, national policies were at best fragmented and episodic. Education or schooling for the ordinary people was particularly neglected when the landlords were expected to pay for educating their serfs, tenants, or laborers. So European literacy levels became generally stagnant after the initial enthusiasm for spreading the Gospels among the people had worn off. New initiatives had to wait for the eighteenth century, and some religious movements such as Pietism helped in this endeavor (McManners 1970; Houston 1988). It was really the rise of an articulate working class and the need for education among the workers that finally led to the achievement of universal literacy in major countries of western Europe.

It is very difficult to determine how many were literate before the nineteenth century, and in what ways. Many might be able to read but not write, some could sign their names but could not recognize any letters; some would not be able to read much else than the letters of their name, and so on. Except for the universities and some privileged schools for the elite, most other schools were run informally, and there was generally no system for collecting statistics about them or monitoring them.

In a pioneering article, Schofield (1968) used three major sources to estimate literacy, in the sense of ability to write, in England before the nineteenth century. The first two were the signatures to the Protestation Oath of 1642, "which had to be taken by all males over the age of eighteen to the effect that they would 'maintain the true Reformed Religion expressed in the Doctrine of the Church of England against all Poperie and Popish Innovations,' and the test Oath of 1723, promising allegiance to George I and renouncing the jurisdiction of the Pope, which had to be sworn by everyone over the age of eighteen" (p. 319). The first source had the grave limitation that even if all the registers recording the Protestations had survived, they would only give literacy levels of males as indicated by their ability to sign their names. The third source is the Anglican marriage register: an act of Parliament accorded "legal validity only to marriages"—with the exception of marriages of Jews, Quakers, and members of the royal family—"registered on Anglican registers and signed by the parties and two witnesses" (p. 320). In effect, a person's ability to sign his name has been taken as the proof of literacy in the preindustrial societies of Europe. However, this test would exclude persons who could read but not write and include people who had learned how to sign their names but did not know how to read or write passages in any language. In the case of counting of signatures, as against marks on marriage registers, this would also involve double counting of spouses who married more than once.

By using the signatures and marks of more than forty thousand men from more than four hundred counties in England, Cressy (1980) estimated male illiteracy in the 1640s to be 70 percent. Female illiteracy was generally far greater. While it might be 88 percent among will makers of Norwich in the 1630s, it might go as high as 98 percent among deponents in diocesan courts in counties far away from London in the period up to 1700 (Cressy 1980). Despite the proliferation of books, pamphlets, and other printed materials, England in the middle of the seventeenth century was overwhelmingly illiterate.

The situation improved only a little in the eighteenth century. On the basis of marks and signatures made by brides and grooms between 1754 and 1837 in a random sample of 274 parish registers, Schofield (1973) found that male illiteracy fluctuated around a constant level of 40 percent between 1754 and the 1790s, dipped a little in the 1790s, but increased around 1800 and began to decline only from the 1820s. The incidence of female illiteracy was about 65 percent in the 1750s, but it declined over the eighteenth century to about 55 percent, increased again (in step with male illiteracy) in the 1810s, and reached just below 50 percent at the end of the 1850s. Using the data available from the Registrar General from 1838, Schofield found that the rate of decline of illiteracy of both females and males accelerated steeply from the 1850s. By the beginning of the twentieth century, illiteracy had been more or less eradicated in England and Wales.

The Dutch of 1500–1800 did not differ from other Europeans in having IMRs between 200 and 300, high birth and death rates ranging between 30 and 40 per thousand, and a low life expectancy, ranging from 27 to 35 years (De Vries and Van der Woude 1997, p. 46). But the Dutch may have outdistanced most other European countries in promoting education and literacy in the early years of the republic. New universities were formed at Leiden in 1575, after the siege of the town by Spanish troops had been lifted (in 1574), at Harderwijk in 1600, Groningen in 1614, and Utrecht in 1634. Because of the increasing toleration of other faiths by the ruling oligarchy, these universities became some of the freest centers of learning in Europe (Clark 1947, pp. 291–92; Israel 1995). According to De Vries and Van der Woude (1997, p. 170), by the end of the eighteenth century, 75 percent of Dutch grooms and 60 percent of brides could sign their names on the marriage registers. In the 1670s, about 70 percent of Amsterdam grooms were able to sign their names. It is an indication of the backwardness of the southern Netherlands that in 1845 Brussels had a literacy level that had already been attained by eleven of the twelve Dutch cities by 1600! It is ironical that by that date Belgium was far ahead of the Netherlands in its degree of industrialization, but again not in respect of survival of children and adults. Within the charmed circle of imperial Europe, diffusion of modern industry could pitchfork a small country like Belgium with relatively low levels of human development into industrialization. Schofield's finding about stagnation or actual decline of male literacy during the most dramatic phase of the industrial revolution in England is consistent with our knowledge of the general standard of living of the English working class during the period. It also tallies with studies of literacy in Lancashire, the home of the cotton textile industry, the leading factory industry of that time. Sanderson (1968, 1972) found that signature rates on marriage registers there declined after the 1750s and began to increase decisively only in the 1830s.

Schofield's work in measuring literacy by counting signatures rather than marks, while pioneering and useful, has severe limitations as evidence of ability to read and write and use education for advancing development and human fulfillment. First, in Christian Europe, putting a sign like a cross was often taken as the equivalent of an oath and even functionally literate people put such a mark in earlier times in lieu of a signature (Cressy 1980). Second, the ability to sign one's name often did not indicate that the person was functionally literate. Third, of course, this method could not be used to measure literacy in societies that used an ideographic script as China did. On the other hand, the systematic variations in the extent of literacy according to class, revealed by the use of this method, does lend a degree of credence to the measured outcome in the context of Europe. In almost all cases, there was a steep decline in degrees of literacy from the gentry and the professional classes through the ranks of artisans and traders down to the lowest orders, namely, common laborers in the countryside (Cressy 1980; Vincent 1989).

The intensity of mass communication or acquisition of knowledge did not always depend on the acquisition of literacy by everybody; on the other side, the rise of mass communication with the advance of industrialization played a major role in advances in literacy. As Vincent (2003, p. 425) put it,

> Reading and writing have to be situated in the connectivity of the population in all its forms. It is at this point that the material inequalities of occupation and residence, which have been all but expelled from the tables of illiteracy, return to the picture.

Industrialization helped the spread of literacy, but differences of state action and class inequality greatly influenced its diffusion. For example, Belgium, with a more industrialized economy than the neighboring Netherlands, displayed far higher rates of male and female illiteracy throughout the nineteenth century. On the other hand, it is also true that the European laggards in industrialization such as Spain, Italy, and Austria showed higher rates of illiteracy than the more industrialized regions such as England, Scotland, France, and Prussia.

STRUGGLES OVER CHILDREN'S SCHOOLING AND
LITERACY IN NINETEENTH-CENTURY EUROPE

Acceleration in the growth of population and a slide in the standard of living, from the 1790s to 1815, increased the supply of child labor in England. This increased supply was matched by an increased demand that hindered children's access to schools rather than paid work in the factories. A decline in philanthropic funding for new schools and the failure of old schools to increase the number of places offered by them compounded the problem of access to schools. Some of Sanderson's findings (1968, 1972), and especially his view that the Industrial Revolution as such had an adverse impact on literacy in the heartland of that revolution, were questioned by Laqueur (1974) and West (1978). But the decline in standards of living that I have referred to elsewhere lends credence to the deteriorating material environment for schooling stressed by Sanderson.

What happened to popular literacy in France, the most populous country of western Europe until the end of the eighteenth century—the country of Louis XIV, the Sun King, the country of the philosophes, the country that witnessed the most comprehensive bourgeois revolution? As Natalie Zemon Davis (1975) has pointed out, it is easy to exaggerate the extent to which *menu peuple* and the peasants could avail themselves of the fruits of the print revolution:

> Rural literacy remained low throughout the sixteenth century. Of the women, virtually none knew their ABC's, not even the midwives. As for the men, a systematic study by Emmanuel Le Roy Ladurie of certain parts of the Languedoc from the 1570s through the 1590s found that three per cent of the agricultural labourers and only ten per cent of the better-off peasants, the *laboureurs* and *fermiers* could sign their full names. (p. 195)

Urban artisans, who had long been more literate than peasants, however, increased their literacy gap with the peasants (Davis 1975, p. 209). But given the low level of urbanization of all European countries except the Netherlands, until the eighteenth century this would not significantly raise overall literacy levels. The European Renaissance meant the acquisition of learning by the elect, not its diffusion among the ordinary people except for some groups of artisans (Graff 1979/1987). The century of Reformation also had only a small impact on popular literacy except in small pockets of what has been called radical Protestantism.

In France, as in England, the ability to sign the marriage document has been taken as proof of literacy. A law of 1667 made it compulsory for the bride and groom to put a mark or signature on the *acte de mariage* (Furet and

Ozouf 1982, p. 7). These signatures or marks provided the basic evidence for a massive survey of the history of literacy in France carried out by L. Maggiolo in the 1870s. (The survey was made against the backdrop of a controversy between republicans and the upholders of the ancien regime regarding the relative efficacy of church education versus republican initiatives in spreading literacy.) Female literacy in a group of provinces at the end of the eighteenth century in France was found to be 9 percent according to Maggiolo's survey and 6 percent on a recalculation of his data (p. 22). These figures are a little lower than the figures of female literacy in a group of provinces at the end of the seventeenth century. Most of the progress in literacy was made from the 1830s: data relating to male conscripts show that whereas 47.4 percent were illiterate in 1831–1834, the percentage had gone down to 34.1 in 1851–1855 and 17.9 in 1871–1875 (Price 1987, p. 330). Taking the index of ability to sign the marriage register, it was found that 32 percent of the men and 48 percent of the women were unable to sign the registers in 1855, but the corresponding figures had fallen to 1.6 percent and 2.7 percent, respectively, by 1913 (Price 1987), thus virtually eliminating the gender gap in literacy.

The spread of literacy among the ordinary people in England even in the nineteenth century was not a smooth or uncontested affair. The first problem was the poverty of most of the working people. In preindustrial or early industrial England, children in peasant, artisan, or laboring families were expected to engage in paying work from the age of eleven or twelve, if not even earlier (Mathias 1969, chapter 6; Malcolmson 1981). The sons of artisans or peasants, if they were lucky, could get themselves apprenticed to a trade, hoping to earn a respectable competence. Otherwise, children of men of small or no property would join the mass of badly paid laborers or servants—the latter might have represented 13 to 14 percent of the national population (Malcolmson 1981, p. 65).

In Jedediah Strutt's mill, children were employed in the 1770s as early as age seven, because they were part of a family or kinship group (Mathias 1969, pp. 202–3). The worst conditions of service occurred where the employer contracted for the supply of labor and the labor contractor contracted for the employment of whole families or kinship networks. Under those conditions, children would work as long as adults and would have neither the opportunity nor the energy to attend school. The Factory Act of 1833 "limited the hours of work of children between 9 and 13 to 8 hours per day, of those between 14 and 18 to 12 hours per day (with no night work). It also outlawed the work of children under 9, and tried to force mill owners to provide elementary schooling" (Mathias 1969, p. 203). An act of 1844 limited the hours of work of children between 8 and 13 to 6.5 hours. But these acts applied at first only to textile factories; in 1853 they were extended to other industries. The Mines Act of 1842 banned all females, child and adult, from work under the ground (Sutherland 1990, p. 130). In the same year Baroness Rothschild wore one and a half million pounds' worth of jewelry to the masked ball of Duc D'Orleans, and John Bright described the women of Rochdale in Lancashire:

> 2000 women and girls passed through the streets singing hymns—it was a very singular and striking spectacle—approaching the sublime—they are dreadfully hungry—a loaf is devoured with greediness indescribable and if the bread is nearly covered with mud it is eagerly devoured. (quoted by Hobsbawm 1962, p. 206)

The restriction of children's work in the factories did not automatically rule out their employment outside the factories nor did that legislation by itself make more schools or school places available to the children of the poor. The establishment of new schools or provision of more places in the schools with government grants ran up against the problem as to which denomination was to be granted such funding. The Anglicans, as represented by the established church, wanted a monopoly of these funds, but their claims were hotly contested by the Dissenters and the Roman Catholics.

"The Whig government of 1833 attempted to side-step the issue by making available a grant for which any voluntary school of any or no denomination, which satisfied certain conditions of efficiency could bid. This was a beginning, but it was a system of 'giving to them that hath'" (Sutherland 1990, p. 131). The Whigs tried to solve the problem of filling the needs of areas of educational destitution by giving grants according to need on a nondenominational basis, but the Tories mobilized against the bill and it was thrown out. Government grants to voluntary, denominational schools continued to rise through the 1850s and 1860s, "but still the money went to localities already making an effort" (p. 131). It was only in 1870 that the Education Act, known as Forster's Act

> at last embodied a commitment to nationwide provision; but the form it took showed the continuing power of the denominational vested interests The act allowed voluntary schools to continue unchanged, with the same committees of managers. But where a proven deficiency of school accommodation existed, or where a majority of the rate-payers demanded it, a School Board could be created. (p. 142)

As in England, so in France, the spread of elementary education among the poor was neither unproblematic nor uncontested. The propertied classes were worried about a possible rise in the cost of labor and losing social control. In a country of revolutions, both the propertied classes and the church wanted to use education as an instrument for instilling respect for the established order in young minds. Hence both administrative intervention and religious control over education went hand in hand. "An ordinance of 19 February 1816 required every commune to make provision for the education of its children and insisted that the very poor should receive free instruction" (Price 1987, p. 310). It was also required that the teachers acquire a certificate of good moral character as well as a *brevet de capacité*. After appointment the teacher's performance was to be monitored by local notables, including the parish priest. However, the church remained unhappy about a state-imposed requirement of competence and obstructed the establishment of low-cost monitorial schools because it was suspicious of the liberal credentials of their chief sponsors.

A breakthrough in elementary education in France occurred under the July monarchy. In 1833 a law introduced by Francois Guizot, then minister of public instruction, "required every commune or group of neighbouring communes to set up and maintain at least one elementary school" (Weber 1976, p. 307); it reaffirmed that every teacher should have a brevet of competence. It also provided schools for training teachers and for an inspectorate of schools. After the abortive revolution of 1848, in the period of transition between the July monarchy and the Second Empire, H. Carnot, the education minister in the provisional government, tried to make elementary education both free and obligatory, but he fell from power before his bill could be presented to the Constituent Assembly (Price 1987, pp. 312–13).

The Second Empire was an epoch of clerical and conservative reaction against all projects of universal and secular education. The first article of a promulgation on education insisted that "the principal duty of the teacher is to give a religious education to the children, and to inscribe on their souls the sentiment of their duties towards God" (quoted by Price 1987, p. 313). Over the years, many teachers suspected of anticlerical and republican sympathies lost their jobs. The requirement of a brevet was sought to be qualified, if not abolished altogether, and the curriculum of teacher-training schools was diluted for fear that too much intellectual content would generate subversive thoughts in the minds of teachers. The clergy became the arbiters of elementary education, with state funding (p. 314). Even the fall of Louis Napoleon and the establishment of the Third Republic did not free elementary education of the clerical incubus or render it accessible to the poor. The conservative regimes further strengthened the church-state ties in education, and the proportion of children taught by priests, who very often had little qualification for teaching, continued to rise. It was only when the republican majority was consolidated in the French national assembly that a law, introduced by

Jules Ferry in 1881, making education in all primary schools free and requiring all aspiring teachers to acquire a brevet, could be passed (pp. 316–20).

In Germany the Thirty Years' War not only took a huge toll of lives but also led to social regression. The power of the feudal lords, especially in the eastern and northern parts of Germany was further consolidated. The princes and electors of the numerous states of Germany were busy elaborating court rituals rather than educating their subjects (Coleman 1961; Carsten 1961b; Gawthrop and Straus 1984). "In a society in which beggars constituted one-fifth of the population and churches and school systems were in desperate need of rebuilding, courtiers and members of urban patriciates flaunted their wealth by dressing in the latest French fashions" (Gawthrop and Straus 1984). It is against this background that the Pietists began preaching that it was absolutely necessary for all Christians to be able to read the Bible to commune with God and be in peace with the world. They found a powerful patron in the Elector of Brandenburg, and gradually their influence spread to other states as well. The competition between different German states for power and loyalty of their subjects also led many of them to found universities and gymnasia (Blackbourn 1984, pp. 176–77). Progress in literacy, however, was patchy and incremental rather than dramatic before the nineteenth century. In eastern Prussia,

> the percentage of peasants who could sign their names rose from 10 per cent in 1750, to 25 per cent in 1765, to 40 per cent in 1800. . . . Best estimates of school attendance in the second half of the eighteenth century range from one-third to one-half of German school-age children. But by the 1830s attendance figures . . . reveal that in many Protestant regions between 76 per cent and 93 per cent of eligible children went to school for at least part of the year. (Gawthrop and Straus 1984, pp. 54–55)

Within Prussia, by 1850 the percentage of bridegrooms who had to sign with marks and therefore were functionally illiterate, went down to 10 percent, whereas the corresponding percentage in England and Wales, in 1853–1854, was still 30 percent (Mitchell 1998a).

Repeated defeats of German armies by the French, succeeded by the abortive revolution of 1848, led to the final dismantling of feudal institutions and an expansion of the civil liberties of the common people. But as in France, the motives of the rulers in advancing education had more to do with exacting obedience to God and the king and producing more efficient soldiers and better-trained artisans than expanding the freedom of the people. Whenever it was felt that these aims were not being realized through the prevailing education system, the authorities interfered directly in the curricula, mode of instruction, and selection of teachers. However, while the ruling apparatus remained deeply imbued with feudal, hierarchical, and militaristic values, the wide diffusion of literacy produced revolutionaries and socialists, along with loyal subjects, in large numbers (Craig 1981; Blackbourn and Eley 1984).

Ever since 1815 the Prussian schools (and what is said of Prussia in this respect was generally true of the other German states) had been administered by men with rigidly conservative views. In the 1820s and 1830s Altenstein, the Prussian education minister, made no secret of his determination that the education in the Volkschulen must not be allowed to "raise the common people out of the sphere designated for them by God and human society"; and his adage was more insistently followed by his successors after the revolution of 1848. King Frederick William IV placed the responsibility for the catastrophe of the revolution at the door of the Volkschule instructors, and once order was restored corrective measures were taken. In 1854 the education minister, von Raumer, issued directives that were to remain in force until 1872 and that made it clear to all teachers that their function was to impress upon their charges discipline, order, and obedience to authority. This command was apparently obeyed (the supposedly revolutionary teachers of 1848 were, a generation later, being given credit for winning the Battle of Königgratz) with the aid of a curriculum that was restricted to religion (with which the school day began), reading, writing, arithmetic, and singing (Craig 1981, pp. 188–89).

So the ruling authorities in Germany, as elsewhere in Europe (and North America), set out to manage and chain the goals of the Enlightenment, and succeeded perhaps too well. Even then opposition to universalizing elementary education was not lacking. Property owners feared the subversive potential of their workers' ability to read, and others, including learned professors and public men, feared the undermining of hierarchy. Friedrich Nietzsche, for example, in a famous series of lectures delivered in 1872, stated that "not the education of the masses can be our goal but the education of individually selected people for great and permanent achievements" and charged that "those who argued for a further extension of Volksbildung were seeking to destroy "the natural order of rank in the kingdom of the intellect"" (Craig 1981, pp. 187–88).

This brief sketch of the advance of literacy among men, women, and children demonstrates how slow that advance was in most countries of Europe before the nineteenth century. While Protestantism and the Counter-Reformation together with the invention of printing might have given a fillip to the increase of literacy, that impetus did not lead to a sustained growth of literacy, especially among women and the poorer sections of society. The right of every child to education and the abolition of child labor required long years of struggle against entrenched reaction in major countries of Europe.

III

THE WORLD BEYOND EUROPE IN THE AGE OF EMERGENCE OF EUROPEAN DOMINANCE

9

China's Economic Development and Quality of Life between the Sixteenth and Eighteenth Centuries

ECONOMIC DEVELOPMENT SINCE THE MING DYNASTY'S END

Many Europeans encountering China, the most populous country in the world, for the first time were struck by the opulence of its major cities and the craftsmanship displayed by its builders and manufacturers. By the beginning of the nineteenth century, however, that admiration turned into contempt and a desire to force the Chinese empire to remove the restrictions on trade with foreigners.[1] Let us then examine the condition of China in the era before European domination or conquest.

China and India were the two most important suppliers of manufactures to the rest of the world before the growth of machine-based manufactures in Britain. In 1750 China produced 32.8 percent of world manufactures, India (meaning the subcontinent of South Asia) produced 24.5 percent, and today's developed countries together produced 27.0 percent (Simmons 1985, table 1, based on Bairoch 1982, tables 10 and 13). China and India had also obviously succeeded in reproducing far larger numbers of human beings than western Europe. Were they doing worse than western Europe in respect of economic growth and human development even before the advent of the Industrial Revolution?

The quality of data and information about various aspects of human development is far better for China than for South Asia. China has provided the livelihood for the largest number of people in historic times, but the conventional wisdom has held, especially since the publication of Elvin (1973), that China was caught in a "high-level equilibrium trap," with no change in technology or productivity, and hence displaying only "extensive growth" at least since the passing of the Ming dynasty in 1644, if not earlier (Maddison 1998,

135

chapter 1). However, the recent work of American, Chinese, and Japanese students of Chinese history has established that late imperial China, meaning the late Ming and Qing dynasty periods up to the 1840s, was a dynamic society, expanding and diversifying under the drives of commercialization, market-induced stratification, and ambitions for upward social mobility, much as European society is said to have been driven by similar forces since the sixteenth century (Rawski 1985; Pomeranz 2000a; Skinner 1971, 1977; Wong 1997). A high rate of commercialization and economic growth were already in progress in the middle of the Ming period (that is, in the fifteenth and sixteenth centuries), until internal turmoil and external attacks (by the Jurchen, who established the Qing dynasty) dislocated the economy and polity from perhaps the 1620s to the 1680s (Mote 1999, chapters 24–26, 29).

Historians of China have followed the lead of Chi'h Ch'ao-ting (1936) in thinking of political economy in terms of three basic macroregions, consisting of the northern and northwestern parts, east-central provinces, and the southwest (Skinner 1971, 1977; Spence 1999). With population growth, the intensification of water-control schemes, effective linking of the regions with the interior and with one another, and the growth of both long-distance and short-circuit commerce, the original loosely linked macroregions differentiated into several more macroregions.

Each macroregion had a core defined by substantial economic activity in major cities, high population density, and comparatively sophisticated transportation networks for conveyance of food and merchandise. And each core was surrounded by a periphery of less populated and developed areas where illegal sects or dissident elements could thrive.

An administrative system that became the hallmark of the Chinese state under successive empires from the Han (206 B.C.E.–220 C.E.) through the Qing facilitated the growth of China's economic resources and population. The Chinese may have been the inventors of the production of silk from cocoons; they were certainly the inventors of the major types of silk-working machinery such as the reeling machine, the twisting and doubling machine, and the flyer; they were also the first people to have applied water power for silk production. According to Francis Bacon, the three inventions that had changed the world were paper, gunpowder, and the magnetic compass; as Needham (1954) pointed out, all three were Chinese inventions. They were transmitted from China to other regions of the world, including Europe, often with a long time lag, however (Needham 1954; Singer, Holmyard, et al. 1956).

The high quality of Chinese manufactures had earned markets for them from antiquity. Chinese textiles and porcelain ware, in which China was the innovator, had long been exported to the rest of Asia and thence to Europe and North Africa. A major route for export was the silk road. It had been opened up by the beginning of the Christian era, and despite interruptions by rebellions among the frontier peoples within the Chinese empire and the nomadic peoples of northeast and central Asia, it remained a major trade route for more than two thousand years. The Chinese economy became more closely linked to the global economy from the sixteenth century when, mainly through the activities of the Portuguese and Spanish merchants, Chinese handicrafts began to be exported to Europe and other continents by ocean routes. The return cargo consisted mainly of silver from Japan and, increasingly, from the mines of Spanish America. This influx facilitated the conversion of most payments of public dues in kind to payments in silver (Rawski 1985; J. Lee 1999).

The increased monetization of the economy under the late Ming stimulated economic growth. The Ming, like earlier and later dynasties, eventually was overthrown when administrative rigor was undermined by corruption, rising taxes led to a major social and political crisis, and multiple revolts led to the Manchu seizure of power and the founding of the Qing dynasty (Wakeman 1985; Mote 1999). The long eighteenth century and the first half of the nineteenth century—down to the start of the great midcentury rebellions—was a period of vast territorial expansion and rapid growth (Chesneaux, Bastid, and Bergère 1976; Rawski 1985; Mazumdar 1998).

The detailed work of William Rowe (1984), Li Bozhong, R. Bin Wong, and Kenneth Pomeranz on the Yangzi basin area convincingly challenge earlier formulations suggesting economic and demographic stagnation in China in the period preceding western aggression. In the Jiangnan region, the delta of the Yangzi, containing Suzhou and Shanghai, was highly commercialized already at the beginning of the Qing period (1644–1911). The population of the region had reached roughly twenty million by 1620 and, following decline during the Ming-Qing transition, reached thirty-six million in 1850 (Li 1998a, pp. 19–20).

Three factors that raised per capita production and productivity in Jiangnan during this period were (1) spread of multiple cropping, generally a paddy crop followed by rapeseed or wheat; (2) intensification of, generally male, agricultural labor; and (3) greater specialization, especially of women in textiles, comprising both cotton and silk fabrics. The growth of the latter activities was supported by greater productivity of male agricultural labor and the allocation of more land to cotton and sericulture. Bray (1984) and Mazumdar (1998) have shown how the technology of wet rice cultivation demanded small-scale agriculture and how that technology delivered growth in productivity and crop diversification. To curb the power of the entrenched nobility, the earlier Song dynasty and, much more emphatically, the later Qing rulers encouraged small holdings and peasant proprietorship, and hence productivity growth. The growth of productivity also stimulated diversification into commercial crops and handicrafts. In Japan, also, agriculture remained small-scale and commercial crops grew as a proportion of total output in the late Tokugawa period, but there was no policy to empower owners of smallhold-ings comparable to that followed by the Qing in China (Smith 1959; Satō 1990; see also chapter 12). The preservation of small-scale production and a degree of public regulation of the market delivered a better performance in terms of human survival than the working of a market guided by the burghers in the Netherlands or the daimyo in Japan.

LONGEVITY AND LITERACY IN CHINA

The detailed studies of the Yangzi delta, Guangdong, and other regions along with data on irrigation (Maddison 1998, p. 30) and population growth from all over China (Ho 1959; McEvedy and Jones 1978; Lee and Wang 1999) in-dicate that the period from 1700 to about 1850 witnessed high demographic growth by prenineteenth-century standards. We do not have estimates of per capita income, but the information on output growth compared with popula-tion increase indicates that, at least in the growth poles, the standard of living went up (Mote 1999, chapters 33–35; Pomeranz 2000b).

Lavely and Wong (1998, p. 721) show that life expectancy in China was a low of 22 years for the Qing nobility during 1700–1710, 31 years for the same group during 1750–1760, and a high of 46 years for the Tongcheng lineages of Anhui Province during 1690–1709. Zhao (1997a) tabulated the very long series of longevity figures, from 0 C.E. to 1749 C.E., for the Wang clan and found that the life expectancy was 34 years. In contrast, the average life ex-pectancy in France was 24.8 years in 1740–1749, 27.9 years in 1750–1759, 33.9 years in 1800–1809, and began to exceed the Wang clan longevity only after that decade. In the case of England, the average life expectancy ex-ceeded the Wang clan figure from 1700 to 1719 but went below it over the next three decades and began to overtake it only from the late eighteenth cen-tury (Livi-Bacci 1991, table 12). As I have pointed out earlier, many experts (for example, Razzell 1993) consider the English longevity figures produced by Wrigley and Schofield (1981) too high, because many infant deaths were not recorded in the parish registers.

Chinese peasants practiced fertility control by various means even during periods of prosperity (Li 1998a; Zhao 1997b). Female infanticide was prac-ticed in prosperous times, but it was more prevalent in periods of distress. But fast population growth between 1700 and 1840 nonetheless indicates an in-creasing level of prosperity as perceived by ordinary people (Lee, Campbell, and Tan 1999).

How literate were the Chinese? It is difficult to define literacy in the case of a people writing a nonalphabetic language such as Chinese (Rawski 1979, 1985; Elman and Woodside 1994; Chartier 1996). Moreover, the attainment of literacy in such a language was far more difficult than in the alphabetic languages. A working definition adopted by the Mass Education movement in the People's Republic of China in the 1950s used the ability to read and to use 1,000 characters as the test of literacy. But this is a far more rigorous definition compared with the signature test used in Europe, for in China "persons knowing fewer than 300 characters were counted as illiterate 'even if able to count and write receipts'" (Rawski 1979, p. 3).

Already in the sixth century C.E., the Chinese government had introduced the system of recruitment of officials on the basis of their proven scholarship in competitive examinations, and the later rulers continued the system (Ho 1962; Balazs 1964). Hence the level of education of a man (women were not allowed to hold any official position) basically determined his position on the ladder of success in the society and polity (Ho 1962). And for each successful examination candidate who obtained official position, there were many others educated in the classics who never passed sufficiently high examinations to obtain official posts. Many of the latter scholars used their literacy to earn a living, mostly as teachers, and thereby attained a certain status in society. Others turned their literacy to use as merchants. Because of the kudos attached to degrees even outside strict officialdom, holders of degrees far outnumbered scholar-officials. For example, "around 1840 there were about a million holders of degrees—twenty-five times the number of civil servants" (Chesneaux, Bastid, and Bergère 1976, p. 14).

Landownership and the bureaucracy were intimately related in China. Educating a boy for competitive positions was expensive, so that wealth, either of the immediate family or from contribution of a kinship group hoping to see a promising boy emerge as a scholar-official, was essential for success in these examinations. Even when scholars did not hold official positions, they performed many supervisory and semiadministrative functions, such as looking after public works and maintaining law and order, especially in times of civil disorder. Many contributed money for local projects that were not funded by the imperial treasury.

Merchants had other incentives for acquiring education. Contracts were generally written, changes in policy or regulations affecting their fortunes were posted in public places, and the ability to read and write was essential for business of any scale. The preservation of family inheritance also required the ability to handle written documents. The demands of this kind became more intense and more diffused among all regions as commercialization spread in late imperial China. The demand for literacy among the poorer classes was less pronounced, but the highly developed skills of Chinese craftsmen also benefited from some degree of literacy.

More prosperous farmers also had an incentive for learning the characters needed to understand contracts and official edicts; the more ambitious hoped to see a son achieve examination success and become a scholar-official. The meritocratic character of Chinese recruitment of officials provides a striking contrast with aristocratic monopoly on official positions in many other societies until the late nineteenth and even into the twentieth century.

The invention of printing and the dissemination of printed books from Song times made increasing numbers of books available for education. Officially sanctioned books such as the Five Classics, proficiency in which was required for passing the competitive examinations, were in great demand. Private publishers and book traders produced and sold books, which were widely diffused through many regions of the country (Rawski 1985; Brokaw 1996; Chia 1996). Under the Ming dynasty the government also endowed schools with libraries (Brook 1996). Both privately run and officially sponsored educational institutions continued to expand under the Qing dynasty as well. Rawski (1985) has estimated that by the beginning of the nineteenth century about a third of the boys of school-going age were going to some school in China. This is not an insignificant achievement in a country whose population was several times that of the whole of Europe at the time, with the additional Chinese handicap of an ideographic script. For comparison, we have to see that, according to the criterion of ability to sign marriage register or wills (which pertains to a wealthier group than the general population), up to 1800 more than 40 percent of the males and more than 60 percent of the females in England were illiterate (chapter 8).

Practically all the state and public efforts in imperial China were directed toward education of boys; girls were left illiterate or, in wealthy or scholar-official families, privately educated. Many experts earlier thought that by the nineteenth century only between 1 and 2 percent of the women were literate. However, in the eighteenth century there was an active debate about the desirability of educating women, in which the women themselves participated (Ko 1994; Mann 1997; Spence 1999). In spite of so many restrictions on their freedom, and partly because of them, the women had emerged, as in eighteenth-century England, as major writers of fiction and of poetry (Bagchi 2004). It is very probable that the earlier estimates of incidence of illiteracy among women are gross exaggerations. A Chinese novel, written by Cao Xueqin and widely regarded as one of the greatest works of fiction, has been translated as *The Story of the Stone* and alternatively as *The Dream of the Red Chamber*. The story revolves around a young scion of a prosperous family, and two young women entwined with his life through love affairs, and the intrigues of his family that blight that love (Spence 1999, pp. 106–10). The description of social life in eighteenth-century China available in this and other novels of the period makes it clear that, at least among the upper classes, women were literate and often able to exercise considerable influence, even though they suffered from many legal disabilities (as in western Europe). As a recent book on Chinese history puts it,

> Westerners who became familiar with conditions in China in Qing times often compared China favourably with Europe, remarking that the masses of ordinary people were well ordered, cheerful, and mannerly, mostly well fed and well housed, and with great capacities for energetic pursuit of their personal and family interests. The general well-being of the society can be inferred from the increasing participation of people at sub-elite and commoner levels in a growing range of organizational contexts, from commerce to philanthropy to religious and civic organizations. Related to that was an increase in literacy; from at least mid-Ming times onward, basic functional literacy was more widespread than in Western countries at that time, including among women at all social levels. (Mote 1999, p. 941)

Eric Jones (1981/1987) in his postulation of European superiority over Asian peoples with respect to prospects of economic growth has claimed that Europeans enjoyed greater security than Asians. A principal type of insecurity ordinary people suffer from is the threat of famine or severe starvation because of entitlement failures. Long before most other governments of the world had even conceived of a systematic policy for preventing distress and death in the case of famines, the Chinese had evolved the concept of "ever-normal granaries" (Will and Wong 1981; Bray 1984, pp. 416–23; Will 1990; Davis 2001, chapter 9). Using this concept, the government procured, stored, and distributed substantial quantities of grain, both to prevent abnormal rises or falls in grain prices and to guard against the ravages of famine. The practice became widespread under the Tang dynasty (618–900), with countrywide stores of grain maintained by the government. The system fell into disuse in periods of political instability, but the idea lived on and was reinstituted under stable administrations. The state encouraged private individuals and local communities to set up ever-normal granaries from which grain would be lent as well as given away in bad years. This assistance was supplemented by public works on which victims of scarcity would be put to work. But unlike under the imperialist dispensation of the British in Ireland and India working on state roads or canals was not made a condition for relief—a condition that often led to the death of the severely malnourished victims who were forced to labor at half the normal wage (Davis 2001, pp. 36–43).

Down to the eve of western military intervention in China, the Qing government had continued the policy of maintaining ever-normal granaries (Will and Wong 1981; Davis 2001, pp. 280–85). Every year, the district authorities would buy grain at the lowest price just after the harvest and sell it at the same price in the spring, so that consumers were not fleeced by speculating merchants. The magistrates would also borrow grain and collect some of it as charity and, correspondingly, give it away, sell it, or lend it as they perceived the people's need in different seasons and the different needs of different groups. Authorities would also store large amounts of grain against years of scarcity (Chesneaux, Bastid, and Bergère 1976, p. 28). The prices at which the transactions were made were examined by the emperor himself and his high officials. According to an estimate in Will and Wong (1981, p. 477), for well over a century, straddling the whole of the eighteenth, the Qing state may have spent as much as 10 percent of its revenues for food security. Moreover, as Davis (2001, p. 283) has pointed out, "In contrast . . . to later Victorian stereotypes of a passive Chinese state, government during the high Qing era was proactively involved in famine through a broad programme of investment in agricultural improvement, irrigation and waterborne transportation."

The question that arises, given multifaceted Chinese inventiveness and the remarkable performance of the Chinese state in its best days to "nourish the people," is why did the Chinese fall so far behind Britain and France in industrial and military technology by the fourth decade of the nineteenth century? I have already discounted the answers given by the culturalist school of Jones and Landes. Pomeranz (2000a) argues that it was due to the serendipitous discovery of the Americas by the Europeans, who were able to exploit the land and the mines of that continent to dominate the rest of the world. This answer is, however, unsatisfactory on several counts. First, for two centuries after the discovery of the Americas, the Europeans were unable to compete on equal terms with Asian manufactures. Furthermore, neither Spain nor Portugal, which were the powers that gained most immediately from the exploitation of Amerindians, was able to make a major dent on the power of the big Asian or Eurasian empires of Ottoman Turkey, China, India, or Persia. Finally, if the import of silver was critical for Europe and its trade with China, and its increased inflow was also important for monetizing the Chinese tax payments and commercial transactions from Ming times, China had a more important source of the metal in Japan up to the seventeenth century than imports from Europe. For example, the VOC imports of bullion from Europe into Asia between the 1640s and 1670s came to 400 metric tons, whereas VOC exports from Japan amounted to 540 metric tons (Pearson 2001, pp. 28–29). Most of these flows either ended up or passed through China. Thus European advantage in being the intermediary for precious flows into China and India may have been exaggerated in the literature. The monetization and commercialization process benefited both Mughal India and imperial China, but Europeans did not hold the key to that process.

Wong's (1997, especially pp. 146–47) distinction between "commercial capitalism," which he claims operated in Europe, and "market economy," which characterized China, is useful to help understand the roots of the great divergence not only between China and Europe from the nineteenth century but between India and Europe from the late eighteenth century as well (see, for more extended treatment, chapter 11). According to him, in China purely competitive operators carried out exchanges in the market, but in Europe transactions were "masterminded by a small number of very rich merchants who [could] set the terms of exchange with producers and consumers to make large profits, often minimizing competition through monopoly and force" (p. 146). The Chinese state controlled merchants with a firm hand and did not allow them to accumulate riches, beyond a point, by exploiting their monopoly power. The policy pursued for creating ever-normal granaries is one important illustration of this. The Qing policy of coastal evacuation to root out the resistance of Ming loyalists simultaneously hampered the growth of a seafaring mercantile class. Be that as it may, in the eighteenth century, seafaring Chinese traders dominated trade with Japan and with Southeast Asia (Hung 2001).

However, Qing commercial policies did not act as a catalyst for an industrial revolution, which remains the key to the great divergence. Property owners were not encouraged to maximize their control of profitable resources. State policies in England, with its parliamentary and private enclosures of open fields and common lands, and Holland, with the rule of the burgher oligarchs, moved to the drumbeat of wealth maximizers. As Allen (1982, 1991, 1992) has shown, efficiency measured in terms of factor use was no greater on enclosed, large farms than on unenclosed small farms in England. But the enclosed farms could privatize part of the commons and put the displaced labor force at their mercy. This applied also to land with exhaustible resources attached to it, such as mines. This ability to concentrate exhaustible resources in a few hands and marginalize and convert the smaller producers into a proletariat generated the economies of scale in production, became the hallmark of the English industrial revolution, and set apart the industrializing countries following the same path. The scientific and technological advances in Europe from the seventeenth century also left China far behind. The methods of using exhaustible resources such as coal and iron on ever larger scales were unknown to the Chinese of the late eighteenth century.

Under the Qing empire, diversification of cropping patterns and increases in productivity through intensified use of labor and fertilizers promoted agricultural growth in central China. The increased production of mulberry leaves and silk cocoons also permitted higher volumes of silk production and their export from this highly commercialized region. Similar market exchanges in southeastern China promoted better technologies for extracting cane juice and refining it and hence the growth of the sugar industry (Mazumdar 1998).

Moreover, as Mote has concluded, rural China was "healthy by premodern standards; the Chinese of all economic levels ate a wholesome diet of cooked foods, drank boiled water or hot tea, and observed some basic principles of community hygiene. Their native traditions in medicine were able to respond to many of the epidemic diseases, such as typhoid and typhus, and by Ming times they regularly practised variolation for the prevention of small pox" (Mote 1999, p. 757; see also Leung 1987). We have to remember in this connection that variolation, or vaccination, was unknown in western Europe until the eighteenth century. The importance of clean drinking water for hygiene was also not appreciated in Europe until the nineteenth century.

NOTE

1. For a brief overview of changing European views of China, see Gunn 2003.

10

India under Mughal Rule and After

DEMOGRAPHIC AND ECONOMIC GROWTH IN THE MUGHAL PERIOD

Let us now take up the case of India (meaning the subcontinent that at present includes India, Bangladesh, and Pakistan), the other densely populated Asian region to succumb to Western domination. As I have noted earlier, in 1500 India and China both had larger populations than all of the western European countries put together. India was under several different monarchies and sultanates and had very varied economic structures as between, on the one hand, port cities, centers of long-distance trade or capitals of major kingdoms, and the core areas surrounding them and, on the other, the forest, semi-desert, or desert regions with sparse populations. Over the next two centuries, the Indian polity became much more unified: beginning with Akbar, successive Mughal rulers brought most of northern India and, subsequently, most of the Deccan peninsula under their rule. The spread of monetary transactions, induced by the Mughal practice of realizing their taxes in money and by the growth of private commerce, led to greater uniformity in economic structures: the scope of the so-called natural economy became increasingly restricted, at least as far as the main population centers were concerned (Habib 1982c; Grover 1966/1994; Subrahmanyam 1994b). But still there were vast areas in which the reach of the Mughal state or of the money economy remained limited.

We have already discussed in chapter 5 why it is reasonable to conclude that the Indian population grew at almost double the rate at which major western European populations increased between 1600 and 1750, when the Indian population is estimated as 190 million. For 1800 most authorities put the Indian population figure at around 200 million. By then a large part of India had come under British dominion. South India and the area between the Ganges and Yamuna in northern India almost certainly suffered a fall in population caused by wars and adverse environmental changes (Lardinois 1989; Mann 1998). The core and most populous part of the British possessions, namely, Bengal, was affected by the terrible Bengal famine of 1769–1770 when a third of the population was wiped out. Moreover, the whole country was devastated by repeated wars in which the British EIC played a leading part. Hence it is reasonable to infer that the Indian population increased at a faster rate during the Mughal and immediate post-Mughal regimes than during the latter half of the eighteenth century.

In the era before the Industrial Revolution, the population of most large countries was essentially influenced by agrarian productivity, and that productivity changed slowly over time. Moosvi (2000, table 3) provides an estimate of the growth of the gross crop area in some of the most important provinces of the Mughal empire between 1595 and 1665. That growth rate comes to about 0.23 percent per annum, marginally higher than the estimated annual rate of population growth between 1600 and 1800. The value of the crops also increased with a shift toward cash crops and increase in double cropping: oilseeds and pulses were sown after harvesting the *kharif* crops, that is, the ones produced June–December. The shift toward cash crops was partly induced by the growth of the textile industry because the dyes used to color the fabrics were vegetable products such as indigo and madder. But there was also growth of the sugar industry: Bengal exported sugar to Southeast Asia in the seventeenth century (Raychaudhuri 1982a; Mazumdar 1998, chapter 2). Similarly, cotton production also spread as the domestic and international demand for cotton cloth went up. Another indicator would be the wages of labor in urban and rural areas. Mukherjee (1939, section 3) tabulated most of the data on wages and prices available from ca. 1595, the approximate date of compilation of the *Ain-i-Akbari* by Akbar's minister Abul Fazl, and 1938. The prices of major food grains are available for northern India for 1595 and 1650 and for Bengal for 1729. The prices of ghee (clarified butter), oil, sugar, and salt are available for 1595, 1661, and 1729. If we use either the prices of food grains or of the more extensive items for deflating the money wages of laborers, then in most cases the resulting real wages are found to have increased over 1595–1729.[1] India in the Mughal and post-Mughal period had huge numbers of cattle, and this was reflected in the consumption pattern of the ordinary people:

> In the Agra region, we are told, butter with rice formed the food of the common people and there was no one in Agra who did not eat it. Similarly, butter was

produced in such plenty in Bengal that besides being part of the diet of the masses, it was also exported. (Habib 1963/1999, p. 59)

Before the defeat of its nawab in the battle of Plassey, Bengal had become both demographically and economically the most dynamic region of Northern India and was expanding its exports, and not only through the European chartered companies. Asian (chiefly Indian) merchants were holding their own in many areas of foreign trade and thus obtained the major share of profits of both inland and foreign trade. Piecing all these fragments of evidence together, it is fair to conclude that the rate of growth of Indian income in the Mughal and immediately precolonial period very probably matched, if not exceeded, the long-run rate of demographic growth in India during the immediate precolonial centuries.

India was probably the biggest exporter of textile manufactures in the world down to the middle of the eighteenth century. We do not have reliable data about intra-Asian trade, but from around the 1610s to 1750, Indian textile exports to Europe by the European chartered companies, especially the English and the Dutch VOC, far exceeded their exports of Chinese silk and porcelain to Europe (Chaudhuri 1978, table C.2; Prakash 1998, chapters 5–6). It is only from the 1760s that the EIC's imports of Chinese tea into Europe began to outdistance its imports of Indian textiles.

While we have reasonably good data bearing on the exports of Indian products by the VOC and EIC, which were the most important European companies trading to Asia in the first half of the eighteenth century (Chaudhuri 1978; Chaudhury 1995a; Prakash 1998), we do not have comparable data on Asian exports out of India. On the basis of reports by European factors of the chartered companies and private traders, Chaudhury (1995a, p. 210) has inferred that around 1750 the total value of textile exports made by Asian traders was around Rs11.5 million, while the total value of textile exports by the European companies would not have exceeded Rs5 million to 6 million. Taking the lower figure of European exports, the textile exports for Bengal alone would come to £1.65 million (£1 = Rs10).

In craft production, Indians enjoyed a comparative advantage down to the end of the eighteenth century. For example, even after forty years of rapacious colonialism had squeezed the economy and the peasants and artisans of Bengal, in 1794 cotton piece goods made up half of the total exports of that province and silk, sugar, and piece goods accounted for about 60 percent of those exports (Colebrooke and Lambert 1795). Other parts of India also exported manufactures, and Bengal was also an exporter of rice, ghee, and sugar, among other commodities, to Southeast Asian countries. Bengal's textile exports went into a terminal decline only after the takeover of the region by the British, and neither Mughal rule nor the post-Mughal Nawabi regime can be blamed for that outcome. Apart from the evidence sketched above, many historians have also stressed the existence of a large class of wealth holders outside the Mughal bureaucracy as a sign of a vibrant commercialized society under the Mughal and post-Mughal rulers (Chandra 1982; Raychaudhuri 1982a, 1982b; Richards 1990).

But then why has Mughal India had such bad press among the mainstream economic historians? One reason was the weight of sheer imperialist propaganda, which portrayed pre-British India as a land of unrelieved misery for ordinary people. A second reason is the arrogant ignorance of many Eurocentric economic historians. Take, for instance, the following statement by Landes (1998, p. 163): "Some of the most important work on Indian history has been done by Indian scholars, yet these, ironically, have had to rely almost exclusively on European records and accounts. Almost no written documentation comes down to us from the Indian side." Landes is talking about Mughal India, and the successor states of the eighteenth century. Enormous volumes of Persian records have come down to us from those times, and most of the work done by the historians connected with the Aligarh School and many others has been carried out on the basis of Persian, Urdu, Marathi, and several other vernaculars as well as European sources.

A peculiarly statist attitude adopted by the Eurocentric historians has also affected their view of pre-British India. When it comes to France under Louis XIV, no good historian would think that the fortunes of Frenchmen could be figured out exclusively by looking at the formal administrative structure of the kingdom and the intentions of Louis. Yet when it comes to Mughal India, many of them think that it is enough to state that the intention of the Mughal administration was to take away half of the gross produce of the peasant and quote the unsupported obiter dicta of one or another European traveler to arrive at an idea of the condition of an ordinary Indian.

Following the lead of Sher Shah Sur, the Mughal bureaucracy tried to assess the productive capacity of the peasants under their jurisdiction and appropriate as much of the peasant produce as possible and convert it into cash. According to Habib (1963/1999, pp. 96–97), the system led to an extreme concentration of the fiscal resources, with 445 officials appropriating 61.5 percent of the revenue income of the empire in 1647. However, the Mughal rulers also attempted to expand cultivation: when new land was opened up, at first the peasants were charged very little, and the tax was exacted at the full rate only after five years (Habib 1963/1999, 1982b, 1982c). When an army marched across some newly conquered territory, it was sometimes accompanied by woodcutters in its train so that forests could be cut down and cultivation expanded. Special rates were provided to encourage the growing of cash crops such as indigo. Moreover, Habib's finding about the extreme concentration of fiscal resources has been contested by other scholars. It has been argued, for example, that "*at least* one-third of revenue under the Mughals was collected in about 1600 by means other than the ones described by Habib" (Alam and Subrahmanyam 1998b, p. 15).

There was a characteristic of the Mughal tax system that raised the peasants' and herders' net income and partly protected India's ecology. Abul Fazl's *Ain* laid down "that if a man kept under pasture such land as was liable to land revenue, . . . a tax of 6 *dams* per buffalo and 3 per cow (or bullock) was to be imposed upon him. But a cultivator having up to four bullocks, two cows and one buffalo to each plough was to be exempted. Moreover, no tax was to be levied upon the *gaushalas* [cowsheds], or herds of cows kept for religious or charitable purposes" (Habib 1963/1999, p. 284). Pastures were generally not taxed under the Mughals, but the herders had to pay a tax, generally at a very low rate, per animal. Indian peasants generally had a much larger complement of draft animals than their Chinese or Japanese counterparts. Large herds of cattle survived into the middle of the nineteenth century. But the refusal of the British to exempt pastures from taxation, their increasing abolition of the rights of the people to common property resources, and their attempts to control seminomadic herders led to the erosion of livestock numbers and the denudation of forests, grasslands, and other common property resources (Bagchi 1976b; Gadgil and Guha 1992).

With increasing trade and use of money and bills of exchange (known as *hundis*) for transferring money and claims, towns and trade centers grew in size and number. Increasing numbers of prosperous merchants, traders and landed magnates, and even artisan traders operated under Mughal and post-Mughal regimes (Grover 1966/1994; Fukazawa 1991; Perlin 1978; Raychaudhuri 1982a, 1982b; Fukazawa 1982b, 1982c). The process of commercialization of the state revenues led to the emergence of well-placed people who benefited from it and who then gained materially by encouraging the production of cash crops (such as the superior grains as well as cotton, indigo, silk, or tobacco). This process was seriously interrupted only when the Europeans, mainly the British, took control over the mechanism for surplus extraction and began remitting it abroad rather than investing it in the country.

For several major regions of Mughal India, such as Bengal, we have a wealth of evidence pointing to a strong growth in demand associated with a growth in the numbers of cultivators, the cultivated acreage, and crop production. Thus the revenue demand for the main districts of Bengal increased between 1595 and 1659 by percentages ranging from 54 to 117 percent (Eaton 1994, p. 199). The deltaic region of Bengal became a growth pole from the 1660s, especially after the Mughal suppression of the disorder caused by the piracy of the Portuguese and the Arakanese *maghs* (Arasarat-nam 1994, chapter 6; McPherson 1993, chapter 3).

As foreign trade carried on by European and Asian traders grew, the Indian rulers benefited from, and by various means encouraged, the inflow of silver and gold into India from Europe via the Cape of Good Hope route and over-land, from China and Japan as well. But it was not just a lust for treasure that motivated them. From the time of Sher Shah Sur (1538–1545) the rulers had roads and hostelries built for travelers on an extensive scale. These roads served military purposes, but also linked important centers of inland and over-seas trade with centers of administration (Alam and Subrahmanyam 1998b). But the circulation of gold and silver was not confined to the towns or centers of trade and administration, nor were gold and silver the only media of circu-lation. Copper was extensively used as a medium of exchange, so that Irfan Habib (1987) speaks of a trimetallic system under the later Mughals. Cowries, seashells gathered from the Indian Ocean islands, remained a universal medium of exchange in villages of eastern India until the British forbade their use for tax purposes (Bagchi 1987a; Perlin 1987). Thus monetization entered into many small-value transactions as well; the survival of an extensive natu-ral economy became a myth in most parts of India with settled agriculture and became increasingly confined to the subsistence needs of hunter-gatherers.

The Mughal empire declined precipitously after the death of Bahadur Shah I in 1712 and it broke up into a number of kingdoms and principalities. There is no proof, however, that before the conquest of Bengal by the British, ma-jor sectors of the Indian economy were in decline. As in the case of China, so for India; it is best to think of economic changes in terms of regions (Alavi 2002b; Marshall 2002). By the beginning of the eighteenth century, eastern India, including Bengal and Bihar had emerged as the most prosperous terri-tory of the Mughal empire. That prosperity was not disturbed by any major war until the conquest of the region by the British. Another successor state, which also retained its prosperity, was Awadh in north India. In both these re-gions, the land revenue realized by the successor states increased, Asian mer-chants continued to hold their own in coastal and intra-Asian trade, and In-dian exports remained buoyant (Alam 1986, 1991; Habib 2002). The Maratha raids proved destabilizing to areas like Rajasthan and parts of central and south-central India, but in the core regions of Maharashtra there were thriv-ing villages and trade centers with a section of the landholders possessing strong proprietary rights down to the time of the takeover of the Peshwa's ter-ritories by the British in 1818 (Fukazawa 1982a, 1982b; Perlin 1978).

The closing years of the Mughal regime were characterized by widespread peasant revolts, the causes of which have been magisterially analyzed by Habib (1963/1999). But those revolts were as much a sign of the increased aspirations of rural magnates as of the oppressiveness of heightened tax demands caused by the expenses of a costly and seemingly never-ending war waged by Aurangzeb, the sixth Mughal emperor. Considering all the evidence, Richards (1997) concluded that the Mughal empire was eminently successful by most criteria, compared with contemporary European realms.

A comparison of the influx of silver with price rise also indicates that, by and large, Indian economic growth was positive until the end of the seventeenth century. There was a considerable influx of silver into India from the sixteenth century along three channels: from the Americas via Europe by the route around the Cape of Good Hope, by an overland route through the Ottoman and Safavid empires, and finally from Japan and the Americas via the Philippines both overland and along the oceanic routes around Southeast Asia (Deyell 1983/1994; Subrahmanyam 1991/1994; Subrahmanyam 1994b; Haider 1996). Yet there was no price inflation of the type that occurred in Europe in the sixteenth century (Habib 1982b; Moosvi 1987).[2] As I indicated earlier, with the growth of long-distance and regional trade, many centers of intense mercantile activity emerged in India during the period. With positive population growth, an active process of urbanization, and the spread of cash crops, the influx of money was used mainly to support output growth, especially because the inflow of high-powered money was encouraged by a state that realized its tribute in money. No estimates are available for the growth of urban centers in the Mughal domains and in the far south of India. However, all the qualitative evidence and the scattered estimates (Hambly 1982; Stein 1982) indicate a degree of urbanization at the end of the Mughal greater than the 10.8 percent recorded for India in 1901 (CSO 1993, table 5a). The available evidence indicates a decline in the population of all major cities in northern and southern India during the nineteenth century. The only cities that grew, in the latter part of that century, were the two port and administrative cities of Calcutta and Bombay as trade and finance became more and more centralized in the major port cities under the dispensation of colonial free trade (Habib 1985, pp. 364–68; Bagchi 1997b, chapters 7–10, 14, 16).

ECONOMIC CHANGES, LONGEVITY, AND LITERACY IN INDIA UNDER BRITISH RULE

Longevity or literacy in any country is affected not only by the economic fortunes of the people but by many other policies, including the expenditure made by the government on education and health care. But we know that the British Indian government spent as little as possible under those two heads. So it is especially necessary to try to figure out what happened after the

British had extended their dominion over the whole of India. Again, the problem is that the evidence not only is fragmentary and scattered but has also been wrongly interpreted by the apologists of colonialism and free trade. I will sketch some of the best evidence and its bearing on the fortunes of Indians under British rule.

By 1795 the British were well on the way toward establishing their paramountcy over most of the north, east, and south of India, leaving only the truncated kingdom of Tipu Sultan in the south, the Maratha confederacy in the southwest, and Sind and Punjab out of their clutches. I had calculated (Bagchi 1973a) the gross domestic material product of Bengal in 1795 per capita on the basis of detailed information on agriculture and handicrafts culled by H. T. Colebrooke, an outstanding British administrator-scholar (Colebrooke and Lambert 1795), and found that it exceeded the gross domestic material product of Bengal per capita in 1895. Because, in 1900, the income from these two sectors accounted for 75 percent of the national income of India (Sivasubramonian 2000, table 6.1), it is reasonable to conclude that, under British rule, Indians were no better off in the richest province than they had been a century earlier. The per capita income of an ordinary Indian in 1895 was probably lower than that of an inhabitant of the province of Bengal, especially since the latter had not been racked by famines like the rest of India, at least since 1873–1874.

The second kind of evidence relates to the record of industrialization or its reverse, deindustrialization. By and large, industrialization in any country has been associated with positive economic growth. If we define deindustrialization as the phenomenon of a decline in the share of the population engaged in the secondary sector, then that is generally associated with economic regression, except in the case of affluent societies in which services have become the growth sector. All the available evidence points conclusively toward the deindustrialization of India on a massive scale over the course of the nineteenth century (Habib 1975/1995; Bagchi 1976a; 1989, chapter 1; Clingingsmith and Williamson 2004). In Gangetic Bihar, for example, the proportion of population engaged in industry declined from 18.6 percent in 1809–1813 to 8.5 percent in 1901 (Bagchi 1976a). In every case, soon after British conquest of a province or region in India, the proportion engaged in secondary industry declined, the reason being not just the abolition of restrictions on entry of foreign goods but the decline in local demand for products of secondary industry. This is how the proportion of Indian industrial output to total world output of manufacturing came down from 24.5 percent in 1750 to 2.8 percent in 1880 and 1.4 percent in 1913 (Simmons 1985, table 1).

There are other kinds of evidence of India's retrogression in economic performance under British rule. I have referred earlier to the real-wage series constructed by Mukherjee (1939) by using prices of food grains as the deflators of money wages. With real wages as 100 in 1600, the real wages of unskilled workers declined to 35.98 in 1812–1820 and 36.48 in 1890. For skilled workers, the decline was even steeper, as we would expect in a process of deindustrialization and associated displacement of skilled artisans: the index declined from 100 in 1600 to 23.58 in 1812–1820 and 21.89 in 1890. The exact variations in the real wages would depend on the basket of food grains used in computing the index, but the picture of a massive decline after the establishment of colonial rule in India would not change. Indeed, real wages of both handloom weavers and agricultural laborers continued to decline in most regions of India down to the end of the nineteenth century (Kuczynski 1965; Bagchi 1972a; Krishnamurty 1987; Bagchi 1989).

Clingingsmith and Williamson (2004) have summarized the major pieces of evidence regarding the deindustrialization of India in the nineteenth century but have given a slightly misleading idea of its course and, more importantly, have assigned a wrong causal nexus for that phenomenon. Contrary to their claim, deindustrialization continued into the twentieth century as the work of Chattopadhyay (1975) and J. Krishnamurty (1983) has shown. According to Krishnamurty (1983, table 6.2), the proportion of the workforce engaged in manufacturing in undivided India declined steadily, from 10.1 percent in 1901 to 8.5 percent in 1931, before increasing marginally to 8.7 percent in 1951. What were the major causes of this decline? Certainly, competition from machine-made goods was a major factor. But in the Indian case, this competition was doubly unfair. First, Indians were deprived of the kind of government patronage and protection against foreign competition that manufacturers in European countries and overseas settlements of the Europeans enjoyed (Sabel and Zeitlin 1985). Second, until the middle of the 1830s, Indian manufactures were made to pay higher duties than the manufactures imported from Britain (Bagchi 1972a, 1976a). From the 1880s, India (along with most other nonwhite dependencies in the British empire) became practically the only major free-trade area in the world, but British manufactures continued to enjoy various kinds of informal imperial preferences in the nonwhite colonies of Britain. "Indian tariffs were about the lowest in the periphery, averaging 3 per cent, compared with 30 per cent in Latin America and the United States, about 17 per cent in eastern Europe and the rest of the newly settled European offshoots" (Clingingsmith and Williamson 2004, p. 6n).

Clingingsmith and Williamson (2004) attribute Indian deindustrialization to a rise in the prices of nontradables and agricultural goods, relative to the prices of major manufactured tradables of India. Implicitly, they also attribute this to growth of agriculture in India exceeding the growth of the workforce. This analysis ignores the long-term compression of domestic demand in India owing to the unrequited export of capital from India, principally in the form of tribute to the British rulers. The analysis also ignores the devastating famines in India, especially in the last third of the nineteenth century (see chapter 18 for details). Their assumption that there was an increase in land productivity after 1860 is also not supported by facts. How could land productivity rise when public expenditure on irrigation or soil conservation remained meager in relation to the needs of a country whose traditional irrigation systems had fallen into decay and that had undergone deforestation on a very large scale?

The estimates of Angus Maddison, in his numerous publications, of Indian income growth in the nineteenth century are accepted by most foreign analysts unfamiliar with Indian sources, and Clingingsmith and Williamson are no exception. However, Maddison's estimates are unreliable because the sources he has used are themselves marred by questionable methods and assumptions that are empirically invalid, as I have previously argued in detail (Bagchi 1989, chapter 1) and in chapter 17.

There is a basic methodological problem in using the specific-factors model in explaining phenomena of long-term de-industrialization à la Clingingsmith and Williamson, because they assume full employment and because they ignore the fact that in a situation of long-term disinvestment (as measured by changes in endowment of capital per person) in an economy, the transformation frontier is all the time pushed inward, and its shape may also change.

Anthropometric data also shed light on the impact of British rule on human development. Brennan, McDonald, and Shlomowitz (1994) have tabulated the data on south Indian migrants to Fiji over the years 1903–1913, who can be taken as representative of the poorer members of south Indian society. The authors conclude that "there was no secular increase in the height of South Indian emigrants going to Fiji and born between the 1860s and 1890s. On the other hand, there was a gradual, but statistically significant, reduction in male chest circumference." The authors then go on to provide evidence for the changes in the conditions of living as indicated by changes in prices of food grains and conditions of harvests in several districts of the Madras presidency. That evidence also points to deterioration rather than improvement of the general standard of living of the south Indian population in the closing decades of the nineteenth century.

Demographic evidence from western and northern India also points in the same direction. For example, between 1872 and 1911, among the major provinces and princely states of British India, only the combined province of Bengal, Bihar, and Orissa experienced positive population growth in every decade from 1872; every other province or princely state experienced an actual fall in population in one decade or another, primarily because of famine, triggering pestilences like diarrhea, cholera, malaria, or plague (Bagchi 1989). Studies of the agricultural development of most of the macroregions of India in the nineteenth century such as Bihar, Central Provinces, western Maharashtra, and Madras fail to reveal any dynamism in terms of productivity or improvement in methods of production (Raghavaiyangar 1893; Bagchi 1976b, 1992; Harnetty 1977; Baker 1984; Baker 1991; Sheel 1992). From the 1840s some extension of irrigation was made, but practically all major projects had to satisfy the criterion of yielding a net financial surplus to the government after meeting all costs, including interest payments on loans. Only a few provinces benefited from those projects and a large part of them accrued only in the twentieth century. Those benefits did not fully compensate for the decline of pre-British, especially small-scale irrigation works nor for the effects of deforestation, soil erosion, and the decline of livestock per head.

As I have pointed out elsewhere (Bagchi 1976b, 1992), the British taxed all land registered in the name of a person, and the tax rates were high. This left the person with no means of maintaining grazing land and livestock at low cost, as he had been able to do under the pre-British system. That meant that he had to gradually deplete his livestock, which served as his major consumer durable, principal consumer good, and the chief source of fertilizer. He was also barred access to forests under the British policy of sequestering most large forests for use by the government, the military, or railway contractors. All this led to the discontinuance of fallows, lower productivity on lands earlier cultivated, increasing use of marginal land, and soil erosion. Many of the earlier systems of small-scale irrigation had been maintained by zamindars or holders of superior rights: the latter also performed some police and judicial functions. Under the so-called Permanent Settlement of land tax in eastern and northern India, the British instituted a set of revenue farmers whose only responsibility was to pay the tax in time. Deprived of their other powers and responsibilities, these new zamindars or taluqdars ceased to maintain local irrigation works, which fell into decay and further depressed agricultural productivity (Bagchi 1976b).

In the case of India, we do not yet have the kind of estimates of longevity of people before the impact of colonialism that we have for China. We have an estimate of the male and female life expectancy in Delhi in 1833, that is, before it came under direct colonial rule. This was in the area "outside the royal palace" and it may have represented the typical condition of ordinary Indians in pre-British urban environments. The expectations of life at birth in the Delhi of 1833 were between 19.8 and 23.1 years for males, and between 22.1 and 24.2 years for females (Visaria and Visaria 1983, p. 473).[3] As we shall see, life expectancy in British Indian provinces went down even below these levels because of famines and epidemics.

It is difficult to measure Indians' literacy before the armed onslaught of European powers led to the disruption of their lives, partly because many of the earlier records perished in the process. Mughal India developed thriving means of communication between mercantile groups and a very active system of gathering of economically and politically significant intelligence. Mercantile exchange and political order depended on some diffusion of literacy among the ruling classes and the trading community (Bayly 1999, chapter 1). This period also witnessed the enormous growth of literatures in the vernacular such as Hindustani, Urdu, Bangla, and Marathi.

In the case of Bengal, three reports by William Adam, who was commissioned by the General Committee of Public Instruction, an official organ of the EIC government, to report on the state of education in Bengal, provide revealing details about how the indigenous system of education had fallen into decay under British rule, without any real alternative being put in its place (Adam 1835–1838/1941; Acharya 1989). Down to the early nineteenth century, in almost two out of every three villages in Bengal, there were elementary schools to teach basic reading and writing in the vernacular as well as arithmetic and the elements of accounting. Since Persian had been the court language under the Mughal and the post-Mughal rulers of Bengal, and continued to be so for some time under British rule, many of these schools also taught elementary Persian. Besides these, almost every district contained several institutions of higher learning in Sanskrit for Hindus with instruction in logic, religious laws, rhetoric, and sometimes astronomy, and similar but less numerous institutions using Arabic and Persian for Muslims (Adam 1835–1838/1941). As in Europe and China, virtually all these institutions were only for boys. Many of the schools were located in the houses of wealthy individuals, and many teachers lacked appropriate qualifications (the last was also true in case of many schools in England [Houston 1988]). However, with the coming of British rule, the avenues of employment of Indians in administration became severely restricted, Persian as the court language lost its cachet, while impoverished Hindu chiefs could not provide patronage for Sanskrit on the earlier scale. As many landlords lost both local power and incomes, they also lost much of the incentive to provide free public education, although some patronage of that kind helped to eke out the meager public funds on education spent by the colonial rulers.

There are other forms of popular literacy, which have so far been overlooked by historians. To take one example, in Sylhet, in today's Bangladesh, a large number of manuscripts on both secular and religious (mainly Islamic) subjects circulated in the early nineteenth century and probably earlier and were read by a significant section of the population. These manuscripts were written in a script that has been styled Sylheti-Nagri, an admixture of the Nagri (the dominant north Indian script), Arabic, and Bangla scripts, but the language was Sylheti, a dialect or a close relative of Bangla (Chanda 1998). There are probably other examples of such popular literacy that have not yet been fully studied.

Christian missionaries also compiled literacy data. Many of them could not enter orthodox Hindu or Muslim households, and hence they tended to underestimate female literacy. The British officials and missionaries tended also to underestimate the role of charitable institutions in inculcating piety through the reading of religious texts and female literacy arising out of it (Raman 1996). Hence the picture of a bleakly illiterate female population painted in official accounts may be wide of the mark in several regions of India. The British Indian government was extremely niggardly in its expenditure on education despite its professed aim of civilizing the natives through English education, and hence illiteracy spread across the land.

"The only educational institutions founded in India during the first half-century of British rule were the Calcutta Madrassa, started in 1781, and the Benares Sanskrit College, established in 1792" (Banerjea 1928, p. 290). When the EIC's charter was renewed by the British parliament, it was directed to set aside the munificent sum of ten thousand pounds per annum "for the revival and improvement of literature and the promotion of a knowledge of the sciences among the people of India" (p. 290). The scale of expenditure can be judged by noting that British India alone must have contained a population of 150 million around 1813, and the revenues of the company's government exceeded seventeen million pounds in 1813–1814 (p. 372). Appropriations out of that fund started only in 1823 and remained equally scanty in later years. By the famous minute of 1835, Macaulay decided to favor only English education, and the program was set afoot to create a tiny corps of clerks, minor officials, and other collaborators of British rule, who would be Indian by birth but English in most aspects of their culture. By 1901, at the high noon of the British imperium, the literacy rate in India was 9.8 percent for males and 0.7 percent for females. By 1941, six years before the independence of India and Pakistan, the corresponding rates had gone up to 24.9 percent for males and 7.3 percent for females, giving an aggregate illiteracy rate of 83.9 percent for Indians (CSO 1993, p. 52). This was the outcome of about two centuries of the civilizing mission as conceived and implemented by the masters of the most populous dependency in the world. The civilizing mission of the metropolitan rulers took a very similar form in other nonwhite colonies.

ENVIRONMENT IN CHINA AND INDIA IN PRE-COLONIAL TIMES
AND SINCE THE NINETEENTH CENTURY

In the contemporary world, many thoughtful people, cutting across ideological divides, have become increasingly worried about the state of the global environment. The question naturally arises, did the Chinese or the Indians take better care of their environment before Western imperialist aggression afflicted them? In one sense, the answer is obvious. From the time humankind domesticated animals, invented agriculture (by domesticating plants), found out how to produce fires, fabricated tools for work and for killing it has affected the environment in many radical ways. Many animals such as the dodo of Mauritius and the Indian *cheeta* of the dog family have become extinct (Rangarajan 2001); elephants have retreated from temperate latitudes to tropical and subtropical habitats; and the cradles of human civilization in the river valleys of the Tigris, Euphrates, Amu Daria, Sir Daria, and Indus have become deserts. So some environmental destruction has become part of human civilization as we have known it.

There are two major difficulties in producing a satisfactory narrative of these ecological changes. First, the evidence has often been written literally in water flow or its disappearance, in the rocky fastnesses of the Pamir plateau, or in the extinction of whole species of flora and fauna before being described or recorded by human beings. Second, the interrelations of the different components of the ecosystem are highly complex, and we are still learning the gross details of those interrelations. The complexity of reasons for the retreat of the elephants from northerly climes is a striking illustration of this. In all those areas, human beings have been responsible for enormous amounts of deforestation going back at least to the first millennium B.C.E., and deforestation has destroyed the habitat of the elephants (Elvin 2004). But Chinese records regarding climate changes have been gathered since about 300 B.C.E., and they show that China (and probably major parts of Eurasia) has gone through several phases of warming and cooling (Marks 1998, pp. 48–52). In particular, there was a distinct cooling down between the latter part of the Han and the transition to the Tang period, and the late Song, the Yuan, the Ming, and the Qing periods were colder than the early Han period (Elvin 2004, figure 1.5). Such long-lasting coldness, in addition to human depredation, may have driven the elephants southward

What we *can* try to do is to form an approximate idea of the part institutions like the state, market, or the complex called capitalist colonialism played in alleviating or aggravating ecological degradation. We must remember that *any* human interference with the environment is likely to be harmful for some living beings, and in many cases a conscious choice of valuing human life more than animal life has to be made. Even now, for example, several persons are killed every year in India by tigers or elephants in the villages bordering tiger or elephant reserves. Attempting to increase the space for animals may mean squeezing the living space of some of the poorest people in the world.

The Chinese, and especially the state, had been active in water control projects from the beginning of their recorded history. They linked up rivers in north China, deliberately redirecting some river courses to try to minimize flood damage or increase their utility as navigation channels. They also reclaimed swamps thrown up by meandering rivers. The Grand Canal, which has been called an artificial Nile, linking the lower Yangzi to the imperial capitals in the north, is estimated to have carried 8.48 million hundredweights of grain by the eleventh century (Chesneaux, Bastid, and Bergère 1976; Mote 1999; Elvin 2004). Other irrigation and water control schemes date from several centuries B.C.E. All these required brilliant engineering skills and massive investments for construction and maintenance.

The water control schemes and erosion of the soil caused by deforestation in the upper reaches of the rivers influenced land formation in the coastal regions. The Xijiang (Pearl River) delta at the confluence of the East, North, and West rivers in Lingnan (consisting of the provinces of Guangzhong and Guanxi) was built up over about a thousand years from the silt brought down by the rivers and the deliberate building up of land by the farmers in the estuary (see the maps in Marks 1998, p. 68). Research by many scientists has also established that from 1194 to 1855, when the Huanghe (Yellow River) in northern China flowed into the sea south of the Shandong peninsula, the silt carried by that river played a major role in building up new land not only near the mouth of the estuary but also along hundreds of miles of coast down as far as the mouth of the Yangzi; seawalls or reclamation of land inside polders by humans also slowed rivers and added to sediment deposition along the coast (Elvin and Su 1998).

The Chinese had probably used their core landmass along the valleys of Huanghe, Yangzi, and Xijiang rivers more intensively by the end of the first millennium C.E. than people in any other large landmass had done until then. This involved clearing of land and cutting down of forests on a stupendous scale (Elvin 2004). But the Chinese also paid attention to silviculture and forest management from the pre-Christian eras (Menzies 1996). When it came to management of forests, although there were enormous variations over the long period of recorded Chinese history, the governments seem to have relied on settlement and management of forests by local administrations rather than on a policy of creating forest reserves from which private persons were excluded (Menzies 1992). Many of the local communities and administrations relied on religious taboos against the indiscriminate felling of trees. Species such as bamboos and cunninghamias (Chinese firs), which were valuable for construction, enjoyed special attention. Because China had been a highly commercialized economy long before Western aggression, extraction of timber and uncontrolled felling certainly led to soil erosion and the disappearance of many species of flora and fauna.

But the process of Smithian growth under the Ming and the Qing dynasties also produced innovations that at least partly rendered development sustainable. For example, in the Lingnan region, sericulture became a highly profitable activity in the seventeenth and eighteenth centuries. Many farmers converted rice paddies into mulberry fields. They dug fishponds and planted mulberry trees along the bordering fields. "Silk worm excrement, leaves from the trees, and other organic material were gathered and thrown into the fishpond, providing food for the carp; the fish were harvested annually, with the muck formed from the fish waste and other decomposed organic matter then scooped out and used to fertilize mulberry trees and rice fields" (Marks 1998, p. 119). Marks is, however, unwilling to consider it a fully sustainable system, ecologically speaking, because it required rice to be imported (generally from northern Chinese provinces) to feed the human beings and thus replace the energy lost. In that sense, any activity that does not directly lead to food production would be considered wasteful. In another context, though, he is willing to grant that Ming-Qing commercialization was radically different from the practices of capitalist colonialism. He approvingly quotes Richard Grove who documented the deforestation and desertification caused by sugar plantations in the Caribbean islands or Mauritius, run on slave labor, and contrasts that with sugarcane cultivation by Chinese farmers on the fringes of the Pearl River delta, which caused no such ecological damage (Grove 1995; Marks 1998, p. 175). The basic institutional reason for the difference was as follows. In China sugarcane was produced on peasants' farms: they could not regard their own labor and the land they cultivated as resources to be mined and thrown away, as slave labor of the slaves and plantation land could be treated as exhaustible inputs by the planters.

I have a feeling that the legitimate worry of many Western (and Chinese) scholars such as Judith Banister, Mark Elvin, and Vaclav Smil regarding the current ecological crisis of China (for a selection of articles reflecting these views, see Edmonds 1998) is being projected back into the history of imperial China. A straight contradiction between the views of two scholars, Anne Osborne and Li Bozhong, regarding the environmental problem on the lower Yangzi delta in late imperial China can be found in Elvin and Liu (1998). Osborne (1998, p. 222) recognizes that, "up to a point, the enclosure of paddies, the building of terraces, and the production of cash crops could significantly increase production without destabilizing the ecology of the region." She also cites examples of innovative schemes to tackle environmental problems such as the proposal of entrepreneurs to raise grass-eating fish in West Lake in Hangzhou as a means of cleaning the water and making a profit for themselves, or the proposal to get kiln households "to set up brick and tile works in the vicinity of the silted-up South Lake in Hangzhou" (p. 222). But her major conclusion is that the growth in that region was "mountain and forest-led" and it became unsustainable from the eighteenth century. Li Bozhong (1998b), however, summarizes the data on land productivity for the most important cereal in the same region and finds that, borne on the spread of double and triple cropping and the cultivation of subsidiary crops such as wheat and beans, the productivity continued to increase from the Ming to the Qing periods, in many cases down to 1850 (see also Li 1986, 1998a)

It is probable that as symptoms of dynastic decline from the time of the later years of the reign of the Qianlong emperor, that is, from, say, the 1780s (Mote 1999, chapter 35), became pronounced, the capacity of the state to adopt measures for correcting ecological degradation declined. Population growth powered by the stability and reasonably well-distributed economic growth also put pressure on scarce resources. The system of keeping grain or, in many cases silver, in stock in official and private granaries against the prospect of grain shortages (Marks 1998, chapter 7; Davis 2001), China's unique system of social security, may have begun faltering, because of corruption and fiscal mismanagement, by the end of the Qianlong emperor's reign (1736–1799). Even then we find the Qing regime spending 2.8 million taels on famine relief in Henan as late as 1785 (Davis 2001, p. 282). Moreover, the growth of the population from somewhere around 275 million in 1700 to around 360–400 million by 1800 (Mote 1999)[4] had not created a subsistence crisis or put an intolerable pressure on the environment. The Chinese peasants had produced many new crops, including the sweet potato, and ingenious adaptations had been continually made in the use of water resources and land.

Apart from the forest cover on steep mountainsides and the disappearing fauna, most of the other resources were renewable and the Chinese capacity for hard work, under proper direction (public and private), could have been harnessed to correct some of these problems. But the forcing of an addictive drug on the Chinese by the British traders in the name of free trade and the Opium Wars, in which the British and the French were the undoubted aggressors, brought about as great a crisis in China as had been caused perhaps by the Mongol conquest of the thirteenth century C.E. (Mote 1999, chapters 18–20). The Taiping revolt was directly triggered by China's defeat in the first Opium War and the humiliating terms of the treaty forced on it. The wars of the Taiping, and other rebels such as the Muslims in Yunnan and the ethnic Hui in the northwest; the countermeasures adopted by the Qing rulers with the help of the Western powers; and finally, the depredations caused by the latter during the second Opium War completed the devastation (Chesnaux 1973; Chesnaux, Bastid, and Bergère 1976, chapters 4–5). In chapter 18, I have quoted some estimates of Chinese deaths caused by the disasters stretching from the Taiping revolt up to the 1890s.

It is difficult to summarize the conclusions reached by experts studying late imperial ecological history in China. In comparison with western Europe, China suffered because of lack of resources, resources commandeered by the imperialist powers; it also suffered because of its failure to meet the challenge of the Industrial Revolution. That failure led to massive deindustrialization in China as in India and made the conditions of artisans especially precarious when food scarcity occurred (Bagchi 1976a; Simmons 1985; Clingingsmith and Williamson 2004). The Industrial Revolution was based on the ability of entrepreneurs to use *nonrenewable resources*: such resources are almost by definition wastefully used under capitalism because the needs of future generations are always undervalued, and humankind has not yet found any way of regenerating nonrenewable resources. The current world conflicts, and especially the repeated aggressions mounted by the United States and its allies in western Asia, can be called energy wars. In the concluding chapter of his magisterial work, Elvin (2004, p. 470) says rightly that China's environmental degradation was partly caused by its lack of "new imperial overseas resources, such as some European countries possessed, and that could be drawn on like an environmental overdraft without any immediate need for further restoration." This statement implicitly recognizes that the Europeans may have escaped paying some of the environmental costs of development only by passing them on to other peoples. That is the logic of the competitive capitalism whose unlovely history I am narrating, but can it be called sustainable development, while the Chinese growth was unsustainable? Elvin does not seem to recognize the direct damage caused by Western imperialism (and Japanese imperialism) on the global environment in general and the Chinese environment in particular.

Finally, I touch on the pre-British record of environmental degradation in India. Surveying the existing literature on the history of deforestation and extension of cultivation until the coming of the Mughals as the paramount power in India, Erdosy (1998, p. 65) concluded,

> after three millennia of cultivation, significant stretches of forest remained. Thus, Xuan Zang in the seventh century C.E. refers to extensive forests between Allahabad and Kausambi, as well as in the vicinity of Kannauj, Sravasti, Kapilavastu,

Kusinagara and Varanasi. The *Ain-I-Akbari*, 900 years later, likewise mentions royal forests near Agra, Meerut, Allahabad and Mathura, as well as in the Punjab, areas nearly devoid of arboreal vegetation today.

Forests and grasslands survived for a variety of reasons, but one basic reason was the varied pattern of human settlement in the immensely variegated topography and climate of India. To that was added human contrivances such as preservation of sacred groves by many communities, particularly in the vicinity of seats of local deities (Kosambi 1962), the segregation of game preserves for hunting by nobles, the protection of plants by physicians and herbalists, and the careful husbanding of water resources through a variety of practices (Chakravarti 1998)—essential for preventing aridity and facilitating the quick renewal of a vegetative cover, especially in areas with scanty rainfall or lateritic soils (Mann 1998).

As I pointed out earlier, the Mughals encouraged agriculture and clearing of forests, as a means both of extending cultivation and breaking down the resistance of enemy chieftains or recalcitrant communities. They also encouraged the cultivation of cash crops by giving exemption from tax for a few years or taxing them at a lower rate than other crops. The amount of arable land in relation to the population was higher in India than in China. The cultivated area within the territory under Akbar's rule around 1595 was only 50–55 percent of what it was around 1900 (Moosvi 1987, p. 65). Although cultivated acreage steadily expanded under Mughal rule, it still left immense amounts of forested areas, especially in the lower Ganges-Brahmaputra delta, in the sub-Himalayan region, in central India, extending into Maharashtra and Gujarat, and in the submontane regions of southern India. The forests and scrubland sheltered vast numbers of wild beasts, including the extinct species of the Indian *cheeta*, tigers, leopards, elephants, antelopes of all kinds, pheasants, peacocks, grouse, and many other kinds of game that provided meat to the people living in the forests, scrubland, and the surrounding villages. The forests were the source of timber for constructing ships and durable structures, fruits, edible plants, honey, musk, and medicinal herbs (Moosvi 1993; Singh 1995). The grasslands provided pasture for the cattle of the peasants and the herders.

There were several checks against headlong destruction of ecological balance that are evident when compared with the situation under British rule. First, the drive for extracting an ever-higher land tax (called *rent* under the convenient British colonial theory that all land had earlier been owned by the king and the British only continued that practice) was much more muted under the pre-British rulers. While the Mughals also tried to extract as much surplus as possible, they were more flexible in their demands. The amount extracted depended on the amount produced, and tax remissions were granted when crops failed. The British imperative to remit a tribute for maintaining an establishment in England and pay a dividend on EIC stock meant that revenue collectors had to extract the maximum possible revenue from forests as well as cropland (Bagchi 1992). The Mughals did not tax horticulture or fisheries (Bagchi 1976b; Gadgil and Guha 1992, pp. 107–8). The Mughal revenue system left considerable room for pastoralists and forest dwellers to live in some kind of symbiosis with the cultivators. Correspondingly, the pre-British rulers also allowed local communities to harvest and manage their water resources in innovative and flexible ways. These allowed water to be better conserved than under British rule, which knew few other ways to use water or forest resources than either bring them under state control or give exclusive property rights to them to people who could pay for them (Hardiman 1998). The Mughals allowed a vast congeries of property rights to continue so long as their authority was recognized. As I noted earlier, their demands for revenue were also variable, depending on the seasons and the harvests. While famine prevention as such appears to have been less systematic than in late imperial China, they regularly remitted significant proportions of revenue in famine-affected tracts, whereas most British administrations showed their zeal and efficiency by jacking up revenue demands even in famine years (Habib 1963/1999, pp. 112–22, 291–92). The Mughals also planted gardens in many of their provincial capitals and preserved forests for royals to hunt in. Some post-Mughal regimes, in particular the Amirs of Sind, managed to create and maintain reserved forests by harvesting water in arid regions. "Between about 1690 and 1830 the Amirs of Sind were responsible for the reforestation of over a million acres of the Indus flood plain with up to eighty-seven *shikargarh*, or hunting and forest reserves" (Grove 1995).The Mughal domains abutted an immense inner frontier, where people lived and subsisted on a variety of field, garden, pasture, and forest products.

The outcome of all this—systematic policies of pre-British regimes, the inefficiency of those regimes, and their incomplete reach—was that India before the advent of the British had vast stretches of forest and systems of water harvesting that conserved soil moisture. This picture would be drastically altered before the first century of British rule had been completed. While we should not entertain any romantic notion about the greater vigorousness of collective concerns for the environment in precolonial days in India or in China before the first Opium War (Rangarajan 1996; Elvin 1998), the impact of armed Western capital with no accountability for the interests of the local people made a more adverse ecological impact within a shorter period of time than the interference of human beings had effected in the earlier centuries.

Under British rule, the Indian environment was imperiled, first, by the ever-increasing revenue demands of the state and its ability to reach much more intrusively into the daily lives of the subjects. The alien rulers had a distinct bias against nomadic herders or swidden cultivators because they were more difficult to control than settled agriculturists. The forest dwellers could take shelter in the dense forests of central and eastern India and defy British power again and again (Rangarajan 1996). Moreover, most British officials thought the forest dwellers occupied land that would pay much more revenue if it was used for sedentary cultivation or raising commercially valuable timber under official supervision. Second, the aggression of mercantile capital, which was restrained by few public policy concerns, also affected the environment adversely. The forests of India, for example, were cut down indiscriminately to build military roads, barracks, and cantonment towns, and military contractors fattened on them. When railway building began, whole forests were cut down to provide timber for the sleepers of the East India Railway, the Great Indian Peninsula Railway, and other major railway ventures (Rangarajan 1996). The construction of these railways also led to deforestation along the route and in many cases the blocking of the usual drainage channels, leading to water-logged areas and swamps that both reduced crop output and became breeding grounds for malarial mosquitoes. On many railways in the early days wood, cheaper than imported coal, was also used as fuel.

The disappearance of forests in British India began to cause concern in official circles from the 1830s because of its impact on land productivity downstream of wooded slopes and the looming scarcity of timber in the regions worst affected by denudation. A comprehensive Forest Act was passed in 1878. The government created two categories, reserved forests and protected forests; the government had full control of reserved forests and regulated protected-forest use on a loose rein. As Rangarajan (1996, p. 74) points out, however, "The creation of extensive government forests had been 'not so much for purposes of forestry' as for the alienation of property rights to land. Many areas were annexed because there was 'no one' whom the government wished to recognize as proprietor." In the name of public regulation, the traditional rights of herders and forest dwellers were abridged or extinguished altogether (Bagchi 1992; Bhattacharya 1995; Rangarajan 1996). We will look at the direst consequences for human survival of colonial policies in India in chapter 18.

NOTES

1. Mukherjee (1939, p. 54) gives a real-wage series that indicates a fall in 1729 compared with 1600 (really ca. 1595). I cannot make out how he derived the figure for 1729.

2. For the best estimates of the coinage of the Mughal empire, see Haider 1996, table 11.

3. The two estimates are based on two assumptions regarding the rate of population growth, namely, 0 percent and 0.5 percent per year.

4. Mote (1999, pp. 744–47) uses the work of Heijdra (1994) to argue that the usual estimate of Chinese population of 150 million in 1650 is much too low. The new estimates of Chinese population are 155 million in 1500, 231 million in 1600, and 268 million in 1650.

Conducting Trade in Asia before and after the European Advent

CONDUCTING TRADE IN ASIA BEFORE AND AFTER THE PORTUGUESE ADVENT

What kind of influence did European armed capital exert on Asian development before the conquest of India by the British? The advent of the Portuguese, followed by the other European powers, affected the fortunes of the major Asian regions in four major ways. One was the expansion or restructuring of international trade; the second was the inflow of precious metals, especially silver; the third was a realignment of political arrangements through the introduction of new military technologies; and the fourth was a reallocation of resources in regions that were involved indirectly or directly in trade with the Europeans. An overarching influence was the introduction of warfare as a means of expanding commerce rather than in the interests of territorial expansion. By and large, Asian kingdoms and empires were land-based and, while the rulers were interested in promoting long-distance trade across the seas as well as overland, they left the actual trading to merchants, occasionally sharing in the profits. Even if some rulers might engage in naval conflicts, they were not conducted with guns and cannon, because Asian ships were not built to withstand attacks by guns.

The best illustrations of the Asian imperial attitude to trade and warfare are provided by the naval venture of Zheng He in the early Ming period and by the decision to forcibly shift the coastal populations of Fujian, Jiangnan, and Guangzhou under the Kiangxi emperor between 1661 and 1683 (Mote 1999, chapters 24 and 32). The Ming emperor Chengzu sent out seven maritime expeditions to promote China's relations with the maritime polities of

southeastern, southern, and western Asia. The seven voyages took place between 1405 and 1433.

> The personnel carried on each expedition numbered from 20,000 to 32,000 men.
> The Chinese ships and their men made a display of maritime strength unknown
> elsewhere until much later in history. Zheng He's larger ships had 2500 tons
> cargo capacity and 3100 displacement; by comparison, the largest of the three
> ships which brought Columbus to the New World in 1492 was 125 feet long and
> had a capacity of only 280 tons. (Mote 1999, p. 614)

Zheng He's ships also had many advanced technical features not known in
other countries at the time. Zheng He deployed diplomacy, not force, in his
missions, bestowing gifts on rulers of the places he visited, carrying sultans
and kings to kowtow to the Chinese emperor and taking them back on his return voyage. Chinese trade and Chinese merchants benefited from the display
of China's power and wealth, but no explicit military force was used to gain
those ends.

When the Manchus defeated the Ming and took over Beijing in 1644, they
had still to face the resistance of Ming loyalists. One of the more redoubtable
of them was Zheng Chongong, whom the Dutch called Coxinga. He used his
fleet to harass the Qing forces along the China coast from Fujian down to
Guangzhou. To deny his forces shelter on land, in 1662–1663 the Qing government forcibly removed the coastal population 40 to 50 *li*s (1 *li* = 0.555
kilometer) inland. Zheng Chongong moved his base from Fujian to Taiwan,
and drove out the Dutch. The coastal evacuation policy was abolished by the
Kiangxi emperor in 1683 after the surrender of the heirs of Zheng to the Qing
(Wakeman 1985; Mote 1999). This coastal removal policy severely disrupted
Chinese trade and caused untold hardship to the people. But the point is that,
despite their ability to defeat the Dutch at sea, the Chinese did not try to use
military power to expand Chinese trade in other parts of Asia, let alone venture across the Pacific. In the long run, the Chinese paid dearly for their neglect of maritime prowess but their whole attention was confined to defending
their land in a literal sense.

The European entry into seaborne trade in Asia effected a number of
changes. First, from the very beginning the European traders sought to monopolize the trade and to use force for that purpose. Vasco da Gama, the first
European commander of a ship to go to India via the Cape of Good Hope
route, was a member of a military order, and everywhere, from Sofala to Cali-
cut, he engaged in unprovoked violence against local rulers and traders (Subrahmanyam 1997, p. 25). After the return of da Gama to Lisbon in 1499, King
Manuel of Portugal assumed the title "Lord of the conquest, navigation and
commerce of Ethiopia, Arabia, Persia and India" (Pearson 1987, p. 30). The

Portuguese commanders and governors were *instructed* to use force and conquest as means of expanding dominion and commerce (Boxer 1973a; Pearson 1987). Luis de Camoens wrote the national epic of Portugal, *The Lusiads*, celebrating the conquests.

The Portuguese brought an utterly foreign innovation to the trading traditions of Asia: the idea that a temporal power can claim lordship of the seas. They set up a protection racket in Asian waters, under which any ship sailing on the seas patrolled by them had to obtain a *cartaz*, or license, showing that it had paid the requisite duty to the Portuguese; otherwise they confiscated the goods or the ship, killing all the passengers, including women and children, or selling them into slavery (Pearson 1987). The Dutch, British, and other European traders in Asian waters following the Portuguese emulated their policy of organizing monopolies of trade by using force as the Portuguese had done with the spice trade. Jan Pieterszoon Coen, who founded the Dutch empire in Indonesia by displacing the Portuguese and defeating some of the major rulers in the area, wrote in 1614 to the directors of the VOC:

> Your Honours should know by experience that trade in Asia must be driven and maintained under the protection and favour of Your Honours' own weapons, and that the weapons must be paid for by the profits from the trade; so that we cannot carry on trade without war nor war without trade. (quoted by Boxer 1973b, p. 107)

This pattern of EIC and VOC trade, with its close ties to state power, had new elements as an institutional form, with no precedent in Asia.

Their honors, the Herren XVII of the VOC, fully agreed with Coen and authorized him to take any and all steps to monopolize the spice trade centered on the archipelago (Boxer 1973b, chapter 4). The English followed the Dutch with similar intentions and flouted the sovereignty of Asian rulers wherever and whenever they could with impunity (Watson 1980). The Portuguese and the Dutch often controlled only certain strategic points. The English in India showed the way to a much more intrusive colonialism. Once the EIC had conquered Bengal, its servants instituted there a system that Burke had characterized, in the famous Ninth Report on the affairs of the EIC, as "coercive monopoly" (Bagchi 1996b).

The Europeans were, however, unable to make a big impact on the volume of Asian trade until the Industrial Revolution. Much of the commerce conducted by the Europeans led to a redistribution of profits rather than a net increase in trade. In the case of trade between Europe and Asia, this meant primarily struggles for redistribution of monopoly profits. This remained true until the Industrial Revolution had made a radical change in manufacturing technology and European military organization had made a decisive advance over those used in southern Asia and China. In the century of their dominance in Asian waters, the Portuguese essentially carried on a redistributive trade. They were never able to close off or monopolize the Red Sea route or the overland route of trade between Asia and Europe via western and central Asia. The Bay of Bengal largely remained outside their control, except as a theater of operation of pirates of Portuguese or Indo-Portuguese origin. While they set up shop in Macau, Chinese commercial and imperial power remained effectively intact in much of eastern and southeastern Asia (Pearson 1987). The major flows of goods between China, southeastern Asia, Japan, and southern Asia far outweighed the trade carried on by Europeans. These trade flows included grains, coarse and fine textiles, spices, medicines, sugar, timber, silver, copper, porcelain, and many other products—not just luxuries. In sixteenth-century Eurasia, in terms of population, trade flows, and probable values of output, the world trading system consisting of China, southeastern Asia, Japan, southern Asia, and Iran far exceeded the size of the one centered on the Mediterranean and the emerging growth pole of western Europe.

When the Dutch had displaced the Portuguese in Indonesia and instituted their own system of coercive monopoly from the 1610s, the character of Asian trade was affected a little more, partly because the Dutch were even more ruthless in pursuing their objectives than the Portuguese. According to Van Leur's estimate, just before the exit of the Portuguese from southeastern Asian waters, the bulk of the southeastern Asian production of pepper went to China (Mazumdar 1998, p. 67). The Portuguese and Dutch attempts to control the trade between China and Japan or Chinese or Japanese trade with other countries failed mainly because of their defeat at the hands of the rulers of the two countries but also because of competition from private Chinese traders (pp. 83–95).

Asian traders held their own in Bengal's commerce until 1760, and it was only political and military might that allowed the British to displace their competitors in the seaborne trade of Bengal (Chaudhury 1995a, 1995b; the contrary argument of Frank 1998, pp. 267–71, is based on flimsy evidence).

The advent of the European captains in Asian waters significantly increased the supply of precious metals, especially silver (Frank 1998, chapter 3; Pomeranz 2000a; Prakash 1998). In economies with widespread monetary transactions, such as those of China and India, the enlarged inflow of precious metals into those lands from the Americas via Europe allowed further expansion of trade and possibly output. Indeed, the absence of a secular price rise in Asian countries, in spite of this inflow, would indicate a much larger elasticity of output in those countries than in the Europe of the sixteenth century (Prakash 1998, p. 320–22). On the other hand, it cannot be too often emphasized that the European import of precious metals into Asia was only an addition to the metals used for circulation and not an innovation in such uses. Long before the sixteenth century, Japan and several other countries of Asia produced precious metals, including copper and silver, and they were circulated in exchange for Chinese and Indian textiles, Chinese or Bengal sugar, Chinese silk or porcelain, and Indonesian or southern Indian spices (Mazumdar 1998). Europeans tried to engage in a redistributive trade in this area also and reap middlemen's or monopolists' profit. Again, Chinese and Japanese governmental resistance and competition of Asian and other European powers generally obstructed those attempts at setting up monopolistic protection rackets. But as soon as the British acquired the revenue-raising rights in Bengal, the EIC stopped sending silver to Bengal and extracted the needed bullion by taxing the Indians. For the European merchants, political power acted as a substitute for trade goods whenever they could obtain control over the levers of the state.

The third area in which Europeans made an impact on Asians' material fortunes was in military technology and organization. Southern Asia had long been dependent on central Asia and the Middle East for the supply of war horses, because it lacked the ecological conditions for breeding sturdy horses on a large scale (Digby 1971/2001; Gommans 1999, chapter 3). After they had obtained a foothold in India, the Portuguese tried to control the naval trade in horses through their *cartaz* system and used it also to deny horses to their enemies (Pearson 1987, pp. 49–51). European advantages in military technology became decisive for India from the late seventeenth century, when several major innovations were made in weapons for arming the infantry (Black 1990; Gommans and Kolff 2001b, especially pp. 26–42). After that, the disintegration of the Safavid empire in Iran and the Mughal empire in India allowed the French and the British to take on the successor regimes and establish their dominion. The Europeans made many advances in military organization, such as close military drill and an established chain of command during the height of the engagement (Parker 1988). But advances were also being made in military technology and organization by the Afghans, and it is by using such advances that Ahmad Shah Durrani in 1761 routed a large Maratha army in the third battle of Panipat near Delhi and eased British ascent to paramountcy in India.

A political system based on the nation-state, rather than just advances in military technology and organization, proved its superiority in aggression over the Asian systems based on patrimonial or semifeudal power. But nonetheless, the ability to sacrifice human lives in a calculated fashion in the cause of mammon was also a driving force behind the improvements in the slaughtering power of the armies and navies of capital. Of course, the disintegration of the Mughal empire made the task much easier in India than in

China, where a centralized state resisted the European aggressors for a longer period. The survival of Japan as an independent nation was due to a complex of internal and external factors. But the ability of its ruling class to learn the arts of war, and technology that might be useful for both military and economic competition played a critical part in that survival.

Did the appearance of European traders in Asian lands and seas improve the allocation of resources and increase the incomes of Asian producers and traders? When the Portuguese seized partial control of the lucrative trade in spices from Asian traders, the incomes of the latter could not have gone up. Or when they simply exacted a protection fee from all traders, the incomes of the traders or the local producers of the goods traded could not have gone up either. The degree of violence to which the Asian inhabitants were subjected went up significantly when the Dutch entered the fray for control of the trade in spices and other valuable Asian products (Furnivall 1939; Boxer 1973a; Bagchi 1982; Van Zanden 1993). Dutch merchants had been active in the southeastern Asian seas from before 1600. By that date Portuguese control over most of the ports of the Indonesian archipelago had virtually collapsed. The Dutch had been entering into contracts with local rulers for monopoly of trade in return for protection against rival rulers (Van Zanden 1993, pp. 70–71). After the formation of the VOC in 1602, the company set out to enforce its privileges against all competitors, including the EIC, French East India company, and Asian traders linking the spice islands, that is, the northern Moluccas, the middle Moluccas comprising Amboyna and other nearby islands, and the southern Moluccas containing Banda Islands—the sole source of nutmeg and mace—and the other islands nearby producing cloves. The Moluccas specialized in the production of spices and exchanged them for Javanese rice and (mainly Indian) textiles brought by Indonesian and other Asian traders. The VOC proceeded to fix the prices of spices and eliminate the Asian traders sailing to the Moluccas. They also confined the production of cloves, nutmeg, and mace to particular islands and destroyed their plants in other islands. When the Bandanese resisted these moves in 1621, the Dutch, led by Governor-General Coen, massacred thousands of the islanders, enslaved the rest, and deported them to Java.

The islanders did not cease their resistance, however. Under the Dutch dispensation, the cost of their subsistence goods went up and the prices of their output plummeted and they were subjected to periodic violence by the Dutch trying to enforce their diktat. The Dutch, for example, had to engage in a bitter war on northern Amboyna between 1641 and 1646 to crush opposition to their policies by eliminating the elite who led the resistance. Between 1653 and 1658, opposition to Dutch policies in the Hoamol Peninsula, near Amboyna, was crushed by decimating its population and deporting the rest to

Amboyna, whose population had declined as a result of guerrilla war against the Dutch (Van Zanden 1993, pp. 71–73). The VOC used corvée labor for raising cloves and other spices in islands confined to their production and used periodic armed raids (the so-called *hongi* raids) to destroy crops on islands not permitted to grow them. Such policies continued throughout the period the VOC ruled Indonesia directly or through their client princes. It would take a brave scholar to argue that the levels of human development of the islanders had gone up under Dutch colonialism.

The situation would be different in territories in which European traders were competing with one another in procuring goods. The producers and the intermediary traders then should be getting better prices for their produce and services. But the competition often occurred in a situation in which one or the other European power was blocking off the access of other traders to the market concerned. Thus, for example, in the first half of the eighteenth century, the Dutch traders had to compete with the English, French, and other European traders for procuring textiles in Bengal. But the Dutch had successfully blocked off much of the trade of southeastern Asia and the access of traders of those regions to the Bengal market. Hence we cannot conclude that any increase in output and income of producers of textiles in Bengal is a net addition to their income, because they might have done far better with the continuance of the tradition of open seas in the years before 1498 (for a contrary argument, see Prakash 1998, chapter 8).

My necessarily brief account of human and economic development in the world economy of Asia before European dominance indicates the reasons why the socioeconomic arrangements of that world economy proved vulnerable to the aggressiveness of European capital. But there is little evidence that peoples of India, China, and other Asian lands lagged Europeans in chances of human survival and living conditions before European capital yoked them to its military- and profit-driven logic (cf. Mazumdar 1998, chapters 5 and 6).

ORIGINS OF THE GREAT DIVERGENCE

Eurocentric history has been recently challenged by historians of eastern Asia and the world (Wong 1997; Frank 1998; Goldstone 1998; Pomeranz 2000a; Arrighi, Hamashita, and Selden 2003). This has led to a new search for the timing and origins of the great divergence between Europe and the rest of the world with respect to economic development.

In the recent debates, however, little of the record of human development and deprivation in the five centuries since Columbus's landfall in the Caribbean islands received serious attention. There is only a very loose fit, however, between the record of aggregate economic growth as convention-ally measured and that of most aspects of human development. In terms of the most fundamental aspect of human development, human survival, the two most populous countries of the world, India and China, seem to have been do-ing no worse than the best-performing regions of Europe down to the middle of the eighteenth century. In terms of commercialization, craft production, and agricultural growth also, China, India, and Japan were performing no worse than major European countries during that period. Additionally, I see little to distinguish most of early modern Europe, except England and the Netherlands, from major states in Asia during the sixteenth to eighteenth centuries, with respect to economic organization, property rights, or civil society—the traits that according to Eurocentric historians marked Europe out for its manifest destiny (cf. Goldstone 1998).

Adapting our perspective to some of the terms of the recent debate, then, we would distinguish not one but two "axial ages," to adopt a phrase used by Janet Hunter (2000), in Europe related to the record of human survival and human development. By *axial age* I mean the years over which some impor-tant components of human development underwent a major change as the country or region turned on its axis, metaphorically speaking. The first lay somewhere between the early to middle decades of the eighteenth century when European population growth, at least outside the Netherlands, recov-ered from its long stagnation in the seventeenth century and the Industrial Revolution began in England. But the longevity or other physical indexes of well-being of Europeans and their overseas cousins had to wait until the 1880s and 1890s to move ahead of what was achieved by population groups in China or India before colonialism. The second axial age would then start from the fourth quarter of the nineteenth century. In the second axial age, the key variable is no longer population growth as such but human longevity and the state of nutrition and education that allow ordinary people and women in particular to exercise control over their reproductive rights. While the poorest nations now have generally much higher rates of population growth, mainly because of some progress in containing infectious diseases, they have yet to attain a long and healthy life (see chapter 22).

My perspective takes in critical dimensions that are often ignored in writ-ings celebrating European exceptionalism. These include the roles of the state and state-backed violence in the competition for territory, control over labor power, raw materials, and markets since the emergence of capitalism (Lane 1958; Wilson 1965; McNeill 1983; Mintz 1985; Parker 1988; Brewer 1989). I was glad to see that the crucial significance of these factors in marking out the eventual victory of European powers has been reaffirmed by Patrick O'Brien (2000) and R. Bin Wong (2002) in recent debates.[1] Social property relations giving secure and totally unencumbered property rights may have been a necessary condition for the rise and growth of capitalism in England (as emphasized by Brenner and Isett 2002) and the Netherlands. But they did not stop the end of the golden age in the Netherlands and its decline into a political dependency of Napoleonic France. Nor did they ensure the victory of British manufactures until the rise of machine-based industry and acquisition of a threshold of military power overcame the Indian rulers and eliminated the competition of Indian textiles (Thomas 1926; Bagchi 1982; Washbrook 1997).

The armed competition between the European states not only heightened the striking power of victorious states but also prepared the ground for the rise of large plantations and factories where labor was subjected to the same kind of discipline as on a military parade ground or on a naval vessel (Thompson 1967/1991; Mintz 1985; Rediker 1987; Brewer 1989).

The conquest of the Americas by the Spaniards and the Portuguese, with the help of superior military technology and the ideology of a superior race (Diamond 1992, 1998), and the subsequent establishment of plantations of sugarcane, cotton, and tobacco with slave labor proved critical in the progress of European capitalism. The flow of precious metals, especially silver, extracted from American mines was essential in settling western Europe's accounts with the Baltic region, Asia, and, much more importantly, the Levant; control of this flow was also critical for expanding the trade of the leading contenders for European hegemony (Glamann 1974).[2] And, of course, millions of hapless Africans captured in not-so-peaceful trade and raids supplied the necessary muscle power for running the plantations whose produce augmented European diets (Inikori 2002). Thus in many instances, the colonial edge was less a product of initial economic or technological superiority in civil production than of advantages won on the battlefield.

The role of colonialism did not cease with the end of the phase of merchant capital in Europe. The final conquest of India and the beginning of the reduction of China to a subsidiary of European powers played important roles in facilitating the progress of the industrial revolution in Britain. The Indian textile industry had probably been the biggest exporter of cotton goods in the world before British mills began spinning yarn with labor-saving machines. The British government severely restricted the import of Indian cotton cloth from 1701—long before they conquered any part of Indian territory. It kept those restrictions in place after the EIC had conquered most of India (Thomas 1926; Mukherjee 1939, Introduction; Bagchi 1973b, 1976a; Washbrook 1997). Moreover, the duties on imports of textiles into Britain for home consumption were increased to prohibitive levels by the end of the eighteenth century. In fact, as was pointed out by the British administrators and traders themselves, under British rule Indian textiles suffered a reverse discrimination: they paid higher duties than English imports. This was happening at a time when continental European states and the United States took measures to protect their nascent cotton mills against imports of British textiles.[3]

The decimation of much of local Indian business, especially in eastern and southern India, combined with the deindustrialization of major regions of British India, also set back indigenous efforts at building up factory industry. India was turned into the biggest consumer of products of the British cotton mills,[4] which for a long time remained the industry employing the largest number of British workers. China after the first Opium War was also rapidly deindustrialized. Other nonwhite colonies of the European powers also became important consumers of the manufactures of a North Atlantic economy on its way to industrialization. Thus colonies played a critical part in the maturing of the first axial age separating Europe and its settler colony extensions from the rest of the world.

The massive surpluses, extracted as tribute and profits of monopolized enterprises by European governments and businessmen and transferred to the metropolitan countries, allowed in turn the flow of foreign investment to colonies of European settlement in the United States, Canada, Australia, New Zealand, and for a brief while, Argentina (Nurkse 1961; Simon 1968; Edelstein 1982, 1994; Platt 1985). That foreign investment helped equip the white migrants to the lands of settlement, raise their incomes, and make possible the private and public welfare measures that led ultimately to the health and longevity transition in those countries. The biggest migration of human beings in history, from Europe to the overseas colonies of settlement over the period from the second half of the nineteenth century down to the beginning of the 1920s, facilitated European ascent to higher standards of living in several ways (Thomas 1954, 1968; Massey 1988). First, it relieved population pressure on European cities and lands and eased the adoption of new measures of public sanitation and water supply. Second, it tightened the labor markets in Europe, improved the workers' bargaining power, and helped raise their real wages and hence living standards. Third, in countries like Sweden, in which the migration left a disproportionately young and old population behind, it induced the government to undertake welfare measures for the children and the old that improved the health and raised the longevity of the citizens. Fourth, by reducing the pressure on the land, it raised the productivity of the intramarginal land and the productivity per worker in agriculture. It also reduced the risk of soil erosion and deforestation because cultivators did not have to resort to marginal lands and cultivation on hill slopes to make a living (cf. Pomeranz 2000a, chapter 5). In this way, Europe exported its environmental problems to non-European lands, and especially to its colonies and semicolonies in Asia, Africa, and Latin America. With its faster rate of re-source accumulation, it also came to be better prepared to correct the regional ecological damage caused by the industrialization process.

NOTES

1. My analysis has many areas of convergence with that of Arrighi, Hui, Hung, and Selden 2002. But they are primarily interested in issues of economic growth rather than those of human development. Also, I find the notion of capitalism as a mode of production still useful for distinguishing, say, China or India of the eighteenth century from England or the Netherlands of the same period. This use is fully consistent with my occasional use of the idea of hierarchies in the circuits of exchange that Braudel (1982, 1984) so fruitfully employed.

2. Glamann (1974) wrote:

> A common feature of all the European trade with Asia is its concentration on imports. The purpose of the trade was not to find new markets for European products but to furnish Europe with those coveted wares that titillated the palate and adorned the body. . . . Except for weapons and ammunition, the "commodity" that could be disposed of in the East was bullion. . . . The successor to spices as the dominant category of imports into Europe is Indian textiles. Around 1700 these accounted for over 40 per cent of the Dutch East India Company's imports. (p. 447)

3. Clingingsmith and Williamson (2004) date the loss of competitive advantage by the Indian cotton textile industry to the 1780s. They, however, fail to factor in the fact of the consequences of British conquest of Bengal, the dominant textile exporting region. The British in India systematically suppressed Asian traders competing with them and coerced handloom weavers to supply goods at prices fixed by them, and the British Parliament legislated to end the import of the higher-value Indian textiles.

4. India took only 0.5 percent of British cotton cloth exports in 1815, but the figure increased to 31 percent in 1860 (Chapman 1972, p. 52).

12

Reconsidering Japanese Exceptionalism

CLAIMS OF JAPANESE EXCEPTIONALISM

Japan has been exceptional among the countries of Asia, as indeed among all the countries inhabited by non-European peoples, in several ways. It began acquiring colonies by the end of the nineteenth century and became a formidable imperial power, competing militarily with the Western powers in eastern and Southeast Asia and ultimately challenging the military might of the United Kingdom, United States, and their allies in World War II. After its defeat in that war, by the 1960s it emerged as one of the most dynamic economies of the world. By the 1980s, its levels of living compared very favorably with that of the most advanced economies of the Atlantic seaboard.

There is a long tradition (see, for example, Kuznets 1960/1965) claiming that all non-European countries were worse off economically at the time of their confrontation with the Europeans. But what are the historians to do with Japan, which was not conquered and, instead, created its own empire that at its peak covered much of eastern, northeastern, and Southeast Asia? One strategy, adopted by *The Cambridge Economic History of Europe* (Habakkuk and Postan 1965; Mathias and Postan 1978), is to include chapters on Japan since, in the judgment of the Eurocentric historians, Japan alone among non-Western countries has made the grade.

The thesis of Japanese exceptionalism takes many forms. One is to claim that the economic growth of Japan was faster than that of China and India in the period preceding the Meiji Restoration, and in particular, it was faster during the Edo or Tokugawa period that succeeded the era of the warring states. The second is to claim that property rights in Japan were of the kind modeled by the theorists of private property rights in Europe. Third, a high degree of

179

commercialization also contributed to the higher economic growth of Japan. Fourth, this economic growth was associated with a higher standard of living for the ordinary people. Fifth, even before the forcing of unequal treaties on Japan by the aggression of the U.S. commodore Perry and other Western powers, Japan was ripe for an industrialization drive.

I accept the thesis that Japan had institutions that made it readier than China and India for emulating western countries in the simultaneous drive for industrialization and imperial expansion and that its pattern of commercialization was in many ways more conducive for accelerated industrialization. I also accept the views of scholars of eastern Asia such as R. Bin Wong, Kaoru Sugihara, and Kenneth Pomeranz that Japan, along with western Europe between the sixteenth and the middle of the eighteenth century, and India and China over the same period, experienced a sustained Smithian growth, based on a high tempo of commercialization of the economy (Sugihara 1996, 2004; Wong 1997, 2002; Pomeranz 2000a). Along with Sugihara and Wong, I find implausible the argument of Eurocentric scholars such as Brenner and Isett (2002) that the lower Yangzi delta of China or the more commercialized regions of Japan had a radically different pattern of commercialization from that of western Europe even before the onset of the Industrial Revolution.

But as I have indicated earlier, I have a less teleological view of human and, more narrowly, economic history than scholars whose sole object is to find out how near a country was to their ideal of an industrialized economy, as if the costs incurred by generations of people while their country is getting there are not to be counted at all. Sugihara (2004) has described Tokugawa Japan's commercialization of agricultural trade and production and a considerable part of the nonagricultural production as an industrious revolution. But Jan de Vries (1993) used the same phrase to characterize the process of economic growth in western Europe before the Industrial Revolution. I find little evidence in the English language literature on Tokugawa Japan indicating that the average Japanese peasant was much better off in 1800 or 1830 than in, say, 1700. Scholars of Japanese economic history agree that the Japanese population, after growing fast between the coming of the Tokugawa peace and the 1730s, stagnated for a century (Satō 1990; Crawcour 1997; Hayami 2001; Hayami and Kurosu 2001). Indeed, the population of the most dynamic region of Japan, namely, Kinai, the region that included Osaka, Kyoto, and other port cities of the southwest, *declined* over this period; the population of the slightly less developed central region *stagnated*. It was the growth of population in the southwestern region that kept the aggregate population at almost a constant figure, between thirty and thirty-three million, over the century when the commercialization of Tokugawa Japan was reaching its peak (Hayami and Kurosu 2001).

I locate the institutions helping Japan to industrialize in Japanese statecraft and an emerging mercantile community that could use that craft just as the new post-Meiji generation of Japanese statesmen knew how to use the services of the aspiring bankers and merchants (Norman 1940). But I find scant evidence that Tokugawa standards of living were superior to those of India up to the middle of the eighteenth century or of China down to the beginning of the nineteenth century (a view supported by Sugihara 1996). We have seen that the Dutch golden age was accompanied in its later decades with increased inequality, fall in the standard of living of the common people, and ultimately, demographic decline. The standard of living of an average person in England also suffered during the Industrial Revolution. Most of the evidence turned up by Japanese and Western scholars also points to the fact that the period of accelerated commercialization in Tokugawa Japan, that is, roughly from the second quarter of the eighteenth century to the first half of the nineteenth century, was associated with increased distress for the common people, signaled most dramatically by a decline in population in the most commercialized locales (Hayami 2001; Hayami and Kurosu 2001). Hanley (1997) has claimed that the physical quality of life in Tokugawa Japan was superior to that of contemporary western Europe in that the housing, food, and clothing of ordinary Japanese were superior to those of their European counterparts and they were therefore more productive in an economic sense. Unfortunately, she presents little statistical evidence that this supposed superiority was translated into longer life or greater satisfaction with their lot. On the contrary, the demographic evidence is strongly against her claim, as is the frequency and intensity of peasant revolts in Tokugawa Japan, especially in the latter half of the Edo period (C. J. Dunn 1969, p. 77; Vlastos 1986).

TOKUGAWA STRUCTURES AND CHANGES

I sketch the economic and social history of Japan from the sixteenth century by starting with Thomas Smith, the author of the classic account of the agrarian transformation of Japan in the Edo period (Smith 1959). Smith documents, with enormous subtlety and attention to detail, the structure of the rural society when Oda Nobunaga, Toyotomi Hideyoshi, and finally, Tokugawa Ieyasu ended the lawlessness of warring lords and established a highly centralized polity at the top while preserving a good deal of decentralized power structure at the village level. The *bakuhan* system—consolidated by the Tokugawa shoguns between the beginning of the sixteenth century and the 1630s—consisted of the *bakufu*, that is, the lands and the military apparatus of the Tokugawa, and the *han*, the domains and castle towns controlled by the lords, or daimyo, under the *bakufu* (Ōishi 1990). The peasantry, or rather, all the people other than the samurai, that is, the lords and their retainers, were disarmed and the samurai were confined to the castle towns. The daimyo were required to keep their wives and children at Edo (modern Tokyo), the seat of the *bakufu*, and under the *sankin kōtai* system the daimyo were required to attend the court at Edo on a fixed schedule (generally every alternate year). The radical separation of the armed retainers from the rest of the people and the confinement of the former in castle towns was the core institution preserving the Tokugawa peace for more than 250 years. The forced periodic migration of the daimyo to Edo and the herding of their retainers in castle towns sowed the seeds of the growth of urban consumption, trade, production, and transport during the Tokugawa period.

The function of the peasants under Tokugawa rule was primarily to supply the *bakufu*, daimyo, and their retainers with rice and other basic agricultural goods. During the first half of the Tokugawa period, according to Satō (1990, p. 43), "peasants were to be so taxed, as the saying went that they 'could not live but would not die,' and the tax rate reached a high of 60 percent" of agricultural output. At this stage, a small number of families in the village were registered as holders of the village land and as the claimants to the use of the commons (Smith 1959, chapter 1). The core or dominant families worked the holdings by using the labor of a large number of dependents. The latter included (1) *fudai*, or hereditary servants, who had been bought by the stem family or whose ancestors had been *fudai*; (2) a class of persons called *nago*, who performed labor services in return for an allotment that housed the *nago* and perhaps included a small plot on which the *nago* would raise subsidiary crops (rice land was generally not included in such allotments); (3) *hōkōnin*, or persons who had been indentured in return for a debt; and (4) collateral branches, or younger brothers or sons, of the family head, because under the usual primogeniture system, younger sons had no right in the land (Smith 1959, chapters 1–4). Smith talks of a cooperative system but, in fact, it was under an extremely hierarchical and coercive arrangement that the dominant household (the head of which was referred to as *oyakata*) secured the cooperation of its dependents. That dependence was naturalized and internalized by every person through a long and arduous process of socialization since early childhood. Even when a family that had earlier been socially and legally dependent on the *oyakata* was separated from the core family and given a holding, which was registered in its name, it did not necessarily become independent. For example, in the case of the *nago*, Smith (1959, p. 34–35) notes, "On the day after registration as a holder, the former *nago* was dependent on the *oyakata*, for housing, for land as a tenant, for capital, for everything except his allotment, and as tightly bound to him by obligations recognized by the community as the day before." This comment would hold equally true of many small holders who might have been a collateral branch of the core family: few of them would be given a holding that would be large enough or the right of access to common property resources that would be broad enough to make them independent of the core family. The obligations would include attendance in the house of the core family on ceremonial or religious occasions and rendering personal service on those occasions.

Even in the beginning of the seventeenth century, patterns of landholding differed between Kinai and most other regions of Japan (Smith 1959; Satō 1990). Kinai was the most commercially developed and densely populated region. Its typical holdings tended to be much smaller and there were far fewer of the very large holdings that dominated the villages of northern Japan or other commercially less advanced regions. This difference in landholding patterns was also associated with a difference in the pattern of dependence of the actual cultivators on the legal holders of land: many more of the dependent peasantry in the Kinai were tenants on rental contracts than *nago*, *fudai*, or *hōkōnin* on long indenture. As commercialization progressed, other regions tended to converge to the pattern observed in the Kinai, but the rate of convergence was uneven and slow in most areas.

The demands of the castle towns of the daimyo and Edo, the seat of the *bakufu*, and the efforts of the merchants and craft producers, first in the castle towns and the major ports and then in the villages, led to an enormous growth in commerce and production for the market (Smith 1959; Hauser 1974; Vlastos 1986; Satō 1990; Nakamura 1990; Crawcour 1997; Sugihara 2004).

The two major products that brought about the transformation in agriculture were cotton and sericulture, followed by sugar. All these products and their techniques of production were introduced from abroad, mainly China. But by the late Tokugawa period, Japan was producing enough for its own needs. As it happened, silk thread became the most important Japanese export for some time after the Meiji Restoration (Allen 1965; Crawcour 1997). The Japanese institutions were adapted to learning from countries with superior technology, and China, for a long time, remained a major source of ideas about governance as well as products and their methods of production (Morishima 1982). As in the case of imports of products, so also in the cases of methods of production, and the Japanese started with imitating the Chinese but improved upon them through their own experiments (Nakamura 1990; Crawcour 1997).

The backbone of Japanese agriculture in the early Tokugawa period was the production of rice; only gradually did other crops such as indigo, cotton, mulberry trees for feeding silkworms, and sugarcane spread in the ecological zones suited for such crops. Agricultural treatises were published recommending cultivation practices, the climatic zones, and the nature and quantity of fertilizers suitable for each crop. In the early Tokugawa period, fertilizers were mostly products of the forest supplemented with night soil. Japan, like China, had only a poor endowment of livestock. So animal manure never formed a major part of the input of fertilizers. However, as the demand for the latter outran supply, through the extension of cultivation and exhaustion of the grasses or forest waste used as fertilizers, the use of commercial fertilizers spread, especially in the regions with diversified cropping. Dried fish, cottonseed cakes, and night soil became the dominant fertilizers in these commercially advanced regions. I have not found any estimates of the increase in land or labor productivity for Japan as a whole as a result of double cropping, application of commercial fertilizers, or crop diversification. Smith (1959, p. 99) reports findings on some individual holdings. On a holding in Kinai, rice yields increased by 75 percent between early sixteenth and early seventeenth centuries. On another holding, this time in the Aki province in southwestern Japan, rice yields increased by about 100 percent between 1787 and 1888. Kinai was already a highly commercialized region in the early sixteenth century. But Aki was in a relatively backward region and the effects of commercialization probably started later in that province. So we should not be justified in adding the gains in productivity in the two holdings over the 250 years.

Commerce and commercial production were both encouraged and inhibited by the Tokugawa regime. The closing of all ports except Nagasaki to foreign commerce and the barring of all Westerners, except the Dutch, from entry into Japan strongly encouraged import substitution. Moreover, the Tokugawa also followed the same mercantilist policy of monopoly or monopsony as the VOC and other European companies chartered by their governments used to aggrandize themselves and thereby enrich their nations. Japan expelled all European traders except the Dutch in 1637 and confined the latter to the island of Deshima off the coast of Nagasaki. The goods imported by them were appraised by the Nagasaki chamber of commerce and prices fixed accordingly. This depressed the profitability for the Dutch but lowered the price of imported goods for the Japanese. This contrasted strongly with the situation in India, where the rulers not only gave privileges to European companies with respect to customs duties but often exempted them from paying internal tolls, thus putting them in an advantageous position compared with the Indian and other Asian traders (Mukherjee 1939; Prakash 1998, pp. 119–27). After the Meiji Restoration, as soon as the Japanese government was able to scrap the unequal treaties with Western powers, it adopted the policy of tightly regulating Japanese trade with foreign countries. This can be considered a major legacy of the Edo period.

During that period, many of the daimyo, officials of the *bakufu* and the *han*, and prosperous farmers or teachers, while conforming to the strategy of keeping foreigners at bay, tried to acquire the knowledge of the Chinese and the arrogant barbarians from the West. The demands of the *bakufu* establishment at Edo produced fiscal crises for both the *bakufu* and many daimyo. The *bakufu* and the daimyo granted monopoly rights to merchant associations (*nakama*), partly to control the direction of commerce and partly to obtain revenues in return for these privileges. Competition drove trade and production in directions in which these guild restrictions did not apply and encouraged a process of protoindustrialization in rural areas (Hauser 1974; Nakamura 1990). When guild restrictions or daimyo monopolies proved too costly, they were removed by the *bakufu*. This process propelled commercialization and incremental innovations further. One index of the degree of commercialization is the percentage share of cash crops in the total value of agricultural output. In 1877, before the Meiji Restoration had really set the process of industrialization going, the percentage of cash crops in the seven major regions of Japan ranged from 10.2 percent in Kyūshū to 25.8 percent in Kinai and 26.8 percent in Tōsan (Smith 1959, p. 72). For the seven regions taken together the proportion was 17 percent. Japan became a relatively urbanized region by the end of the eighteenth century. About 10 percent of the population lived in towns of five thousand or more, Edo alone contained a million people and became the largest metropolis in the world; the three metropolises of Edo, Osaka, and Kyoto together housed nearly two million persons. The growth of towns and cities; the requirements of literacy that the village officials had to meet because of their duty of record keeping, tax payments, and the preservation of law and order; and the enrichment of merchants and the more enterprising peasants and craftsmen led also to the growth of literacy (Dore 1965; Moriya 1990). The demand for books and other printed materials was met by a steady growth of publishing houses: it has been estimated that by the nineteenth century in Tokugawa Japan, there were 494 publishing houses in Kyoto, 504 in Osaka, and 917 in Edo (Moriya 1990, p. 115).

Smith shows how the rigidly hierarchical society of the early part of the Edo period changed radically toward a network in which commercial exchanges determined most social relations. But he also records that even through the late eighteenth century and beyond, parents were basically selling children to be adopted by wealthier people and entering into a contract that their sons would serve the adoptive family to a late age (up to age forty in one recorded case; Smith 1959, chapters 2–3). We have seen earlier how changes in legal status of servants and servile peasants failed often to free them from social and economic dependence on the larger holders of land. Thus commercialization failed to deliver real freedom of choice to vast numbers of the

Japanese peasantry (see also Dore 1959). The commercialization process in the late Edo period certainly enriched merchants and created a class of literate professionals, aware, despite the semiclosed nature of the Japanese economy from 1640 to 1853, of the advances made by the Western nations in technology, science, and the military arts. But the gains of the majority of the Japanese from this process in terms of greater freedom or higher living standards remain rather problematic.

The fast commercialization process carried its own cost. First, the distribution of ownership of land tended to become more unequal over time, with a much larger proportion of holdings becoming marginal in the sense that the holders could not make a living without supplementing their farm income with work on others' fields or some nonagricultural work. There was also a growth of very large holdings. These latter were worked by tenants at rack rent, because many peasants were reduced to a state of landlessness. But agricultural work remained highly labor-intensive (Smith 1959; Dore 1959). Peasants apparently gained in freedom as their obligations as hereditary servants, *nago* or *hōkōnin*, declined. But it is important to note that even as late as 1801–1820, there were *hōkōnin* bonded up to fifteen years and that debt bondage was so burdensome that such indentured workers received only a tenth of the wages of workers bonded for one year (Smith 1959, p. 121). Moreover, as I have already pointed out, the ascent of dependent peasants to the status of legal holders of land did not necessarily free them from social and economic dependence on large holders. When, after the Meiji Restoration, the customary servile tenures were overhauled, the larger holders took advantage of the situation to jack up their rents. The following example, cited by Smith (1959, p. 28) is probably quite typical:

> An *oyakata* in northern Japan, for example, between 1872 and 1920 commuted labour services into money payments for about half of his *nago*: the resulting loss of labour, for which he had received monetary compensation, he made good by increasing the labour services of the remaining *nago*!

The practices of the Tokugawa regime were often carried into the polity of an industrializing Japan and provided the means for the military-feudal elements to pursue their ends (Norman 1940, chapters 2–3).

Not only was the distribution of land ownership more concentrated at the end of Tokugawa rule than in its beginning but almost certainly consumption also became much more unequally distributed (Hauser 1974; Crawcour 1997). From the late eighteenth century, rice prices declined relative to prices of luxuries such as silk cloth and other nonagricultural goods and cash crops. The decline caused a crisis in *bakufu* finances because the tax was reckoned and collected in quantities of rice, which were then sold through rice brokers for defraying *bakufu* expenses. Part of this decline was due to rice prices being controlled but not the prices of competing commodities. This was occurring when peasants were urged, with the threat of penalties including imprisonment and expulsion from the village (which provided them with whatever legal rights the family enjoyed), to be industrious and produce as much rice as possible. The relative price of rice was also adversely affected because the prices of cash crops or competing products were jacked up by the monopolies mentioned earlier. But part of the explanation of the relative decline of rice price must lie on the demand side. The shift in incomes toward the more wealthy meant that they could consume more of the luxuries, whereas rice and other inferior cereals still accounted for the bulk of the expenditure of the poorer peasants and landless workers, and the shift of incomes away from them affected rice prices adversely. (Repeated attempts by the *bakufu* to restore the balance between rice and other prices did not produce a durable result [Hauser 1974; Vlastos 1986; Crawcour 1997].)

In contradiction to some unsubstantiated claims about the high rate of economic growth in pre-Meiji Japan made by Hanley and Yamamura (1977), Yamamura (1985) shows that even Tokugawa bannermen, a very privileged group of people (retainers and officials of the central rulers), experienced a steady decline in fertility. This was in turn caused by shrinking opportunities of economic and social mobility and not by expanding incomes. For poor people who had little land or other resources, *dekasegi*, or internal migration in search of wage employment, became a way of survival, and such mobility was a major reason for long separations of spouses, widely spaced births, and low fertility (Hayami 1985; Sasaki 1985).

There were significant differences in the rates and patterns of fertility among the three major macroregions of Japan: the northeast, the central region (containing Kinai and Kantō, the region around Edo), and the southwest (Hayami 2001; Hayami and Kurosu 2001). In the northeast, the age at marriage was low: about twenty-two years for men and seventeen years for women. But many women went on service (*dekasegi*) soon after marriage and the marital fertility was low; the population in this macroregion declined. In the central macroregion, a large proportion of men and women went on service, but they did so before marriage. The average age at marriage tended to be in the late twenties for men, and early twenties for women. Marital fertility was higher than in the northeast and the population remained stagnant. "Many families in the lower strata [of society] were unable to have enough children to be able to avoid termination of the lineage (*zekke*)" (Hayami and Kurosu 2001, p. 309). The southwest experienced the highest rates of population growth during 1721–1846: the population of the provinces of Hokuriku, San'in, San'yo, and Shikoku increased by 50 percent over this period (Hayami

2001, p. 48). In the southwest also the age at marriage was relatively high (about twenty-five years) but extramarital births were common and there was a more relaxed attitude to cohabitation and divorce compared with the other two regions (Hayami and Kurosu 2001, pp. 310–11).

The aggregate population of Japan was just about kept up by the contrasting trends in the three macroregions. In the central region, the preponderance of cities tended to lead to a high mortality, which was partly compensated by migration of people from within the region and from the poorer northeastern provinces. There is some evidence of bias against girl children in birth rates both in the northeastern and central regions. Much of the low fertility in the northeast must be regarded as coercive, since *dekasegi* was a major contributor to this outcome. Moreover, *dekasegi* was far more prevalent among the tenants (both men and women) than among the landlords (Hayami 2001, pp. 137–53).

The stagnation of the population may also be partly due to famines. Japan was visited by numerous famines in the eighteenth century. The major famines occurred in 1732–1733 (Kyoho famine), 1755–1756 (Horeki famine), and 1783–1786 (Temmei famine). The environmental changes caused by the compulsion to raise production and diversify into cash crops were contributory causes of food scarcity and famine. For example, in the Hochinhoe domain in the northeast, the peasants had to shift to cash crops, such as soybeans, and clear forests to expand production. This led to an expansion of the wild boar population. When in 1749 crops failed, humans had to compete with wild boars for tubers and other food, and boars even moved into the castle town and attacked humans (Walker 2001). An estimated 10 percent of the Hochinhoe population died in the resulting famine. And then in the nineteenth century the Tempo famine struck between the years 1833 and 1838. This series of famines and the increasing impact of fluctuations in prices of essential commodities caused many peasant uprisings, which were often led by the lower ranks of samurai, whose standard of living was also badly affected by the lower purchasing power of their rice stipends. The latter were often in arrears because many daimyo were themselves financially bankrupt and could carry on only with the help of loans extended by rich merchants and bankers (Norman 1940, chapters 2–3; Vlastos 1986). One of the most dangerous of these uprisings was that led by Oshio Heihachiro—a scholar and minor police official—in Osaka, the heart of the financial and trading network of Tokugawa Japan (Norman 1940, pp. 33–34; Hayami 2001, pp. 47–50).

During times of food scarcity or famine, the people fell back on help from the self-help groups (*kō*), charity of more prosperous neighbors, or loans from the *bakufu* or daimyo, which were given out from the land tax fund of the peasants. The loans carried a 30 percent interest rate and had to be repaid within a fixed period (Satō 1990, pp. 57–58). The Tokugawa had no policy resembling that of the maintenance of an ever-normal granary under the great Chinese emperors.

MEIJI-ERA DEVELOPMENTS

The collapse of the Tokugawa regime in 1867–1868 was not a sudden affair: it had been challenged by dissident and powerful daimyo of Choshu, Satsuma, Tosa, and Hizen for years, if not decades (Norman 1940, chapter 3). It had been a complex and turbulent process, with merchant capital and disaffected daimyo and samurai playing supporting roles. The ultimate spark igniting the powder keg that blew off the Tokugawa regime was the forcing of the closed doors of Japan by the bombardment of Edo by Commodore Perry and the signing of the first unequal treaty with a Western power, the United States, in 1858. But the daimyo of the southwestern domains of Japan had been aware of the power of the Western nations for a long time. Some of their statesmen and scholars had been trying to spread the learning of Dutch science. Many important books on scientific advances were translated from Dutch into Japanese: these included Vesalius's *Anatomy* (translated in 1774), Copernicus's theory (in 1798), Newton's theory (in 1798), and so on (Watanabe 1987, p. 185). Rutherford Alcock, the first British consul to Japan, was greatly impressed by the ingenuity of Japanese craftsmen and their eagerness to learn new technologies of the West (Alcock 1863, cited by Watanabe 1987, pp. 181–83). From the early 1850s, the daimyo and their advisors became seriously perturbed by the incursions of the British and other foreign powers into Japanese waters. They then began importing technicians and machines from Britain and other European countries to set up reverberatory furnaces and iron foundries and to manufacture cannon in imitation of the advanced Western models.

Much of the early industrialization under the Meiji regime was driven by military and strategic considerations. The statesmen guiding the Meiji Restoration knew that if they could not compete with the barbarians on their terms, Japan would meet the same fate as China, with the barbarians walking over its prostrate body (Norman 1940). The Japanese leaders considered that the only way to get rid of the humiliating unequal treaties imposed on them from the 1850s and to compete effectively with the Western powers was to "Enrich the Nation and Strengthen the Army" (Watanabe 1987, p. 186). Unfortunately, this conviction became so ingrained in the minds of the reforming bureaucrats and military leaders that it gave an imperialist cast to both the foreign and the domestic policy of Japan. Almost immediately after the restoration, some of the leaders wanted to mount an expedition against Korea; when that scheme was squashed by the more cautious leaders, the aggressive ones had to be satisfied with a punitive expedition against Formosa, on the grounds that some Formosan tribesmen had killed some Japanese fishermen (Norman 1940, pp. 88–91, 197–201). Under the constitution of 1889, the military authorities were more or less freed from civilian control: the former would report directly to the emperor without going through the prime minister (Norman 1940, chapter 6; Gow 1993, pp. 50–56). The military leaders were determined to expand Japan's foreign possessions as a means both of defense against foreign imperial powers and of building up Japan's economy. Japan was deficient in coal, iron ore, and minerals compared with most other imperialist nations; moreover, the constriction of the home market because of a poverty-stricken peasantry meant that Japan's industries had to conquer foreign markets. These considerations also fed Japanese imperial ambitions.

The civilian-controlled Diet (the Japanese parliament) tried from time to time to arrest the headlong expansion of the Japanese army and navy, but after at most a pause, the drive for expansion continued (Duus 1988b; Harries and Harries 1991; Gow 1993). After defeating China in 1895, the Japanese took control of Formosa and also received a huge indemnity. They used this indemnity, along with increased taxes, to prepare for war against Russia, because they saw Russian expansion in the Far East as a direct threat to Japan's security. Japan gained the Liaoning peninsula as a result of its victory over Russia in the 1905 Russo-Japanese war. Soon after this victory, Japan formally annexed Korea. The acquisition of the colonies on the Asian mainland, instead of diminishing the anxiety of the Japanese about their security, increased it and goaded both the army and the navy to demand more resources for expansion from the public exchequer (Duus 1988b; Harries and Harries 1991, chapter 7). Already between 1896 and 1903, military expenditure had virtually doubled and had accounted on average for 40 percent of the national budget (Harries and Harries 1991, p. 64). In view of mounting interest charges on Japan's foreign and domestic loans, and inability to honor some of the domestic obligations, in spite of emergency measures, the Diet, for a little while before World War I, was able to retrench the military demands on the national budget.

But Japan's search for national security and the drive for industrial development as a means for enhancing security continued apace and pushed it on a path of aggressive militarism. I will sketch that development and its implication for the Chinese and other victims of Japanese aggression in chapter 20. We will also consider the deaths caused by Japan's Asia Pacific War in that context. Here we consider the cost inflicted on its own people by Japan's militarism.

Despite imperial Japan's rapid strides in developing industries, the drain of its resources in military preparations did not leave a great deal for improving the standard of living of the ordinary people. At the beginning of the Pacific War, 50 percent of the workers were still engaged in feeding the country, and Japan had still to import 20 percent of its needs from its colonies in Formosa and Korea (Coox 1988, p. 377). Because of growth in per capita income and some improvement in nutrition, the biological standard of living improved in Japan, but it did so rather slowly between the two world wars. According to the data provided by Mosk (2000, tables 1 and 2), the nutritional index of an average Japanese increased only from 118.2 to 118.7 between 1921–1930 and 1931–1940. The average heights of military recruits increased from 157.2 centimeters in 1900–1904 to 159.1 centimeters in 1920–1924 and then only to 160.3 centimeters in 1935–1939.

As in the case of other imperialist countries, such as Britain and Germany, the concern of the rulers for the health of army recruits led to the adoption of welfare measures such as provision of better and more extended health care and introduced a degree of egalitarianism in such provisions. In 1936 "the army medical bureau announced that the number of men failing their draft physicals had risen from 25 per cent in 1922–26 to 35 per cent over 1927–32 and 40 per cent in 1935" (Kasza 2002, p. 423).[1] Immediately after this, the government announced welfare policies such as a national health insurance scheme, under the control of the cooperatives. But these welfare measures could not by themselves augment resources available for consumption, especially after Japan had ventured on its Pacific War. In 1941 the food availability left an average Japanese barely above the minimum calorie intake needed for subsistence. In 1943 the government took away almost 60 percent of the gross domestic product (GDP) for war expenditures, leaving only 40 percent for consumption expenditure, including taxes (Hoyt 1987, p. 371). By the end of World War II, Japan was completely devastated by Allied bombing, including the two atom bombs that reduced Hiroshima and Nagasaki to radioactive deserts, and by its loss of its most active generation in wars abroad. An estimated three million Japanese perished in the Pacific War (Kasza 2002).

Japan's rise as a capitalist world power between 1868 and 1941 illustrates in a concentrated form the combination of the drive for pelf and power and the ideology of a civilizing mission that we have witnessed in the case of other major capitalist powers in Europe and North America. The Japanese ruling class spread the slogan of creating a Greater Asia Co-Prosperity Sphere even as they perpetrated unbelievable cruelties on the conquered peoples and especially the Chinese.

If we look back at the history of Tokugawa Japan, we can see that from the eighteenth century, many aspects of its economy were rapidly commercialized, and new technologies were imported and adapted to the requirements of the country. It also threw up a ruling class, which was intensely nationalist. A merchant and rich farmer class developed in the interstices of a highly hierarchical society. But the peasantry remained under an extreme degree of subjection. Some of them gained a measure of freedom, but very often at the cost of a loss of their customary right of access to land as a source of employment and livelihood. The Meiji Restoration legally released the peasants from some of their servile obligations, but by giving unrestricted property rights, including legal rights of sale, to a few holders of land, it aggravated the problem of landlessness and enabled the landlords to increase their take to up to 60 or 70 percent of the produce of the tenanted land (Norman 1940, pp. 70–80 and chapter 5; Ladejinsky 1947/1977; Dore 1959, chapters 1–5). But as I noted earlier, even on the eve of World War II, 50 percent of the people of Japan depended on agriculture for their livelihood.

Under these circumstances, it was very unlikely that the ordinary people could have a high standard of living at the close of the Tokugawa period, despite claims to the contrary made by Susan Hanley (1983). As Yasuba (1986) showed in a critique of Hanley (1983), Japanese workers in spinning mills in the nineteenth century were paid even lower wages than Indian and Chinese textile workers at the time. Since the wages of the textile workers in China, India, and Japan were related closely to the earnings of small peasants or agricultural laborers, it is unlikely that the general run of Japanese peasants earned much more than Indian and Chinese peasants at the time. We must remember, by the way, that India had suffered more than sixty years of deindustrialization by the 1880s (Bagchi 1976a; Clingingsmith and Williamson 2004).

For all the eagerness of the progressive rulers and scholars in late Tokugawa Japan to learn those sciences and technologies of the foreigners that would make the nation stronger militarily and economically, they were rather late in introducing smallpox vaccination, although smallpox was probably the single biggest cause of fatality among children (Walker 1999; Jannetta 2001). Vaccination was introduced first among selected groups such as the Ainu and among the temple population since the 1880s. It is the gradual diffusion of vaccination from then on that was responsible for bringing down the IMR to 150 by the early 1920s (Bramall 1997, p. 554). The failure to bring it down further by that date must be linked to the priorities of a Japanese ruling class bent on winning in the interimperialist competition rather than on raising the standard of living all around. It is typical of mainstream histories that questions of the actual standard of living of the Japanese in the prewar period are hardly addressed in them (see, for example, Lockwood 1968; Ohkawa and Rosovsky 1973).

For all its military prowess, Japan was still a rather poor country in the 1930s, with a low life expectancy (the life expectancies of Japanese men and women even in 1920–1925 were forty-two and forty-three years, respectively [Cornell 1996, p. 30]). Steckel (1999) tabulated the heights of samples of population in eight developed countries (United Kingdom, United States, France, the Netherlands, Sweden, Germany, Australia, and Japan) in the so-called preindustrial phase, the early industrial phase, middle industrial phase, and late industrial phase. In Japan's case the early industrial phase was supposed to last from 1868 to 1880 and the late industrial phase from 1920 to 1940, whereas the corresponding phases are supposed to have been 1720–1760 and 1830–1870 in the case of the United Kingdom. Japanese statures were much lower than those of all of these European populations in all the phases. Steckel (2001, p. 6) found a strongly negative relation between stature and urbanization and also that Japan was the most urbanized country in the preindustrial phase: "the congestion and turnover associated with urban living increased the chances of exposure to pathogens," while a "large number of poor people . . . lacked access to food, clothing and shelter that would have increased resistance to disease." But there is a paradox in the Japanese case. Although Japanese longevity lagged behind those of the advanced industrial nations in the first half of the nineteenth century, that longevity was in fact higher than that of the United Kingdom in most of the corresponding phases (Steckel 2001, table 1). Was this the result of the continuation in the social arrangement under which the Japanese peasants could not live but were not allowed to die either? But the effect of the failure of the Japanese state to spend any substantial funds for public welfare and of the deterioration of nutrition can be seen in the worsening of the average life expectancy between the 1890s and 1920s: life expectancy for males was 42.8 years over 1891–1898, declining to 42.0 before rising to 46.92 in 1935–1936. Life expectancy for females was 44.3 years, 43.20 years, and 49.63 years, respectively, in the three corresponding periods (Japan Statistical Yearbook 2002, table 2–27).

In Japan both economic growth and human development really took off after its defeat in what the Japanese style as the Pacific War (Tsuru 1993; Bagchi 2000). Pro-peasant land reforms and concentration of all national resources on civilian production and research played a very important part in this acceleration, as did the policies that are anathema to market fundamentalists—namely, a severely protectionist foreign trade regime and closing of the national economy to foreign capital.

NOTE

1. We must remember that Japan had a policy of national conscription, and the dragnet for the draftees was made continually wider, so that the army had probably to recruit less and less able-bodied persons as the war preparations progressed.

Capitalist Competition, Colonialism, and the Physical Well-Being of Non-European Peoples

DIFFUSIONISM AND ITS FAILURES

By the beginning of the twentieth century, industrial capitalism had provided the knowledge and most of the technology for improving the longevity of human beings and the quality of their life. However, until the end of World War II, the benefits of those advances remained largely confined to lands settled by whites, and even there, the benefits were differentially distributed along lines of class, gender, and race, thus belying the claims of universalism proclaimed by the primary ideologies of capitalism (Wallerstein, "Capitalist Civilization," in Wallerstein 1995, pp. 113–63). In this chapter I recapitulate some part of the history of the non-European peoples subjected to the domination of European powers to show why diffusionist optimism was falsified.

FATE OF THE NATIVE AMERICAN POPULATIONS UNDER EUROPEAN IMPACT

The first non-European victims of the European drive for profit backed by the power of the state were the native peoples of the Canary Islands in the Atlantic and the black Africans on the western coast of Africa, who were either enslaved or killed off in the maritime ventures of the Portuguese prince Henry the Navigator in the fifteenth century. But the demographic impact of the intra-European competition for finding new territories and new groups of people to exploit was felt most fatally by the native American people in the Western Hemisphere after Christopher Columbus had pioneered the route across the middle Atlantic to the Caribbean.

As we have seen earlier, down to the eighteenth century European nations had neither conquered much of Asia nor surpassed the quality and price competition of Indian and Chinese textiles, ceramics, and other manufactures. They paid for Asian textiles and spices in silver or gold (and later, guns and other armaments). Large quantities of silver and gold could be obtained only from the Americas, or the coastal regions of Africa. But mining required labor; so first the Spanish conquerors of the Aztec and Inca empires in the Americas turned to coerced labor of the Amerindians of Mexico, Central America, and Peru. European powers other than Spain and Portugal had to acquire the silver and gold by selling goods, and increasingly slaves, to Spain and obtaining a hold over Spanish commerce in general through trading networks and finance. Slaves from Africa were used in increasing numbers in Spanish and Portuguese America, because (1) it was found difficult to enslave Amerindians; (2) in New Spain, Spanish conquest was attended by a demographic disaster of massive proportions; and (3) Spanish theologians persuaded the Spanish monarch to halt the enslavement of Amerindians (but not Africans) within the Spanish dominions (Pagden 1986); and (4) plantations of tobacco and sugar in the Caribbean and South America used up slave labor in very large numbers.

Serious research into the demographic consequences of the impact of the Europeans on the Americas by Carl Otwin Sauer (1935, 1939), followed by Woodrow Borah, Sherburne Cook, and Lesley Simpson—his associates at the University of California, Berkeley—have given us approximate estimates of the numbers dying in New Spain and the Americas in the wake of Spanish conquest (Denevan 1976a).

The native Tainos of Hispaniola, the first island to be occupied by the Spanish conquerors, were extinct by the 1520s, if not earlier (Lovell 1992; Cook 1998). When the native inhabitants of the Caribbean islands put up a resistance against European marauders, the latter demonized them by deriving the word *cannibal* from *Caribe*, which meant *daring* in usage of that time.[1] The Caribs died out because they starved when the Spaniards commandeered their food and their labor without payment; they were hunted down when they tried to resist the Spaniards; many were tortured and killed by sadistic Spaniards; and they died of newly introduced diseases to which they had not developed resistance. New diseases rather than deliberate manslaughter appear to have been the principal cause of the demographic disasters on the mainland and the islands of Spanish America. But as we know, malnutrition and oppressive labor can be powerful allies of germs in killing people. The main diseases identified are an influenza epidemic, which may have been spread from swine introduced by the Spaniards, and smallpox. Denevan's (1976b, p. 291) estimated population of the Americas in 1492, that is, just before the incursion of Columbus on Hispaniola, is shown in table 13.1.

Table 13.1.   A Conservative Estimate of
the Population of the Americas in 1492
(Figures in Thousands)

North America	4,400
Mexico	21,400
Central America	5,650
Caribbean	5,850
Andes	11,500
Lowland South America	8,500
Total	57,300

The figure for the population of North America has been recently revised upward (Diamond 1992, 1998; Trigger and Washburn 1996). The Mississippi valley alone may have contained as many as 20 million people before the advent of the Europeans (Diamond 1998, chapters 3, 18).

For central Mexico, Cook and Borah (1971, p. viii) estimated that the Amerindian population fell from a total of 25.2 million in 1518 to 1.1 million in 1605, less than a century later, as reproduced in table 13.2.

Initially, the greatest toll of Amerindian life was taken by disease, the forcible exaction of Amerindian labor with or without permission of the Crown in the form of *encomienda*, and the takeover of Indian lands by Spaniards for pasture and for crops. Slave raids also took a toll of native lives until the campaign of Fray Bartolomé de Las Casas and other Spaniards siding with him led to the banning of private enslavement of natives (Gerbi 1955/1973; Pagden 1986, chapters 6 and 7; Wade 1999). All the contestants in the famous debate between Las Casas and Juan Ginés de Sepúlveda in Valladolid in 1550–1551 accepted the Aristotelian idea that there were natural slaves and masters; the difference lay in the differing views of Las Casas and his supporters on the one hand and their opponents on the other as to whether Amerindians fitted into the category of natural slaves and whether, even if they did, the Spaniards had the right to enslave them. Already by 1542, slavery of the natives had been banned in Spanish colonies, and Portugal also imposed a ban later (Wade 1999, p. 1127). But the banning of formal slavery for Amerindians hardly improved their lot. The Portuguese, and especially the so-called *bandierantes* of São Paulo, continued to enslave Amerindians in their search for exploitable bonded labor. In the Spanish colonies, the Spaniards

Table 13.2.   Native Population in Central Mexico, 1518–1605 (in Millions)

1518	1532	1548	1568	1580	1595	1605
25.2	16.8	6.3	2.7	1.9	1.4	1.1

converted whole communities of Amerindians into bonded labor in the service of the state or the *encomenderos* who obtained rights of exploiting their labor and resources.

In a remarkable twelve-hundred-page *Letter to a King*, composed between 1585 and 1615 (quoted by Lovell 1992, p. 437), Waman Puma pointed out the numerous ways the Spaniards usurped the possessions of the natives and thereby impoverished both the natives and the realm. In particular the Spaniards had taken over and destroyed irrigation channels that Amerindians had constructed with great skill over centuries, and now the land could not produce enough food because of shortage of water. Moreover, the fields of the natives were ravaged by the grazing of mules, horses, and other animals owned by the Spaniards.

The decline of pre-Columbian water conservation and irrigation systems under Spanish rule hastened the demographic collapse in the Americas. Apart from the forcible dispossession of the natives through royal grants of lands to Spaniards and plain illegal usurpation of the latter, the introduction of private property rights led to further dispossession of a dwindling Amerindian population (Bagchi 1982, chapter 3; Prem 1992).

The population of the six major nations of western Europe (England, Holland, Germany, France, Italy, and Spain) in 1600 has been estimated as 55.4 million (Livi-Bacci 1991, p. 6). By a generous estimate of demographic growth in the sixteenth century, the population of these countries, including Portugal, might have increased by 15 million (assuming an annual growth rate at least as high as during 1600–1750). Even if we accept the rather conservative estimate of the American population in 1492 made by Denevan (1976b), his figure of 57.3 million exceeds the population of the western European countries, and if we take more realistic estimates of the North American population, it far exceeds that number. Thus reckoning one human life as equal to another, the spread of European dominion over the Americas in the sixteenth century was a negative-sum game for the human population as a whole, even without taking into account the devastation caused in Africa by the Atlantic slave trade.

TRADE IN ENSLAVED AFRICANS AND THEIR USE IN THE WESTERN HEMISPHERE

Africans were captured and sold for use as beasts of labor by the Portuguese from the second half of the fifteenth century. After Bartolomeu Dias, Vasco da Gama, and their followers discovered the route around Africa to Asia, the Portuguese established bases from which they made raids for slaves or bought slaves from other Africans who had captured them in war or by some other means. However, this trade did not acquire its demonic magnitudes until the interlopers from northwestern Europe, and in particular the Dutch, the English and the French, emerged as slave traders. The demand for slaves made a quantum jump as the Dutch demonstrated the profitability of plantations, first in northeastern Brazil; then, after their expulsion from Brazil, in the island of Curaçao; and finally in Surinam on the Guyana coast (Postma 1990). The British and French did not lag far behind. Jamaica, other Caribbean islands occupied by the British, and the island of Hispaniola, which the French captured from the Spaniards and renamed St. Domingue, became highly profitable possessions run by a small planter class employing hundreds of thousands of slaves. As the demand for African slaves grew, so did their supply. Slave traders and slave raiders extended their reach from the coast of western and west-central Africa to the deep interior of Sub-Saharan Africa, central Africa, and even parts of eastern Africa. It has been estimated that altogether between 11 million and 12 million Africans were exported by the Europeans between 1450 and the end of the slave trade around 1900 (Lovejoy 1983), giving an annual rate of 26,000 Africans exported across the Atlantic (table 13.3). Recent estimates of slave exports from Africa range from 11,569,000 for the transatlantic trade in 1519–1867 (Behrendt 1999, p. 1867) to 15.4 million for the global trade (Inikori and Engerman 1992b). Slave exports accelerated over the period 1450–1800: in the eighteenth century alone 6.47 million slaves were exported from Africa (Behrendt 1999, p. 1869). As the British emerged as the most powerful European nation during the eighteenth century, they also became the leading slave traders of the world. According to Richardson (1989), between 1698 and 1810, British slavers exported more than 3,046,000 slaves from Africa. In the peak years of the 1780s, 100,000 persons were enslaved and exported annually from Africa. One reason why so many slaves had to be imported is that they died off very quickly because they were made to work so hard regardless of their state of health (Dunn 1987).

The first case of abolition of black slavery occurred in Haiti, with a revolt led by Toussaint-Louverture, around 1789. The British abolished slave trade in 1807 and slavery within the British empire in 1833. The British imposed an embargo on the Atlantic slave trade by all nations and enforced it by deploying warships along the western African coastline. But slaves were smuggled in large numbers into Brazil and Cuba and other slaveholding Latin American countries, as the figures in table 13.3 indicate. Moreover, internal trade in slaves in the United States and Brazil continued unabated and may have been accelerated by the external embargo. around 900,000 slaves may have been sold by the old South to the new South slaveholding states in the

Table 13.3.   Slave Exports from Africa: The Atlantic Trade
1450–1900

Period	Number	Percentage of Total
1450–1600	367,000	3.1
1601–1700	1,868,000	16.0
1701–1800	6,133,000	52.4
1801–1900	3,330,000	28.5
Total	11,698,000	100.0

Source: Lovejoy 1983, p. 19.

United States and a similar number was traded within Brazil before slavery
was formally ended in the two countries (Eltis 1987, p. 8). More insidiously
still, slavery became entrenched in most parts of Sub-Saharan Africa as slaves
became cheaper, and many African societies came to use them both for production of commercial crops and for domestic service. As we shall see, the
British and French conquered most of western Africa with the abolition of
slavery as a declared objective but continued to tolerate it in practice for the
sake of minimizing the cost of rule and maximizing the tribute raised from the
conquered peoples. This is yet another illustration of the contradiction of
the promise of freedom and its effective suppression under the dispensation
of capitalist colonialism.

The nature of slavery within African societies, especially in precolonial
times, had been profoundly different from the chattel slavery of the Americas,
as M. G. Smith (1954) pointed out when he contrasted slavery in the Jamaica
plantations with slavery in Zaria in northern Nigeria. In Africa slaves could
be trusted ministers of chiefs and given favorable conditions, their descendants could merge into the society of freemen as equals: this is something that
could rarely happen when the masters were white and the chattel-slaves were
blacks. African societies were demographically badly disrupted by the slave
trade, because the majority of the slaves were young adult males, leaving broken families of survivors behind (Eltis and Engerman 1992).

After taking into account the loss of life caused by slave raids and associated wars and the loss of life in the terrible middle passage, when about a
sixth of the slaves died, Basil Davidson estimated that the five centuries of
the Atlantic slave trade had led to a loss of at least 50 million in potential
African lives (Davidson 1961). Recently, Manning arrived at the same number after taking into account regional variations in slave exports and assuming an intrinsic growth rate for African populations of 0.5 percent per annum: he concluded that without the hemorrhage of slave trade Africa's
population in 1850 would have been 100 million instead of 50 million (Manning 1990, p. 85).

The slave-run plantations and mines in the Americas made major contributions to the earnings of the European capitalists and to the calorie intake of the European population, especially in the eighteenth century. By 1787 the islands in the possession of the English and French states were exporting 106,000 and 125,000 tons of sugar, respectively, out of a total export of 286,000 tons of sugar from the New World (Blackburn 1997, p. 403). The profit rates of British plantations in the West Indies over 1689–1798 have been estimated as 3.4 percent in the worst years and 14.9 percent in the best years (Ward 1978). Moreover, as Blackburn (1997, chapter 10) and others have pointed out, the plantations were only a part, though a vital part, of an enterprise in which the owners also were bankers and traders, while monopolizing political power in the island oligarchies.

Neither slaves nor other victims of rampant capitalism submitted to formal or informal servitude without resistance. They repeatedly bid for freedom and demanded equality with their exploiters (Craton 1982, 1987; Blackburn 1997, especially pp. 404–6, 473–77, 591–92; Linebaugh and Rediker 2000, chapters 5–9). When the English navy during the Cromwellian regime took Jamaica from Spain, a large number of slaves fled into the forests and created a liberated zone, raising their own crops and exchanging them with tradesmen and sailors. Not only in Jamaica but in other Caribbean islands and on both shores of the Caribbean, the Maroons remained a hydraheaded multitude disturbing the ease of the slave owners. Together with plantation slaves, sailors who had deserted, just been laid off by their captains, or had mutinied; Irish prisoners who had been exiled to the Caribbean; and other rebellious poor hatched conspiracies, blew up forts and planters' houses, and invited the enemies of the ruling power to help them. The rulers tried to break the spirit of the exploited by meting out savage punishments to the rebels, but they never succeeded fully nor did they feel fully secure in their mansions. In Jamaica, for example, the authorities had to sign a truce with the Maroon leaders Colonel Cudgoe (Cudjo) and Captain Accompong in 1739 and recognize their freedom and their possession of 1,500 acres of land (Blackburn 1997, p. 404; Linebaugh and Rediker 2000, pp. 194–96).

The ending of the Maroon War of Jamaica did not bring peace to the plantation societies of the Caribbean or the mainland Americas. All through the eighteenth century there were numerous conspiracies and rebellions all over the region. The activities of the rebels reached into London, the heart of the metropolis, and joined with other revolutionary elements to strike terror in the hearts of the property-owning gentry and led them to engage in the state terror inflicted on democratic elements in the 1790s. Fear of uncontrollable slave insurgency in Jamaica and other islands as much as the earlier work of abolitionists such as Granville Sharp and William Wilberforce led to the formal abolition of slavery by the British government.

INDENTURED LABOR REPLACES SLAVERY

Slaves had been introduced into the Americas in larger numbers in the sixteenth and seventeenth centuries because the supply of white indentured labor from Europe proved to be inadequate and costly. When slavery was formally abolished in the British dominions in the 1830s, a system of indentured labor took its place for running the plantations in the Caribbean, Fiji, Mauritius, Natal, Sri Lanka, Assam, and other centers of white-run plantations (Tinker 1974; Northrup 1995). Contrary to conventional wisdom, the legal abolition of slavery or the slave trade by the British did not lead to the end of slavery or severe bondage in the British dominions (Sarkar 1985; Anderson 1993; Lovejoy and Hogendorn 1993). The Jamaican planters complained about the shortage of labor after the abolition of slavery because many of the freed slaves refused to work on the plantations. The British authorities tried to remedy the situation by finding new sources of (necessarily cheap) labor for them. The rulers of a country that had been vociferous in abolishing slave trade set about devising a scheme for retransporting across the Atlantic the freed slaves who had been settled in Africa (Green 1984). Even when bolstered by a government subsidy, this did not work. Then the British rulers allowed planters to recruit workers, mainly in India and China, with harsh conditions of indenture that differed little from those of slavery. Table 13.4 provides summary data on exports of indentured labor from the most important sources to various destinations over 1831–1920. The data show that China and India provided 83 percent of the world total.

Indentured Europeans were favored with a subsidy. In any case, their import as bonded laborers virtually ceased after 1860, when the mass migration of Europeans to the United States and other overseas former colonies surged upward. The Japanese migrated primarily to Peru and Hawaii and went into better-paid occupations such as trade or craft work, partly because they were better educated than the Chinese and the Indian migrants. The mortality among the migrants was generally very high, especially in new-disease environments, such as those of Malaya (Shlomowitz and Brennan 1992), as table 13.5 indicates.

The Indian indentured laborers in the plantations of Perak in Malaya and Assam in India fared very badly, as table 13.5 shows. In the 1860s, going to work in the Assam plantations was even more murderous for the indentured workers: according to the *Report of the Commissioners Appointed to Enquire*

Table 13.4.   Numbers of Indentured
Laborers Exported from China, India,
and Elsewhere, 1831–1920

Africans	96,032
Chinese	386,901
Europeans	56,027
Indians[a]	1,336,030
Japanese	85,202
Javanese	19,330
Pacific Islanders	96,043
Total	2,075,565

Source: Northrup 1995, pp. 156–57.
[a] *Indians* means South Asians but most were
recruited from the southern, central, and
northern parts of today's India.

into the State and Prospects of Tea Cultivation in Assam, Cachar and Sylhet (Calcutta 1868, quoted by Shlomowitz and Brennan 1990, table 1), the mortality rate (per thousand) in the Assam tea gardens was more than 301.6 in July–December 1865 and 182.6 in 1866. The situation improved a little later on, but it remained grim for new immigrants (Shlomowitz and Brennan 1990, 1992). The mortality of the laborers on their way to work was also reminiscent of the deaths of enslaved Africans during the infamous middle passage.

    The horrendous levels of mortality of slaves and indentured laborers were only extreme examples of the kind of governance and exploitation to which ordinary people in nonwhite dependencies were subjected. There was very little investment by the colonial masters in public health facilities or hygiene of the natives; moreover, because of the working of the capitalist market and colonial extraction of tribute, they suffered endemically from entitlement failures and deprivation of even their habitually low levels of nutrition. This meant that cholera, smallpox, malaria, and bubonic plague took a vast toll of

Table 13.5.   Average Mortality of Indian[a] Labor, 1871–1910 (Death Rate per Thousand per Year)

	1871–1880	1881–1890	1891–1900	1901–1910	1871–1910
Assam	79.8	59.0	50.3	40.9	52.6
Fiji		31.3	20.9	15.4	19.8
Surinam	53.6	20.9	16.8	14.1	22.3
Province Wellesley[b]	57.3	39.7	49.6	56.9	48.0
Perak		57.0	73.7	85.7	79.6

Source: Shlomowitz and Brennan 1992, table 6.
[a] *Indian* means South Asians but most were recruited from the southern, central, and northern parts of today's India.
[b] Province Wellesley was Malaya, part of today's Malaysia

human lives at a time when the means of their eradication was known to medical scientists and when European countries were on the way to conquering most of these diseases through the improvement of nutrition and public health facilities (Kunitz 1986). During 1900–1951 life expectancy in most western European countries and North America rose from 45 to 60 years and above. In India life expectancy was 22.9 years in 1901–1911 and had moved up to 32.1 by 1941–1951 (CSO 1993, p. 33).

AFRICAN AMERICANS IN THE UNITED STATES OF AMERICA

The condition of the African Americans in the United States is an extremely significant example of the continuation of unequal development and its reproduction under capitalism. The bloodiest struggle in U.S. history was waged to decide between freedom and slavery of the African Americans as well as between the desire of the more advanced industrial states of the northern United States to pursue a centrally directed policy for further industrial growth and the determination of the planter- and slaveholder-dominated southern states to go their own way and bring further territories under plantation slavery (Du Bois 1935/1992; Marx 1998, chapter 6). As we shall see, in the most powerful capitalist nation in the world, slavery ended but African Americans remain a severely disadvantaged community.

As Du Bois (1935/1992) documented in his great book on the antecedents and immediate aftermath of the American Civil War, free African Americans had not been disenfranchised even in the colonial period. But they were disenfranchised as the United States evolved as an independent, white-dominated republic. Even then the southern free African Americans in the antebellum era were as tall as the whites (Bodenhorn 1999), suggesting that their overall standards of nutrition and health approximated to those of the whites. When the Civil War started, 200,000 African Americans fought on the side of the Union, and many simply deserted the slave-operated plantations. These moves as well as the strong abolitionist drive prompted the U.S. government to abolish slavery—but only piecemeal at first. It was abolished by proclamation of the Union government in 1862 in the territories of the Confederate states and then throughout the United States by the Thirteenth Amendment to the U.S. Constitution, passed in December 1865.

In the brief period of Reconstruction, African American and white workers fought side by side to establish genuine democracy: the rights of newly enfranchised African Americans were enforced through the presence of federal troops and public money was used to fund elementary education (Du Bois 1935/1992). The result was an enormous improvement in the condition of the

African Americans: "black literacy rose from 10 to 50 per cent between 1865 and 1890, black landownership rose, and per capita real income of blacks increased 46 per cent from 1860 to 1880" (Marx 1998, p. 130). However, a backlash from the majority whites and the need of the northern Congressmen to appease southern whites as a way of reuniting the nation led to reassertion of the power of the dominant white interests and passing of legislation effectively disfranchising the African Americans, reversing most of the gains they made during the radical Reconstruction period (Du Bois 1935/1992, chapters 14–15; Margo 1990; Marx 1998, chapters 6, 9). Jim Crow laws and mob violence led to the lynching of at least 2,000 African Americans (Marx 1998, p. 141), with law-enforcing authorities watching and implicitly or explicitly condoning it. These developments set African Americans back in terms of most indexes of human development. In the late nineteenth century, the ratio of public expenditure on an African American pupil to that on a white pupil, which had already been lower than 1.00 by 1890 in most of the southern states, declined further. Table 13.6 gives expenditures per pupil and the ratio of expenditure per African American pupil to that on a white pupil in selected southern U.S. states between 1890 and 1935. By the latter date only a little of the lost ground had been recovered by the children of African American parents, and their schooling continued to suffer, condemning them to low-paid jobs as they grew to adulthood.

Systematic discrimination in the workplace and much poorer access to hospitals and medical facilities rendered the average African American more malnourished and shorter-lived than the average white, even though these whites included immigrants from much poorer regions of Europe, who were vulnerable to U.S. diseases. Table 13.7 gives the estimated longevity of whites and African Americans in selected years since 1900.

In 1900 the gap between the life expectancies of whites and African Americans was 14.1 years in the case of males and 15.2 years in the case of females. But it fell significantly after World War I. Ironically enough, the gap declined more speedily in the two periods straddling the two world wars than in peacetime. The passage of the U.S. Civil Rights Act of 1964, ending formal electoral discrimination and introducing affirmative action for African Americans and women, made a difference only from the 1970s. In 1984 the life expectancy at birth (e_0) of white males was 71.8 years and that of African American males was 65.3 years; for white females and African American females the corresponding figures were 78.7 years and 73.6 years, respectively (see table 13.7). But as an aftereffect of policy changes made in the Reagan years, while the life expectancy of whites continued to move upward, though rather slowly, African American life expectancy for both males and females declined or stagnated. In 1994 the life expectancy of white males was 73.3 years and

Table 13.6.   Per Pupil Expenditures on Instruction, Selected Southern States (in 1950 U.S. Dollars)

	Expenditure per Pupil ($) and Ratio of African American (A) to White (W)	*ca. 1890*	*ca. 1910*	*ca. 1935*
Alabama	A	8.80	10.39	17.50
	W	8.89	33.51	53.18
	A/W	0.99	0.31	0.33
Florida	A	13.12	9.95	34.66
	W	26.66	36.05	84.74
	A/W	0.49	0.28	0.41
Louisiana	A	8.29	9.03	19.91
	W	16.57	53.76	74.60
	A/W	0.50	0.17	0.27
Maryland	A	27.88	27.88	80.63
	W	42.82	47.34	102.84
	A/W	0.65	0.59	0.78
Mississippi	A	9.27	7.67	13.36
	W	18.62	27.88	58.61
	A/W	0.50	0.28	0.23
North Carolina	A	7.75	9.28	32.92
	W	7.67	17.25	51.43
	A/W	1.01	0.54	0.64

Source: Margo 1990, table 2.5.

that of white females was 79.6 years, while life expectancy of African American males was 64.9 years and that of African American females was 73.9 years. From 1995 the life expectancy for all four groups moved upward again and in 2001 the life-expectancy gap between white males and African American males had narrowed to 6.4 years; between white females and African American females, 4.7 years. The continuance of the gap in the survival chances of whites and African American is the outcome of the public neglect of the health care needs of working-class African Americans and market forces, which condemn them to low-paid jobs and long stretches of unemployment, interspersed with prison terms, especially in the case of young male African Americans (Beardsley 1987; McBride 1989). For African Americans, however, the experience of slavery and racism in daily life may cast a long shadow. The death of enslaved Africans in middle passage occurred mainly because of dehydration. The survivors had a higher salt-retaining capacity than average. So today's African Americans may suffer more hypertension because

Table 13.7. Life Expectancy at Birth (in Years) of Whites and African Americans in the United States, Selected Years, 1900–2001

	White		African American	
Year	Male	Female	Male	Female
1900	46.6	48.7	32.5	33.5
1910	48.6	52.0	33.8	37.5
1920	54.4	55.6	45.5	45.2
1928	57.0	60.0	45.6	47.0
1930	59.7	63.5	47.3	49.2
1940	62.1	66.6	51.5	54.9
1950	66.5	72.2	59.1	62.9
1960	67.4	74.1	61.1	66.3
1970	68.0	75.6	60.0	68.3
1980	70.7	78.1	63.8	72.5
1984	71.8	78.7	65.3	73.6
1990	72.7	79.4	64.5	73.6
1994	73.3	79.6	64.9	73.9
2001	75.0	80.2	68.6	75.5

hypertension-prone genes are overrepresented in their gene pool. An alternative but reinforcing factor may be that anger against everyday racism in the United States causes hypertension among them (Wilson and Grim 1992; Inikori and Engerman 1992b).

Moreover, the acceleration of financial liberalization from the 1990s seems to have put a premium on only the highly skilled and thereby increased the disparities in the average earnings of African Americans and whites. Thus according to the U.S. Census Bureau data, there were 22,844,000 high school graduates out of 76,722,000 non-Hispanic white males age 15 and above as against 3,998,000 high school graduates out of 11,821,000 African American males. The total number with professional degrees and doctorate degrees was 2,799,000 among non-Hispanic white males of the 15 and older age group as against only 128,000 among African Americans males of the same age group. It goes without saying that female educational attainments were lower among both racial groups (U.S. Census Bureau, 29 June 2004, www.census.gov/population/socdemo/education/cps2003).

NOTE

1. *The Shorter Oxford English Dictionary*, 1959. Supriya Chaudhuri (1996) has an insightful discussion of the myth of the non-European cannibal in the European Renaissance discourse.

14

Civilizing Mission and Racialization: From Native Americans to Asians

RACIALIZATION OF SUBJUGATED PEOPLES: THE NATIVE AMERICANS

When Columbus and his companions first encountered the Tainos and the other peoples of the Caribbean, they meant to trade with them. Unfortunately, however, apart from iron goods and weapons of a kind that the Tainos had not encountered before, they had very little to sell. So they took forcibly what they wanted. Naturally the situation turned ugly and the first steps were taken toward the extermination of these peoples (Seed 1993). The Spanish sovereigns had reconquered the whole of Spain from the Moorish kingdoms by the middle of the fifteenth century. They had also conquered the Canary Islands from the Guanches, the original inhabitants of the islands. The conquerors saw their mission as one of Christianizing the conquered, while enserfing them to Spanish overlords and exterminating those who did not see eye to eye with their civilizing mission (Parry 1973, chapter 1). The Roman Catholic Church set up the Inquisition to test the genuineness of the conversion of the heathen and eliminate heretical tendencies, and the conquered peoples suffered the horrors depicted in various contemporary paintings.

The Spanish legitimacy for the conquest of the Americas was based on papal bulls issued by Alexander VI, who was himself a Spaniard. (A similar justification for the conquest of Ireland by the Norman kings of England had been provided in 1154–1155 by Pope Adrian IV, himself an Englishman, although Ireland was already a Christian country [Simms 1989, p. 56].) In 1493 after the return of Columbus from the Caribbean, the most important of the bulls, *Inter caetera*, was issued. It drew "an imaginary boundary line from north to south a hundred leagues west of the Azores and Cape Verde Islands, and provided that the land and sea beyond the line should be a Spanish sphere of exploration. . . . The bulls of 1493 constituted for Spaniards the basic legal claim of the Spanish Crown to the lands of the New World" (Parry 1973, pp. 22–23). In 1494 the two kingdoms signed the Treaty of Tordesillas, which gave to the Portuguese most of the islands of the south Atlantic, the soon-to-be-explored land of Brazil and the monopoly of exploring the route to India round Africa.

Portugal had a long history of slave raiding on the Moorish kingdoms of North Africa and farther down the western African coast. They had been accused of enslaving even the Christianized Guanches of the south Atlantic. Justification for enslaving black Africans, or "Ethiopians," was often found in their supposed descent from Ham, who was cursed by Noah because he had found Noah in an uncovered state (Boxer 1973a, chapter 11; Stocking 1987; Blackburn 1997). From time to time, there were attempts by some theologians and some high officials such as Pombal to end legal discrimination against non-European subjects of the Portuguese Crown, but in general purity of blood was retained as a condition for obtaining any respectable position in the secular or religious establishment within the Portuguese empire.

Conquest of an alien people almost at once led to the stigmatization of the conquered as inferior beings, as happened to the exterminated Caribs, whose memory was desecrated with accusations of cannibalism down the centuries. Jews, Moors, and non-Christians in general were generally depicted as inferior races in the medieval European literature, although many theologians contested this depiction.[1] The racialization had no operative impact on non-European peoples until the European powers were able to use their prowess in warfare to subjugate peoples of other continents. Moreover, this did not happen at the same time in all the continents. Hence the pattern of racialization also varied over time.

Soon after the Spanish conquest of the Caribbean islands and much of mainland America, Fray Francisco de Vitoria argued that papal authority could not be invoked to justify the conquest of the peaceful Americans living under the rule of their own princes: the pope might authorize a Christian prince to use armed force to protect missionaries but that would not amount to the authorization of war or conquest (Parry 1973, p. 126; Pagden and Lawrence, "Introduction," in Vitoria 1991). Vitoria ultimately fell back on the inadequacy of Amerindian institutions—as evidence of which their alleged practices of cannibalism and human sacrifice were commonly cited by Europeans—to provide a weak justification for Spanish dominion over the Americas and the Amerindians (Parry 1973, pp. 126–29; Pagden 1986, pp. 67–80). But these arguments also provided the rationale for Amerindians to be treated as children needing to be educated by more civilized people (Pagden 1986, chapter 4).

I have referred in chapter 13 to the debate about the justification or otherwise of enslaving the Amerindians between Fray Bartolomé de Las Casas, the so-called apostle of the Indians, and Juan Ginés de Sepúlveda, a famous humanist, who argued for the legitimacy of enslavement. Las Casas, a Dominican friar, had a long experience as a settler and then a priest in Spanish America. Sepúlveda, on the other hand, had never set foot on lands across the Atlantic, and argued, like James Mill three centuries later, that direct empirical knowledge was not needed to pronounce on the state of society of non-European peoples.[2] The famous debate at Valladolid in 1550–1551 between Las Casas and Sepúlveda (Pagden 1986, p. 108) appealed to two different theories of the constitution of the state and the duties of the sovereign as well as to the supposedly natural state of the Amerindians and their mental capacities. Las Casas appealed to a theory of kingship, under which only the king or his specifically authorized agents had power over his subjects, and no other subjects had any powers of dominion over his subjects. The Amerindians were subjects of the Spanish Crown and, therefore, enjoyed the same rights as other subjects of the Crown. Except in special cases, subjects of the Crown could not be enslaved, and this prohibition applied to the Amerindians as well as to the true-born Spaniards, especially after the Amerindians had obtained the benefit of the Gospel (Parry 1973, pp. 129–32; Pagden 1986, chapters 2–3). Sepúlveda, on the other hand, appealed to Aristotle's formulation (Aristotle 1988, p. 2) that there were natural slaves as well as natural masters and to a theory of the state under which the authority of the sovereign is mediated by an aristocracy of natural masters. He argued that Amerindians were by nature slaves, and permanent tutelage under the oversight of the natural masters, the settlers and conquerors from Spain, was the right condition of civil existence for them (Parry 1973, pp. 133–38).

In theory, Las Casas won the debate, not least because his arguments strengthened the claims of royal authority over the settlers and their descendants, the criollos. The Spanish Crown treated the Amerindians as free subjects, restricted the power of the *encomendaros* who were entitled to receive tribute from Amerindians, and appointed *corregidores*, who were supposed to look after the interests of the Amerindian subjects (Bagchi 1982, pp. 48–49). In practice, the condition of the Amerindians approximated to that of legal serfs of the Spanish Crown, which distributed them to the service of royal projects, such as literally killing labor in the silver mines, road construction, and so on, and also to favored private Spaniards and criollos.

The prohibition of enslavement became the only pragmatic policy when it was realized that Amerindians were dying out fast and their indefinite enslavement would seriously damage royal projects. A major plank of those who would permit the enslavement of the Africans while opposing the enslavement of the Amerindians was that the former were not subjects of the Spanish Crown and that they had already been enslaved when they were imported into Spanish America. Las Casas, who had condoned in 1516 enslaving the Africans on the grounds that they suffered less than the native Americans under the harsh treatment meted out to them by their masters, is said to have bitterly regretted this connivance in his old age (Blackburn 1997, p. 136).

In the period around the Spanish conquest of the Americas, serfdom was widely prevalent in Spain, although slavery was supposed to have virtually disappeared in northern Spain. But Muslims in the territories wrested from the Moorish kingdoms were frequently enslaved, and slaves were also obtained as trade goods from North Africa and other regions bordering the Mediterranean (Parry 1973; Blackburn 1997, pp. 49–54). Portugal conformed to the same pattern; moreover, Portugal was further ahead in the capture or purchase of slaves from Africa and the conquest of islands in the Atlantic to the west of the Iberian kingdoms (Boxer 1973a).

It has been suggested that the failure to recognize other human beings living under different conditions as kin was responsible for their treatment as the horrible Other (cf. Pagden 1986, chapter 1). However, treating the unfamiliar as the Other does not always lead to their demonization or dehumanization. For example, the native peoples of Africa and the Americas encountering Europeans for the first time often treated them as miraculous beings, if not gods. It is the desire and the ability of particular groups of Europeans (or for that matter, the Japanese aggressors in Korea and China) to dominate that led to the construction of an uncivilized Other needing the healing or enlightening tutelage of the dominant group (Allen 1994; Roediger 1991).

One of the best illustrations of this occurs in the case of the treatment of the Irish people by successive English governments, after the Norman conquest of Ireland. Ireland was the oldest colony of Britain. But before the reign of Queen Elizabeth I of England, the English settlers in Ireland more or less became part of the dominant culture. The religious divide between Protestant England and Roman Catholic Ireland became much sharper after the consolidation of a capitalist nation-state in England. The Irish were racialized by the English, and as the Irish broke out in revolts, English oppression intensified. After the defeat of the Irish by William of Orange, who became king of England after the so-called Glorious Revolution, the Catholic Irish were subjected to penal laws that have very few parallels in history (Burke 1760–1765/1988; Lecky 1912, chapter 2). The Irish migrated to the United States en masse after the great famine of 1845–1850, which wiped out a million of the Irish population under a laissez-faire regime even when Ireland was legally part of the United Kingdom, economically and politically the most powerful nation of the time. Unfortunately, many of the Irish adopted the racialist attitude of the U.S. conservatives toward blacks, even though they had suffered what amounted to English racism directed toward them. (Please see appendix 2, available on the Rowman & Littlefield website at www.rowmanlittlefield.com/ISBN/0742539202, for further details.) The racist attitude of the ruling coterie in Israel toward Arabs provides a tragic parallel in our own times of victims of racism themselves turning racist.

UNIVERSALIST CLAIMS OF THE ENLIGHTENMENT DISCOURSE VERSUS SCIENTIFIC RACISM

One of the most remarkable statements of universalist values of the European Enlightenment was penned by Montesquieu:

> If I knew something useful to me, but prejudicial to my family, I would reject it from my mind. If I knew something useful to my family, but not to my country, I would try to forget it. If I knew something useful to my country but prejudicial to Europe, or useful to Europe and prejudicial to the human race, I would regard it as criminal. (Charles, Baron de Montesquieu, *Pensees*, as translated and cited by Gay 1969, p. 38)

But along with these universalist premises there were inegalitarian tendencies in many strands of the Enlightenment discourse. The same thinker could be egalitarian in one respect and consciously or unconsciously harbor discriminatory assumptions in another part of the argument. Rousseau, for example, traced the origin of inequality among human beings to the invention of private property and civil society rather than to any innate differences between men and men. However, in his ideal society, the patriarchal family would serve as the basic unit, with women being subjected to the authority of men (Rousseau 1755/1984).

The conquest of Bengal in 1857, the rapid buildup of the British Indian empire, and the further prospect of conquering parts of the Ottoman Turkish domains and the immense empire of China lent a special virulence to the ideologies of imperialism, racism, and Orientalism (Curtin 1971; Said 1978, pp. 73–110; Symonds 1986; Stocking 1987). With the dawning of this phase, we have prominent figures of the Scottish and French Enlightenment as well as evangelists, prominent scientists such as Georges Cuvier and Charles Darwin, radical democrats such as James and John Stuart Mill, and defenders of the aristocratic Whig order in England providing the rationalization for various racializing and dehumanizing ideologies and drawing up projects for civilizing the non-European natives. In many of these cases the same ideologies were used to justify repressive methods of social control for civilizing the workers in their own countries.

In his *Esprit des Lois*, Montesquieu described what he considered to be the characteristics of oriental despotism and provided an environmental explanation of how it was sustained. In the era of European dominance, Montesquieu's universalist message, previously quoted, was obscured by his characterization of non-European societies. Turgot followed up Montesquieu's characterization of Asian states as Oriental despotism with the specific idea that the ease of communication and fertility of the rolling plains of Asia fostered despotism whereas broken or difficult topography fostered republics (this is not far from the hypotheses of Jones 1981/1987). Voltaire, with his contempt for the common run of *Homo sapiens,* rapidly passed from an admiration for Chinese sages to an idea that human civilizations can be hierarchically ordered with European society at the top (Stocking 1987, pp. 13–15). As European capitalism expanded its reach, European ideologies of domination also proliferated.

As I have noted earlier, Malthusianism and social Darwinism became part of the intellectual baggage of upper-class men in many countries from the nineteenth century. They provided justification not only for racist attitudes and policies but also for discrimination against poorer people everywhere in public policies, employment, and health care. Through the nineteenth century and beyond, in comparative philology, in the budding discipline of anthropology, archaeology, history, literature, art, and practically all expressions of the human mind, we have a torrent of outpourings of ideologies of white and European dominance, the civilizing mission, the white man's burden. The main currents of ideas that shaped highly discriminatory official policies in the dependent colonies can be illustrated by looking at the pronouncements of some of the most influential figures shaping British policy in India and Africa, such as James and John Stuart Mill, Thomas Babington Macaulay, Henry Sumner Maine, James Fitzjames Stephen, Evelyn Baring (later Lord Cromer), and Frederick Lugard.

IDEOLOGY OF CIVILIZING INDIA THROUGH BRITISH RULE

In some ways, James Mill stands at the head of these imperial *epigoni* because of the very comprehensiveness of his denunciation of the society, laws, and religion of India and indeed of all countries to the east of Europe. In his *History of British India* (1817/1858), Mill contested the notion, put forward earlier by Sir William Jones, that the Hindus, meaning basically the inhabitants of India or Hindustan, had attained a high standard of civilization. Mill posited that whatever advance had been made by them had occurred a long time back and that both the society and state had later stagnated into a condition of barbarism. Mill never visited India and did not know any of the Indian languages or Persian, in which much of the official business was conducted well into several decades of British rule. He justified his ignorance on the grounds that he was therefore less likely to be misled by the testimony of credulous people. In fact, Mill had constructed what Said has called an image of the Orient, and his descriptions are an elaboration of that image. His book was also an argument for a despotic style of British rule in India, in which the Indians should have as little share as possible. Not content with deploring the moribund and stagnant state of India, he accused the Indians, all 150 million of them, of criminality, debauchery, and unnatural sexual appetites.[3] He recommended that as large a proportion of the surplus produced by the land—the main source of income of Indians and government revenue—be extracted through taxation of the rent element, as the price for imposing law and order on a lawless people. But he had no proposals for educating the people. Those apostles of democracy, the Mills *pere et fils*, always treated India as a special case, to be governed in the pattern of Oriental despotism, although the supposedly evil consequences of Oriental despotism had been used as a justification for the British conquest of India.[4]

J. S. Mill had probably a more nuanced view of what civilization meant (Mill 1836/1875). But he had some curious notions of the behavior of the people he called savages (mainly hunters and gatherers, who lived in villages). He thought that they were incapable of cooperation with one another. However, the very survival of hunters and gatherers and pastoralists depended on intense cooperation with one another and often with settled agriculturists as well, particularly where transhumant or migratory pastoralism was involved. According to Mill's definition, the degree of civilization was to be judged by the ability of a particular society to deliver material prosperity (Francis 1998).

Despite such a view of civilization that would have required Indian surpluses to be invested for raising productivity, John Stuart insisted, like his father, that the government of India should cream off the surplus in the form of tribute as the price for giving the natives good government. It is no surprise that he succeeded his father as the chief examiner of the EIC's correspondence and was chosen to write a defense of the company's governance of India just before the assumption of that government by the British Crown.

Macaulay was far more astute than James or John Stuart Mill about the "civilizational" requirements of British rule in India. His famous minute (1835) on

education for Indians was aimed at producing a set of native intermediaries between the British rulers and the general populace of the country:

> We must at present do our best to form a class who may be interpreters between
> us and the millions whom we govern, a class of persons Indian in blood and
> colour, but English in tastes, in opinions, in morals and in intellect. To that class
> we may leave it to refine the vernacular dialects of the country, to enrich those
> dialects with terms of science borrowed from the Western nomenclature, and to
> render them by degrees fit vehicles for conveying knowledge to the great mass
> of the population. (Macaulay 1835, as quoted in Curtin 1971, p. 190)

This was the classical formulation of the central policy for every successful colonialism.

Although Macaulay envisaged spending more for educating this class of
brown Englishmen, he was not exactly overflowing with generosity for
achieving his purpose. As I pointed out in chapter 10, until 1813, there was
no regular provision in the budget of the EIC's government for education, and
the government had founded only two educational institutions for training jurists in the Hindu and Muslim scriptures and related laws.

The sum that Macaulay was willing to spend for achieving his grand objectives, £10,000 per annum, was the same amount that the British parliament
had directed the company to spend in 1813, at the time its charter was renewed. But he wanted the money to be diverted from the teaching of Oriental texts (which he considered to be quite worthless) to the teaching of Western literature and the sciences. It may be mentioned that in 1834 the total
amount spent on education by the company's government was a little more
than Rs400,000, or £40,000, when the total receipts of the government in
1834–1835 were more than £26.8 million and total expenditure was £16.7
million (Curtin 1971, pp. 292–93, 373). It is no wonder that India became a
country of illiterates, the glitter of a tiny educated elite hiding the educational
darkness of the vast majority.

When in 1835 Macaulay decided in favor of the Anglicists as against the
Orientalists, the program was set afoot to create a tiny corps of clerks, minor
officials, and other collaborators of British rule. The real losers in this battle
for the allocation of a derisory sum for education were the ordinary people of
India, who sank ever deeper into illiteracy (see chapter 10 for data on Indian
literacy under British rule). The civilizing mission of the metropolitan rulers
took a very similar form in other colonies, namely, ruling over an illiterate
and poverty-stricken population with the help of a small group of native collaborators, spending as little as possible on public health or education, and using exemplary brutality when people broke out in revolt.

The propaganda about the civilizing and racializing process directed toward the subjugated peoples continued throughout the period of colonialism and beyond. Sir Henry Sumner Maine became the first law member of the British Indian Viceroy's Council in 1862. He was succeeded by James Fitzjames Stephen, a close friend and, like Maine, a Tory. Maine was critical of Jeremy Bentham and his followers for their failure to recognize the influence of history and customs on law (Feaver 1991). In his *Ancient Law* (1861) and *Village-Communities in the East and West* (1871), Maine advanced the proposition that the surviving communal and customary institutions in India showed how the comparable European institutions worked in earlier centuries. In his speeches he was eloquent about the responsibilities of a progressive race to oversee the steady administration of the rule of law in a hitherto stationary society, meaning India (Feaver 1991, p. 45). A defender of private property, in his Rede Lecture of 1875, he advanced the view "that 'nobody is at liberty to attack several property and say at the same time that he values civilization'" (Burrow 1991, p. 60).

The racialization of the conquered peoples became part of the common sense of the ruling classes. When in the 1850s there was a move to grant the Indian subjects of the British rulers the same legal rights as were enjoyed by the British, it was opposed by virtually all European residents of India. The crux of their argument was admirably phrased by Theodore Dickens, a practicing barrister:

[You Indians] are one of the conquered race, who have, therefore, no original and strictly political right to be well-governed; you are at the mercy of the conquerors. But I am one of a nation who have their rights guaranteed by such things as Magna Carta, the Bill of Rights, the Act of Settlement and a few other conditions, upon whose due and faithful observance by the Crown my allegiance to it depends. I cannot, therefore, allow that you are politically my equal. (Dickens 1857 as quoted by Bose 1981, p. 101)

In the 1880s, Sir Courtenay Ilbert, a successor to Maine and Stephen as the law member of the Viceroy's Council, introduced a bill that sought to bring Europeans as well as Indians under the jurisdiction of duly appointed legal officers of the British Indian government, overturning the earlier practice of allowing Europeans to be tried only by European magistrates and judges. Both in India and Britain, the whole European community mobilized against the bill, and the government was forced to withdraw it. Stephen allied himself with the protesters and wrote in a letter to the *Times* of London, dated 1 March 1883,

[The Government of India] is essentially an absolute Government founded not on consent, but on conquest. It does not represent the native principles of life or government, and it can never do so until it represents heathenism and barbarism. It represents a belligerent civilization, and no anomaly can be so striking and dangerous as its administration by men who, being at the head of a Government founded on conquest, implying at every point the superiority of the conquering race, of their ideas, their institutions, their opinions and their principles, and having no justification for its existence except that superiority, shrink from the open, uncompromising, straightforward assertion of it, seek to apologize for their own position, and refuse from whatever cause, to uphold and support it. (quoted by Sinha 1995, pp. 39–40)

The imperial proconsuls often traveled from one colonial posting to another and that journey only reinforced their racialist prejudices. Evelyn Baring, later Lord Cromer, had been finance member of the Viceroy's Council in India and had there earned his sobriquet of "Overbaring." He then became more or less the supreme ruler of Egypt, under successive British administrations. In his account of Egypt under British rule (Baring 1908, vol. 2, as cited by Said 1978, p. 38), quoting Sir Alfred Lyall, another and earlier proconsul of British India, he wrote: "Sir Alfred Lyall once said to me: 'Accuracy is abhorrent to the Oriental mind. Every Anglo-Indian should always remember that maxim.' Want of accuracy, which easily degenerates into untruthfulness, is in fact the main characteristic of the Oriental mind" (Baring 1908, vol. 2, p. 164).

But, of course, the imagination of the middle-class European demanded the clothing of naked power in garments of love. For this purpose, history was worked over repeatedly to create new legends, and new tales were told not only of the glories of the Raj but also of the loyalty displayed by the civilized native. Espionage and skullduggery acquired a new romantic halo, for example, in Kipling's novel *Kim* (1901). In the justly forgotten opera of Giacomo Meyerbeer and Eugene Scribe *L'Africaine* (1865), we have a Vasco da Gama rescuing an Indo-African Queen Selika from the slavers. Selika promptly falls in love with Vasco, and when Vasco, a Christian, is about to be slaughtered by vengeful Brahmins after he had been shipwrecked, Selika gives out that they are already betrothed and thus saves him. But in the same scene, Vasco becomes reunited with his real love, the Portuguese lady Ines, and Selika gives Vasco up to her and dies in a final celebration of pure love. Thus Vasco's heroism and nobility of character are celebrated, the propensity of high-born non-Europeans to fall in love with European adventurers is recalled again (remember Pocahontas and John Smith?), the purity of blood is preserved, and the principle is established that true love, if it happens between Europeans will be rewarded in this life but the love of others for a European can be consummated only in God's embrace (Subrahmanyam 1997, pp. 1–6).

EUROPEAN CONQUEST OF AFRICA AND
THE CIVILIZING MISSION

The European powers embarked on the conquest of mainland Africa after the slave trade ended. This drive attained a crescendo in the last three decades of the nineteenth century. The Portuguese had been in nominal occupation of some territories from the sixteenth century, but they had been used more as trading outposts and bases for slave raiding than as plantations or colonies of exploitation. The scramble for Africa had its roots in interimperialist rivalry for getting hold of the resources of the continent, for protecting, in the case of the British, the route to India against rival powers, and for exploiting the markets. The scramble led also to the Anglo-Boer war, starting in 1898. This was triggered by not just the imperial ambitions of adventurers like Cecil Rhodes but also the British need to control the richest veins of gold that would sustain London's financial supremacy in the era of the international gold standard (Ally 2001). With the British and French conquest of most of Sub-Saharan, central, eastern, and southern Africa, there was a new outpouring of speeches and writings on the objectives and methods of the civilizing mission in Africa.

One of the most influential formulations of the methods of European rule over African populations and the associated civilizing methods occurred in the dispatches and writings of Frederick, Lord Lugard, the imperial proconsul in Nigeria under the British (see especially Lugard 1929; Curtin 1971, pp. 234–68). Faced with a densely populated country with earlier structures of states, Lugard formulated a theory of indirect rule, something that the British rulers had already practiced in the territories under the nominal rule of the so-called native princes of India and in most parts of the Indian countryside under direct British jurisdiction. Keeping many of the erstwhile rulers, particularly those who had displayed a spirit of submissive collaboration with the British, would economize on the costs of administration, conciliate the general populace, and preserve existing structures of social control. Lugard wanted Africans to be educated but only up to a standard at which a few of them could act as intermediaries between the British officials and the ordinary people. In particular, he did not want to train up a set of discontented intellectuals who might threaten the very endurance of British rule. In the interest of trouble-free rule, Lugard and his successors tolerated slavery in Nigeria down to the 1930s, although the need to end the slave trade and, less emphatically, slavery had been part of the justification of the conquest of Nigeria by the British in the first place (Lovejoy and Hogendorn 1993). Not only were many of the old structures of unfreedom preserved under the complaisant eyes of the European merchants and officials of the ruling powers but, in many cases, new structures of bondage were forged under Western supervision.

NOTES

1. See in this connection papers from the symposium on European racist ideology in *The William and Mary Quarterly*, third series, 54(1), January 1997, with contributions by David Brion Davis, A. T. and Virginia M. Vaughn, Emily C. Bartels, Robin Blackburn, J. H. Sweet, and Jennifer L. Morgan; for a linguistic study of stereotyping see Tista Bagchi 1999.

2. The irony was, of course, that Sepúlveda was supposed to be armed with the new knowledge of the humanists, and James Mill was a radical and a founder of democratic political theory. One can see how Said (1978) arrived at his transhistorical concept of Orientalism as constructed by the Europeans, however undialectical that conceptualization may be (cf. Ahmad 1992, chapter 5).

3. James Mill was severely taken to task for his mistakes of fact, his deliberate ignorance, and his biased judgments by his editor, the great Sankritist, Horace Hayman Wilson (see "Preface" by Wilson, in Mill 1817/1858, vol. 1, pp. vii–xxxvi, and his running footnotes on Mill's text).

4. James Mill's evidence tendered in 1831 and 1832 before the Select Committee of the Parliament on East India Affairs showed him to be even more authoritarian in his view of how India was to be ruled (Mill 1831, 1831–1832a, and 1831–1832b; Barber 1975, chapter 10).

15

Civilizing Mission in Lands Taken by European Settlers from the Original Inhabitants

Norbert Elias, whose idea of the civilizing process has been used by many as a motif for state formation and control in Europe and by Europeans elsewhere, was himself a victim of the Nazi terror. When writing about the recent history of the Germans (Elias 1989/1996), he deplored the breakdown of civilization, which he saw as the primary cause of the emergence of the Nazis. But the racist underpinning of the Nazi terror was an extreme form of a kind of civilizing ideology shared by European nations in their encounters with, and establishment of colonial rule over, non-European peoples. Entire peoples were dehumanized in the name of race, their labor was forcibly extracted, and hundreds of thousands were exterminated or uprooted when they proved obstreperous or when their removal was necessary for allowing the European settlers to grab their land. As Frantz Fanon emphasized, settler colonialism was based on the naked use of violence as a systemic feature (Fanon 1961/1967).

I have already briefly sketched the character of the civilizing mission mounted by the Spaniards in the territories they conquered in the Americas. It remained basically a paternalistic despotism, seeking to preserve many of the older structures of social control and keeping most Indians in place, for the sake of securing their labor and tribute. The Indian communities were transformed but not destroyed (Wolf 1982, pp. 145–49). This strategy proved most successful where Amerindians had already created centralized state structures with settled agriculturists at the base of exploitation. As the Spaniards went farther north or moved east from the tributary domains of the Aztecs, they encountered looser state formations and populations that combined hunting and gathering with agriculture, or more properly, horticulture.

The Spaniards then had to rely on less formal methods of control, depending on negotiation and conciliation through trade and the giving of gifts (Adelman and Aron 1999).

Approaches that left local tenure relations more or less intact were shared in varying degrees by the French, and to some extent, the English, down to the middle of the eighteenth century. But after the victory of the British over the French in the Seven Years' War (1756–1763), European settlers increasingly sought the land themselves. Thereafter, the history of the native peoples of the Americas became mainly a story of dispossession, desperate resistance, further dispossession and displacement, further bouts of extermination, miraculous survival of small groups, and slow recovery in residual pockets of territory from the middle of the twentieth century (Brown 1970, 1994; Wolf 1982, chapter 6; Diamond 1992; Dickason 1992; Green 1996; Salisbury 1996; O'Brien 1997). The story of the dispossession of the native inhabitants by European settlers was repeated also in eastern and southern Africa, Australia, and New Zealand and assumed grim proportions in the nineteenth century.

The difference between the grabbing of land for settlers by the European powers in the Americas and Australia and their different strategies for controlling the resources of the natives in India, China, and Southeast Asia had a number of reasons behind it. The most important, perhaps, was that the Asian countries had more developed state structures and were more densely populated, and it was much more economical to extract a profit from them by using and adapting the earlier structures than by resorting to wholesale slaughter. Second, except for north China, most of the Asian lands had tropical or subtropical climates, which were unattractive to potential migrants from Europe. Settler colonies grew up primarily in regions with temperate climates, including, for example, the Kenya highlands populated by whites.

In eastern and northeastern North America, the native populations such as the members of the confederacy who came to be known as the Iroquois had not developed centralized state structures (Wolf 1982, p. 165). The spread of European microbes at once led to a fall in the Iroquois and other native populations of the eastern seaboard of an estimated 50 percent (Adelman and Aron 1999; O'Brien 1997). As the native peoples became involved in trade relations with the European traders, they came to specialize in particular products, such as fur and tobacco, and often gave up their traditional subsistence horticulture, consisting typically of a combination of corn, beans, and squash, the so-called three sisters (Dickason 1992). The Amerindians welcomed the iron tools, kettles, and other household goods brought by the Europeans. But the advent of the Europeans changed more than the pattern of specialization for the Amerindians.

Even before the arrival of the Europeans, the different Amerindian nations had been engaged in competition and occasional warfare for the control of cultivable land, hunting and fishing grounds, and water bodies. Moreover, the different Amerindian nations were caught up in the interstate conflicts of the European powers. For a time, the former managed to retain some autonomy and most of their land because the Europeans needed allies among the native peoples. But as the intra-European conflict was resolved in favor of the British and colonists from Britain, the century and a half of relative Amerindian autonomy ended and they were mercilessly pushed out of their lands, hunted down like wild animals, and confined to reservations.

The example of the Huron will serve as an illustration of the way the fate of the Amerindian nations was settled by intra-European struggles. Up to the 1640s, they were the main trading partners and allies of the French. The Huron were not just hunter-gatherers but farmers as well. The Huron and their allies soon became embroiled in rivalry and endemic warfare with the Iroquois confederacy for hunting grounds and the major share of the fur trade. The French tried not only to trade with the Huron but also to settle them in villages and Christianize them (Dickason 1992, p. 127). However, the Amerindians resented the attempt to eliminate their communal ceremonials. Many missionaries allowed the observance of those rituals to their Christian converts that were judged not to violate the basic tenets of Christianity. In 1634 smallpox began killing the Montagnais, another native people in the Great Lakes region and soon affected the Huron: "Within four years two-thirds of the latter were gone." (Dickason 1992, p. 129).

The Iroquois confederacy had access to both the Dutch and the English for trade and the supply of arms. They were victorious against the Huron in the seventeenth century. But the Iroquois were pushed out of their hunting grounds by English settlers, and different groups within the confederacy found themselves divided when European powers came into conflict (Wolf 1982, pp. 165–70).

The trend in English territories since the arrival of the Pilgrim Fathers of the Protestant Englishmen was one of ruthless grabbing of Amerindian lands. Once the French lost Quebec in the Seven Years' War and ceded the whole of the area above the Great Lakes, the fate of the Amerindians was sealed. In the American Revolution many of the Amerindian peoples sided with the British, because they saw the imperial government in London as a restraining influence on settler expansionism. They paid dearly for this. The Cherokees, for example, attacked backcountry settlements in the summer of 1776. These produced devastating retaliatory attacks by armies from Virginia and the Carolinas. "While many people fell before them, the invaders did most of their damage against the villages, homes, and granaries of the Cherokees. Soldiers burned fifty towns, and tens of thousands of bushels of corn and beans; they cut or burned hundreds of acres of fields and orchards, and killed or confiscated several hundred heads of livestock. Such destruction drove many thousands of Cherokee people into the forested Appalachians to eke out a subsistence on nuts, wild plants, and game" (Green 1996, p. 463).

With the birth of the United States, the Amerindians were pushed from their dwelling places again and again, and were hunted down when they resisted this policy (Brown 1970, 1994). European arrogation of authority to decide the fate of non-Europeans again played its role in handing over Amerindian peoples to the tender mercies of the settlers and the U.S. army. When the Amerindian nations entered into treaties with European powers, they thought that they were allowing the foreigners only rights of use of some of their land. But the foreigners interpreted it as the surrender of their whole land (Merchant 2002, p. 27). By the Peace Treaty of Paris, which concluded the U.S. Revolutionary War, the new nation acquired sovereign rights over the vast territory bounded by the Great Lakes to the north, the Mississippi river to the west, and Spanish Florida to the south (Green 1996, p. 465). As the European settlers pushed the Amerindians farther and farther west, and did not spare even those like the Cherokee who had become civilized by European criteria, many of them tried to resist that relentless expropriation of all their rights. But that resistance was ruthlessly suppressed. Even the attempt of John Marshall, the celebrated chief justice of the United States, to protect their legal rights was spurned by the U.S. administration (Merchant 2002, chapter 5).

The attitude of the colonists and the Founding Fathers of the United States toward the rights of African Americans and American Indians between the eighteenth and nineteenth centuries was pitted with contradictions. On the one hand, the Constitution embodied the declaration of the rights of all men (Tocqueville 1848/1964; Du Bois 1935/1992, chapter 1). On the other hand, prize money was regularly paid by the thirteen state governments or the federal government for scalps of Amerindians, including those of women and children (Diamond 1992, chapter 16, appendix).[1]

The Amerindians were in effect pushed back to levels of civilization below those they had attained before the arrival of the Europeans. In desperation Amerindian warriors raided European settlements. In return, U.S. army men and free-ranging adventurers killed Amerindian groups like vermin. This was a war of a powerful modern state against groups of retreating survivors, and there were many acts of savagery, especially on the winning side. In 1868, for example, Colonel George Armstrong Custer, commanding the Seventh Cavalry unit of the U.S. army, wiped out an entire Cheyenne village (Brown 1994, p, 414).

In 1889–1890, a millenarian movement for restoration of the world before the advent of the white man swept through the Amerindian peoples, and the U.S. government sent the army in to quell the movement. An aged Chief Sitting Bull, then leading a peaceful life, was killed while being arrested in 1890. Big Foot, chief of the Sioux, tried to move his group to Pine Ridge Reservation but was intercepted by a 500-strong U.S. army unit at Wounded Knee Creek, on 29 December 1890. After demanding surrender, the army began firing and killed 153 Sioux, more than half of them women and children (Brown 1970, chapters 18–19). By the end of the nineteenth century, the process of civilizing the Amerindian peoples by exterminating them or confining them to impoverished or marginal lands as reservations was more or less complete.

The Amerindian peoples fared better, but not much better, in Canada. For a start, Canada's interior was much more forbidding from a climatic point of view and most settlers headed toward the United States rather than British America.[2] The British administration had also pursued, partly in emulation of and competition with the French, a policy of negotiation—offering gifts and signing treaties with the natives for taking over their land. These treaties had no validity in European international law, because they were not between recognized sovereign states, nor did they even have validity in the eyes of the British parliament, because they were not ratified by it. Moreover, in 1763 when a proclamation was made with the formal surrender of French Canada to the British and in 1783 when peace was concluded recognizing the independence of the thirteen colonies forming the United States, the contending powers extinguished all the treaty rights of the Amerindians. In a landmark case, *St. Catherine's Milling v. The Queen*, ultimately decided by the British Privy Council in 1888, it was held that the underlying right to all Indian land was held by the Crown and could be extinguished by the decision of the competent authorities of the government of Canada. It was typical that in a case that vitally affected the livelihood and rights of all the Amerindian peoples, it was not considered necessary to consult any of them (Kulchyski 1994, chapter 1).

The idea of civilizing the natives continued to affect the fate of native peoples in Canada as in other regions of European dominance. The fact of Amerindian decimation through contact and conflict was used in Canada as in the United States as an argument for confining them to reserves (Dickason 1992, p. 225). From 1879 to 1986, the Canadian government ran a system of residential schools for children of native peoples. The aim of this system was "violent in its intention, to 'kill the Indian' in the child" (Molloy 1999, pp. xiv–xv). The children were taken away from their parents and made to forget their own language. Many died of infectious diseases sweeping through badly constructed living places. They also died of malnutrition because many of the missionaries stole the funds and kept the children on short rations (Molloy 1999, chapter 5).

Whole groups of people died as a result of contact with the Europeans. The Caribs disappeared in Hispaniola, the Beothuks in Newfoundland, and the Yahi tribe were killed off by the Californian settlers between 1853 and 1870 (Diamond 1992, pp. 270–71). One of the cruelest and best-recorded acts of genocide was carried out by white settlers in Tasmania in the 1820s and 1830s (Stocking 1987; Reynolds 1992; Diamond 1992). This case of brutality was paralleled, among others, by the deliberate slaughter of the San people (known to the Europeans as Bushmen) in South Africa by Dutch and British settlers (Sparks 1991, pp. 10–12).

The inhabitants of Tasmania, known to the Europeans at the time as Van Dieman's Island, had been cut off from the mainland of Australia for an esti-mated 1,000 years and had probably the least advanced technology among all human groups in the world (Diamond 1998, pp. 312–13). They had their first contact with the Europeans in 1772, but a longer exposure occurred in 1802. Francois Peron, the self-styled anthropologist of that expedition, later de-scribed the Tasmanians as "the realization of those brilliant descriptions of happiness and simplicity of the state of nature of which I had so many times in reading felt the seductive charm" (quoted in Stocking 1987, p. 275). A group of settlers was sent out next year by the British authorities, who founded Hobart Town, the capital of Tasmania today. The settlers included twenty-four "incorrigible" convicts, and they inflicted inhuman cruelties on the natives, such as "killing them for their women, or to feed their own dogs, even roasting them alive" (Stocking 1987, p. 276). From 1820 a more sys-tematic hunting down and killing of the natives was put into operation. The editor of the *Colonial Times* in 1826 advocated the removal of the natives by the government or destroying them like wild beasts. "The following July the *Times* reported the killing and wounding of sixty Tasmanians in retaliation for a settler's murder; in another incident that year a party of constables trapped a 'mob' of seventy among some rocks, 'dragging the women and children from crevices . . . and *dashing out their brains*'" (italics in original; Stocking 1987, p. 277).

The Tasmanians fought bravely with their primitive weapons against these civilized brutes and in a few years had dispatched 150–200 of the settlers (Reynolds 1992, p. 89). With the help of a missionary, George Augustus Robinson, the government removed in 1831 some 200 Tasmanians, the only known survivors, to Flinders Island, where the Tasmanians just dropped off like flies. When the last man, William Lanner, "died in 1869, competing teams of physicians, led by Dr George Stokell from the Royal Society of Tas-mania and Dr. W. L. Crowther of the Royal College of Surgeons, alternatively dug up and reburied Lanner's body, cutting off parts of it and stealing them back and forth from each other" (Diamond 1998, p. 253). All this was done in the name of science and progress because the doctors wanted to see whether the Tasmanians could be a missing link between apes and true men!

At around the same period, at the other end of the Eastern Hemisphere, the final act was being played out in the extermination of the San and the Khoikhoi peoples of southern Africa. Ever since 1652, when a group of Dutchmen under the command of Jan van Riebeeck decided to set up an outpost at the Cape of Good Hope for the victualing of VOC ships, they had come into conflict with the cattle-grazing Khoikhoi and the hunter-gatherer San peoples in that region. The Dutch settlers took away the grazing and the hunting grounds of the Khoikhoi and the San, confiscated the meat and the cattle, and relentlessly pushed them inland as they occupied more and more of their land (Boxer 1973b, chapter 9; Sparks 1991, chapters 1–2). The British acquired the Cape Colony from the Dutch during the Napoleonic Wars and retained it at the time of the post-Napoleonic peace treaty. In 1820 the British authorities allowed the immigration of 20,000 British settlers into the colony, and the competition for land among the Boers intensified further (Oliver and Atmore 1981, chapter 5; Sparks 1991, chapter 3). Their treatment of the San was vividly recorded by Thomas Pringle, a journalist who accompanied the British settlers. Pringle quoted the testimony of a Boer farmer who was part of a commando force out hunting bushmen (i.e., San):

> When the firing ceased, five women were still found living. The lives of these, after a long discussion, it was resolved to spare, because one farmer wanted a servant for this purpose, and another for that. The unfortunate wretches were ordered to march in front of the commando; but it was soon found that they impeded our progress—not being able to proceed fast enough. They were, therefore, ordered to be shot. . . . The helpless victims, perceiving what was intended, sprung to us, and clung so firmly to some of the party, that it was for some time impossible to shoot them without hazarding the lives of those they held fast. Four of them were at length despatched; but the fifth could by no means be torn from one of our comrades, whom she had grasped in her agony; and his entreaties to be allowed to take this woman home were at last complied with. (Thomas Pringle, *Narrative of a Residence in South Africa*, Cape Town, 1966, p. 226, as quoted by Sparks 1991, p. 11)

The Boers may perhaps be blamed for their fundamentalist beliefs as Calvinists and racists (Oliver and Atmore 1981, pp. 53–54; Brink 1991). But educated Europeans, imbued with ideals of civilizing the natives, also followed policies that almost invariably aided dispossession and, in some cases, decimation of those natives. To take an example almost at random, Sir George Grey, who grew up in an evangelical circle and wrote an ethnographic account of Australian Aborigines, proved his prowess as a civilizer by depriving the Maoris and the Xhosas of thousands of acres of their land in his two stints as governor of New Zealand and a stint as governor of Cape Colony and high commissioner for South Africa (Stocking 1987, pp. 81–87; Gump 1998). There was method in the kind of "naïve humanitarianism" displayed by Grey, because this kind of policy created a proletarianized and in most cases unfree labor force to be used by European farmers, mine owners, and planters. When Grey managed to quell a resistance movement among the Xhosas (taking advantage of a famine raging in their territory), he indentured nearly 30,000 Xhosas for work in the Cape Colony and forcibly opened up the territory of Chief Sarhili as well as British Kaffraria to white settlement (Gump 1998, p. 100).

As I have mentioned, the overseas migration of Europeans had beneficial effects on the people who stayed back. The greatest beneficiary of the overseas migrations of Europeans and the foreign investments made by the European powers, however, was the United States. As we have seen, the settler government there also cleared the land for European population by systematically dispossessing and exterminating the Indians. But the clearing and settling were also aided by resource transfers from nonwhite dependencies of the Europeans. We turn to an analysis of that process in the next chapter.

NOTES

1. Diamond cites statements of Benjamin Franklin and George Washington regarding Amerindians that are worth quoting (Diamond 1992, p. 277). Franklin: "If it be the Design of Providence to Extirpate these Savages in order to make room for Cultivators of the Earth, it seems not improbable that Rum may be the appointed means." Jefferson: "This unfortunate race, whom we had been taking so much pains to save and to civilize, have by their unexpected desertion and ferocious barbarities justified extermination and now await our decision on their fate."

2. For vivid descriptions of the problems faced by the settlers in the first half of the nineteenth century, see the firsthand accounts of the Strickland sisters (Traill 1836/1989; Moodie 1852/1989).

16

Intercontinental Resource Flows Sustaining the Ascent of the European Powers

INTERCONTINENTAL RESOURCE FLOWS IN THE AGE OF MERCHANT CAPITAL

The marauding European traders and conquerors used a variety of instruments for transferring resources from other continents and increasing the profits of capitalists and the financial and military resources of the European powers. As I noted earlier, until the end of the eighteenth century, Europeans had very little to sell to the Asians. But they wanted Indian textiles and Chinese tea—the latter in ever-increasing quantities. Some of the payments were made out of profits in intra-Asian trade, but a large fraction still consisted of payments in silver and gold. (It was more silver than gold, partly because the price of silver in relation to gold was higher in Asia than in Europe.) But the Dutch paid very little for what they obtained from Indonesia, because most of the spices and coffee were obtained directly or indirectly as colonial tribute. The British conquered Bengal in 1757 and by 1799 they had conquered most of southern and northern India. The EIC then ceased to ship bullion to India, for it obtained its so-called investments simply as tribute. The tribute extracted from Bengal has been estimated as anywhere between 5 and 10 percent of the gross domestic product of that province (Bagchi 1973a; Habib 1975/1995). The payments for Chinese tea and silks were effected by sending bullion, cotton, and increasingly opium from Britain's Indian possessions (Bagchi 1982, chapter 4). Down to the 1780s, the slave-run plantations in the Caribbean were also a major source of profit to England. In 1774 it was estimated by Edward Long, a leading West Indian planter, that the annual income of Great Britain from trade with Jamaica alone was £1.25 million (Long 1774, p. 507, as quoted by Sheridan 1965, table 9). England also possessed the intra-European colony of Ireland, another source of the imperial surplus.

The British drive for securing paramountcy in the whole of India after they had conquered Bengal led to the deaths of thousands of people in direct conflicts and many more in the dislocation caused to communications, supply lines, and husbandry. Following a policy of forcing "subsidiary alliance" on those Indian rulers whose territories they did not occupy directly, the alien conquerors forced the latter to station British troops on their own territory and pay a tribute ("subsidy") for the upkeep of the troops. The troops became instruments in the hands of the British for keeping watch over their allies and for annexing their territory if the ruler proved restive under the British yoke or was unable to pay the subsidy (Majumdar, Raychaudhuri, and Datta 1978, pp. 668–764). The British rulers used the British Indian army, kept at the expense of the Indians, to quell any rebellious tendencies among Indians, protect their other allies in Asia, and sustain an aggressive stance against other powers in Africa and central Asia. Self-ransoming became one of the devices for continued extraction of a tribute from the protected peoples. Meanwhile, with the help of slave labor, and capital and credit extended by England and other European countries, the economy of the thirteen colonies of Britain in North America forged ahead as an overseas extension of European dominion (Solow and Engerman 1992).

By the last quarter of the nineteenth century, all of Africa (barring Ethiopia) was finally brought under European dominion. Excepting Japan and a few nominally independent states, and the mainland of China, all of Asia was reduced to a vassal status by the major European powers. In Latin America, formal Spanish and Portuguese rule was ended but the regimes that followed were controlled by criollos claiming European descent and were dependent for most of their ventures into modern industry and communications on British or other European capital (Bagchi 1982, chapter 3).

From the last thirty years of the nineteenth century, the manufacturing towns receiving European emigrants were located not only within Europe but in the United States, Canada, Australia, New Zealand, Argentina, Uruguay, or South Africa. As new immigrants came into the eastern United States, old immigrants moved farther west, and many of the new immigrants with some capital at their command were encouraged to become farmers, through the device of the Homestead Act and other official measures encouraging settlement of the land by working farmers.

The direct and indirect exploitation of Asia by the European powers did not really attain great heights until the second half of the eighteenth century. The conquest of the Americas yielded silver and gold, which were essential for western Europe to carry on trade with the Baltic countries and with countries to the east of the Mediterranean. The European gain from the exploitation of the labor of colonies and slaves in the Western Hemisphere is partly reflected in the figures of European import of bullion from the Americas and its export to other regions (table 16.1).

The surpluses of bullion arrivals over exports were used by the Europeans to support the rapidly intensifying exchanges among European countries. And for extra-European exchanges with Asia and the Baltic region, the only means of settling the large European deficits was bullion. Table 16.2 gives a minimum estimate of the exports of silver and silver bullion from Europe to the Baltic, the Levant, and the part of Asia that was linked by the EIC and VOC. Tables 16.1 and 16.2 both show a rapid rise of exports of bullion from Europe, primarily to Asia until 1750 and a decline thereafter. That decline was almost certainly due to the British conquest of Bengal. The EIC ceased to ship bullion to India for trade thereafter. Moreover, part of the payment for the rapidly increasing European (mainly British) demand for Chinese tea was met by exports of cotton and, increasingly, opium from India. In interpreting tables 16.1 and 16.2, we should also remember that a part of the American production of bullion also found its way directly across the Pacific to Asia via Manila—to China, Southeast Asia, the overland route to India, and even to Japan, though Japan probably remained a net exporter of silver in the seventeenth to the eighteenth centuries.

The exports of silver by VOC increased in the eighteenth century as the Netherlands declined as an economy, and it was as yet unable to convert Indonesia into the highly profitable plantation colony that it became in the nineteenth century. On the other hand, as the British obtained possession of the trade and revenues of Bengal after 1757, the remittance of bullion of the EIC tapered off.

Table 16.1.   Estimated Average Annual Production of American Silver and Movement of Silver Equivalent into and out of Europe, 1501–1800 (in Metric Tons)

Period	American Production (Column 1)	European Arrivals (Column 2)	Column 1 Minus Column 2 (Column 3)	Exports from Europe (Column 4)	Net Balance: Column 2 Minus Column 4
1501–1550	170	145	25	n.a.	n.a.
1551–1600	530	410	180	n.a.	n.a.
1601–1650	735	535	200	225	310
1651–1700	945	700	245	285	400
1701–1750	1,200	915	285	400	515
1751–1800	1,760	1,190	570	410	780

Source: Barrett 1990, table 7.3.
Note: n.a. = not available.

Table 16.2.   Estimates of Average Annual Exports of Silver and Silver Equivalent from Europe, 1600–1780 (in Metric Tons)

Period	To Levant	Via VOC	Via EIC	To Baltic	Total
1601–1625	50	8	—	43	101
1626–1650	50	9	10	56	125
1651–1675	50	10	10	59	129
1676–1700	50	21	32	53	156
1701–1725	50	43	42	53	188
1726–1750	50	45	56	59	210
1751–1775	50	51	50	65	216
1776–1780	50	34	40	71	195

Source: Barrett 1990, table 7.7.
Note: According to Pearson 2001, the figures given by Barrett of exports to the East via the Levant are serious underestimates, but this does not affect my argument.

The exploitation of the Americas with the help of Amerindian labor and African slave labor enabled the Europeans to sustain nutrition and living conditions in an urbanizing environment down to the eighteenth century. Between 1815 and the 1920s, the European exploitation of Asian colonies and semicolonies enabled the European countries to channel a strong flow of investment to the colonies of European settlement overseas. That flow in turn supported the largest flow of migrants in recent human history as recorded between the 1870s and 1920s (see table 7.1). As I have shown in chapter 7, that flow not only led to the peopling of the United States and its rise as the most economically advanced country in the world but also helped improve the living conditions of Europeans left behind. Contrariwise, the mechanisms of exploitation used by the European powers in the colonies and the surpluses removed by them from those dependencies left a legacy of unfree civil societies, coercive state apparatuses, and low-productivity technologies trapped in pervasive poverty and low human development.

MECHANISMS OF EXPLOITATION FROM THE
AGE OF MERCHANT CAPITAL IN EUROPE TO THE
MATURING OF INDUSTRIAL CAPITALISM

Many of the mechanisms of extraction of surplus from their overseas dependencies used by the emerging capitalist powers remained unchanged between the age of merchant capital and the era beginning with the Industrial Revolution. What I shall attempt to do here is to elaborate further on the mechanisms of exploitation and provide estimates of surpluses extracted from some of the major nonwhite dependencies of the metropolitan powers.

As I have observed, in the nineteenth century and beyond, British investment in the United States had as its counterpart large trade deficits with the United States. In the balancing acts that supported the British empire, before World War I, Indian exports generated large surpluses with the United States even as India had a nominal and increasing deficit with the United Kingdom (Saul 1960). India sent a large tribute to Britain in the shape of Home Charges (that is, costs of British civil and military establishment in India maintained by Indian revenues along with interest on British loans to India), and British traders, shippers, and insurers realized a profit, going up to 40 percent of India's external trade (as against the 5 or 4.5 percent assumed by Imlah [1958]); most of that trade was monopolized by European—mainly British—traders (Bagchi 1982, chapter 4; Banerjee 1990). Much of British investment in India owed its origin to the reinvestment of profits made in India. While some of those profits originated in new enterprises, the Europeans had privileged access to those resources such as land for plantations, charters for railways, or mining properties that made the enterprises profitable (Bagchi 1972a, 1972b).

The size and even the direction of flow of surpluses from the dependencies have been obscured by the conventional methods of calculating the value of foreign trade. The profits realized by the importers, financiers, shippers, or insurers based in the metropolitan country and the tribute exacted by the ruling power as expenses of administration and defense do not figure directly in the trade accounts. Hence the surplus flowing out of the colony is grossly underestimated in conventional estimates. Interestingly enough, some of the metropolitan officials, traders, and planters had recognized and analyzed the problem in the eighteenth and nineteenth centuries (Long 1774; Colebrooke and Lambert 1795; Bagchi 1989a), but many of the modern apologists of colonialism (such as Davis and Huttenback 1986) have ignored this phenomenon altogether. The issue is clearly set out by Braudel (1982, pp. 277–78), while describing the relation of St. Domingue and other tropical colonies of France in the eighteenth century to Bordeaux, the main French port importing the products of those colonies:

> The wholesalers, commissioners and shippers of Bordeaux, who obliged the islanders to use the services of their boats, their captains (who often had instructions to sell cargoes for them), their warehouses and their life-saving advance payments, were thus the masters of the machine that turned out the riches of the colonies. . . . Now all this hardly seems to correspond to the overall statistics of colonial trade. In Bordeaux, where half of all French trade with the colonies was carried on, exports only amounted to a third, later a quarter, later still back to a third, of the imports to Bordeaux of products from St. Domingue, Guadeloupe and Martinique. And there is a similar imbalance in the figures for Marseilles. . . . And

yet St. Domingue, to take only one example, was constantly drained of her pias-
tres: they were smuggled in from nearby Spanish America and did no more [than]
pass through the island. The extraordinary truth was that they went straight to
Bordeaux—in huge quantities after 1783.

The folk wisdom of most economists and economic historians (for example, Woodruff 1966) plays up the significant role of European investment in
developing the rest of the world. In spite of the work of Nurkse (1961), Simon (1968), and others, it is not realized that most of that investment went to
overseas colonies settled by the Europeans. There is even less recognition of
the fact that not only was there little net investment by the European powers
in their nonwhite dependencies but a massive amount of profits and tribute
was extracted from those dependencies.

Most of the existing work by distinguished economic historians has concentrated on the costs and returns of investment made by the nationals of the
metropolitan countries and has not considered the returns obtained without
any productive investment made by the colonial powers (Bagchi 2002b).
What investment did the slave traders make in the countries from which they
procured their victims? What investments did the EIC make in India before
the coming of the steamships, the railways, or the large irrigation canals? Precious little, as Marx had pointed out in 1853 in his articles on India. A later
commentator, Jenks (1927/1963, p. 207–8), aptly observed,

> The subjugation of successive portions of the decrepit Mughal empire to the
> Company's authority paid for itself. Subsequent wars and annexations were fi-
> nanced by rupee loans, floated in Calcutta, in which the civil and military ser-
> vants of the Company invested for safe-keeping their accumulations, which in-
> cluded not a little booty. And as independent mercantile establishments grew up
> to carry on the trade and to engage in exchange banking, they too were financed
> from the savings and plunder of the Company's servants.

The major portion of gain from the colony accrued from the tribute realized from the colonial subjects in the form of land revenue and other taxes,
from the utilization of what Edmund Burke had characterized as "coercive
monopoly," and from the profits of internal and international trade, a large
part of which functioned as a means of effecting the transfer of the tribute.
Some of the earlier students of the nature of British trade and investment were
more clear-sighted about the size and direction of the resource transfer than
most of the recent analysts. For instance, Keynes (1909, p. 14) discounted the
exaggerated figures of private British investment in India and estimated that
over 1902–1909, the remittances from India by foreign investors in private
enterprises exceeded the investments made by them in those enterprises. Pan-

dit (1937, p. 125) found that in the sixteen years from 1898 to 1914 Great Britain's investments in Indian private firms was positive in only two years (1900–1901 and 1905–1906) and negative in all the other years. The net outflow on account of private enterprises in which British investors were involved, according to Pandit's estimate, came to Rs233.2 million, or £15.5 million, over these years. During the late nineteenth century, top British officials and spokesmen of British business clearly recognized that Indian surpluses with the Americas performed a vital function in balancing British balance-of-trade deficits with those countries, especially the United States (Bagchi 1989a, 1997a).

Contrary to the assumption of even some analysts who recognize the role of imperialism (for example, Washbrook 1981; Cain and Hopkins 1987; O'Brien 1988a, 1999), the introduction of formal free trade in Britain in 1846 did not lead to the pursuit of economic gain under the rules of purely competitive markets. The cases of India and Indonesia vividly illustrate the numerous ways the members of the ruling race rigged the market in their own favor.

Let us take the example of the construction of railways. Some wealthy Indians had shown a great deal of interest in the construction of railways in the 1840s (Chakrabarty 1974), quite a few years before the first railway company began construction. But none of them could be promoters since none were British citizens with access to the British parliament: you needed the sanction of the parliament to secure a charter for a joint-stock company and you needed the government of India's grant of land for pushing through the railway line. The situation did not change even after the EIC's rule over India formally ceased and the parliament assumed direct rule over India. Nor did it change when the new Companies Act, framed in imitation of the British legislation, allowed joint-stock companies to be floated in India. It was unthinkable that any purely Indian company should have secured a land grant for the construction of railways from the British Indian government.

Could the Indians have anything to do with the running of the railway companies? Again, the prospects were bleak. The head offices were in Britain; the directors were all European; the recruitment of officers took place in Britain from among exclusively British or from among non-British whites; and the purchase of railway engines, rails, and for some time, even sleepers was made from Britain or white settler colonies such as Australia. If there were any Indian shareholders, they could have no say in any of these matters (Bagchi 2002b). In the actual operation of the railways, internal Indian trade and Indian-controlled ventures were systematically discriminated against: freight rates were higher for transport between two internal points than between a point in the hinterland and the port. Goods produced in India paid higher freight rates than similar imported goods. When there was a shortage of wagons, European companies (which were organized into trade associations and chambers of commerce that formally or informally barred the membership of Indians) obtained preferential allocation. The list could be extended very far to include many other examples of monopolistic behavior.

Let us take another instance—shipping companies. One way of minimizing initial losses of the major shipping companies, and of ensuring various contracts later on, was to acquire government custom, in particular, the privilege of carrying royal mail. These privileges were granted only to British-controlled companies, such as Peninsular and Oriental or British Indian Steam Navigation Company. If any Indian companies dared to challenge British companies on any of their profitable routes, these big companies, with deep pockets and official patronage, set out deliberately to ruin them through cutthroat competition. The first major Indian company to have survived these tactics did not emerge until the twentieth century, and that had something to do with the intensification of the anti-imperialist struggle in India (Jog 1969, 1977).

Not only in these major transport enterprises but in trade, banking, access to land, the exercise of control over labor, and supply of stores to the government, being British or European gave an enormous advantage to the owners, managers, and promoters. Let us take the example of plantations. For ordinary Indians, the continued recognition of a title to land was contingent on a prompt payment of an annual rent, euphemistically called *land revenue*. But when land was made available to prospective British planters, it was granted for a low price and under fee simple, that is, as absolute private property without the burden of an annual revenue payment. A similar discrimination was practiced in virtually all nonwhite dependencies of Britain (Bagchi 1992).

Take joint-stock banking with limited liability. Before the introduction of an act in the 1860s authorizing the establishment of joint-stock banks with limited liability, any banks with that privilege could be organized only under a charter granted by the British parliament. The government of India had such banks organized in the three presidencies of India—in 1809 in Bengal, in 1840 in Bombay, and in 1843 in Madras. The first of these banks had one Indian director for the first two years and no other Indian on the board thereafter, and the Bank of Madras had no Indian director except in the very last year of its existence. All three banks were closely connected with the government and were the biggest domestic banks. Because of some historical factors (Bagchi 1972a, chapter 6; Bagchi 1987a, parts 1 and 2), the Bank of Bombay had a complement of Indian directors and lent to Indian and European borrowers in a reasonably even-handed manner. But the other two banks discriminated against Indians in their lending policies. All of them recruited their officers only from among British citizens, denying the Indians all opportunities of promotion to supervisory positions.

In the few manufacturing companies that grew up in colonial India, on the basis of government patronage in areas such as the production of rum or other spirits and saddleries and other army stores, the Europeans acquired local monopolies or in some cases even India-wide monopolies or cartels. Access to foreign and especially transoceanic trade was denied to the Indians in most parts of India except Bombay and for trade with Southeast Asia, Sri Lanka, and Madras. Control of channels of foreign trade and large-scale finance by Europeans ensured, for example, that when the jute industry grew up near Calcutta, Indians would have no share in it until World War I led to the breakdown of the European monopoly of foreign trade (Bagchi 2002b).

As in the case of the jute industry, oligopolistic control was exercised by European-controlled plantations companies, tea marketing companies, and the final sellers of tea in the world market, which were organized in a tight network radiating from Mincing Lane in London to all the major producing regions in the British empire. As a result, the companies were able to organize a quantity-regulating cartel to fight the worst effects of the depression of the 1930s even before the officially negotiated International Tea Agreement of 1933 (Gupta 1997, 2001).

The imperial network allowed the privileged British firms to make supernormal profits in several other ways: for example, when sugar prices were depressed in the late 1890s and early 1900s, India paid much higher prices for Mauritian sugar than for Indonesian sugar, because the former was produced and marketed by British companies (Banerjee 1999, p. 102). On the other side, Indian raw cotton exported to the United Kingdom fetched lower prices than exports to Japan or the continental European countries (Banerjee 1999, p. 112).

The oligopolistic control exercised by the incumbent Anglo-Indian business groups and the clear regional division of India between spheres of influence of big European business houses discouraged investment in private enterprises by foreigners who had not acquired a foothold in some sector of business. Thus investment in India by genuinely multinational foreign enterprises was quite insignificant until after Indian independence.

17

Colonial Tribute and Profits, 1870s Onward

SURPLUS EXTRACTED FROM INDIA AND BURMA

We can arrive at a minimal estimate of the surplus extracted by Europeans by determining the unrequited export surplus of a colony. However, because the nominal figures of exports in the official trade accounts do not take cognizance of the profits made by Europeans on those trades, they have to be separately included in the estimates. By comparing the series of figures of exports (FOB, or free on board) from India with the series of imports from India (CIF, or cost, insurance, and freight) into Britain in the late nineteenth century, Banerjee (1990) found the average difference to vary from 14.5 percent to more than 40 percent. I have, therefore, raised the values of exports, including the profits made by European traders, shippers, bankers, and insurers, by 20 percent and 25 percent; allotted different shares of Europeans in the external trade in the major ports of British India, including Burma (Myanmar); and arrived at the figures of the export surplus of India including and excluding Burma for the years 1871–1916 (for a more detailed account of the method of estimation, see Bagchi 2002b).

I have estimated the export surplus of India accruing to the Europeans using these assumptions about the average rate of gross profit made by European shippers, insurance agents, exporters, and agency houses involved in international exchange. The justification for taking Burma explicitly into account is that most of Lower Burma was already under British rule by the 1870s and the British conquered the rest in the 1880s.

The value of the surplus annually transferred from India including Burma came to £25.4 million (with the profit rate assumed to be 20 percent) or £27.7 million (profit rate 25 percent) in the quinquennium 1871–1876, rising to

£46.6 million (profit rate 20 percent) or £53.4 million (profit rate 25 percent) in the quinquennium 1911–1916. These values combined with those of British foreign investment formed more than half of British investment flows (in fact they exceeded them in some years) as estimated by Imlah (1958, pp. 70–75) up to the 1890s and were a very substantial fraction still of British foreign investment in the peak years before World War I.

It may be argued that not all foreign trade was monopolized by the Europeans in the colonies. But most of it was. In the dependent nonwhite colonies, most of the so-called invisible earnings of the metropolitan country contained varying elements of (1) a political tribute, which was often in the nature of self-ransom as, for example, the principal and interest charges for the British Indian government debt contracted for quelling the so-called mutiny of 1857–1858 or the debt contracted by the Netherlands East Indies government for fighting numerous counterinsurgency wars in Indonesia and (2) monopoly rents on business from which natives were formally or informally excluded and in which competition from other competing metropolitan powers was also sought to be minimized (Bagchi 1982, chapters 3–4).

Britain was the single most important destination of Indian exports, and her share, even after declining over the years, remained above 60 percent up to World War I. Moreover, the exports from Bengal ports, which were the most important origin of Indian exports, were practically monopolized by the Europeans. Exports from the Madras ports were partly consigned by Indian traders, and the latter had a bigger share in the exports from Bombay and Sind. European, mainly British, companies monopolized all the profits from banking, insurance, and shipping services on virtually all exports.

Furthermore, much of the surplus was directly appropriated by the British as Home Charges and transferred to Britain. The British also maintained a large military presence in all sensitive areas east of Suez, and the major cost of that would not show up in foreign trade accounts. Finally, most British officials and merchants maintained a lavish lifestyle, the resources for which came out of taxes raised by the colonial government and the profits made by the merchants. Again, these would not show up in foreign trade accounts. The Europeans controlled not only the major part of imports and exports but also a large part of the wholesale trade in the colonies. To take these factors into consideration, I have made an alternative assumption that the Europeans in India and Burma (Myanmar) controlled all foreign trade and the profits on that trade were eventually transferred abroad. The Home Charges were by definition transferred out of the revenues of the colony to be spent in London. By clubbing these profits and Home Charges, we can get an estimate of the upper limit on the surpluses transferred out of India and Burma, presented in table 17.1. This approximate measure still does not cover the enormous expenditures of the colonial officials and businessmen within the colony.

Table 17.1 indicates that the annual surplus extracted from India and Burma by the British state and European businessmen can be reasonably estimated as having been a minimum of £21.4 million and a maximum of £28.9 million in the 1870s and risen to a minimum of £52.9 million and a maximum of £65.3 million on the eve of World War I.

The profits of productive investment in India were only a fraction of the total amount realized by the British. Much of this was the price of protection, or self-ransom, exacted from the Indians. For example, in 1893–1894 the gross expenditure of the government of India incurred in England came to £15.83 million. Of this amount, military charges amounted to £3.61 million; pensions and other charges of civil administration came to £2.11 million; interest on, and the cost of management of, Indian government debt amounted to £2.55 million; and only £0.35 million can be considered to be on account of purchase of capital goods (Banerji 1982, table 15). Interest on debt and other obligations, incurred, for example, in connection with the guarantee of minimum rates of return on private railways, amounted to £8.25 million. Most of the government debt, other than that incurred for the guaranteed railways, was accumulated as payments for self-ransoming (such as the cost of quelling the Indian revolt of 1857–1858) over and above the normal revenues.

Table 17.1. Alternative Estimates of the Total Tribute Extracted and Profits Made by Europeans Connected with India and Burma, 1871–1916 (in Thousands of Pounds)

Five-Year Average	5% Profit on Imports (£)		10% Profit on Imports (£)	
	20% Margin on Exports	25% Margin on Exports	20% Margin on Exports	25% Margin on Exports
1871–1876	21,472	23,309	23,322	25,159
1876–1881	24,519	26,825	26,634	28,940
1881–1886	29,223	32,085	31,946	34,808
1886–1891	28,822	31,686	31,824	34,689
1891–1896	28,779	31,467	31,232	33,919
1896–1901	28,864	31,664	31,514	34,315
1901–1906	42,907	46,837	46,661	50,591
1906–1911	51,943	53,580	57,239	58,876
1911–1916	52,914	58,963	59,203	65,252

Sources: The data on "Drawings of the Home Government" have been taken from *Statistics of British India, vol. 2, Financial Statistics* (Calcutta: Superintendent of Government Printing, 1918). The data on imports and exports of merchandise and treasure are taken from *Statistics of British India, part 2, Commercial, 1908 and 1913* and *Statistics of British India, vol. 1, Commercial Statistics, 1918* (Calcutta: Superintendent of Government Printing).

Note: The totals have been arrived at by adding the Home Charges to the estimated margins on exports from and imports into India, including Burma. The imports include net imports of treasure.

The profits made by European traders, financiers, and the like. are either ignored altogether or grossly underestimated in the usual accounts of benefits of imperialism to the ruling countries (e.g., Offer 1993). The underestimation of the tribute and profits of monopolistically organized trade, finance, and processing industries together with acceptance of dubious figures of national income originating from apologetic sources naturally also leads to a gross underestimate of the burden of imperialism on the dependency (see, for example, Foreman-Peck 1983, pp. 24–27).

My recalculation of the surplus extracted by Britain from India and Burma demystifies the surprisingly large proportion British foreign investment formed of its gross national product (GNP) and the apparently perverse desire of the British to retain an empire that was less profitable than, say, investment in the United States. Pollard (1985) has pointed out that the interest on the estimated portfolio investment by British residents would be enough to more than counterbalance the estimated outflow of private capital from the late 1870s or 1880s. If we take the incomes from foreign payments of all kinds, then even after deducting all British lending abroad and funds taken by British emigrants, a large surplus would remain in Britain, except in the peak foreign investment years of 1900–1913 (Pollard 1985, table 4). The mystery of the apparently enormous foreign investments made by Britain in the years from 1870 to 1913 virtually disappears when it is realized that the British income from the colonial possessions of Britain has been grossly underestimated.

The usually accepted figure of total British investment worldwide in 1913–1914 is composed very largely of the reinvestment of returns on accumulating balances of those investments and compounding them at the normal rate of interest or profit (Pollard 1985). Therefore to compare that total to the accumulating balances of Indian surpluses for which the Indians received no recompense, we have also to apply compound interest rates to the surpluses from the time they accrued to the year 1914. Applying a compound rate of interest of 4 percent to the figures of table 17.1 yields the figures shown in table 17.2.

The extraction of the surplus from a dependent colony was achieved through the maintenance of highly imperfect markets, with direct government intervention preventing the emergence of free markets in land, labor, and cap-

Table 17.2. Accumulating Balances of Unrecompensed Indian Surpluses (Figures from Table 17.1) Compounded at 4 Percent (in Thousands of Pounds)

	5% on Imports 20% on Exports	5% on Imports 25% on Exports	10% on Imports 20% on Exports	10% on Imports 25% on Exports
Total (£)	3,199,320	3,482,374	3,498,898	3,779,264

ital. Even where labor was not subjected to explicit bondage, such as in Madras under early British rule, local authorities sought to depress the wages of labor below what a free market would throw up (Ahuja 1999). To set up models of capital markets with the implicit or explicit assumption of free competition in factor and product markets, then, appears to be an exercise in fantasy rather than real history.

The debate surrounding the issue of whether India should have been allowed to adopt the gold standard in the 1870s and 1880s indicates that most of the British policy makers and opinion shapers such as Walter Bagehot and George Goschen were aware of the interconnections between the tribute originating in the dependent colony in the East and the opening up of the land of opportunity for British finance and British migrants in the West (Bagchi 1989a, chapter 2; 1997a).

SURPLUS EXTRACTED FROM INDONESIA AND OTHER DEPENDENCIES

The export surpluses extracted from Indonesia played a very important role in supporting Dutch public finances, Dutch investment, and Dutch external balances (Bagchi 1978; 1982, chapter 4). In the 1830s the Dutch introduced the so-called cultivation system, which was a way of reducing peasants to the status of government serfs on the land they occupied and extracting most of the produce as a tax. It has been estimated that in the period 1830–1880, the net transfers from Java to the Netherlands amounted to 8–10 percent of the Javanese GDP and 3–5 percent of the Dutch GDP (Van Zanden 2003). This was a substantial addition to Dutch resources when the Netherlands was trying to catch up with other European nations that had left it far behind after the Napoleonic Wars. From 1878 to 1900 the average annual export surplus of Indonesia increased from about 48 million guilders, or about £4 million, to about 60 million guilders, and by 1913 it had increased to 207 million guilders, or £17.25 million (CEI 1987, table 1).

As in the case of India and Burma, I have used the basic data on exports and imports to calculate the unrequited export surplus transferred by the Dutch and their metropolitan associates from Indonesia. Table 17.3 reproduces the results of those calculations.

The estimated profit transferred by the Europeans from Indonesia comes to between about 109 million and more than 116 million guilders per year over 1871–1875 and to between 241 million and 260 million guilders per year over 1910–1914. Taking a British pound to equal 12 Dutch guilders during this period, the transfer of profit and tribute from Indonesia rose from

244 Chapter 17

Table 17.3. Estimated Export Surplus (Annual Averages) Generated by Indonesia after Taking European Profits into Account (in Million Guilders)

Period	Low Estimate	High Estimate
1871–1875	109.4	116.4
1876–1880	77.8	85.2
1881–1885	89.2	97.0
1886–1890	101.0	109.0
1891–1895	80.0	88.2
1896–1900	117.6	127.4
1901–1905	157.8	170.4
1906–1910	221.8	238.2
1911–1914	241.0	260.4

Source: CEI 1987.

about £10 million in the 1870s to more than £24 million per year on the eve of World War I (for the method of estimation, see Bagchi 2002b).

Over time, the number and earnings of Europeans (predominantly Dutch citizens) working in Indonesia increased at a high rate. Hence the export surplus becomes less useful in later years as an indication of incomes earned by the Dutch in Indonesia. A series of national-income calculations, differentiated by origin or citizenship of earners, shows that in 1925 (CEI 1979), for example, Indonesians (including those of Chinese origin) earned 4,116 million guilders out of a total Indonesian income of 5,023 million guilders and incomes of Europeans, government export income, and incomes of nonresidents accounted for the rest. That is, almost a fifth of the national income was earned by Europeans in Indonesia.

The period from the 1870s to the end of the 1890s has been characterized as the Great Depression, primarily because of a fall in prices, which was led by the fall in gold prices of agricultural commodities. This in turn was precipitated by the outflow of grain and other agricultural products from the United States, Canada, Argentina, and Australia but also from India and other nonwhite dependencies. While the export stream from the white-settled colonies was generated by extension of transport and acreage of lands emptied of Amerindians or other native peoples, the food grains and other agricultural products exported from India were pushed out by poverty-stricken peasants having to find money for taxes and necessities in an increasingly commercialized economy. The enforced absorption of silver—a rapidly depreciating metal—by India and other eastern lands, when most of the European economies adopted the gold standard, also depressed gold prices (Bagchi 1997a). This availability of cheaper grain made a significant contribution to improved nutrition and reduction of mortality rates in western Europe.

Table 17.4. Figures of Annual Average Export Surplus Generated by Indonesia (in Million Guilders)

1916–1920	1921–1925	1926–1930	1931–1935	1936	1939
654	600	507	165	344	257

Source: Boeke (1940–1953, p. 199, as quoted by Gordon 2004, table 4).

In my earlier writings, I had argued that the Eurocentric historians of Europe had not paid any attention to the contribution made by the exploitation of Indonesia to the reemergence of the Netherlands as an industrialized economy of Europe (Bagchi 1978; 1982, pp. 71–72). Together with the figures of table 17.3, table 17.4 shows that the profitability of Indonesia to the Dutch was still substantial in the interwar years.

Maddison (1989) has used essentially the same method of using the unrequited export surplus for estimating the amounts remitted by the colonies of India and Indonesia to Britain and the Netherlands, respectively. But Maddison has used the official figures of exports and imports without taking into account the profits on exports FOB and imports CIF made by European merchants. Even then, Maddison comes to the conclusion that income remitted from Indonesia represented a net addition to Dutch domestic product of "about 5 per cent from 1840 to 1870 and . . . around 8 per cent in 1921–38" (Maddison 1989, p. 646). Moreover, according to his estimate, about 10.6 percent of the Indonesian domestic product was remitted annually over the period 1921–1938 (Maddison 1989). The regular drain of a proportion of income that had been enough to launch most European countries on their road to industrialization and eventual human uplift would be enough, even without the other repressive associations of colonialism, to condemn the Indonesians to the low level of human development at which the Dutch left them after more than three centuries of indirect and direct rule. But the extracted surplus added very substantially to the invested funds of the Netherlands, thus advancing its material and human development.

Maddison's estimates of the amount remitted from India and its proportion to India's national income in the same article are gross underestimates: the surplus is underestimated for reasons I have spelled out here. The estimates of national income are taken by him from Heston (1983), who ultimately bases himself on Atkinson (1902). Atkinson, as the accountant general of India had to defend the government's record against attacks by Indian nationalists such as R. C. Dutt and Dadabhai Naoroji and liberals such as William Digby. He did it simply by assuming, against the background of the famine holocausts of 1876–1879 and 1896–1901, and other local famines before and between those dates, that areas under cultivation and productivity per acre went up continually in British India in the last thirty years of the nineteenth century. Atkinson's estimates are no better than the assumptions he started with. Hence Maddison's estimates of Indian income in the colonial period in his numerous publications are also quite unreliable.

We do not have comparable estimates of the surplus extracted from Malaya. But Drabble (2000, p. 40, as quoted by Gordon 2004, p. 375) has estimated that between 1870 and 1920 Malaya's imports averaged only 70 percent of its exports and that proportion declined below 70 percent from the 1890s. For the period 1912–1922, the capital invested in Malayan rubber plantations was £11.85 million, but the net profit realized came to £18.39 million (Gordon 2004, table 5). During the interwar period, Indian export surpluses shrank and the balancing of the British imperial accounts was largely accomplished by Malayan surpluses (Kahn 1946, chapters 11–15).

India, Indonesia, and Malaya were, of course, not the only profitable colonies of the European powers in the nineteenth and twentieth centuries. The whole of Latin America was virtually an informal dependency of Britain after its formal liberation from Spanish and Portuguese rule down to 1914 and beyond as I have noted elsewhere (Bagchi 1982, chapter 3). British merchants, financiers, mine owners, and railway builders and operators earned enormous profits from that informal empire. There were rich pickings from other parts of European dependencies also.

One of the richest prizes obtained by the British imperialists in the late nineteenth century was Egypt. That country had been nominally part of the Ottoman Empire for a long time. But Muhammad Ali, an Albanian by birth, virtually became an independent ruler in early nineteenth century. He started on a modernization drive and tried to build cotton mills and other modern factories under state patronage. However, the Anglo-Turkish treaty of 1838 enforced a regime of free trade on the Ottoman Empire, including Egypt. The problems caused by that treaty were compounded by those of building up viable factory industries in a society of largely illiterate peasants and artisans, dominated by landlords and officials, and ended this early experiment in a forced march to industrialization (Hershlag 1964; Marsot 1984).

Muhammad Ali's son, Muhammad Said (1854–1863), and his successor, Khedive Ismail (1863–1879), came under the influence of European bankers. Partly under their influence, Ismail embarked on a series of expensive projects, which pushed the country into an external debt trap. The Suez canal, linking the Red Sea and the Mediterranean, was dug during his rule. But its control passed almost at once into the hands of the British, who had managed to acquire most of the canal company shares, including those originally allotted to Khedive Ismail. Egypt effectively passed into the control of European financiers because of Ismail's inability to repay his debt.

A group of nationalist army officers led by Arabi Pasha staged a coup in 1881 and took over the Egyptian government. But in 1882 the British invaded Egypt and defeated Pasha. Thus began the chapter of British rule over Egypt. Egypt was valuable for maintaining British rule over India because it lay directly on the route to India. It was valuable in other ways too. It became a major source of high-quality cotton for the British mills. The output of raw cotton grew from 1.7 million cantars (1 cantar = 50 kilograms) in 1878 to 6.5 million cantars in 1897. In 1897–1898, Egypt's raw cotton exports amounted to 5.177 million cantars (Britannica 1902b, p. 692). Egypt, like other profitable colonies, also generated an export surplus: for example, in 1899, the monetary value of exports amounted to 15.35 million Egyptian (E) pounds (which equaled pound sterling and six pence) and the imports to 11.44 million E pounds. Egypt had lost first its financial and then its political independence. The subsequent colonial exploitation of Egypt also involved a large external debt and its servicing charges. Table 17.5 indicates the burden of interest charges on the Egyptian economy over 1880–1919.

Colonial governments often borrowed abroad for purposes that had little to do with the welfare or human development of the subject peoples and then charged the revenues of the colony with the debt-servicing costs. In fact, the cost of conquest of the colony and pacification or counterinsurgency operations was routinely borne by the conquered peoples themselves (again justified as the cost of civilizing the natives). Underinvoicing of exports, overinvoicing of imports, and transfer pricing in various forms were also used to siphon off capital from developing countries by both their own nationals and by foreign enterprises. Increasingly, from the late 1970s, embroiling the developing lands in debt has become a favorite method of transferring resources from them. From that point of view, the method used in Egypt from the 1860s to extract surpluses by foreigners provided a foretaste of the future.

Table 17.5. Burden of Interest Payments on the Egyptian Economy, 1880–1919 (Currency in Egyptian Pounds)

Period	Average Annual Interest	Average Annual Government Revenues	Average Annual Exports	Annual Interest as Percentage of Government Revenue	Annual Interest as a Percentage of Exports
1880–1889	4,137	11,488	11,871	36	35
1890–1899	3,920	11,220	12,575	35	31
1900–1909	3,673	14,909	15,769	25	23
1910–1919	3,455	20,666	32,908	17	11

Source: Hershlag 1964, p.116.

In the Indian case, the interest on the debt accumulated by the British Indian government had almost from the beginning of British rule (originally in the form of dividend on EIC stock) provided a method of extracting and transferring a part of the surplus. But after World War I, as the tribute became less important as a component of the total surplus, the interest on the Indian debt became more important for extracting and transferring the surplus, and became a powerful argument for pursuing a basically deflationary fiscal and monetary policy throughout the period between the two world wars. Again, those earlier imperial policies throw an interesting light on the policy stance of the Indian central government today.

18

Demographic Disasters
in the Colonies and Semicolonies in the
Heyday of European Colonialism

FAMINES, WARS, AND DEMOGRAPHIC LOSSES IN CHINA
IN THE NINETEENTH CENTURY

British traders and the gunboats backing them became increasingly aggressive in illegally pushing opium into China in the 1830s. This aggressiveness erupted into the first Opium War, which was fought by Britain to force a government of another country to accept the import of a severely harmful and addictive drug (Greenberg 1969; Bagchi 1982, pp. 94–98). As the booty of their victory in the war, the British acquired the island of Hong Kong and exacted a war indemnity of $21 million (Chesneaux, Bastid, and Bergère 1976, pp. 64–65). Other trophies included the opening of five Chinese ports—Canton, Shanghai, Ningbo, Amoy, and Fuzhou—as treaty ports for the foreign powers, including the United States and France, to establish trading establishments. "Chinese customs duties were limited to 5 per cent—which was 60 to 70 per cent lower than the previous tariffs. In each treaty port the Westerners were granted extraterritoriality, which meant that they were subject only to the legal jurisdiction of their consul" (Chesneaux, Bastid, and Bergère 1976, p. 65).

The demonstrated feebleness and disarray of the Qing administration then precipitated the Taiping Rebellion. It was joined by the Nian rebellion in north China and by rebellions among groups of Chinese Muslims from Yunnan in the southwest to Kashgar in the west (Chesneaux 1973; Fairbank, Reischauer, and Craig 1969, pp. 128–46). In terms of the number of deaths, the Taiping Rebellion is regarded as the most sanguinary civil war in history. This revolution was ultimately crushed with the help of the British and French governments, which had inflicted another opium war on China—on the flimsiest of excuses, namely, insult to a British flag—and defeated it. The Qing regime continued to be wracked by rebellions even after the last of the Tai-ping rebels had been disposed of with exemplary ferocity. The situation of China was sketched as follows in 1865:

> Smiling fields [in the rich Yangzi valley] were turned into desolate wildernesses; "fenced cities into ruinous heaps". The plains of Kiang-nan, Kiang-si and Chehkang were strewn with human skeletons; their rivers polluted with floating carcasses; wild beasts descending from their fastnesses in the mountains roamed at large over the land, and made their dens in the ruins of deserted towns . . . no hands were left to till the soil, and noxious weeds covered up the ground once tilled with patient industry.[1]

The other parts of China fared no better: "Most of Guizhou, Yunnan, and the Northwest were in a similar state, as well as several regions in the North China plain. Shenxi had lost nine-tenths of its Moslem population and Gansu two-thirds, amounting to 3 million inhabitants; the rest had been deported. Half of the population of Yunnan had been wiped out" (Fairbank, Reischauer, and Craig 1969, p. 149). Tens of millions lost their lives in the Taiping, Nian, and Muslim rebellions, in the counterinsurgency operations mounted to sup-press them, and in the famines accompanying the disturbances (Chesneaux 1973).

In the areas worst affected by the Taiping wars, Ho (1959, p. 241) has esti-mated the population losses to lie between 40.2 percent and 88.2 percent. Ac-cording to his calculations, for four large provinces of China, namely, Zhe-jiang, Anhui, Jiangxi, and Jiangsu, the population in 1953 at 117 million was lower than their population in 1850, which was 136 million (Ho 1959, p. 246).

Meteorologists have established that the rapid warming or cooling of the eastern Pacific (an El Niño or a La Niña event, respectively) is connected with droughts or floods, respectively, in the whole of the southern tropical and subtropical mainland from China to Brazil. Such combinations are dubbed El Niño southern oscillation (ENSO) events.

As we have seen in chapter 9, before the nineteenth century, the Chinese rulers had tried to control the effects of droughts or floods with policies for succoring the affected people. In contrast to the policies pursued earlier, the Chinese bureaucracy acted in a callous and uncaring fashion when, as a result of an ENSO event in 1876–1877, a severe drought hit China. The adminis-tration had been by then totally enfeebled and demoralized by repeated de-feats by the Western powers and the hemorrhage of the Taiping, Nian, and Muslim rebellions. Estimates of famine deaths in China during the three years of drought, 1876–1879, range from 9.5 million to 20 million (Davis 2001, p. 7). Drought struck again with equal ferocity in 1896–1901 and again the Chi-nese counted their dead in millions.

As a result of defeat in the China-Japan War of 1894–1895, China ceded Formosa (Taiwan) and the Pescadores to Japan and also had to agree to the payment of an indemnity of 230 million taels. Other concessions included permission to the Japanese (and by extension to all other foreign powers) to open industries in the treaty ports (Chesneaux, Bastid, and Bergère 1976, chapter 9). The current revenues of the Qing government were totally inadequate for the payment of the huge indemnity. So Russian, British, and German financiers had a field day arranging loans for the Chinese government, in the process making more profits and extracting further concessions from the Chinese government.

Repeated defeats of the imperial authorities and resentment against the enforced foreign presence on Chinese soil led to enormous popular discontent. The famine starting in 1896 led to the emergence of bands of desperadoes looking for some way to make a living. There were patriotic elements who wanted to throw out the foreign powers. The first stirrings of revolt that culminated in the Boxer Rebellion started in Shandong. There members of a secret society, the Big Swords, who shared the popular idea that the presence of foreigners was at the root of all the troubles of the common people, murdered two German missionaries. The Germans retaliated by seizing Jiaozhou and burning villages. When the drought hit northern China and famine and unemployment affected vast numbers of peasants, popular opinion attributed it to the displeasure of the gods caused by the presence of foreigners and the spread of Christianity (Cohen 1997, part 2). The agitation of the Big Swords was joined by another secret society, the Boxers, who claimed to be invincible. The imperial court had already been thoroughly discredited, but the reactionary officials who were opposed to any major reform of the system of governance had gained the upper hand (Gray 1988, chapter 6; Cohen, part 1). The Beijing court dithered about suppressing these popular revolts. As the revolt spread and the activities of the foreigners became more provocative, the court supported the Boxers: the slogans of the secret societies had by then changed from destroy the Qing and restore the Ming to support the Qing and throw out the foreigners. Thus erupted what has been styled as the Boxer Rebellion in the Western press.

The imperialist powers — Austria, Britain, France, Germany, Italy, Japan, Russia, and the United States — forgot their rivalries and sent an international expedition to punish the Boxers and also the imperial authorities. When the troops left for China, Kaiser Wilhelm II of Germany, a grandson of Queen Victoria by the way, declared, "Peking should be razed to the ground. . . . Show no mercy! Take no prisoners! A thousand years ago, the Huns of King Attila made a name for themselves which is still formidable in history and legend. Thus may you impose the name of Germany in China for a thousand years" (quoted by Chesneaux, Bastid, and Bergère 1976, p. 334).

The imperialist troops entered Peking (Beijing) on 14 August 1900, and did their best to carry out the kaiser's instructions. They massacred thousands in Beijing, sacked the whole city, including the imperial palace, and went on to slaughter people and burn villages in areas in which missionaries had been attacked. The Chinese government had already incurred a cost of 120 million taels in waging its war against Japanese aggression in 1894 and, besides losing Taiwan to Japan, it had to pay an indemnity of 263 million taels (about $200 million) in gold. When the foreign powers had brought the Qing court to its knees, they imposed an indemnity payment of 450 million taels on a bankrupt government.[2] Chinese borrowings for construction of railways, telegraph lines, and industry, often under highly onerous conditions (Bagchi 1982, chapter 4), came to about 360 million taels from the 1890s to the interwar period (Gray 1988, 165–67). Thus indemnity payments far exceeded loans taken for modernization, and of course, as in the cases of the European colonies in Asia, the profits remitted for those modern enterprises generally were paid for through the forced generation of an export surplus.

The demographic cost of this conjunction of imperialist onslaught and El Niño drought in China has been estimated as 10 million excess deaths. I have not calculated the amount transferred from China to the metropolitan countries, for the reason that it is very difficult to make an estimate of that amount. But the sheer values of the indemnities from the period of the first Opium War would suggest that the amount exacted from China was enormous.

DEMOGRAPHIC LOSSES IN INDIA UNDER BRITISH RULE IN THE NINETEENTH AND EARLY TWENTIETH CENTURIES

Indian territories that came under British occupation were racked by famines from the very beginning of British rule. One of the worst famines occurred in Bengal in 1769–1770, twelve years after the British victory over the last independent nawab of Bengal and five years after the EIC obtained a *sanad* (charter) from the Mughal emperor in Delhi to directly levy the land and other revenues in Bengal. Ten million out of an estimated population of 30 million are supposed to have perished in that famine (Visaria and Visaria 1983, p. 528). The unprecedented mortality was primarily due to the policies of the EIC. The servants of the company so zealously extracted the taxes from the prostrate population that the total revenues of the government increased in the famine years. Because of the continuous export of silver and other specie as tribute of the company, there was acute shortage of media of exchange and of purchasing power, in addition to purchasing power declining because of harvest failure. And, of course, the government took no steps for relieving the people's distress.

The British government had no policies in place for famine relief before the 1870s, and the character of those policies was such that many people died after they received relief (Davis 2001, chapter 1). Famines affected estimated populations of 8 million in western and northern India, 18 million in western and southern India in 1824–1825, and 22 million again in 1832–1833 in roughly the same region. In 1853–1855 drought and excessive floods caused famines in Rajasthan and southern and western India, involving 20 million persons (Visaria and Visaria 1983, pp. 528–29). For many other famines over this period in British India, estimates of neither the population affected nor of mortality are available. For the 1860s, we have the following estimates: in 1860–1861, 13 million persons in Punjab, Rajasthan, Uttar Pradesh, and Gujarat were affected and excess deaths amounted to 2 million. In 1866–1867, famine in Orissa wiped out between a quarter and a third of the affected population of 3 million. Famines of smaller magnitudes struck other parts of India in 1866–1867 and 1868–1870 (Visaria and Visaria 1983).

Excluding those famines for which calculations of excess mortality have not been made, Visaria and Visaria (1983, pp. 528–31) put deaths in famines in India during 1876–1900 at 10,850,000 persons. Between the 1870s and the 1920s, the death rates in India varied between about 40 per thousand and 50 per thousand and the IMR between 278 and 295 (Visaria and Visaria 1983, p. 501).

When the El Niño drought hit India in 1876, the British Indian government adopted a policy of famine relief that has itself become a synonym for infamy in the annals of food security and human survival. The then prime minister of Britain, Benjamin Disraeli, an avowed imperialist in his policies, chose Lord Lytton as viceroy of India, because he rightly believed that Lytton would follow an aggressive policy toward Russia and Afghanistan in central Asian affairs (Dutt 1906/1960, pp. 305–6). By launching a ruinously expensive and futile war against Afghanistan, Lytton added enormously to the costs of British Indian administration and to the woes of the starving Indians. Queen Victoria expressed a desire to add to her royal style and titles. She was then crowned Empress of India, in absentia, in Delhi—the historic capital of India but not yet of British India—on 1 January 1877, with pomp and ceremony, in the middle of a famine ravaging most of southern India (Cohn 1983). Victoria assumed the title of Kaiser-I-Hind, which according to Lytton and his advisers, would convey the grandeur of the queen better to the oriental mind.

Sir Richard Temple, then lieutenant governor of Bengal, had sanctioned a living wage, equivalent to 2,500 calories, for heavy labor to famine victims in the Bengal presidency in 1874—the only occasion in British India on which famine relief had been provided on an adequate scale—and had been chastised for his efforts. When famine broke out on a large scale in 1876, the governing council of India in London gave the following instruction to Lytton and Temple, as the finance member of the Viceroy's Council, "The task of saving life irrespective of cost, is one which it is beyond our power to undertake. The embarrassment of debt and weight of taxation consequent on the expense thereby involved would soon become more fatal than the famine itself" (quoted by Davis 2001, p. 37). A pliable Temple carried out the instructions thoroughly. The infamous "Temple wage" was fixed at a level (1,627 calories for heavy labor) that was even lower than the ration given to the inmates of Buchenwald, the Nazi prison (Davis 2001, p. 39). People had to prove that they were truly starving before they would be accepted for the relief works opened by the government. Thereafter, even if they could reach the relief camps in time, heavy labor on the Temple wage would kill them through further weakening and the onset of cholera or malaria, if they did not drop off from sheer exhaustion before that (Davis 2001, pp. 38–54). Maharatna (1996, p. 15) has estimated the Indian death toll in the famines of 1876–1878 as 6.2 million.

The Indian famines of 1876–1878 are a paradigmatic illustration of the lethal effects of the joint dance of the counting house, conquest, and the civilizing mission on a hapless dependency of European capital. The India Office in London, and the viceroy in India had all the time to calculate the pecuniary cost of whatever they wanted to do because, come hail, drought, or holocaust of Indian lives, they had to remit the Home Charges to London. The Indian rupee had been depreciating in tandem with the value of silver since the end of the Franco-Prussian War and the move of most of the European powers to join the bandwagon of the gold standard. The British officials managing India wanted India to join the gold standard because that would reduce the cost of remitting the tribute and render their task easier. However, the London financial and commercial interests, represented, among others, by Walter Bagehot, the editor of *The Economist*, did not want the gold standard for India, because it would interfere with London's function as the financial hub of the capitalist world by raising the cost of gold. And, of course, in the conflict between broader imperial interests and the narrower interests of the managers of Indian affairs, the imperial interests won. The cost to India continued to mount as silver depreciated.

The rest of the story of human survival in British India can be shortly told because it all fits into the same pattern. In province after province, rates of population growth in many of the decades between 1872 and 1901 were negative (Bagchi 1989a). In the 1890s, famines struck Punjab, United Provinces (Uttar Pradesh today), Bengal, practically all of western and southern India;

in 1896–1897 and again in 1899–1900 most of India was visited by harvest failure and some regions were severely affected by famine. In the middle of all this came the extravaganza in connection with the Diamond Jubilee of Queen Victoria; the Anglo-Boer war; the ostentation of the proclamation of Edward VII as the successor to Victoria in a Delhi durbar of 1903; the grandest extravaganza mounted by the British rulers of India, namely, the coronation of King George V in the Delhi *durbar* of 1911; and finally World War I. The extravaganzas and the wars, of course, given the imperatives of imperial governance, added to the number of Indian deaths from famine, plague, malaria, cholera, and other pestilences.

If we take the figure for 1896–1897 given by Visaria and Visaria (1983, p. 531) and add it to the lower estimate of excess deaths in 1899–1900 given by Maharatna (1996), the total numbers of excess deaths in the end-of-century famines comes to 8.15 million. This was not the last of the famines in the high noon of the British Indian empire: a famine in 1907–1908 killed between 2.1 million and 3.2 million persons (Maharatna 1996), and other famines lay ahead.

The imperialist policies followed by the British and other Western governments were denounced by British liberals such as William Digby and J. A. Hobson and by Indian nationalists and poets such as R. C. Dutt and Rabindranath Tagore. But of course, their protests could not halt the progress of the Maxim guns of imperialism. Between the 1870s and the 1920s, life expectancy fluctuated between 20.2 and 25.5 years, with no upward trend (Visaria and Visaria 1983, p. 502). It is only from the 1920s that all the basic indexes of survival began to show an upward movement. The literacy rates of the population were also abysmally low. Only about 6 percent of the population was barely literate as revealed by the censuses of 1891 and 1901.

British rule ended with the great Bengal famine of 1943–1944. Estimates of excess deaths over the years 1943–1946 caused by that famine have varied from 1.8 million to 2.4 million (Maharatna 1996) to 2.62 million to 3.05 million (Sen 1981) and 3.5 million to 3.8 million (Greenough 1982, pp. 299–309).

While El Niño events, combined with warfare and the ceaseless extraction of the incomes of the colonial countries, produced the megadeaths in China and India, the destructive impact of colonial rule was not confined to the famines nor can the devastation caused by the sudden shock of El Niño events be understood without looking at the ecological disaster let loose by armed capitalist marauders in the preceding decades (or centuries, in the case of Latin America and coastal Africa). I will sketch some aspects of the environmental change and the health situation of the Indians under British rule as an illustration of the processes let loose by colonialism—processes that are often continuing under the class-ridden, dependent postcolonial regimes (see also chapter 13).

Arguably the most destructive impact of British conquest on India's environment occurred in the first century of British rule. When conducting military campaigns and flushing out communities resisting dominion, the British often followed a scorched-earth policy, cutting down forests and destroying all natural obstacles against the rapid march of the army. Many of the fortresses in northern India were ringed by forests. The British systematically destroyed the forests while besieging the forts and as a preventive against future rebels using them as refuge (Mann 1998, p. 409). Much of the soil between the Ganges and Yamuna rivers was saliferous, and one of the trees that thrived on that soil was the dhak tree. The destruction of the forests exposed the topsoil to rapid erosion and brought the saline layers nearer the surface. In eastern and western India, many of the resisting autochthonous communities saw their means of livelihood deliberately destroyed by conquering British troops. Not content with such destruction and the abolition of the Mughal practice of exempting gardens and groves from taxation, in a large part of today's western Uttar Pradesh they also forbade the plantation of new mango groves, because they were supposed to be potential shelters of rebels and other mischief makers.

Large irrigation projects were executed by the British on the upper reaches of the Yamuna without providing adequate drainage. Problems of waterlogging soon became serious in the irrigated areas and threw thousands of acres out of cultivation (Whitcombe 1972, 1995; Mann 1998).

Many British geologists and engineers working in India wrote about the problems caused by such thoughtless interference with the environment (Whitcombe 1972, pp. 285–289). Between the 1830s and 1840s, several surgeons in the service of the EIC such as Alexander Gibson, E. G. Balfour, Hugh Cleghorn senior and his nephew, Hugh Cleghorn junior, had warned the governments of Bombay and Madras about unchecked deforestation and soil erosion causing harvest failures, revenue losses, and famines. Some of them also made a connection between water pollution and cholera and the effect deforestation could have on water supply (Grove 1995, chapter 8). These arguments led the Bombay government to set up in 1847 the first forest department of the country for conservation. Eventually, following the recommendations of a German expert on forestry, Dietrich Brandis, an imperial forest department was established (Rangarajan 1996, chapter 2).

Dictates of imperial revenue made the recommendations of the surgeons largely an exercise in futility. But as we have noted in chapter 10, in a move to protect timber supplies for various imperial and commercial projects, the government fenced about a fifth of the surface area of British India as forests under its management. That may have checked deforestation in some areas, but it led to the further dispossession and marginalization of many population groups that had depended on forests and grasslands for their livelihood.

In Bengal and Bihar, the territory the British conquered first and that remained the chief source of their land revenue, the backbone of the colonial structure of exploitation, the new rulers instituted the so-called Permanent Settlement of land revenue. Under this system, revenue farmers, called zamindars, were given the power of collecting the land tax from the people claiming to be the occupiers of the land, retaining a part of it themselves and paying the rest to the government treasury. Before British rule, there had been zamindars who claimed the first right to a share of the produce. They had the responsibility for looking after the agricultural infrastructure, generally with the help of the leading families in the villages. These included harvesting water by building temporary dams across suitable inclines and releasing it into reservoirs or peasants' fields as the need arose, digging field channels, excavating tanks, and so on. These superior-right holders also enjoyed limited police and judicial powers. The zamindars instituted by the British were deprived of their magisterial powers except that they were allowed to use virtually any degree of coercion on the peasants so long as it was exercised for facilitating the collection of the land tax and so long as they did not dare to challenge British authority directly. They were also rendered irresponsible in the Permanent Settlement areas because they had somehow to pay the demands stipulated by the state as the only condition for retaining their revenue farming rights. As a result, vast areas of eastern India, which had earlier been protected against drought by local irrigation works, now became repeated prey to want and famine (Bagchi 1976b; Sengupta 1980).

The British resorted to indiscriminate felling of trees for burning the bricks and clearing the land to build barracks, prisons, and roads. Indian railways, whose construction started in 1853, became gigantic devourers of trees and wreckers of the environment. First, the laying down of tracks took no account of any local damage that might be caused by the route chosen. Forests, natural drainage channels, traditionally used trade routes all became victims. The railway sleepers then consumed immense numbers of trees. Finally, before the coalfields of eastern India had been properly explored and exploited, most rail engines used either wood or imported coal as fuel (Whitcombe 1972; Mann 1998). The opening up of mines in Bengal-Bihar destroyed many of the forests and pauperized the forest peoples of the region. Vast numbers of trees in the sub-Himalayan tract were cut down only to rot, because they were difficult to transport to places where they would be used (Rangarajan 1996).

If forests were destroyed almost wantonly during the first century of British rule, wildlife did not fare any better. The cult of the masculine ruler as sportsman inspired many a British official to engage in enormous slaughter of big game and led them to kill some animals, such as the elephant, that had in pre-British times been outside the purview of deliberate hunting as a form of sport (Lahiri-Choudhury 1999b; Rangarajan 2001). However, some lovers of wildlife began to worry about the effect of this slaughter on the availability of future game and even about the possibly adverse effect on the sustainability of the natural resource base.

After conquering the Arakan region and the Tenasserim peninsula in 1852, the British adopted the practice of getting local people involved in teak replanting. The practice of so-called *taunguya* forestry, that is getting the hill people to grow teak plantations on their own land, had precedents in the practices of earlier Myanmarese governments, but the British efficiency in enforcing regulations led to considerable resistance (Bryant 1994). The British tried this coercive inclusiveness in only a few cases. Elsewhere they created a hierarchy of rights between fully reserved forests in which all forest products and game were the property of the government, partially reserved forests and grasslands to which private persons were given access on the payment of a fee or under special conditions, or forests to which rights were given to private persons.

Generally speaking, the government recognized few common property rights. The government regarded itself as the owner of all land and decided how it was to be used. Under this dispensation shepherds lost out almost universally as did the general run of peasants who had treated grazing land as free for use. They also used cow dung as manure and leaves and timber from the forest for a variety of purposes. The immense numbers of Indian cattle failed to reproduce themselves in many regions, and this had a deleterious effect on land productivity and on the availability of fats and protein for most peasants (Bagchi 1976b; Baker 1984; Bhattacharya 1998). The imperial forest policies adversely affected the income and life patterns of the swidden or settled cultivators, food gatherers, and shepherds and naturally provoked resistance, including many open rebellions (Rangarajan 1996; Saldanha 1998).

The response of the colonial state remained tardy and woefully inadequate in delivering the benefits of scientific advances made in the nineteenth century in terms of medicines and prophylaxis. Until the late nineteenth century, when the discoveries of Louis Pasteur, Robert Koch, and Ronald Ross percolated to the medical fraternity, the doctors trained in Western medicine knew very little that practitioners of Ayurvedic or Unani medicines or surgery did not know. Often the shoe was in fact on the other foot. Also, many diseases were the direct result of poverty, squalor, and starvation. People died in large numbers of cholera, diarrhea, and malaria after the peak of the famine scarcity was over, because they had become badly weakened by long periods of nutrition below basal metabolic levels (Guz 1989; Arnold 1989, 1993; Maharatna 1996).

The long delay in the eradication of smallpox in India illustrates the problems faced by the capitalist-colonial regime in British India and other dependencies, even when they tried to do something to tackle a dread disease. Pre-British India had a system of variolation that had been described in detail in 1767 by J. Z. Holwell and in 1831 by Radhakanta Deb (Arnold 1993, chapter 3). This depended on taking the matter for injection from human subjects. Jennerian vaccination was sought to be introduced in India soon after its use in Britain, for the protection of the Europeans to begin with. But it proved difficult to transmit the vaccine to India by arm-to-arm method. When the system grew up of sending the vaccine as lymph, it often became ineffective on arrival or at the point of use because of defective methods of preservation (after all, refrigeration also was a late nineteenth-century technology). It took considerable amount of innovation and adaptation to get vaccines produced in India for there to be anything like an adequate supply of the vaccine (Arnold 1993; Bhattacharya 2001). In any case, where the government's expenditure on public health was a negligible fraction of the budget, it was ridiculous to expect very much from the official campaign for smallpox vaccination. The official excuse for the ill success of the campaign often was the caste prejudice against vaccination with cow lymph or blood of polluted humans. Certainly, there was prejudice of that kind among many upper-caste Indians. But that prejudice was strengthened by the frequent failure of vaccination or, worse, infection caused by degraded vaccine.

I will end this part of my narrative by citing estimates of the rate of growth of population and of the expectation of life in late colonial India.

Tables 18.1 and 18.2 tell their own story. Until 1921–1931 there is no sign that the minuscule supply of modern medicine and public health care was at all effective in raising Indian life spans beyond what they were before the 1870s. The decade of the 1930s again saw a stagnation in South Asian longevity. Then came World War II and the final stage of the South Asian independence. The record of the postcolonial governments of South Asia, except for Sri Lanka and some state governments of India, notably Kerala, in providing basic health services to the people has been anything but glorious. But whatever advances have been made in this area have been made under independent regimes—not under the civilizing British rulers.

Table 18.1.   Rates of Growth of Population and the Expectation of Life in India as a Whole, 1891–1941

Decade	Rate of Growth of Population (Percentage per Year)	Life Expectation at Birth (Years)	
		Male	Female
1881–1891	1.86	26.3	27.2
1891–1901	0.18	22.2	23.4
1901–1911	0.56	25.3	25.5
1911–1921	0.03	21.8	22.0
1921–1931	1.05	29.6	30.1
1931–1941	1.36	29.5	29.6

Source: Dyson 1989a, p. 6.

DEMOGRAPHIC LOSSES IN OTHER LANDS PEOPLED WITH NONWHITES IN THE LATE NINETEENTH CENTURY

The nineteenth century recorded huge losses of population in other countries settled by nonwhites. Great uncertainty surrounds estimates of initial population and hence of the losses in Africa caused by various jihads and by the final scramble for Africa on the part of the European powers. Losses through wars and war-related dislocations of the African economies, societies, and seasonal population movements can only be conjectured. These losses added to the numbers of Africans sacrificed to the five centuries of African slave trade. The combination of ENSO drought and the onslaught of Western imperialism caused the decimation of the peasantry in Tanzania, Mozambique, and southern Africa and provoked resistance by the desperate peasantry and brutal reprisals by the invading European powers (Davis 2001).

The aggression of capital backed by arms did not cause misery only in formal colonies or countries directly invaded by European armies. In the nineteenth century it wrought untold misery also in Latin American countries. The latter had been brought under oligarchic criollo rule after the demise of the formal Spanish and Portuguese empires in that continent. We will take up the case of Brazil, which for much of the nineteenth century remained the destination of the largest nominal flow of British investments in Latin America, until its place was taken by Argentina (Rippy 1959). Brazil had become, by the eighteenth century, virtually a dependency of Britain since its formal ruling power, Portugal, had passed into a condition of vassalage to England (Manchester 1933). The Anglo-Portuguese trade treaty of 1703 formalized this economic vassalage. Portugal obtained the privilege of exporting wine to England on favorable terms in exchange for giving Britain the right to export manufactures to Portugal, and hence to Brazil, on privileged terms. The

Table 18.2.   **Expectation of Life at Birth (in Years) in Different Regions of India, 1881–1921**

Region	Year or Period	Male	Female
Bombay Presidency[a]	1881–1891	27.27	25.98
	1891–1901	11.93	16.12
	1901–1911	20.63	18.99
	1911–1921	12.38	11.39
United Provinces[a]	1881–1891	21.60	23.58
	1891–1901	16.29	19.55
	1901–1911	14.97	13.83
	1911–1921	12.63	12.07
Madras Presidency[a]	1881–1891	33.90	32.98
	1891–1901	29.90	28.76
	1901–1911	29.03	26.69
	1911–1921	19.80	17.00
Madras, Ghulam Mahmud's khandan[b]	1881–1890	27.4	23.6
	1891–1900	34.7	27.9
	1901–1910	24.3	29.6
	1911–1920	28.0	19.0

Sources: [a] Clark 1989, table 1. The life table was based on the United Nations South Asia model. [b] Vatuk 2002, p. 250. The United Nations South Asia model life table was used.

inability of either Portugal or Brazil to protect their manufactures against foreign competition ensured that neither could start on a path of industrialization for another two centuries (Furtado 1963).

England further cemented its privileged position in Brazil from 1808, when Dom Joao, the Portuguese king, fled the invading French and sought refuge in Brazil under British protection. Under various treaties, culminating in that of 1827, Britain obtained major trade concessions and extraterritorial privileges from Brazil. The treaty of 1827 was the price Brazil's new rulers had to pay to gain recognition for the independent empire of Brazil (Manchester 1933/1966). Inevitably, Brazil became specialized in the export of primary products. The two biggest exports of Brazil in the nineteenth century were sugar and coffee, until the older export, sugar, was eclipsed by coffee altogether.

The northeast of Brazil had long been its major sugar-producing region and become notorious in the geography of world hunger and oppression. The working force for the sugar *engenhos* (plantations) was provided by captured slaves from Africa (Furtado 1963, chapters 1–7). From the eighteenth century, the Brazilian industry entered into a long phase of declining profits as sugar prices came down and as the Caribbean islands of Jamaica, St. Domingue, and Cuba produced sugar at a lower cost. The plantations survived by withdrawing from market transactions as far as possible. But Brazilian plantations proved to be a great killer of African lives: Brazil was the last country in the Western Hemisphere to formally abolish slavery, and that happened only in 1888. Even after agreeing, under British pressure, to ban slave trade, more than a million slaves were smuggled by Brazilian slavers (Curtin 1969, p. 268). Unlike in the United States, no successful slave-breeding regions grew up in Brazil, and imports were used to replace the huge numbers of Africans perishing in the cane fields of the northeast.

Alongside the sugar industry, a stock-raising industry, generally operated by free labor, also grew up in the northeast. The standard of living of that labor was generally higher: when markets for their products failed, the pastoralists could use their herds as their main source of consumption. When the ENSO droughts of 1876–1879 and 1896–1897 struck Brazil, however, the slaves, the dependent peasantry, and the herders were all badly affected (Davis 2001). The *Nordeste* (northeast) had already experienced grievous deforestation and uncompensated environmental destruction as adventurers scoured the land in search of minerals, timber merchants cut down forests to feed distant markets, and planters of sugar and cotton cleared land in frenzies of speculation. When drought struck, the affected people had no recourse but to make long treks to towns and ports in search of food and water. Many never reached there and died on the way. Those who did found little succor and were often forcibly turned away. A slaveholding oligarchy had little respect for other people's lives, particularly the lives of blacks and shirtless half-castes. Some of these oligarchs had their determined inhumanity steeled by the same logic as had formed the ideological armor of the likes of Lord Lytton and Sir Richard Temple in British India in the same epoch.

The British had influenced Brazilian society not only through economic might but also by shaping the world outlook of the oligarchs. Most articulate members of the Brazilian ruling class were advocates of laissez-faire and admirers of Britain as the most successful practitioner of the political economy of free trade (Graham 1968). To laissez-faire political economy was added the Comtean and Spencerian ideals of progress. The Republic of Brazil had the Comtean slogan "Order and Progress" emblazoned on its flag. The order would come from preserving the existing social system and its racist hierarchy as much as possible; the progress would come from scientific education and a process of natural selection as proclaimed by Herbert Spencer and his eugenicist acolytes (Graham 1968).

When the drought began driving *retirantes* (refugees from the *sertão*, or backlands of the interior) toward the cities and the ports, Caetano Estelita, the president of Ceará, the province most affected from 1877, tried to organize relief. When the drought persisted, he and his allies tried to provide them with doles. However, the minister for imperial affairs, Antonio da Costa Pinto, had first to guard the fragile imperial treasury (Britannica 1902a, p. 350). The parlous state of Brazilian finances was partly due to its dependence on customs duties for most of the revenues because the oligarchs refused to pay direct taxes and because, as a consequence, Brazil owed a large debt to foreign, mainly British financiers. Costa Pinto and his allies argued that, while the Brazilian constitution guaranteed subsistence to every citizen, it did not mean that they had to encourage idleness (Davis 2001, pp. 82–90). So starving people, put on manual work, died as surely as they might have done if no official hand had been stretched toward them. The famished died also of attacks by vigilantes of the rich in the cities. They died when they were forced on boats leaving for the Amazon region, sometimes against the protests of landlords who feared a labor shortage owing to the exodus. In the two famines of 1876–1879 and 1896–1900, 2 million people are estimated to have died in Brazil (Davis 2001, p. 7). Another untold number died in another intervening famine of 1888–1891. These were huge numbers in a country whose population in 1900 has been estimated as 17.98 million (Sánchez-Albornoz 1974). The awesome scale of the holocaust is better appreciated if we realize that the population of the worst-affected region, namely, the *Nordeste*, could not have exceeded 3–4 million (Britannica 1902a, p. 348).[3]

Several millenarian, or apocalyptic, movements sprang up among the famine-affected *sertanajes* (inhabitants of the dry region) (Davis 2001). The leader of the most remarkable of them, Antonio Conselheiro, preaching the Christian gospel of equality and declaring the oligarchs in the cities to be anti-Christian, gathered his faithful followers and built up the city of Canudos— 435 miles inland from the port of San Salvador—as a refuge for the hungry. The city was on land supposed to be the property of a powerful *fazendaro* (owner of a *fazenda*, or large estate). The Brazilian authorities had to mount three expeditions, each more ruthless than the last, between 1896 and October 1897 before they could subdue Canudos and raze it. By then only four of the resisters survived: an old man, two other full-grown men, and a child (Euclydes da Cunha, as quoted by Davis 2001, p. 193).

Brazilian oligarchs faced the problem of inadequate social reproduction of labor, which became especially acute as the slave trade had finally to be wound up. Instead of trying to solve it by making sure that the majority of people could survive and reproduce they tried to "whiten" the race by bringing in European labor on privileged terms. But European immigrants had more attractive destinations than the sugar plantations of the *Nordeste*, the mines of Minas Gerais or the coffee plantations of São Paulo. Most of the attempts to create prosperous colonies of European immigrants ended in failure (Furtado 1963, chapter 22). After all, an economy that had run for centuries on slave labor wastefully used could not generate the kind of dynamism that was displayed by the United States, Canada, or Australia. Brazil remained an underdeveloped agrarian economy run on racist principles down to the 1930s. As in the case of casteism in India, the ideology of race is still dying a lingering death in Brazil.

On the basis of our brief review of the environmental destruction and loss of lives caused by capitalism armed, we can hazard the generalization that these effects are the more extreme the greater the difference in the technologies of the marauders as against those of the resisters, the greater the drive for quick accumulation and conquest on the part of the aggressors and the lesser the social cohesiveness among the resisters, and the deeper the inroad doctrines of competition and social Darwinism have made among the ruling strata of the resisting population.

NOTES

1. *Journal of the North China Branch of the Royal Asiatic Society*, 1865, vol. 2, p. 143, as quoted in Chesnaux, Bastid, and Bergère 1976, p. 149.

2. Some of that indemnity was used to spread the light of western ways of thinking among the Chinese (Smedley 1972, p. 56).

3. In my account of environmental destruction under capitalist colonialism, I have concentrated on China, India, and Brazil mainly because they starkly illustrate the typical processes of damage to nature and humankind under the dispensation of capital. For a more general account of environmental damage under capitalism and the struggles of conservationists and other concerned citizens to stem it, see Foster 1994.

IV

THE TWENTIETH CENTURY: ANTISYSTEMIC STRUGGLES, WARS, AND CHALLENGES TO GLOBAL CAPITAL

19

Setting the Stage for Megawars

INTERIMPERIALIST CONFLICTS, FASCISM, AND ANTISYSTEMIC MOVEMENTS

The foundations of the twentieth century were laid between the 1880s and 1913 as the European powers completed their conquest of Africa, and the competition for redivision of imperial spoils came to a boiling point. This is the era in which the military-industrial complex, familiar to all students of the twentieth century, came into active operation in all major capitalist counties (McNeill 1983, chapter 8). We have seen in part 2 how superior military organization often yielded victory to a European power with smaller resources of manpower in inter-European conflicts. The organization of work in the new modes of naval and army functioning then was transferred to civilian modes of organization of factories. As private enterprises came to service military requirements, advances in civilian technology then became useful inputs in military conflicts (Brewer 1989). This feature became much more pronounced as the industrial revolution and the exploitation of fossil fuels made it possible to overcome earlier constraints imposed by human and animal energy or easily renewable energy such as water or wind power. Many of the more capital-intensive innovations came to depend on state patronage, and that patronage was generally more easily procured when military needs came to the fore. This feature is well illustrated by the spread of techniques of mass production from the United States to European countries. For a number of reasons, such as the higher wages of labor, the abundance of natural resources, the difficulty of retaining highly mobile skilled labor (see "Introduction" by S. B. Saul in Saul 1970), U.S. manufacturers such as Eli Whitney, Blanchard, Hussey, and McCormick had pioneered methods of manufacturing guns, machines, tools, and other products on a mass scale by using interchangeable parts. After the exhibition of these advances in the Crystal Palace exhibition of 1851, British manufacturers and politicians became aware of U.S. superiority in these areas and after a parliamentary inquiry a government arsenal was set up to manufacture guns using American methods; with some encouragement from the government, private companies also began manufacturing small arms using similar methods (Ames and Rosenberg 1968/1970). But until naval competition renewed between European powers in the 1880s, private manufacturers sustained themselves by selling guns to sportsmen as well as the government (McNeill 1983, pp. 234–36). A partnership between private arms manufacturers and the government in the development of armaments had already begun. But this partnership became much more pronounced as competition between France, Britain, Germany, and Russia intensified from the 1880s. Battleships became bigger, better protected against guns, and were mounted with superior guns; the lethal quality of small arms and artillery was steadily upgraded; and with those improvements went necessary changes in tactics in land and naval wars.

This is also the period when Japan emerged as a new imperialist power with ambitions of expansion along the eastern Pacific rim and the United States expanded its imperial ambitions from domination of the Western Hemisphere to the Pacific (Zimmermann 2002). Japan surged ahead as an imperialist power. It grabbed Taiwan from China by defeating it in 1895; it signed a treaty of alliance with Britain in 1902, defeated Russia after launching a surprise attack on its naval base at Port Arthur before declaring war[1] in 1904 and established its presence on the mainland of Asia, and then took over Korea in 1910. In 1898 the United States took over Cuba and the Philippines and annexed Hawaii by a congressional resolution. China, with its crumbling empire but vast resources, became the coveted prize for all the imperialist powers. But the fateful armed conflict for control of the Pacific and northeastern Asia would center on the United States and Japan—two powers that expanded into the Pacific basin from the late nineteenth century.

The end of the nineteenth century also marked the end of British dominance of world trade, finance, and industry. In Europe Germany became the biggest producer of industrial output, with best-practice technologies in a range of products, from steel to synthetic fertilizers, rubber, and electrical equipment. Across the Atlantic, the United States emerged as the richest country in the world, rich in agricultural, natural resources, as well as industrial output. A special urgency for carving out an empire drove particularly those newly industrializing countries in which firms became organized in cartels or outright monopolies, eager to extend cartels to territories in which they had privileged access. Germany sought a larger presence in Africa through a consolidation and extension of the gains it made in the 1880s. It also eyed parts of the Russian dominions and the areas vacated by the Ottomans, possibly as direct dominions or dependencies of the new Reich created by wars and diplomacy since 1866 (Craig 1981; Raff 1988; Hobsbawm 1992). German aspirations for acquiring a formal or informal empire in central and eastern Europe were in direct conflict with the expansionist goals of czarist Russia, which hoped to gain a part of the crumbling Ottoman empire while extending its control over the central Asian sultanates and khanates.

Benefiting from massive flows of immigrants and capital (chapter 7), by the early twentieth century, the United States emerged as the most affluent and powerful capitalist nation. With an ideology of manifest destiny, it had created a privileged domain in the Western Hemisphere through continental expansion and the promulgation of the Monroe Doctrine. In an early demonstration of its military power in the 1840s, it had dismembered Mexico and expanded its territory by half. A new opportunity arose with the revolt in Cuba and the Philippines against Spanish rule; in 1898 on the pretext of helping end the oppressive rule of Spain, the United States installed its own regime over those two lands (Williams 1981, chapter 13; V. Jones 1996; Zimmerman 2002).[2] While Cuba came to be formally ruled by politicians subservient to the United States, the Philippines was colonized after a bitter war and was not granted formal independence until after World War II. The strategy applied in Cuba of preserving informal imperium in formally liberated colonies had been perfected in most countries of Latin America by Britain from the nineteenth century and would be extended by the United States and others on a global scale after World War II and the rise of anticolonial movements.

With Germany as the main challenger to British hegemony in Europe, World War I, as a lethal tournament among the imperialist powers with the lives of their citizens and subjects as pawns, was played out primarily in the European theater. But it extended also to the Middle East as the Ottoman empire entered the lists as an ally of Germany and Austro-Hungary. Japan had concluded an entente with Britain in 1902 and, partly taking advantage of that, had launched a war against czarist Russia in 1904 and obtained parts of northeastern Asia as its colony (see also chapter 12). Japan entered World War I on the Allied side. In 1915 it presented a set of twenty-one demands to the Yüan Shih-k'ai government, seeking to turn China into a protectorate, in addition to establishing Japanese predominance in Shandong, Manchuria, Inner Mongolia, and the southeastern coastal provinces (Chesnaux, Barbier, and Bergère 1977, p. 17). In the Versailles settlement of 1919, Japan obtained the colonies of Germany in the Pacific and the Shandong peninsula. But even before the war, its rulers regarded the occupation of China to be essential for Japan's power and prosperity. This objective, of course, put it on a collision course with not only the United States, the other major imperialist power in the Pacific, but with all the other Western powers with interests in Asia as well.

The word *imperialism* came into vogue in the period from the 1870s, and some publicists and statesmen proudly called themselves imperialists (Hobsbawm 1992, p. 60). By the beginning of the twentieth century, several politicians and publicists were elaborating theories of imperialism, which they regarded as a new phase of human history. The major theories of imperialism date from the early 1900s. The names of J. A. Hobson (1902), J. Hilferding (1910/1981), Rosa Luxemburg (1913/1951), Nikolai Bukharin (1917/1964), and finally, V. I. Lenin (1917/1964) are associated with those theories.[3] The factors behind interimperialist conflicts and wars included contests over markets and supplies of raw materials, drives to invest the surplus extracted from domestic or foreign operations in profitable channels, the rapidly increasing concentration of economic power in the hands of big corporations with their attendant designs to limit competition as much as possible, and finally the determination of old imperialist powers such as Britain, France, and the Austro-Hungarian empire to retain their foreign possessions and, as noted above, new imperialist powers such as czarist Russia, Germany, and Japan, to get a bigger share of the European dependencies.

The theorists of imperialism stressed different aspects of the looming conflict. Hobson stressed the move in advanced capitalist countries from competitive capitalism and free trade to the organization of monopolies and rise of protectionism (the mother of monopolies) as being responsible for a persistent tendency toward underconsumption. As monopolies spread, the workers, the main consuming class, received a smaller share, and consumed a lesser proportion, of the national product. The capitalists then had to find new fields to invest their capital. That led to a demand for new colonies in which the surplus capital could be invested. Hobson also saw a special role for a coterie of financiers who egged their governments on to conquest. But as a liberal, he considered the situation to be remediable through the restoration of free trade and appropriate social policies. Virtually all the other theorists of imperialism were avowed Marxists, but some, and especially Lenin, were also influenced by Hobson's view, tracing the aggravation of the problem of underconsumption under capitalism to the growth of cartels, trusts, and monopolies. Hilferding firmly linked the rise of big capital and the emergence of high finance and styled the amalgam *finance capital*. In this he was drawing on his knowledge of Germany where there was a far greater linkage of large banks and big firms than in Britain.

Rosa Luxemburg alleged that there was a persistent tendency under capitalism to give rise to underconsumption. Thus according to her, capitalism always needed external markets for the incentive to invest to be kept up. These external markets were to be found in the colonies where capital extended its sway by breaking down natural economies. Luxemburg also contended that investment of new capital on an extended scale logically needed continually expanding spheres of investment that could only be provided by conquering new colonies. Bukharin criticized her by showing that, logically, investment could simply be supported by new investment in a closed economy. That argument did not have much explanatory power in the real world of capitalism because it was periodically plagued by overproduction crises. Moreover, as we have seen, capitalism was from the beginning a system fomenting wars and conflicts for new markets and colonies. But another strand of Bukharin's critique had more force: Luxemburg ignored the stimulus to productive investment that competition between firms and states organized on the basis of the class power of capitalists provided (Bagchi 1986). However, Luxemburg focused on the role of military expenditure in enlarging effective demand in the capitalist countries, very often at the expense of the workers' share of the national product. In fact, as in the past, military projects also led to an increase in economies of scale, innovations, and increases in productivity. Improvements in aviation technology, use of nuclear power, and the initial advances in computer technology are some of the best examples of this potential. The Promethean drive of capitalism armed has, however, continued to deprive billions of people of the benefits that those improvements could have conferred as a result of the destruction of wars.

Bukharin and, finally, Lenin welded the elements from Hobson's and Hilferding's theories to produce a rationale for the eruption of World War I. In Lenin's view, by the end of the nineteenth century, capitalism had taken on the characteristics emphasized by Hobson and Hilferding, so that the tendency toward underconsumption and inadequate incentive to invest on the basis of the domestic market had become a general tendency. But because the whole world had become parceled out among the major imperial powers, as formal or informal colonies or spheres of influence, and their interests were mutually irreconcilable, it was inevitable that war between them should break out and the conflict would become global. Moreover, as I observed elsewhere (Bagchi 1986, p. 27), imperialism was characterized by "a persistent tendency of *mature* capitalist state systems to generate conflicts."

I have one major difference from most of the theories that I have sketched so briefly. Building partly on the work of Ragnar Nurkse and Matthew Simon, I have shown (Bagchi 1972b, 2002b) that the nonwhite colonies were primarily sources of surplus extracted by the capitalist powers and were not destinations of their net investment, except perhaps in certain brief phases. In short, the colonies were not merely objects of conquest; they also provided a significant surplus to their colonizers.

Imperialism used not only the military power of the advanced capitalist states but also nationalist ideology whose development accompanied the growth of capitalism in Europe and spread to other countries. A nationalist ideology undergirded the expansionist plans of all imperialist powers, including the United States (Greenfeld 1992; Hobsbawm 1990; Hastings 1997). Not only dictators and monarchs but also politicians and media in formal democracies deliberately fanned the fumes of jingoism.[4] Between 1875 and 1900, Britain, already the world's greatest empire, added a territory measuring some 5 million square miles and containing at least 90 million people. By 1900 Great Britain ruled over 13 million square miles of territory populated by 370 million subjects, 300 million of whom lived in its Indian empire (Cole and Postgate 1961, p. 403). Between 1884 and 1900, France added 3.5 million square miles with nearly 40 million subjects to its African empire (Cole and Postgate 1961, pp. 403–4). German rulers likewise wanted their economic and military power to be reflected in a bigger presence in Africa and central and southeastern Europe. In Africa, Germany occupied southwestern Africa (today's Namibia) and Tanganyika.

Nationalism almost inevitably transformed itself into imperialism as far as the major capitalist countries were concerned. On the other hand, people struggling against alien rule also generally found the nation to be the most effective collective unit for building solidarity to fight imperialism. It is hardly an accident that Lenin was writing extensively on the right of nations to self-determination at the same time he was sketching the etiology of imperialism (Bagchi 1986). The social, political, and territorial borders of nascent nations were often contested territory and some of them harbored their own imperialist ambitions. Japan is the most important example of a nation facing the threat of domination by expansive colonial powers that itself became a colonial power. The logic of intercapitalist competition, using arms and state power as strategic instruments, spurred Japan's emergence as a ferocious imperialist power.

The seeds of two sets of intertwined antisystemic struggles began to germinate during this epoch of global conflict between major capitalist powers. On the one hand, the doctrines of Marx and Engels were adopted by the German Social Democratic Party, which emerged by the 1890s as the biggest mass party in the world. The beginnings of Russian communism also can be dated to this period. The Bolshevik Party, which spearheaded the Russian Revolution of 1917, was born in the first decade of the twentieth century.

Another strand of these struggles, as I have mentioned, was the rise of movements for self-determination of peoples all over the world. In Egypt this movement began almost as soon as the country came under British rule in the early 1880s. Some of these movements also became imbued with goals of social transformation that would grant them the civil freedom that European powers had promised, only to render that promise into a mockery.[5] Some others harked back to a traditional, patriarchal society. The struggle between these contradictory goals and their protagonists stored up troubles for many of the lands that gained formal independence from colonial rule during the twentieth century.

In India and many other non-European colonies and dependencies of the imperialist powers, organized struggles for self-determination began during the latter part of the nineteenth century. In the European dependencies of the imperialist powers, such as czarist Russia, the Austro-Hungarian empire, the German Reich, and the Ottoman empire, a settlement of territories on the basis of claims of national identity took place after World War I. But the non-European dependencies had to wait for formal independence until the end of World War II.

There was no dearth of imperial ideologies in the older empires such as Britain and France. The period from the 1880s saw an outpouring of such ideologies among virtually all the major capitalist countries. Some of these ideologies stressed imperialism as a means of social uplift of the poor in metropolitan countries (Semmel 1993). Some others relied mainly on theories of scientific racism and the civilizing mission (Curtin 1971). The latter had a close affinity with fascism, which would abolish freedom for not only inferior races but also lower-class whites in Europe. In Germany, for example, even as large numbers of workers rallied to the Social Democrats, the more authoritarian sections of the ruling class were busy designing rationales and laws that would deprive dissenters of the right to speak freely (Craig 1981; Raff 1988).

Although fascism got its name from the movement that Mussolini used to overthrow a democratically elected government in a putsch, its virulence reached a peak with the coming of the Nazi Party to power in Germany in 1933. The horrendous success of Nazism in the brief period of its glory between 1933 and 1942 inspired fascist movements and takeovers in other countries such as Austria.

Fascism is a system under which the legislative, executive, and judicial powers are collapsed under the same authority, which brooks no challenge, competition, or scrutiny of its actions. Ironically, it is premised on a preexisting separation of these functions in the state, and succeeds the birth of a rational-bureaucratic state apparatus. It invariably seeks to preserve or restore previous holders of power and property. Its rise to climax in a state with the largest socialist movement in western Europe is not accidental. Not only was it directed against the antisystemic movement of the workers but it also used the mobilization of the masses that the socialists in Germany had carried out

for decades. Similar observations may be made with regard to the fascist and
Falangist mobilization in Italy and Spain, respectively. Fascism can be seen
as a preemptive measure to preclude the installation or continuation of a democratic regime that threatens the established order.[6] In a country such as Germany, the erstwhile rulers continued to harbor imperialist aspirations, and
their spokesmen sought to subjugate other peoples to the rule of the chosen
volk. We have already seen that racism gave a cutting edge to the ideology of
conquest in non-European countries. What the Nazis did was to turn that
racism inward and build on the anti-Semitic traditions of the Christian church
and the absolutist states of Europe, especially since the fifteenth century, that
is, exactly when the Portuguese and the Spaniards were pioneering the strategy of armed trade against non-European peoples.

Not all antidemocratic, anticommunist regimes that proliferated in Europe
between the two world wars professed an explicitly fascist ideology: the authoritarian regime of Antonio Salazar, for example, professed a "corpora-
tivist" ideology, claiming to represent economic and occupational groups and
being ruled by technocrats and bureaucrats from above (Hobsbawm 1995,
chapter 4). But when France, the most powerful country in continental Europe, fell to the Nazis, many right-wing regimes found it expedient to ally
with fascists or maintain a tactical neutrality between the Allies and the Axis
powers during World War II.

In the ex-colonial countries or countries ruled by coteries closely allied with
major imperial powers, a fascist regime could be externally imposed or could
sustain itself through external support. Such a regime should really be called
military-repressive rather than fascist, depending as it does on the police, the
military, and the secret service rather than on mobilizing the masses. (Of
course, the fascist regime also used these arms of the state but it also perfected
mobilization techniques and turned ordinary people into informers and, when
occasion demanded, murderers.) Thus the fascist regime of General Suharto
installed itself in Indonesia in 1965, killing up to a million Indonesians (Dwyer
and Santikarma 2004), with the active support of the United States and its allies. The perceived threat in that case was the growth of the Communist Party
of Indonesia, which had emerged as the largest communist party in Asia outside China. Similarly, U.S. support played a critical role in the overthrow of
the democratically elected administration of President Salvador Allende by
General Pinochet and in assuring the subsequent durability of Pinochet's
regime. In South Africa the almost century-long innings of a racist regime,
which severely abridged the freedom and human rights of the vast majority of
its inhabitants, could be played only with the active or tacit support of Britain,
the United States, and other Western powers. This was primarily a racist-
repressive regime run in the interest of white property owners who bribed the

white workers by treating them better than their black brethren. But it acquired a fascist character in relation to the white population because it severely curbed the freedom of dissenting whites as well.

WORLD WAR I

World War I was actively fought by the major imperialist powers of Europe, with the United States joining the war in 1917; Italy and Japan also joined the war partly because of the imperial ambitions of their ruling classes and partly out of fear that they might be deprived of any share of the spoils if they did not also pitch in. As indicated earlier, all the major European powers were locked in an arms race, especially with regard to the building of warships from the 1880s. The army was also fitted out with weapons of increasingly lethal effect. Because the quality of armaments and training differed among the major powers, a single figure such as the number of men in arms no longer conveys the differential capacity of different powers in waging war. For example, even though Russia's military expenditure of £88.2 million in 1914 exceeded the £76.8 million spent by Britain (Taylor 1954, pp. xxviii–xxx), in a global war it would be less effective than the British whose navy at the time had a presence in all the strategic waters. Moreover, in a race with Germany and France, the British had spent more and more of their defense expenditure on the navy, so that in 1914 the navy accounted for £48.8 million out of the total of £76.8 million military expenditure (McNeill 1983, p. 287). In any case, relatively poor empires like czarist Russia and the Austro-Hungarian empire were spending upward of 6 percent of their national income on the military and even then were unable to match the prowess of Britain and Germany, which were spending a lesser proportion of their national incomes on the same head (Taylor 1954, pp. xxviii–xxx).

Britain enjoyed two substantial advantages over all the other European powers. In its far-flung empire, it possessed unparalleled resources and armies, which could be thrown into the war. In particular, the large Indian army effectively defended the British empire in Asia and eastern Africa. During the war, combatants from the Union of South Africa, Australia, New Zealand, and Canada also fought alongside British soldiers. The French also mobilized their colonial possessions; but they were far less extensive than British dependencies and dominions. Second, no power could match the strength of the British navy.

Russia and Germany both mobilized approximately 13 million persons during World War I, whereas the United States, entering the war only in 1917, mobilized 3.8 million (Kennedy 1989, table 25). But Russia and Germany were both devastated by the war, whereas the United States came out much stronger than before. It faced no attack on its soil, sustained few casualties, and its enormous economic potential was invigorated by a booming market for its products. Japan gained the former colonies of Germany in Asia and the Pacific and Britain and France gained the German colonies in the Middle East and Africa under the Treaty of Versailles and the so-called Mandate of the League of Nations. But the latter two powers were weakened by the hemorrhage of the war.

No major war can be considered to be the *sole* result of planning for profit by capitalists (cf. Hobsbawm 1992, p. 315). But calculation of profit always figured prominently in the exercise of power *and* the conduct of war as a means of defending or extending that power. The interests of capitalists in the belligerent nations of western Europe, wedded to aggressive nationalisms, played a major role in the eruption of World War I.

The twentieth century has been called a century of megadeaths, most caused directly or indirectly by imperialist wars or by such peaceful processes of the working of a vastly unequal international economic order as differential rates of infant mortality, disease, and life expectancy. I will here focus mainly on deaths that can be laid at the doors of major wars. According to Kennedy (1989, p. 278), the losses in World War I for the extended period 1914–1919 "might have been as much as 60 million people, with nearly half of these losses occurring in Russia, and with France, Germany, and Italy also being badly hit." Hobsbawm (1995, p. 26) provides another perspective on the losses:

> The French lost almost 20 per cent of their men of military age, and if we include the prisoners of war, and the permanently disabled and disfigured. . . . Not much more than one in three French soldiers came through the war without harm. The chances of the five million or so British soldiers surviving the war unharmed were just about even. The British lost a generation—half a million men under the age of thirty. . . . One quarter of the Oxford and Cambridge students under the age of twenty-five who served in the British army in 1914 were killed. . . . The Germans, though the numbers of their dead was even greater than the French, lost only a smaller proportion of their much larger military age groups—13 per cent.

By the end of the nineteenth century, the major capitalist powers had vanquished practically all the precapitalist states and empires in the world. Japan was fast learning the military and industrial arts of the barbarians and had already tested them on a crumbling Chinese empire. Advanced military technology had diffused among all the major powers through domestic state patronage of private armament makers and through arms trade. The drive for more power and profit was, then, bound to lead to armed conflict among powers some of whom sought to protect their existing colonies, while others wanted a bigger share in the colonial loot. War was also a way of derailing movements for social change in countries like Germany and Russia. World War I ended in a stalemate for at least two countries with unsatisfied imperial ambitions, Germany and Japan, and sowed the seeds of World War II.

NOTES

1. In this, it was following the precedent of Lord Nelson of Britain who attacked and destroyed the Danish fleet off Copenhagen even though Britain was not at war with Denmark at the time (Liddell Hart 1973, pp. 227–28).

2. The uprising in Cuba against Spain started in 1895 and in the Philippines in 1896. The power of the media to whip up jingoistic sentiments among the general public, which was to be witnessed repeatedly in the twentieth century and beyond, was demonstrated in the U.S. decision to invade Cuba and the Philippines, ostensibly to free oppressed people from thralldom. The "yellow press" publishers "saw in the Cuban situation an opportunity to increase circulation. They sent swarms of reporters and artists to cover the conflict. . . . 'You furnish the pictures,' one publisher allegedly instructed a reluctant artist, 'and I will furnish the war'" (Williams 1981, p. 318). The distinction between the yellow press and others has virtually disappeared as far as the newspapers and TV channels controlled by media barons are concerned.

3. For representative selections from these theories see Fieldhouse 1967; Wolfe 1972. For analysis, see Arrighi 1983; Patnaik 1986; Bagchi 1986; and Hobsbawm 1992, chapter 3.

4. *The Shorter Oxford English Dictionary*, 3rd edition, vol. 1 (Clarendon Press, Oxford 1959) defines *jingo* (originally a music hall refrain, "By Jingo!") as "a nickname for those who supported the policy of Lord Beaconsfield [then British prime minister] in sending a British fleet into Turkish waters to resist the advance of Russia in 1878; hence a blatant 'patriot', a 'Chauvinist'."

5. Ireland, the oldest colony of England, seemed likely to be granted home rule under the Liberal administration that was elected in December 1910. Sir Edward Carson, who had been solicitor general under the Conservatives from 1900 to 1905, provided leadership to the Protestant Ulstermen of Northern Ireland, who armed themselves to fight the move of the legally elected British government, and that government looked the other way (Beckett 1981, chapter 22; Foster 1988, chapter 19). That was one of the decisive points of history at which the political division between the Catholics and Protestants of Northern Ireland became virtually permanent.

6. A definition of fascism provided by Georgi Dimitrov, the Bulgarian communist whom Hitler tried to incriminate for burning the Reichstag in Berlin on 28 February 1933, still seems to be apposite in the context of a developed capitalist economy. In his address to the Seventh Congress of the Communist International on 2 August 1935, Dimitrov, quoting the Thirteenth Plenum of the Executive Committee of the

Communist International defined fascism as, "the open terrorist dictatorship of the most reactionary, most chauvinistic and most imperialist elements of finance capital." Elaborating his point further, Dimitrov asserted that fascism is not "power standing above class, nor government of the petty bourgeoisie or the *lumpen-proletariat* over finance capital. Fascism is the power of finance capital itself. It is the organization of terrorist vengeance against the working class and the revolutionary section of the peasantry and intelligentsia. In foreign policy, fascism is jingoism in its most brutal form, fomenting bestial hatred of other nations" (Dimitrov 1935, p. 4).

20

Revolution, Nazism, Japanese Militarism, and World War II

RISE OF NAZISM AND ITS FALL-OUT

World War I ended with a revolution triggered by the mutiny of the German soldiers and workers against continuing the senseless slaughter. By the end of October 1918, sailors at Wilhelmshaven refused to put out to sea and engage the enemy. By 7 November the revolt spread to Munich and then to Berlin where workers joined the revolting soldiers (Raff 1988; Stackelberg 1999). The kaiser fled the country. The task of suing for peace fell not to the military high command and the courtiers who had plunged the country into war but to the Social Democrats who led the interim government. Generals, such as Erich Ludendorff and Paul von Hindenburg, and right-wing politicians could then claim that it was the civilian, mainly socialist, politicians who were responsible for signing the humiliating peace terms imposed on Germany. From the beginning of the revolution ending the war, one section of the Social Democrats, led by Karl Liebknecht and Rosa Luxemburg, had favored pushing at once toward a socialist transformation of the state and society. A January 1919 uprising of this group, who were called the Spartacists, was crushed by moderate Social Democrats and centrist politicians with the help of the so-called Free Corps, consisting mostly of disbanded soldiers led by their officers. Liebknecht and Luxemburg were both murdered. The crushing of this revolt with the help of vigilantes boded ill for the future of the emerging democracy.

Under the Treaty of Versailles, Germany lost all its colonies in Africa, which were grabbed by Britain and France under the fig leaf of a League of Nations mandate. The Austro-Hungarian empire vanished, as did the Ottoman

empire, with the result that much of western Asia became either direct dependencies or informal colonies of Britain and France. All of southeastern
Europe now became free of Ottoman rule. But the borders of the successor
states remained disputed.

The German aristocrats, military leaders, and capitalists were thoroughly
unhappy about the democratic regime that succeeded the Prussian empire
(Stackelberg 1999). Since the national assembly for drafting the constitution of the new republic met at Weimar, the home of Goethe, the new
regime in Germany came to be known as the Weimar Republic. That constitution had two features, which were used by antidemocratic, right-wing
forces to destroy the republic. First, deputies were to be elected on the basis of proportional representation. In a multiparty system, with severe class
conflicts and a host of parties professing irreconcilable ideological positions, this often meant that no party or combination of parties could obtain
a majority that could form a government. Consequently, there were frequent
elections and changes in government. To meet a situation in which no government could work, under article 48 of the constitution, the president of
the republic was given emergency powers, including that of dismissing or
appointing chancellors, meaning prime ministers, when no party or coalition commanded a majority in the parliament. This safeguard would prove
to be the Achilles' heel of German democracy, as we shall see. Hindenburg
became president of the republic in 1925 and was elected for a second term
in 1932.

The German people resented the enormous indemnity that the victorious
Allies imposed on them. Within May 1921 alone, the reparations to be paid
by Germany were supposed to amount to 20 billion gold marks (Craig 1981,
p. 437). The occupation of the Ruhr by the French, when the payments of
reparations fell behind schedule, added to the sense of national humiliation
and a desire for revenge. The hyperinflation that raged up to 1923 ruined most
middle-class families and added to the misery of the working class.

During the 1920s the Social Democrats usually formed the government, often in coalition with centrist parties. However, the newly founded Communist
Party also attracted a large following. Large sections of the middle class and
businessmen resented the gains made by workers, in the shape of security of
employment and a voice in the running of the workplace, and were alarmed
by the growth in popularity of the Communists. When the world economy
was engulfed in its worst depression after the stock-market crash of October
1929, time also ran out for the Weimar democrats.

In the 1920s, German scientists led the world in physics, chemistry, and
many other branches of the natural sciences. In literature, architecture, and
the plastic arts Germans were also among the avant-garde. But as has been

noted by Berghahn (1987, p. 84), even in the arts, many must be "placed in the camp of those who wanted to reverse the historical trends of the past two hundred years. . . . What united them was their elitism and rejection of liberalism and Marxism, of rationalism and 'materialism.'" Although Germany was a newborn democratic republic and as such should have attracted the sympathy of older democracies such as Britain and France, the ruling classes of the latter were far more concerned with crippling Germany's economic and military power than in helping its democracy to survive the assault of monarchists, militarists, and other forces of the extreme right. This was the significance of the heavy reparations imposed on Germany.

Heinrich Brüning, a Center Party leader, became chancellor in 1930. With the support of President Paul von Hindenburg, he proceeded to ignore the parliament, ruling through emergency decrees. His deflationary economic policy further worsened the disastrous condition of the German economy: despite a severe decline in prices and a steep rise in unemployment, he imposed wage cuts and slashed government expenditure (Craig 1981, chapter 15; Raff 1988, pp. 255–61). The Nazis, who had earlier been insignificant in electoral terms, won a large number of seats in the elections when Brüning dissolved the parliament and fresh elections were held. Frantz von Papen, a right-wing politician and Hindenburg's choice as successor to Brüning in June 1932, failed to revive the economy or arrest the violence of the Nazis. In January 1933 Hindenburg appointed Hitler as chancellor. Ludendorff, who had participated in Hitler's failed putsch of 1923, sent him a prophetic letter:

> By appointing Hitler as *Reichskanzler* you delivered our sacred German fatherland into the custody of one of the greatest demagogues of all times. I solemnly predict that this man will be the ruin of the Reich and will bring down unspeakable sufferings on our nation. Coming generations will curse you in your grave for this deed. (quoted by Raff 1988, p. 263)

Once Hitler became chancellor, he adopted both illegal and quasi-legal means to consolidate his power. His *Sturmabteilung* (Stormtrooper) thugs beat up and killed political opponents while the police looked away; in Prussia they were made into an auxiliary police force. Hitler called for fresh elections to be held on 5 March 1933 (Craig 1981, chapter 16; Berghahn 1987, chapter 4). On 27 February, a fire destroyed the Reichstag, the parliament building. A Dutch vagrant with a dubious past had been seen clambering down the walls. On this evidence alone, Hitler accused the Communists of setting the fire[1] and arrested 4,000 of them and many other left-wing politicians. The historical consensus supports the view that the fire was set by the Nazis. Hitler persuaded Hindenburg to sign an emergency decree suspending the civil liberties of all German citizens accused of any threat to law and order without right of appeal. Right-wing and centrist cabinet members failed to object to the signing of this decree.

Even with the terror unleashed against them, the Communists still received 10.9 percent of the votes cast on 5 March 1933; the Social Democrats retained their share of more than 16 percent, and the Nazis polled 38.7 percent of the votes. Thus the Nazis could get a majority in the Reichstag only with the support of other centrist and right-wing parties. On 23 March 1933, Hitler had his dictatorship legalized by the Enabling Act, granting him absolute power for four years. To ensure the two-thirds majority in the parliament, he had arrested many of the Social Democrat and all the Communist deputies, and surrounded the opera house, where the parliament met, with Nazi thugs. In the end, only the remaining ninety-four Social Democrat deputies voted against the act. Hitler consolidated his regime with the full knowledge of the major capitalists, landowners, higher ranks of the professional classes, and the military. As it turned out, many of them would pay a very high price for their preference.

Behind the rise of fascism, and especially the growth of Nazi power, lay not only the earlier traditions of authoritarianism and militarism but also the crisis in international capitalism and the fear of, and hatred for, communists in ruling-class breasts after the Bolshevik triumph in Russia. In many ways, Germany's defeat in the war, the apportioning of blame for that defeat, and the acceptance of the punitive Versailles treaty imposed on Germany facilitated the rise of German fascism. The onerous terms imposed by the Versailles treaty enabled the Nazis to pose as the defender of German honor and livelihood. In the year of the Versailles settlement, all the European armies were treating Bolshevism as the common enemy, and the hatred of communism persuaded many members of the upper classes to support fascist and Nazi efforts to crush the communists (Mayer 1967). Because in many countries Jews were also among the leaders of the socialists and communists, the hatred of communism easily fused with the anti-Semitism of many members of the liberal bourgeoisie (remember T. S. Eliot and Ezra Pound?) to provide the bacterial culture for the kind of racism that Hitler and the Nazis took to its genocidal heights.

The Nazis imprisoned millions of people, including Jews, Gypsies, Catholics, and homosexuals, and herded them in concentration camps, where they were tortured and killed. In a century of horrors, Nazis set new standards of man's inhumanity to man. There has been a long history of the persecution in Christian Europe of the Jews, who often fled to other countries.[2] In the eleventh century, Pope Urban II called for a crusade to liberate the Holy Land from the Muslims. During the long and difficult trek to the Holy Land, many of the crusaders, joined by the local people, indulged in an orgy of killing of the Jews—much easier targets than the Arabs or the Turks (Mayer 1988, pp.

26–27). Jews in most of the Christian countries of Europe were forbidden to engage in many occupations open to others and to hold any public office. Active persecution and pogroms flared up in moments of conflict or consolidation of particular powers.

The Nazi decision to rid Germany of the Jews might have been taken as early as 1939, but it was in 1941 that final plans for implementing that decision were taken in hand (Breitman 1997). On 20 January 1942, at a high-level meeting in Berlin, the so-called Wannsee Protocol was drawn up. At this conference the task of effecting "the final solution of the Jewish problem" was handed over to Himmler, the head of the Schutzstaffel (SS), the Nazi stormtroopers, and the German police, "without regard to geographical borders." The systematic extermination of Jews and Gypsies in all the territories under the control of the Nazis and their allies was then carried out with military precision (Raff 1988, pp. 308–9). But from the very beginning of Nazi rule in Germany, concentration camps had been set up, and death was the lot of most of the millions of inmates. They included communists, social democrats, liberals, and Jews—any group the Nazis considered to be *untermensch* or a threat to their power. The systematic extermination of Jews started after Hitler had invaded and overrun Poland. All the most notorious extermination camps—five in all, beginning with Auschwitz (Oswiecim)—were set up in Poland. The Polish Jews, three million of them and the largest in number in any European country, became targets of extermination and of the euthanasia experiments of the Nazi doctors (Raff 1988, pp. 228–41).

In his postwar book on the Germans, Norbert Elias tries to explain how civilization broke down in Nazi Germany. A German Jew whose family perished in the Nazi genocide, Elias had survived by finding asylum in Britain. However, he found the Nazi decision to exterminate all the Jews in Europe almost inexplicable. The pogroms and the gas chambers did not increase the military power of the Germans nor did the genocide of the Jews free any lands for the Aryans among Germans (Elias 1989/1996, pp. 309–10).

The breakdown of civilization in Germany can hardly be explained in fully rational terms, because the cluster of events had a profound unreason buried in their center. It can be seen as the culmination of an assault of the upper strata of German society against the aspirations of workers. The rational state constructed with the help of the civilizing process made its servants such as Karl Adolf Eichmann immune to merely human appeal, because they thought they were only carrying out orders (cf. Bauman 1989). Reason as an instrument had completely defeated reason as the constitutive element of human life.

The instruments of this instrumental reason had been fashioned by some of the greatest inventors and scientists of Germany. Haber, the inventor of the production of nitrates by synthesizing atmospheric nitrogen and winner of a

Nobel Prize, directed the production of poison gases during World War I. Other scientists, including Otto Hahn and James Franck—both winners of the Nobel Prize in later years—assisted him (Rhodes 1986, pp. 92–93). The military machine itself had been perfected in the successful campaign Prussia had conducted for defeating the Austro-Hungarian empire and France. German industrialists had enthusiastically assisted German war efforts before and during World War I, and they continued so to support Hitler's war plans after the Nazis seized power.

The Nazi hatred of the Jews was an extreme expression of the racism that had become part of the common sense of the European upper classes. The Jews were considered to be outsiders, immigrants from an inferior continent. Moreover, they had the effrontery to beat the typical European at things that they considered to be a peculiarly (white) European domain, namely, science and profit making in modern industry and finance. As has been aptly put, the Nazi cadres were bent on attaining equality in injustice, since the capitalist system, as the ordinary Germans knew it, had denied them justice in equality (Adorno and Horkheimer 1944/1979).

But the irrationality of genocide became an epidemic in the twentieth century, as in country after country—in Bosnia, Croatia, Kosovo, Rwanda, and Liberia—one group or another considered themselves true inheritors of the land other groups shared and proceeded to murder all the members of other groups for no other fault than their professing another religion, speaking another language, or having another (often mythical) stem of descent. One major reason for this has been the collapse of hope and disenchantment with ideologies embodying a message of equality as a central element. The irrationality of a doctrine of human progress through a process of natural selection is to be found in most genocidal projects.

DEATHS IN WARS AND IN THE NAZI AND JAPANESE EXTERMINATION CAMPAIGNS

World War II erupted when, after occupying Austria and Czechoslovakia without serious opposition by Britain and France, Hitler invaded Poland. After achieving victories through lightning strikes against Norway, Denmark, Belgium, the Netherlands, and France, Hitler attacked the Soviet Union in June 1941. The European war became truly global when, on 7 December 1941, Japan attacked Pearl Harbor, the main U.S. naval base in the Pacific, and the United States entered the war on the side of Britain, France, and Russia.

From the time of World War I, the attention of Japanese leaders was directed toward China as a limitless source of land and natural resources (Harries and Harries 1991, chapter 11). From the 1920s, Japan began various aggressive moves against China, and from 1931, partly with the help of the appeasement policy of the Guomindang, which was far more interested in crushing the communists than in fighting the foreign aggressor, Japan seized Manchuria. But even after the conquest of Manchuria with its coal and iron resources, Japan remained greatly dependent on sources of basic raw materials and particularly oil, which was controlled by Western powers. Japan invaded China on a wide front in 1937; in September 1940, it entered into an alliance with Germany and Italy. Taking advantage of the fall of France, Japan tried to turn French Indochina and Dutch Indonesia into its protectorates. In July 1941 the United States and Britain imposed an embargo on supplies of oil to Japan. This decision further inflamed the party advocating war against the Western powers, for without assured oil supply Japan could not carry on its long-drawn-out war against China, let alone fulfill the ambition of creating a Japan-dominated Co-Prosperity Sphere in eastern and Southeast Asia (Liddell Hart 1973, chapter 16).

Japan achieved extraordinary success in the initial phases of its war against the United States, Britain, and the Dutch. By 15 February 1942 Japan had occupied Singapore, the principal naval base of the British in eastern Asia and had conquered British Malaya. By 6 May it had ended U.S. rule of the Philippines, and by August 1942 it was master of the whole of Southeast Asia and of the seas from the Japan Sea to the Bay of Bengal on one side and the southwest Pacific on the other (Liddell Hart 1973, Chapter 17). However, there was a severe mismatch between the resources of Japan and its two chief antagonists among the Western powers, the United States and Britain. For example, the output of oilfields controlled by Japan was 1.9 million barrels as against the U.S. output of 1.4 billion barrels (Harries and Harries 1991, chapter 40). The disproportions of the U.S. and Japanese outputs of coal, steel, munitions, ships, and aircraft were almost equally large. Its merchant marine was also very small (six million tons) for a nation entirely dependent on shipping for essential raw materials, including fuel (Liddell Hart 1973, chapter 16). Moreover, Japan's industrial weakness is indicated by the 1938 index of industrial potential of Japan, Britain, and the United States as 88, 181 and 528, respectively, as calculated by Kennedy (1989, p. 201). Finally, China never surrendered to Japan and Japanese land forces became bogged down in trying to keep its conquests in that country. These factors ultimately led to the defeat of Japan.

By 1941 France had capitulated to the Nazis, and General Charles de Gaulle led a rump of the French army and navy in the name of the government of Free France. Hitler's army was largely destroyed in his war against the Soviet Union. The Soviet Union received critical aid in the form of food

and materials from the United States, but it was the Soviet Union that bore
the lion's share of the fighting and dying that led to the defeat of Hitler but
also the devastation of the Soviet Union. The war ended first in Europe with
the entry of armies of the Soviets and the Western powers into Berlin in June
1945 and in Asia with the United States dropping atom bombs on the Japanese cities of Hiroshima and Nagasaki and the entry of Russian forces into
Manchuria in August 1945.

The number of war-inflicted deaths from the beginning of the twentieth
century up to 1991 has been estimated as 187 million, or more than one in ten
of the global population in 1900 (Hobsbawm 1995, p. 12). Excess deaths in
western Europe were mainly due to wars, including civilian casualties and the
people killed in deliberate campaigns of extermination by the Nazis. Estimates of war losses, like losses from famine, can have wide margins of error,
because apart from fatalities of persons in uniform, it is necessary to include
civilian deaths from direct military attacks; epidemics; shortages of housing,
food, and medicines; and famines resulting from wartime dislocation.

The losses in World War II were much larger, especially in the Soviet
Union, Germany, eastern and central Europe, China, Japan, and among cate-
gories of people especially targeted by the Nazis and their allies, of whom the
Jews and the Gypsies were the worst sufferers, than they had been in World
War I.

> Most of Europe and East Asia were in ruins. Vast stretches of both continents
> were destroyed twice, first when they were conquered and again when they were
> liberated. . . . It is impossible to know the complete toll in human lives lost in
> the war but some estimates run higher than 70 million people. (McWilliams and
> Piotrowski 1997, p. 12)

As a people, the Russians paid most heavily in both world wars, but especially in World War II, with Soviet losses estimated at between 20 million and
40 million.

> At least 15 million Soviet soldiers lost their lives, including some 3.5 million
> soldiers who were deliberately starved to death or killed by other means in
> camps run by the Wehrmacht [the German army] or SS. Poland suffered even
> greater losses in proportion to their population. Some 6.5 million Polish citizens
> lost their lives, half of them Jewish. (Stackelberg 1999, p. 213)

In another account, we read,

> Poland lost 5.8 million people, about 15 percent of its population. Germany lost
> 4.5 million people, and Yugoslavia 1.5 million. Six other European nations—

France, Italy, Romania, Hungary, Czechoslovakia and Britain—each lost more than half a million people. In Asia, perhaps as many as 20 million Chinese and 2.3 million Japanese died in the war, and there were large numbers of casualties in various Asian countries from India in the south to Korea in the northeast. (McWilliams and Piotrowski 1997, p. 12)

Half of the war dead were civilians. The proportion of civilian casualties to those of combatants went on increasing over the twentieth century as the great powers perfected weapons capable of mass slaughter, particularly those associated with bombing (Selden 2003). While in World War I only a twentieth of the dead were civilians, in World War II "an estimated 12 million civilians were killed" in direct military action and untold millions of civilians died as a result of deliberate military attacks on cities and in famines and epidemics caused or exacerbated by the war. By using gas chambers, concentration camps, and forced labor, the Nazis exterminated 12 million people— "Jews, Slavs, gypsies, the conscientious objectors, and political opponents (mainly Communists)" (McWilliams and Piotrowski 1997, p. 12).

The holocaust of European Jewry at the hands of Hitler and his goons is the most notorious legacy of the Nazi terror. In their map of the extermination camps, Calvocoressi and Wint (1974, p. 233) provide an estimate of 5.4 million killed by 1945 out of a population of 8.5 million Jews in the lands occupied by the Nazis and their allies.

Since the Japanese aggression against China lasted for well over fifteen years—from 1931 to 1945—and there were encounters on such a wide front, it is even more problematic to estimate the number of people killed in that war than the people killed by the Nazis. One of the notorious atrocities committed by the Japanese soldiers was the Nanjing massacre, in which, after attacking Nanjing in December 1937, they deliberately killed soldiers who had laid down arms and thousands of other men, women, and children after raping the women and subjecting the victims to gruesome torture (Xingzu et al., 1962/1996; Selden 2003). Informed estimates of the deaths in that massacre range from 80,000 (Japanese scholarly estimates; McCormack 2004a; Askew http://japanfocus.org/article.asp?id=109) to official Chinese estimates of 300,000 or more. A recent estimate of the deaths in all the theaters of what the Japanese term the Asia-Pacific War has put it as 11 million civilians and 4.5 million soldiers on all sides (White 2004; this includes the casualties in Burma, Indonesia, and other Southeast Asian countries).

The question can be asked, "Can the Japanese militarists who launched the war against China and then attacked Pearl Harbor be called fascists, in the sense that, having suppressed an actual Japanese democracy, they proceeded to fan mass nationalism as a springboard for launching aggressive wars that eventually carried them to domination of much of Asia?" My answer would be a qualified yes, because both before World War I and in the 1930s, prime ministers answerable to the Diet had tried to restrain military expenditure and further military adventures. They had either been replaced or assassinated. Through the cult of the emperor, and universal education, the Japanese people had been mobilized in the service of extreme nationalism, and in Japan as in Germany, these processes were generally supported by large capital in the form of the *zaibatsu*, the large financial-industrial combines that dominated the Japanese economy. As in any comparison, there were of course significant differences. Japan lacked an equivalent of the Nazi party with its mass mobilization of the population to suppress its enemies, nor was there any equivalent to the extermination of the Jews.

The second question that arises is, "Why has there been a rash of genocides since the Nazi holocaust of the *untermensch*?" First of all, let us concede that genocides are not a new phenomenon in human history. We have already seen how Tasmanians, the native peoples of South Africa, and American Indians were deliberately hunted and exterminated by white invaders in the nineteenth century (see chapter 15). So one motive for genocide could be the acquisition of resources. In a world made mobile by forces of global capitalism and awash with ideologies of competitiveness and winner takes all, such a motive could ignite genocidal campaigns on the part of Hutus and Tutsis in Rwanda as well as white settlers in the United States.

A second motive could be to create terror in a population resisting conquest and domination by demonstrating the sheer killing power of the invader. This motive acts powerfully, especially in cases in which the invader feels utter contempt for the civilizational level of the invaded people. This could be the motive of the atrocities committed by the United States in Vietnam as well as those committed by the Japanese against the Chinese and the Koreans during its Pacific War. It is characteristic of the ultimate irrationality of such motives that the atrocities increase in intensity as the intended demoralization of the enemy fails to materialize. The last stage of irrationality is reached in phenomena like the Holocaust, which destroyed vast human resources that Hitler could have used to wage war and created social divisions within the German population. If we take modern warfare to be essentially the extrapolation of the heart of the capitalist principle that everything is fair in search of profit and an advance of competitive prowess, we see the sheer irrationality of central principles of the modern world. The ultimate irrationality of the working of markets supported by state power and arms manifests itself in the irruption of famines, endemic hunger, and environmental destruction that is unprecedented in human history even as the productive capacity of the system outstrips that of all earlier civilizations.

The Cold War between the Soviet bloc and the Western powers started almost as soon as World War II ended. The end of the war saw the growing challenges of liberation struggles in India, Indonesia, Korea, Vietnam, and throughout Asia. The first flash point in the form of an armed conflict between members of the Soviet bloc and the U.S.-led Western powers occurred in Korea. Korea was divided after the end of World War II into two parts, North Korea under the Communists led by Kim Il Sung and South Korea under the U.S.-backed dictator, Syngman Rhee. Neither Kim nor Rhee was reconciled to this division (Cumings 1990; McWilliams and Piotrowski 1997). There were skirmishes across the border in 1949 and 1950 conducted by both sides and then the North Korean army launched a massive attack on 25 June 1950 and almost drove the South Korean army out of the peninsula. Although the United States had earlier not considered Korea vital to the defense of the Western bloc, under the policy adopted in the same year of opposing the Communists at every point of threat, the United States, using the excuse of a UN authorization, sent an army into the conflict zone. When the North Koreans were driven back to the Yalu River, the border between China and Korea, Chinese forces opposed the advance of the U.S.-led invasion and the UN forces were moved back to the thirty-eighth parallel, the border currently dividing North and South Korea. During this conflict U.S. authorities several times threatened to use atomic weapons against the Communist opponents,[3] but ultimately fear of a nuclear holocaust, if Russia entered the lists, deterred them. After a long stalemate, a truce was signed in 1953. The U.S. army was now permanently stationed in Korea and both sides of the demilitarized zone between North and South Korea remain heavily militarized. According to Cumings (1990) the total number of fatalities in the Korean War for all the combatants came to 2 million. The pattern of the not-so-cold Cold War was set by that war.

The sharpening conflict between the Soviet bloc and the advanced capitalist powers provided expanded space for the freedom fighters in these countries. But it also meant that the eastern and Southeast Asian countries and, a little later, most of the newly liberated African lands became ensnared in the toils of the Cold War. The Soviet regime persecuted many intellectuals suspected of subversive activities and put down uprisings in Hungary (1956) and Czechoslovakia (1968) through armed intervention. For its part, the United States sometimes supported independence movements, but in cases where communist forces emerged at the center, the United States suppressed liberation movements or installed and supported repressive pro-Western dictatorships in nations including Vietnam, Korea, Iran, Syria, Indonesia, Guatemala, Chile, Congo, and scores of other countries of Asia, Latin America, and Africa. While the Soviet regime eventually collapsed, the attempt to suppress all movements challenging U.S. capital and U.S. military power continues.

NOTES

1. "The evidence collected by an international committee headed by Walther Hofer of Berne strongly supports the conclusion that the blaze was set by an SA/SS Sondergruppe under the direction of Himmler's associate, Reinhard Heydrich, and the director of the division of police in the Reich Ministry of the Interior" (Craig 1981, p. 573). Heinrich Himmler was the leader of the Schutzstaffel (SS), another of the Nazi paramilitary formations that played a major role in the extermination of the Jews and the people of the lands conquered by Nazi Germany.

2. The great philosopher Baruch Spinoza, for example, was a descendant of Spanish Jews who had found a refuge in the Netherlands.

3. As Cumings (2004) has pointed out in the current controversy surrounding the possession of nuclear weapons by North Korea, it has been forgotten that the United States had used nuclear weapons against Japan and repeatedly threatened to use chemicals and nuclear weapons against northeast Asia during the Korean War.

21

Imperialism and Wars in the Late Twentieth Century

WARS AND DEATHS

World War II ended with the United States dropping atomic bombs on Hiroshima and Nagasaki on 6 and 9 August, respectively, 1945. Already the United States had destroyed most of the major cities in Japan by firebombing and killed hundreds of thousands of civilians (Craig 1979). Once it was known that an atomic bomb could be developed, the top policy makers in the United States, led by President Truman and Secretary of State Henry Stimson, U.S. generals in the know, and the top British politicians such as Prime Minister Winston Churchill committed to its deployment to force Japan's surrender (Liddell Hart 1973, chapter 39; Craig 1979, chapter 4). Only one group of scientists led by James Franck had opposed the dropping of the bomb that would kill so many innocent civilians. The Japanese surrender was hastened by the entry into the war of the Soviet Union on 8 August and U.S. assurance that the position of the emperor would not be impugned by the terms of surrender. The decision to use the bomb was made to force surrender to save American lives by avoiding an invasion and to forestall the possibility of the Russians landing on Japanese shores (Rhodes 1986, pp. 679–93; McWilliams and Piotrowski 1997, pp. 15–22). The cost in civilian lives up to 1950 in Hiroshima and in Nagasaki has been calculated as 340,000 (Rhodes 1986, pp. 735, 740–42). Many more lived out aborted lives as cripples, suffering from diseases caused by heat, blast, or exposure to radiation or giving birth to malformed children. The distrust of its Soviet ally displayed by the U.S. government in deploying the bomb and refusing to share the technology with its allies laid the basis for U.S.-Russian rivalry from 1945. The carnage of the

Korean War, the Vietnam War, and other wars were the fall-out of that not-so-cold war between the two superpowers. The end of the Cold War with the fall of the Soviet Union did not end the carnage. Civil wars in the constituent states of erstwhile Yugoslavia and various African conflicts were followed by the unilateral wars against Iraq and Afghanistan under U.S. leadership.

THE COLD WAR, COLLAPSE OF THE SOVIET UNION, AND CONSOLIDATION OF THE U.S. EMPIRE

World War II sapped the power of the old imperialists—Britain, France, the Netherlands, Spain, and Portugal—and eliminated the empires of Japan and Germany. Japan had played a very important role in fatally weakening colonialism everywhere, most notably French colonialism in Indochina; British colonialism in Burma, Malaysia, and Singapore; Dutch colonialism in Indonesia; and U.S. colonialism in the Philippines, both by defeating the former colonial masters and inciting nationalism. The British recognized the writing on the wall and took astute steps to transform the old imperial designs, handing over power to regimes it deemed friendly (exceptions were Malaysia and Kenya where the British subsequently waged murderous counterinsurgency operations). But the French, Dutch, Portuguese, and Spanish rulers did not give up their empires so easily. Whenever liberation forces included any major section professing communist ideology, the United States intervened on behalf of the imperial power or the local rulers. The massive U.S. aid to the Guomindang after the start of the civil war in China in 1946 was paradigmatic of the U.S. determination to stop the communists in every theater of conflict.

The U.S.-Vietnam war was emblematic of the counterrevolutionary interventions of the United States and its allies in the Third World. In 1940 Japan invaded Indochina and threw out the French, who had conquered the country in the nineteenth century. The Vietnamese, under the leadership of the Communist Party headed by Ho Chi Minh, fought a guerrilla battle and liberated most of the country before the final defeat of the Japanese. After the victory of the Allied powers, they founded a republic. When the French refused to recognize Vietnam's independence, war began. From around 1950, when the U.S.-Korean War started (like all U.S. wars since World War II, it was an undeclared war), the United States began supplying military and financial aid to the French and the anti-Vietminh forces. After the decisive battle of Dien Bien Phu in 1954, the French withdrew, leaving the United States to wage war against the Vietnamese people.

Recognizing that in any free elections the communists would win, the United States flouted an agreement arrived at in Geneva in 1954 to hold free elections. Using the pretext of an alleged attack on the U.S. destroyer *Maddox,* which was within the twelve-mile limit of Democratic Republic of Vietnam (DRV; or North Vietnam) territorial waters gathering military intelligence, U.S. president Lyndon Johnson persuaded Congress to support an undeclared war against North Vietnam. Savage bombing by U.S. forces reduced most of the cities of North and South Vietnam to rubble, millions of Vietnamese were forced off the land into strategic hamlets or into the cities, and the toxic chemical Agent Orange, was sprayed to defoliate hundreds of square kilometers of forests and cultivated lands. Mass murders were carried out against both insurgents and noncombatants.

The attitude of the U.S. military in Vietnam, and subsequently in their war against Iraq, Kosovo, and Afghanistan, is illustrated by the statement of a U.S. army major who was involved in the bombing of Hue, the old imperial city of Vietnam. When asked why they had done it, his reply was, "We had to destroy it in order to save it" (McWilliams and Piotrowski 1997, p. 209). Massive protests by students and other sectors of civil society against the senseless slaughter of the Vietnamese forced the U.S. government to withdraw its troops in 1973. In April 1975 DRV liberation forces entered Saigon, the capital of South Vietnam, without facing any resistance.

The U.S. government had systematically destroyed the environment of Vietnam, Laos, and Kampuchea with chemicals, bombs, and land mines. The strategy of destruction of the lives and elementary facilities of survival of civilians, developed by the United States in Japan and Korea, became the centerpiece of subsequent U.S. wars, in direct violation of the very laws of war that the United States had put in place. It was extended in Vietnam by shifting the focus of such attack from city to countryside with the use of Agent Orange. The numbers of people killed by the U.S. war in Vietnam have been estimated as lying between one million (plus or minus one hundred thousand) (Hirschman, Preston, and Loi 1995) and two million (Chomsky 1998; Ellsberg 2003; Mirsky 2003), along with another six hundred thousand killed in Cambodia (McNally 2002, p. 162). But even in 1997, half a million babies were born in Vietnam with deformities caused by the chemicals dropped by the United States (p. 162).

In their determination to defeat what they regarded as a worldwide communist conspiracy, successive U.S. governments have used all instruments of subversion and armed aggression against any country in which they have sensed the possibility of establishment of a regime that will not be subservient to the dictates of American power, both military and economic. With that objective, they have sustained the kings of Saudi Arabia as the fountainhead of Islamic fundamentalism and a bulwark of American power throughout the Middle East from World War II to the present while maneuvering to assure pro-U.S. regimes throughout the region (Achcar 2002; Prashad 2002; Klare 2004). Saudi Arabia's possession of the largest reserves of easily exploitable oil in the world seals this U.S. support. However, the fact that Saudi Arabia possesses the holiest shrine of Islam, namely, the Qaaba of Mecca, would make it both a frontline state in fighting secular Arab nationalism, typified by Gamal Abdel Nasser of Egypt, and a source of contention throughout the Arab world. Nasserism's assertive nationalism would eventually be crushed by the successive victories of Israel against Egypt and its other neighbors such as Jordan and Syria.

Two events of the 1970s further underlined the importance of Saudi Arabia as a loyal U.S. ally. One was the Iranian revolution of 1979, in which the shah of Iran was thrown out and Ayatolla Ruhollah Khomeini, an anti-Western and anti-Soviet fundamentalist cleric, came to power. The other was a revolution in Afghanistan in the same year in which Soviet-backed communists assumed leadership of that country (Ali 2002, chapter 17). Almost at once, the U.S. government, using the Pakistani military dictatorship headed by Zia ul-Haq, began sending money and arms to the tribesmen in Afghan villages to foment civil war. Falling into the trap set by the U.S. Central Intelligence Agency (CIA), the Soviet leader, Brezhnev, sent a unit of the Russian army into Afghanistan. As the war heated up the mujahideen, warriors from across the Middle East fighting a jihad against the infidel communists, were recruited, armed, and financed by the CIA and its allies.

A principal leader of these recruits was one Osama bin Laden, the scion of a Saudi business family close to the Saudi kings and to the family of George W. Bush, a future U.S. president. The Soviet army withdrew from Afghanistan in defeat in 1989, but the civil war in Afghanistan continued. By the middle of the 1990s, except for some pockets of resistance in the north, an army of the so-called Taliban, orphans of the civil war who had been trained in a militant form of Islam in madrasas in Pakistan, was in control of Afghanistan. On 11 September 2001, planes crashed into the World Trade Center in New York, destroying its twin towers, and also plunged into the Pentagon in Washington, the headquarters of the U.S. defense establishment. An estimated twenty-eight hundred died in the attacks. The United States charged that Osama bin Laden, leader of al Qaeda, was responsible for the attacks. (Fifteen of the nineteen hijackers were Saudis.) The United States demanded that Afghanistan should give up bin Laden and his associates into U.S. custody. When the Taliban government, following international law, requested evidence of bin Laden's involvement before he could be arrested and extradited for trial, the U.S. government, with the support of its NATO allies, invaded Afghanistan in October 2001.

Zbigniew Brzezinski was the national security adviser to U.S. president Jimmy Carter at the time the United States began arming and financing the mujahideen. In 1998 Brzezinski was asked whether he regretted having helped form the Taliban regime. He said that he had no regrets: "What is most important to the history of the world? The Taliban or the collapse of the Soviet empire? A few crazed Muslims or the liberation of Central Europe or the end of the Cold War?" (Ali 2002, p. 208).[1] The 2001–2002 U.S. attack against Afghanistan pulverized a country that had already been devastated by more than twenty years of war. The 4.6 million refugees in Pakistan, Iran, and other neighboring counties were joined by hundreds of thousands more. Most of the promised U.S. help for reconstruction of the country never materialized as U.S. and international donor interest quickly shifted elsewhere. Bin Laden remained at large, warlords continued to rule many regions while the United States established a puppet regime in Kabul and new U.S. military bases in the country.

Long before the declaration of jihad on terrorism, as I have pointed out, the U.S. government and its allies used every means to defeat any challenge to their dominance of the world economy and their control of vital resources, including that vital commodity, oil. Emblematic was the 1953 U.S. deposing of Mohammed Mossadegh, the democratically elected prime minister of Iran, who had nationalized the British-controlled Anglo-American Oil Company. The United States replaced him with the Shah as an American client. In neighboring Iraq, the United States encouraged the activities of the fundamentalist Muslim Brotherhood and used the Baath party to destroy the most popular communist party of the Middle East (Ali 2002; RUPE 2002). Saddam Hussein ultimately became the dictator of Iraq as leader of the Baathists, building a formidable army with the oil resources of the country. After the ouster of the Shah in the Iranian revolution, the United States supported Saddam Hussein's 1980 invasion of Iran. For example, the United States provided the know-how for the poison gas that the Iraqi army used against the Iranians. The U.S. arms industry sold much of the arms and ammunition to both sides. The eight-year-long war left both sides enfeebled.

But when Saddam Hussein invaded Kuwait in August 1990, it was a different story. Not only was Kuwait a loyal ally, its emirs were useful to keep an eye on Iraq and Iran. The security of Saudi Arabia and U.S. oil interests would be jeopardized if Hussein got his way. Moreover, by this time the Soviet bloc had disintegrated. While playing an active behind-the-scenes role, the United States had until then avoided a direct military role in the region. President George H. W. Bush persuaded the United Nations to impose economic sanctions against Iraq and then proceeded to build up a force of more than half a million U.S. soldiers and another one-hundred-thousand-plus allied troops for the invasion of Iraq (RUPE 2002). U.S.-led allied forces invaded Iraq in January 1991. In this war between two vastly unequal forces, the invading forces dropped an average daily tonnage of bombs nearly equal to that used during World War II on two continents. Thousands of civilians died in air raids televised by CNN to admiring watchers in the United States, Britain, and others worldwide. The war was over by 26 February, when the Iraqi dictator accepted the terms of the invading powers. Between one hundred thousand and two hundred thousand Iraqi soldiers died, most of them while fleeing toward the Kuwait-Iraq border (RUPE 2002, p. 34).

Iraq remained under a regime of UN sanctions, which were to be lifted only after Iraq had destroyed all "weapons of mass destruction" and paid heavy compensation to Kuwait. Because the verification of all the conditions would take years and because an embargo on the sale of oil, Iraq's main resource, made it virtually impossible for Iraq to pay the reparations demanded, the country entered a tunnel of precipitous economic decline accompanied by long drawn-out processions of deaths of innocents, caused by lack of food, medicines, clean water, and hospital facilities destroyed by U.S. and British bombing during the Gulf War and in repeated raids between the war of 1991 and Gulf War II of 2003. Estimates of excess deaths of Iraqi children caused by the sanctions range up to a million. In a confidential report just before the United States was about to launch Gulf War II, the UN Office for Coordination of Humanitarian Affairs estimated that in Iraq the IMR was 2.5 times higher than in 1990, that half of pregnant women were anemic, and three million depended on state handouts to avoid starvation (Jones 2003). Many U.S. soldiers also suffered long-term maladies because of exposure to depleted uranium weapons during the war.

The Gulf War set the pattern for subsequent wars conducted by the United States and its allies: In Kosovo the Western powers intervened to check the atrocities committed by the Serbian army and left the country in ruins and in the hands of Kosovan victors whose atrocities were comparable to those committed by the Serbian army. In Somalia the U.S. army left the country without a visible state when it withdrew after losses. In Afghanistan the invading forces led by the U.S. continued their occupation with few signs of reconstruction of the economy and with most of the country remaining in the hands of warlord armies beyond the control of the U.S.-imposed regime of Hamid Karzai, whose power was largely limited to the capital, Kabul.

The pattern of disproportionate casualties on the part of resisting local forces had, of course, many precedents in the history of colonial wars, for example, in the battle of Omdurman (1898), in which the British army decimated the Sudanese Mahdi's army, Japan's China war in 1931–1945, or the

U.S.-Vietnam War. The disproportion was again witnessed in Gulf War II, in the invasion and occupation of Iraq in April–May 2003 by the forces of the United States and Britain—an invasion in total disregard of international law and in the teeth of opposition by people around the world, including many Americans and British. Already under UN sanctions, in compliance with the intrusive demands of UN arms inspectors, and savaged by U.S. and British attacks on civilian and military targets, the Iraqi army was a shadow of the force that was vanquished by the U.S.-led force in Gulf War I. The U.S.-British attack was launched with the ostensible object of finding weapons of mass destruction, even though successive UN inspectors had certified that, by 2001, Iraq had no such weapons. While killing thousands of Iraqi soldiers and more Iraqi civilians in savage bombing raids in a war that lasted barely three weeks, the invading forces lost less than 150 soldiers. But the Americans had underestimated Iraqi resourcefulness and resistance. By the end of 2004, Iraq remained unpacified while more than a thousand U.S. soldiers had died in attacks by Iraqi insurgents and tens of thousands of Iraqis had died in attacks by U.S.-led forces and by insurgents: the U.S. rubric for all resistance forces is terrorists, a fact that conceals U.S. state terrorism.

After the end of the Cold War, the United States and its allies invented a new bogey, that of terrorism, more specifically, in most cases, Islamic terrorism. This witch hunt suits U.S. purposes of mobilizing resources and troops to fight to preserve U.S. domination of the oil resources of the Middle East as a principal lever for controlling the world economy and simultaneously assuring the continued power of an Israeli regime that has been the major beneficiary of U.S. wars in the Middle East even as it deprives the Palestinian people of the most basic human rights.[2] Islam is an enemy that legitimates the surge of new U.S. military bases throughout the Middle East and central Asia and the prospect of a permanent U.S. military presence in an oil-rich region on the Soviet border. But the very acts of the global marauders breed terrorists as Karl Marx observed long ago while discussing the origins of the revolt of the Indian soldiers and their peasant partisans in 1857 (Marx 1857; Achcar 2002).

The unbounded U.S. aggression from 1990 against everybody the incumbent administration regarded as its enemy was a consequence of the elimination of the Soviet Union as a power capable of challenging the U.S. militarily. Does this mean that the strongest military power can be restrained only by the arrival of another big bully, even if the latter starts with a different ideology than that of armed competition for the limited resources of the world? My perspective suggests that there are more humane possibilities and those possibilities must be struggled for if we want human survival and a fortiori if we value the human fulfillment of everybody.

CONSTRUCTION OF THE U.S. EMPIRE

To understand how the United States has come to occupy the position of the sole superpower in the world, we have to refer to the flow of foreign investment and migrants from Europe that built up its strength in the nineteenth century. With the growth of its economic power, its imperial ambitions were publicly proclaimed by its leading statesmen and found partial fulfillment in the annexation of Puerto Rico, the Philippines, and Hawaii in 1898. U.S. enterprises were already spreading to other countries and continents with their branch offices and factories before World War I (Wilkins 1970). The United States was a net debtor until 1913, but by 1938 it had emerged as the second most important creditor nation in the world, just after the United Kingdom (Dunning 1964/1972). By then the United States already had probably the largest multinational enterprises in the world in the areas of steel, petroleum, and automobiles. Despite the nationalization of the Mexican oil industry in 1940, petroleum ranked just after manufacturing and utilities with respect to U.S. direct foreign investments abroad (Wilkins 1974, table 8.2). The growing U.S. supremacy was also based on new methods of organization of production such as Taylorism and Fordism, and the innovation of new ways of organizing large enterprises in general, such as the multidivisional enterprise (Chandler 1977).

World War II not only pulled the United States out of a decade-long depression but also catapulted it into the position of the leading creditor nation and, much more importantly, the source of massive flows of foreign direct investment to the war-devastated European countries (Wilkins 1974). The Marshall Plan and the foreign direct investment flows were a factor in helping narrow the technology gap between western Europe and the United States. But Japan followed a strategy of securing more advanced technology through licensing agreements with foreign firms but preventing foreign enterprises from controlling any major industrial or financial sector. The successful newly industrializing countries in eastern Asia followed Japan in this respect until the beginning of the 1990s. Of course, the flow of technology and investment between Europe and the United States was not a one-way affair, but at least until the 1960s, U.S. companies were larger than their foreign counterparts in most major industries (Hymer and Rowthorn 1970). This was particularly true in the case of oil companies. That dominance has continued, but in an attenuated form, to the beginning of the twenty-first century. Of the top twenty-five nonfinancial TNCs in the world in 2000, six were based in the United States, but another eighteen were based in Europe or Japan, with a single company, Hutchison Whampoa, based in Hong Kong, China (UNCTAD 2002b, table 4.1). Interests of U.S. TNCs, and especially those of the oil companies, and the interests of the U.S. state have been closely intertwined since World War I. But during the Cold War, the western European and Japanese governments and TNCs based in them also became dependent on the United States for providing military security, markets, and technology. So long as the threat of Soviet communism as an ideological rival continued, the inevitable contradictions of capitalist competition found only an occasional outburst, for example, in the pronouncements of the French president Charles de Gaulle. Nevertheless, western European countries pushed forward with their plan of creating a European Union, with a common currency and common political setup, that might challenge American economic and financial might. While the major countries of continental Europe introduced a common currency, the euro, from 2000, the British remained outside the Euro zone. Politically also Britain remained a much more steadfast ally of the United States than France and Germany. Apart from the link of English-speaking traditions, Britain was a pioneer of financial liberalization and had a strong presence in the global oil industry, with the interests of its ruling class being firmly wedded to those of the City of London, and this common economic interest further strengthened their alliance.

U.S. leadership of the capitalist world has been accompanied throughout the twentieth century and beyond by a determination to enforce its interests by the force of arms, and the arms industry has become an autonomous power center in U.S. politics (Prestowitz 2003, chapter 6). In 2002 U.S. military expenditure accounted for $335.7 billion while that of the next highest spender, Japan, was $46.7 billion. In 2003 the U.S. military expenditure amounted to $417.4 billion and Japan's to $46.9 billion. In both years the United States spent more on arms and armed personnel than the next fourteen top spenders. The military expenditure of China, which U.S. policy makers have designated as a strategic competitor, came to $32.8 billion in 2003. U.S. military expenditure accounted for 43 percent and 47 percent of global military expenditure in 2002 and 2003, respectively (SIPRI 2003, 2004). The United States is also the biggest seller of arms in the world, and it directly spends about 70 percent of the military research and development worldwide (Prestowitz 2003, p. 164). In terms of military expenditure and hardware, the United States has no rival.

U.S. military bases now encircle the globe and dot the land and sea of every subregion of the world. As of September 2001, fifty-nine countries and territories had U.S. military bases, and the number of bases acknowledged by the Defense Department was at least 725 outside the United States. But after 9/11 the number of U.S. bases and countries in which they were located increased fast and the number of bases might have reached 1,000. The bases are there for global surveillance. A base at Guantánamo Bay in Cuba the United States acquired in the Spanish-American war of 1898; bases in former Soviet central Asia and Japan now encircle both China and Russia, two powers the U.S. government watches with particular vigilance; not to mention the numerous new bases in the oil-rich and war-torn Middle East (MR Editors 2002; Johnson 2004). The United States also regularly conducts military exercises with many more countries, such as India, in which it has no formal bases.

U.S. supremacy was built, both on its military prowess that penetrated every advanced and backward capitalist country via its grid of bases and attendant flows of expenditure and on the incorporation of other advanced capitalist countries, into what Gowan (2003) has styled a hub-and-spokes arrangement. The United States acts as the hub for investment, technology, and markets, with the other countries inserted into the hub as spokes. The ideology of success as measured by financial power is spread worldwide through control of the major electronic and print media. The United States has also been a major destination for educated and skilled personnel from all over the developing world, particularly countries such as India, which trained a highly educated professional corps but failed to provide sufficient jobs and pay matching their skills and aspirations. The United States has either generous quotas for skilled immigrants or relaxes them in their favor when it suits the interests of its rulers. For example, among Latin American countries, the proportions of professionals and administrators admitted as legal immigrants into the United States between 1990 and 1999 increased from 32.2 percent to 60.7 percent in the case of Argentina, from 29.0 percent to 60.7 percent in case of Brazil, and from 43.6 percent to 63.7 percent in case of Venezuela (Portes and Hoffman 2003, table 8). According to the Inter-American Development Bank, remittances home by Latin American expatriates amounted to $23 billion in 2000 (Portes and Hoffman 2003, p. 74). The United States has also trained military officers from all over the world, first in the School of the Americas in the U.S.-controlled Panama Canal Zone and then in many other locations all around the world. Many of the school's graduates became dictators or the bulwarks supporting dictators in Latin America, so that the School of the Americas became known as the school for dictators (Prestowitz 2003, p. 167).

But the hub-and-spokes arrangement is rather unstable: it is vulnerable to challenges from a country like China, which is not penetrated militarily by the United States and has become the most dynamic economy of the world. Some of the other advanced countries also have a partly antagonistic relationship with the United States. The contradictions among the G7 countries have deep economic and political roots (Mayer 2003). The quadrupling of oil prices in 1973 by members of the Organization of Petroleum Exporting Countries (OPEC), with the tacit consent if not the active collusion of the United States and its oil companies, hurt the oil-importing economies of continental western Europe and Japan, while raising the profits of oil companies and chan-neling enormous amounts of petrodollars into the coffers of U.S. and British transnational banks. The U.S. determination to keep control of global oil sup-plies was evident not only in Gulf wars I and II, but also in its unilateral ab-rogation of all contracts made by the legally constituted government of Sad-dam Hussein with countries like France and Russia after the U.S.-led forces had occupied Iraq at the conclusion of Gulf War II. The Anglo-U.S. invaders of Iraq in 2003 were strongly criticized by their close allies in NATO, espe-cially France and Germany, which were derided by U.S. proponents of Gulf War II as the so-called Old Europe.

Even though the United States has become the world's biggest debtor and the dollar has been on the decline since 2001, the dollar remains the key cur-rency of international transactions, not least because it is the medium of global transaction for key commodities, especially oil. I earlier mentioned the growth of U.S. TNCs. TNCs based mainly in G7 countries have acquired a stake in the global order that the United States presides over. In 1990 the sales of TNCs equaled world exports; by 2001 they were twice as high as total world exports. By 2001 foreign affiliates of TNCs accounted for one-tenth of world GDP and one-third of world exports. While the gross product of the foreign affiliates of TNCs increased by a factor of nearly six between 1982 and 2001, the more than twelvefold growth in their assets from $1.959 billion in 1982 to $24.952 billion in 2001 was even more dramatic (UNCTAD 2002b, "Overview," table 1). A very large part of that growth occurred not through investment in new production facilities but through mergers and ac-quisitions. In 2000 alone, the foreign assets of the 100 largest TNCs increased by 20 percent, their foreign employment by 19 percent and their sales by 15 percent (UNCTAD 2002b, p. 2).

Ever since the 1890s, tendencies toward greater concentration of economic power through mergers and acquisitions had been evident in the evolution of U.S. and global capitalism. But these tendencies were periodically slowed and at times reversed by wars, antitrust laws in the United States and some Euro-pean countries, and public control of public utilities. They were slowed also by the emergence of competitive pressures through new technologies; the appear-ance of new industries such as computers and electronic industries; the emer-gence of new growth poles such as Germany, France, and Japan in the 1960s and 1970s; and the appearance of eastern Asian firms in steel, automobiles, and branches of computer hardware. However, active support of the giants by the neoliberal regimes since the 1980s, the privatization of many firms in devel-oping countries in waves of repressive structural adjustment at heavily dis-counted prices, and the waves of megamergers and acquisitions across borders without any international body to police them have led to unprecedented

degrees of concentration in old and new industries such as banking, stock bro-
kering, telecommunications, drugs and pharmaceuticals, and computer soft-
ware and media (Du Boff and Herman 2001). The deregulation of financial
markets and the inauguration of the World Trade Organization (WTO) regime
in the areas of patents, crossborder capital flows, and trade in services are likely
to increase these tendencies toward oligopoly of the whole global economy.

Imperialism and capitalism, like all systems that rest on hierarchy, require
ideologies justifying the privilege of the few. We have seen how social Darwinism and scientific racism have served as the pillars of discriminatory policies supporting capitalist control and exploitation. The effort to create new
bases for these ideologies by causally associating intelligence with heredity
continues unabated, in spite of the demonstration by eminent scientists that
Sir Cyril Burt, a major pioneer of this kind of construction, cooked his data
to suit his conclusions (Gould 1981). Lately, Herrnstein and Murray (1994)
have claimed to find a strong association between intelligence as measured by
the usual IQ tests and heredity. However, social scientists, biologists and
practitioners of cognitive sciences (Helms 1997; Valencia and Suzuki 2001)
have persuasively disputed such claims, showing that the methods of the conventional psychometrists fail to take proper account of socioeconomic variables and aspects of intelligence that are not captured by standard IQ tests. In
most societies, class, gender, and ethnic factors are heavily loaded against
members of socially and economically disadvantaged groups and depress
their IQs as they are conventionally measured. The ideological marker of the
neoliberal order is the notion of freedom as equated to American values and
the right of the chosen people of the United States to impose those values and
the interests of the chosen people on the rest of the world with the threat of
devastation in case of refusal (Pieterse 2004). When social Darwinism is
combined with religious righteousness and enormous military power, it creates an explosive potential for mass murders.

Ideologies of the neoliberal order are instilled by the global media, which
have come to be controlled by a small number of giant corporations such as
Fox News and CNN (Herman and Chomsky 1988; Herman and McChesney
1997). Consent to inequality and submission to the U.S.-run imperial order is
manufactured by the media.

The advance of financial liberalization, deregulated behavior of large business, the bashing of trade union rights, and the decimation of most developing country economies through structural adjustment policies have been associated with a steep increase in inequality in almost every major country of
the world. To take the example of the United States, the workers who had
gained in working conditions, wages, and security through struggles and
unionization from the 1930s to the 1960s have lost on all counts since the

1970s. The proportion of union membership of workers has gone down from a high of 33–36 percent in the 1950s and 1970s to 13.3 percent in 2003, much of it in the government or public sector, the hours of work have increased, labor has become disposable, subject to hiring and firing with little redress in law, working conditions have worsened, and for large sections of workers, especially in declining industries, real wages have not risen at all since the beginning of the 1980s. When new workers are lucky enough to get jobs, many are forced to work part-time at miserable wages (Goldfield 2004; Merrifield 1999; Yates 2001). The footloose rich of the world provide a major support base for the ongoing process of further enrichment of the wealthy and the further marginalization of the poor (Atkinson, Rainwater, and Smeeding 1995; Atkinson 1999; Milanovic 2002). The global regime of free capital and service flows across borders mandated by the WTO that came into being in 1995 is likely to aggravate the tendency toward inequality everywhere.

NOTES

1. Interview of Brzezinski, published in the French weekly *Le Nouvel Observateur*, 15–21 January 1998, and cited in Ali 2002, p. 208.

2. The Israeli government has violated the largest number of UN resolutions among all the members of that body. It has torn up practically all the agreements arrived at in various peace initiatives brokered by the United States. It continues to deny basic human rights, let alone citizenship rights, to the Palestinians and has constructed a wall that more or less imprisons Palestinians within the shrinking territory available to them. Extreme forms of racism continue to pour out of Zionists in Israel and their supporters outside. Rabbi Ovadia Yosef, the spiritual leader of Israel's ultraorthodox Shas party, in a sermon delivered 9 April 2001 to mark the Jewish festival of Passover called for the annihilation of Arabs: "It is forbidden to be merciful to them. You must send missiles to them and annihilate them. They are evil and damnable" (BBC 2001). When the president of the Palestinian Authority, Yasser Arafat, went to France for medical treatment and lay dying in a Paris hospital, on 30 October 2004, the American Board of Rabbis called upon the Jewish people everywhere to boycott everything French because France had harbored "Master Terrorist" Arafat (PRWEB New York, 30 October 2004). This, of course, fits in very well with the ideology of the U.S. supremacists.

22

Capitalism and Uneven Development in the Twentieth Century

TWENTIETH-CENTURY DIFFERENTIALS BETWEEN RICH AND POOR COUNTRIES

As I have noted earlier, from the late nineteenth century, the development of the germ theory of disease and invention and spread of new prophylactics against infectious diseases led to major advances in human survival in ordinary times. However, there were enormous differences in the provision of public sanitation, prophylactic measures, and improvement in nutrition between poor, mostly ex-colonial lands on the one hand and advanced capitalist countries and, in the period up to the beginning of the 1980s, those of the Soviet bloc on the other. As I have noted, more people died in wars, between countries and within countries, than ever before in history. Millions of people still died in famines, most of them due to policy failures at the national and international levels.

The spread of knowledge and technology of control of infectious diseases led to a decline of death rates in most countries and hence population growth picked up in most of the ex-colonial countries of the world, notably since World War II. But this was not accompanied by a rapid decline in IMRs or increases in life expectancy in most of the developing countries, and in the case of Sub-Saharan Africa, some of the gains have been reversed from the 1990s (Deaton 2004). The leaders and laggards among the developed economies have converged with respect to decline in IMRs: over 1901–1905 and 1946–1950 Norway and Sweden had reduced their IMRs from 80 and 91 to 31 and 24, respectively, but the IMRs of Germany and Italy had come down from 199 and 167 to 71 and 77, respectively, between the two periods. However, by 1986–1990, the IMRs of Norway, Sweden, Germany, and Italy had

305

come down to 8, 6, 8, and 9, respectively (Masuy-Stroobant 1997). In 1900–1904, Mexico had an IMR of 220; by 1950–1954, it had come down to 45, but it was still 24 in 2001 (Mitchell 1998b; UNICEF 2003).[1] In 1960 the IMR was 215 in Afghanistan and was still 165 in 2001. Comparably high levels of IMRs and slow rates of decline could be found in most countries of Sub-Saharan Africa and in a number of countries in Asia and Latin America as well.

The differentials in the chances of survival were to be found not only between rich and poor countries but also between classes and between privileged and deprived population groups within countries. Table 13.7 shows the differentials in survival chances of whites and African Americans within the United States. In 1956 when the IMR for whites had come down to 23.2, it was 42.1 among African Americans, that is, not very different from the Mexican average. In combination with large African American–white differences in adult death rates, there ensued large differences in expectation of life.

As noted earlier (chapter 5), declines in IMRs in Europe and North America and a sustained rise in life expectancy are largely a twentieth-century story. In the most rapid phases of industrialization and urbanization in the countries of the Atlantic seaboard, men and women almost always lost in height (Steckel and Floud 1997). In many countries this phase lasted till the last quarter of the nineteenth century; sustained gains in height are again mainly a twentieth-century phenomenon. Because whites in early nineteenth-century United States were better nourished than their European counterparts, they tended to be unusually tall. By 1830 the native-born white males in the United States were 174 centimeters tall on average, but they lost 4 centimeters during the next fifty years. Recovery in height began by about the 1890s, and by the 1970s the heights of native-born white males in the United States on average came to 178 centimeters (Costa and Steckel 1997).

Until the post–World War II period, Japan's gains in human development lagged behind its apparent military prowess (Bagchi 2000). The heights of Japanese men were about 157 centimeters in the late nineteenth century and may have even fallen in the 1920s and 1930s because of a high degree of urbanization and poor nutrition (Steckel 1999, p. 17). In 1950 the height of young adult men in Japan was 160 centimeters. With rapid economic growth and improvements in nutrition recorded since then, the Japanese have gained most rapidly among all population groups for which data are available: by 1995 their height had reached almost 172 centimeters (Bogin 1999, pp. 242–44).

From the 1970s, major figures in the corporate world in the United States such as Edmund Pratt, the chief executive officer of Pfizer, the biggest drug company of the world, were looking for ways of blocking competition from new challengers. Their effort led ultimately to the inclusion of so-called intellectual property rights in the document establishing the World Trade Organization (WTO). Under this patent regime, the U.S. practice of giving patents for twenty years and for products rather than processes has been extended to all members of the WTO. This regime has pushed up drug prices everywhere and will go on doing so as more and more developing countries are forced to adopt the so-called trade-related intellectual property (TRIPs) rights clauses of the WTO. The GATS (general agreement on trade in services) clauses of WTO also have mandated free trade in services, including health care and education. As most developing country governments have become fiscally enfeebled and have been ideologically pressured to withdraw from public provisioning of even basic necessities such as elementary education and primary health care, the gap has been increasingly filled by private providers who charge high prices and often supply low-quality services. Under this triple jeopardy of an enfeebled state, enforcement of TRIPs and GATS regimes of the WTO, and highly inegalitarian distribution of incomes in poor developing countries, they are unlikely to soon, if ever, close the gap with developed economies in human fulfillment.

GOLDEN AGE OF CAPITALISM, RISE OF EAST ASIA, AND THEIR AFTERMATH

The improvement in longevity, education, income, and other indexes of human development in the North Atlantic seaboard was sustained by the boom in the world economy stretching from 1950 to roughly 1973 that has been characterized as the Golden Age of capitalism (Armstrong, Glyn, and Harrison 1984; Marglin and Schor 1990). In western Europe it was distinguished by the combination of high growth, peace, and the welfare state. During 1950–1973, GDP per capita increased at the rate of 3.9 percent in western Europe, 2.4 percent in the countries Maddison (1995) calls "Western Offshoots" (that is, overseas settlements of Europeans led by the United States), and 4.9 percent in southern Europe. These rates were far higher than those achieved in those regions for any comparable period since 1820. There was little convergence in rates of economic growth in Europe before 1945 (Maddison 1991; *The Economic Journal* vol. 106:1016–69). But there has been a strong convergence after that date, so that many of the laggard countries such as Italy, Austria, and more recently Spain, Ireland, and Portugal as well have joined the club of OECD countries with high incomes and high human development. Quite a few of today's OECD countries became members of the club with high levels of education, technological competence, low levels of fertility, and near-universal literacy only after World War II. Birth rates in many of these countries stayed above or around 20 per thousand up to the 1940s (in the common sense of racism, high birth rates are supposed to be the monopoly of nonwhites, but are in fact mostly the result of poverty and female illiteracy) and educational levels were also much lower than in the most advanced countries of the group such as Denmark, Sweden, Germany, and France.

After World War II, virtually all the western European democracies, whether ruled by Social Democrats, Christian Democrats, or conservatives or liberals of one variety or another, adopted social democratic policies and spent massively on education and health (cf. Milward, Brennan, and Romero 1992). They also adopted policies directed toward achieving high levels of employment, and that increased the bargaining power of men and women workers. That improvement in turn was reflected in the governments adopting policies of the welfare state. These policies led to the empowerment of labor and women. With a high degree of capacity utilization, productivity rose and Europe (and Japan) came close to bridging the technological gap with the United States. High levels of expenditure on research—much of which was funded directly or indirectly by the state—also helped in this process. Both human and economic development went up in tandem.

Thus increases in productivity and per capita income are extremely important for achieving a sustained expansion of human capabilities and functioning. However, the causes of such expansion are far more complex and the roles of public and collective action in promoting human development have been much more important than market fundamentalists would like to believe.

During 1973–1992 the rates of growth in per capita incomes declined to 1.8 percent in western Europe, 1.4 percent in Western offshoots, and 1.7 percent in southern Europe (Maddison 1995, table 3.1). According to Maddison's estimates, most other regions of the world followed the same pattern. But in their case the decline over 1973–1992 in rates of growth of GDP and GDP per capita were far more drastic: in the case of Africa and eastern Europe the rates of growth of per capita income became negative. The only exception—and it was a major exception—was Asia, where annual per capita GDP growth declined only marginally, from the high level of 3.8 percent in 1950–1973 to 3.2 percent in 1973–1992.

The countries of east Asia beat the world trend and continued their fast growth in the decades of the 1970s and 1980s. Maddison (1995, table 3–2) estimates that while over 1950–1973 the per capita real GDP in China, South Korea, and Taiwan grew at annual rates of 2.9 percent, 5.2 percent, and 6.2 percent, respectively, the rates for those countries accelerated or stayed constant over 1973–1992: the corresponding rates of growth were 5.2 percent for

China, 6.9 percent for South Korea, and 6.2 percent for Taiwan. Japan, the biggest and most advanced economy of east Asia, experienced a slowdown in the growth of GDP per capita over the two periods, from 8 percent to 3.2 percent, but during 1973–1992 it remained higher than that of all western European countries, the United States, and Canada. Whether China is to be considered a capitalist country still remains doubtful. But in the period since its opening up, China has certainly used all the peaceful tools of capitalist competition to conquer world markets and increase productivity. The increases in longevity and fall in fertility also occurred at much faster rates in China, South Korea, Japan, and Taiwan after World War II than most demographers had anticipated. Growth theorists might debate the relative merits of the various economic models in explaining these changes (cf. Crafts and Toniolo 1996), but the institutional and policy regimes that account for them are pretty clear. In western Europe, the Marshall Plan floated by the United States as an aid to the reconstruction of the war-devastated continent and an instrument for containing the advance of communism helped in launching a renewed growth process. But the continuation of that process required the expansion of investment and rapid technological change that would hold up business profits. Business confidence was promoted by repressing militant labor movements and at the same time providing an institutional framework for peacefully negotiating demands for higher wages (Armstrong, Glyn, and Harrison 1984). The impetus to technical change was provided by the enormous gap that had opened up between U.S. and western European technology in most fields of manufacturing: the war had devastated western Europe but had quickened investment in more productive technologies in the United States. As European and Japanese investment rates accelerated from the 1950s, the average ages of their machines and technologies came down and their productivity rose fast. By the late sixties, the manufactures of many of these countries began to drive U.S. products out of the market, because they were newer and cheaper. The fast growth in wages and government spending on welfare measures for the workers, especially in western Europe helped the expansion of effective demand and kept the profit rates up. In all the countries, release of workers from old machines and stagnant sectors helped expansion of the effective labor supply. In Japan this was augmented by the release of enormous numbers of peasants for work in the industrial sector as land reform and mechanization led to increased productivity in agriculture and freed labor from the land. In western Europe, immigration from Turkey, North Africa, southern Europe, southern Asia, and the Caribbean islands considerably eased the labor market.

The boom in the United States was powered by its initial advantage as the economy with the most advanced technology in most fields of production and its ready access to all markets outside the Soviet bloc. The United States also gained from the stability in the international payments system that had been underwritten by the establishment, through meetings of the major Allied governments at Bretton Woods (United States) in 1944, of two organizations, the International Bank for Reconstruction and Development (popularly known as the World Bank) and the International Monetary Fund (IMF). The former was entrusted with the task of postwar reconstruction and development. U.S. surpluses were supposed to provide the core funding of that body. It was agreed among the Allied powers that the instability of exchange rates, sudden reversals and drying up of international capital flows, and unregulated devaluations of currencies in the effort to boost exports at the expense of competitors — thereby aggravating their problems of unemployment—were major factors facilitating the spread of fascism and militarism in the 1930s. Hence the IMF was established and entrusted with the task of maintaining the stability of the international payments system; the value of the dollar was pegged in terms of gold, and the dollar became the dominant currency of international trade.

But as other advanced capitalist countries upgraded their investment and technology, the United States was increasingly unable to compete with them, its balance of payments surplus narrowed, and its rates of investment in civilian technology suffered relative to those of West Germany and Japan. Its productive capacity was also overstretched as it increased its military expenditures to fight the long-drawn-out and costly U.S.-Vietnam war. Simultaneously, U.S. business corporations continued to export large amounts of capital overseas as they established subsidiaries to help penetrate foreign markets and take advantage of cheaper labor abroad. Of course, European firms also invested in the United States but there was a net outflow of capital from the United States. It was the logic of capitalist competition—and armed preparedness against threats to the global capitalist-imperialist order—that overheated the system and by the late 1960s made it impossible for the United States to maintain the external value of the dollar pegged to $35 per ounce of gold. Its balance of payments turned negative to an unsustainable degree and it could not generate the surpluses that had earlier fueled the mechanism of global capital flows. On 15 August 1971, the U.S. government announced that the dollar would no longer be convertible to gold (Carli 1994).

By the end of the year, a set of fixed exchange rates, with the dollar devalued by about 9 percent, had been worked out by the so-called Smithsonian Agreement between the major capitalist powers, including Japan. But these exchange parities were soon invalidated because the yen and the deutsch mark were floated soon after, and the dollar was devalued in relation to those currencies by more than 20 percent. The era of floating exchange rates began. Along with these international factors upsetting the Bretton Woods system, internal factors in major capitalist economies also affected their profit rates, business confidence, and investment rates. These centered around the increased power of the working class that had raised their real wages and share of national income and, at the same time, made it more difficult to meet the obligations of the welfare state without imposing higher tax obligations on the upper income groups. Increased international rivalry prevented governments of the major powers from adopting measures of coordination that might have got them out of the difficulty (Armstrong, Glyn, and Harrison 1984, chapters 10–12).

Ironically, the action of the biggest producers of petroleum, most of whom were Third World countries ruled by monarchs or dictators, in quadrupling the price of oil in 1973 provided the trigger mechanism and the opportunity for the U.S. administration and its allies to mount a counterattack against the working class, its challengers in exports such as Germany and Japan, and the developing countries that were clamoring for a new international economic order. The massive increase in flows of petrodollars was routed through transnational banks domiciled in Europe or the United States, thus increasing the liquidity at their command. The access of new sources of liquidity was accompanied by deregulation of banking on a wide scale, and new financial instruments such as derivatives proliferated and made international financial markets much more risky for small operators and for poor countries. The latter were unable to weather drastic declines in their asset values because of totally unanticipated changes in sentiment originating in some remote corner of the world.[2] The rise in oil prices along with wage inflation, coinciding with declines in rates of investment, produced the phenomenon of stagflation, that is, inflation coinciding with high rates of unemployment in capitalist countries.

The Organization of Petroleum Exporting Countries (OPEC) raised oil prices again in 1979. The accretion of petrodollars realized resulting from increases in oil prices were recycled by lending massively to Third World countries, and especially to those ruled by dictators or military juntas that were considered to be friendly to the Western bloc. Some of the governments of the major oil producers, such as Nigeria and Mexico, went on a spending spree and at the same time greatly liberalized their inflows and outflows of capital and goods. The real rates of interest charged by banks were low, sometimes lower than the rates of inflation. But the situation in the international debt market changed drastically as Ronald Reagan, elected U.S. president in 1980, and Paul Volcker, chief of the Federal Reserve Bank, ordered a drastic increase in the U.S. rates of interest. Since most Third World debts were contracted at floating rates, the servicing obligations on their account mounted to unsustainable levels. Moreover, as the currencies of these countries became

increasingly overvalued and their current balances turned negative, large volumes of capital flew out of them, legally and illegally. As governments borrowed from abroad, the politicians and businessmen at once exported a large
part of the borrowed funds, thus increasing the debt burden of the poor countries. From 1982 most Latin American countries could no longer service their
debt. In the name of rescheduling their debt and helping them to repay it
through belt-tightening and structural-adjustment policies, the IMF and the
G7 governments led by the United States pushed most of them into deep recession and a state of permanent indebtedness to foreign banks and multilateral funding organizations.

This financial counterattack of big capital against the developing countries
aspiring to a place in the sun was accompanied by direct or indirect armed intervention by the United States in most theaters of struggles for liberation in
the Third World. Such interventions included giving help to the mujahideen
seeking to overthrow the communist-led secularist government in Afghanistan
and escalating supply of arms and other military help after the Soviets had
stepped in to support the incumbent government; armed intervention to suppress the democratic Sandinista movement against the brutal Somoza regime
in Nicaragua; active help to the racist government of South Africa trying to
suppress the black liberation movements in its own territory and all the lands
bordering it; and so on. Within the G7 countries savage attacks were mounted
against the trade union movement and workers' rights in Britain under the
leadership of Margaret Thatcher as prime minister and in the United States under President Reagan. As I will argue later, the repressive measures in the
United States also included frontal attacks on the substance of democratic governance while retaining the forms (Blum 2002).

I have noted earlier that the only region of the world where growth rates
held up between 1950–1973 and 1973–1992 was Asia. In fact, Asian growth
kept up till the financial crisis of 1997–1998 and had resumed again by the
beginning of the twenty-first century. The fastest growers in real terms from
the 1970s in Asia (excluding Japan) were the Republic of Korea (South Korea), Taiwan, and the two city-states of Hong Kong and Singapore. They were
followed by Thailand, Malaysia, and Indonesia (Bagchi 1987b, 1998). They
have been joined by China, which in the 1990s and subsequent years recorded
the highest rate of industrial growth in the region. According to Wu (2002),
the annual rate of industrial growth in China was 9.7 percent over 1949–1977
and it rose to 10.0 percent over 1978–1997. How did the east Asians buck the
trend?

The east Asian economies had all along resisted the U.S. and IMF pressure
to open up their economies to unregulated flows of foreign capital and goods;
they had carried out thoroughgoing land reforms and had introduced mea-

sures to universalize education and continually upgrade educational standards. Because they had avoided financial liberalization and taken various measures to discipline the capitalist class, the rates of saving and investment remained high, in fact higher than in all the other regions in the world over the 1980s and 1990s.

It is interesting to note that, apart from failure to introduce land reforms, some large economies of Latin America had pursued policies similar to those of east Asia until the middle of the 1970s, and their rates of growth were not too different from Asian growth rates during 1960–1980 (UNCTAD 2003). The annual rate of growth of real GDP of Brazil, for example, at 8 percent over 1960–1980 was only about 0.5 percent lower than those of South Korea and Hong Kong and higher than those of Thailand and Malaysia. One reason for the subsequent collapse of Latin American growth, most dramatically illustrated by the decimation of the Argentine economy starting in 2001, is the obedience to the neoliberal dogma of free trade managed by big capital and its clients: unregulated borrowing abroad pushed up the value of the currency, made debt levels unsustainable, and gave the handle to the U.S. and transnational capital lobby to bleed the Latin American economies.

In Asia the economies of Thailand, Indonesia, and South Korea were most battered by the financial crisis of 1997–1998 because their governments had given their capitalists an unlimited license to borrow, at different times from the middle 1980s to the early 1990s. Taiwan and the People's Republic of China, which regulated transborder capital movements, and Malaysia, which introduced controls on such movements when the crisis hit, were less affected than the others (Bagchi 1998; Stiglitz 2002). China and Taiwan continue to regulate the inflows and outflows of capital, and east Asia, while slowing down, still displays greater dynamism than most other regions of the world.

Major east Asian countries gained in human development as they pushed their growth forward. In fact, it is their ability to improve literacy, education, and health care that enabled them to reap the benefits of policies of protection and government patronage that often proved disappointing in their results in most other developing countries. Between 1970 and 1997 in South Korea, Singapore, and China, for example, IMRs declined from 54 to 6, from 22 to 4, and from 85 to 38, respectively, and life expectancy improved from 60.1 years to 72.4, from 68.8 to 77.1, and from 62.0 to 69.8 in the respective countries. Advances in literacy and education took place in tandem (UNDP 1999). Belying the fears of the neo-Malthusians, east Asia has also experienced a rapid fertility transition. In South Korea, Singapore, and China between and 1975 and 1997, the total fertility rate declined from 3.4 to 1.7, from 2.1 to 1.7, and from 3.9 to 1.8, respectively (UNDP 1999). Their current fertility rates are comparable to those of the developed countries and are much lower than those of most other developing countries. But it is an example of the ever-emerging contradictions of neoliberal capitalism that the decline in fertility and rise in life expectancy are posing new problems for the management of pension funds and the stability of the financial system.

The roots of the earlier lag of the developing countries in respect of economic growth, as we have seen, are to be found in the policies that were imposed upon them by the metropolitan powers in the earlier epochs. During the period when most of the continental European countries, the United States, Canada, and Australia were following Britain in adopting factory-oriented technologies and changing their agrarian economies into industrial societies, they had a highly protectionist regime. Protection against foreign manufactures raised the rate of economic growth in the continental European countries (Bairoch 1993, chapters 2–4; O'Rourke 2000). When British manufactures threatened to decimate handicrafts in continental European countries and the United States, their governments raised tariff barriers against foreign imports and developed their own textile and other manufacturing industries (Sabel and Zeitlin 1985). The self-governing British dominions such as Canada and Australia followed suit and extended government help for a range of private activities, including white immigration.

In contrast, most of the nonwhite dependencies, including India, were forced to adopt policies of free trade and received minimal government help, except when necessary to protect the interests of European businessmen or the security of the colonial state (Bagchi 1972a, 1973b). Most of these colonial countries experienced slow economic and industrial growth until the middle of the twentieth century, and their indexes of human development also suffered. To portray the history of economic development as the triumph of free trade and minimalist government is to fly in the face of compelling historical evidence. The twentieth-century differentials in economic and human development, and the contradictions caused both by the global capitalist order and the incompleteness of antisystemic struggles, are most tragically illustrated by famines and I turn to sketch their genesis in the next section.

FAMINES IN THE TWENTIETH CENTURY

In the twentieth century, according to an estimate by Devereux (2000, table 2), more than 75 million people died in famines. While Devereux has accepted the high figure of 30 million for famine deaths in China during the Great Leap Forward period (1958–1961),[3] he has ignored deaths in minor famines under colonialism, such as the famines in British India over the years 1905 to 1908 that affected a population of 50 million (Visaria and Visaria

1983, p. 531). The excess mortality in the famines of 1907–1908 has been estimated as lying between 2.15 million and 3.22 million (Maharatna 1996, p. 15), but Devereux does not mention them.

Famines in most, but not all, cases were caused by what Sen (1981) has termed an entitlement failure, that is, the failure of the starving people to get access to food. The most devastating famines were caused by both entitlement failures and severe food shortages. These combinations frequently occurred in countries that were involved in wars, internal conflicts between groups claiming differences in ideology or ethnic affiliation, and antisystemic struggles.

In terms of their etiology, famines may be protocapitalist, colonial, and antisystemic.[4] Famines of the type experienced in ancien régime France or other countries of continental Europe may be called *protocapitalist* famines. Markets had developed but they remained badly segmented by obstacles in communication networks and channels of transmission of price signals and opening up of alternative sources of purchasing power and entitlements. State unresponsiveness to distress, of course, multiplied the starvation toll. *Colonial* famines occurred because the authorities were not accountable to the affected population for their actions and could ignore native deaths if they did not upset their hedonistic calculations. The great Bengal famine of 1943, which killed an estimated 3.5 million, was a colonial famine par excellence (Sen 1981; Maharatna 1996). While there was a short harvest in Bengal in 1942–1943, the British authorities, in their keenness to deny the advancing Japanese any advantage, ordered the destruction or sequestration of most means of transport, so that grain could not be moved from storages to areas of shortage. Grain was also procured by the authorities for the army on a priority basis. As prices soared, the administration made no attempt to provide public relief or introduce rationing until it was too late.

Regimes that came to power after major antisystemic struggles often experienced major famines. First, the regimes that they overthrew had presided over low levels of productivity and thin margins between starvation and survival. Any major shock could tilt the balance toward mass deaths. Second, postrevolution regimes generally faced severe opposition from the leading capitalist nations and were, therefore, reluctant to reveal their weakness to the outside observer. They rightly assumed that the information would be used not to help people in distress but merely to malign the new regime and weaken it. In the famines in the Ukraine in Soviet Russia in the 1930s and the Chinese famine of 1958–1961, another factor that played a part was the unwillingness of local party leaders to admit that things were going badly wrong and not according to the plans of the top leaders, who would be displeased by such unwelcome information (Devereux 2000; Drèze and Sen 1990a, 1990b,

1991). This antidemocratic tendency was fostered and reinforced by the isolation of Russia and China under the dominance of global capital. In the event, there was no prospect of assistance from the rich capitalist nations at the height of the Cold War.

A final example of famines would be what can be called a *globalization* famine. This is the destruction of food security of ordinary people in countries or regions that have experienced the devastation of subsistence economies through the unregulated working of the market, without securing new, market-mediated entitlements to food and other necessities. Under the impact of globalization, many poor countries have specialized in the production of crops such as soybeans and coarse grains to fatten the livestock to produce the rich man's meat and milk. In the absence of a public provisioning system, when the prices of such crops collapse or the country experiences a balance of payments crisis, the poor cannot buy food or get access to it.

The series of famines afflicting Ethiopia throughout the late twentieth century are tragic illustrations of protocapitalist, antisystemic, and globalization famines (Sen 1981, chapter 7; Kumar 1990; UNCTAD 2002a; almost any media source such as the BBC). Until 1974, Emperor Haile Selassie had ruled Ethiopia. Although Selassie had deservedly acquired fame for his resistance against Mussolini's aggression against Ethiopia, his empire remained archaic in its social structure, with feudal chieftains and court officials lording it over a largely illiterate and short-lived population of peasants, agricultural laborers, herders, and rural artisans. The Orthodox Church of Ethiopia was itself a great landowner, and landowners and the Church extracted their tribute from basically subsistence agriculture and pastoral activities (Read and Legum 1969; Kumar 1990, p. 177). That vast land also had poor communications. But most tragically, ordinary people had few entitlements they could invoke when drought destroyed crops and animals and also severely curtailed their purchasing power. When the rains failed in 1972 and the people of the northern province of Wollo became subject to starvation and tried to migrate to cities, they were turned back by the police. The imperial government called the news of famine a "fabrication." "The emperor voiced his views about the famine in an interview: 'Rich and poor have always existed and always will. Why? Because there are those that work . . . and those who prefer to do nothing. . . . Each individual is responsible for his fate'" (cited by Kumar 1990, p. 180). In 1973 "starvation and misery stalked the land while grain was sold abroad to pay for oil, industrial and luxury exports" (Freund 1984, p. 255). A revolt, led by the military but supported by radical elements, overthrew the empire. The Dergue, as the junta presiding over the new regime was called, however, failed to solve Ethiopia's myriad problems, and it turned into a repressive regime. It also tried to hold on to Eritrea, which Haile Selassie had occupied as the inheritor of the short-lived Italian empire. Ultimately, after a brutal and costly war, Eritrea obtained its independence in 1993 only to plunge again into war with Yemen and Ethiopia. These wars were among the factors that created the conditions for famine in Ethiopia and also in Eritrea. Two major famines in Ethiopia in extended over 1972–1975 and 1982–1985. In both cases, international aid proved inadequate for meeting the needs of millions of starving people (Kumar 1990). The repressive governments interfered with some of the famine relief, but the stark fact is that geopolitical considerations generated callousness among the major powers about the sufferings of people who lacked economic or military clout.

Both Ethiopia and Eritrea remain among the poorest countries of the world. In 1999 the per capita GDP was $107 for Ethiopia and $180 for Eritrea (UNCTAD 2002a, p. 247). In the decade of the 1980s, the per capita income of Ethiopia declined at the rate of 0.6 percent per annum (UNCTAD 1999, p. 177). Ethiopia, of course, was not alone in this disastrous experience. Of the forty-three countries of the UNCTAD tally of least developed counties, twenty-three suffered absolute decline in incomes in the decade of the 1980s (UNCTAD 1999, p. 177). For 1990–1999, of the forty-four least developed countries, twenty suffered a regression in per capita incomes (UNCTAD 2002a, p. 247). Among them, the Democratic Republic of the Congo, Burundi, and Sierra Leone suffered declines in per capita GDP of 8.3 percent, 4.9 percent, and 6.4 percent per annum, respectively.

Famine again threatens the Horn of Africa, including Ethiopia, Eritrea, and Kenya. By the beginning of 2003, 14 million people were directly afflicted in the three worst-affected countries, Eritrea, Ethiopia, and Kenya (Famine 2003; Mavunduse 2003; Q&A Ethiopia 2002). The common element in these famines is drought affecting both peasants and pastoralists. In many ways, pastoralists, who form a significant part of the population in this part of the world, are the worst hit. The livestock die in droves because of lack of fodder and water, thus directly depriving the herders of their protein and much of their calories. Moreover, the livestock and their products, such as milk and meat, are their major salable commodities. With declines in crop production and peasant incomes, the demands for livestock and their products decline drastically, thus leading to a crash in their prices.

Already in April 2000, an estimated six children a day were dying because of drought-related conditions in Ethiopia. The UN was warning of a possible total of 16 million people at risk of starvation in ten counties of east and central Africa (Kriner 2000). By 2002–2003, observers were warning of a famine in Ethiopia and Eritrea that could be worse than that witnessed in 1984. In some of the worst affected areas, half the cattle had perished by the beginning of 2003. In Eritrea more than half the population of 2.4 million was in need of food aid. In both Ethiopia and Eritrea, food aid from international agencies often takes time to arrive, and when it arrives, it is difficult to deliver it because of bad or nonexistent roads. The state is quite disabled for these tasks by lack of funds and by ideological pressure from the World Bank, IMF, and U.S. Agency for International Development (USAID) to keep the state away from provisioning the poor or engage in any economic activities. According to Dr. Tewolde Egziabher, head of Ethiopia's Environmental Protection Authority, the international agencies had not allowed the Ethiopian government to borrow money for constructing food stores as buffers against future scarcity (Kirby 2003). Ethiopia and Eritrea have both become highly dependent on tardily delivered international aid to avoid utter disaster and millions of starvation deaths (Fisher 2003), but extreme malnutrition has become endemic in the country. This occurred in the context of a glut of food supplies, especially in developed market economies, which continued to subsidize their rich farmers. The famines in Africa have again starkly exposed the doubletalk of free trade, the ending of the Cold War, and the collapse of the Soviet Union leading to plenty for all. The twenty-first-century international political order can bully the poor but not deliver them from hunger, starvation, and untimely death.

NOTES

1. In 1960 just about the time the Cuban revolution took place, Cuba had an IMR of 39; by 2001 it had come down to 7, the same level that was to be found in the United States, a country with a per capita income that was about ten times that of Cuba (UNICEF 2003; UNDP 1999, "Human Development Indicators").

2. It is not coincidental that the formula for options pricing was constructed in 1973 in two separate papers by Fischer Black, and Robert Merton and Myron Scholes. The last two authors were awarded the Nobel Prize for economics in 1997 (Black had died before that date. Merton and Scholes played a not-so-noble role soon after in the collapse of the firm Long Term Capital Management [Prestowitz 2003, pp. 57–58]).

3. For a critique of the usual estimates of famine deaths, see Utsa Patnaik 2002.

4. I am ignoring famines under precapitalist conditions. By the twentieth century, no part of the globe was outside the pale of capitalism.

23

Destruction and Renewal in the Neoliberal Global Order

STOCK MARKETS, FINANCIAL LIBERALIZATION, AND DEMOGRAPHY

One of the central tendencies of the move toward liberalization is to throw all the assets into the casino of the stock market. The resemblance of the stock market to a casino had been powerfully demonstrated by Keynes in chapter 12 of his classic *The General Theory of Employment, Interest and Money* (1936). Basically, the price of a share in a freewheeling market depends, not on the intrinsic value or profitability of a company, but on the opinion of other operators in the market as to how the share price will change. Even if shareholders believe that the price should be say, higher than what the market judges it to be, they may not be able to take advantage of it, because by holding on to the shares while their price goes on falling, they may lose most of their wealth, their creditors will call in their loans, and the shareholders may ultimately be ruined. Thus there is no point in being rational in the sense of judging share prices by what economists call expected value, because the stock market operates on the basis of herd behavior and irrational impulses rather than on that of rationality as defined by neoclassical economists.[1] Of course, professionals with deep pockets know this and pocket their profits before the crash of the individual stock or the market. In case of a stock-market crisis, banks advancing money to stockbrokers may also be unable to meet their obligations to their depositors because their borrowers are unable to repay their debts. This kind of crisis occurred in the Great Depression that began with the New York stock-market crash of 1929 and led the U.S. Congress to enact the Glass-Steagall Act, which strictly separated banking and stock-market operations. In Germany and Japan, firms were financed mainly by banks—which might also hold equities—rather than through the operation of stock markets. In India and most other developing countries also, following the pre-1970s traditions of English banking, banks did not finance stock-market operations.

All this changed with the financial deregulation starting in the 1970s. As deregulation of the domestic financial system was accompanied or followed by deregulation of movement of capital into and out of the country, the stock-market crisis was accompanied by a banking crisis and a currency crisis. When borrowers in a particular country were unable to repay debts contracted in times of "irrational exuberance" (cf. Shiller 2000), a run on the currency followed. After a while the country would officially declare its inability to pay its external debt and apply for an IMF bailout. The latter would then offer a package after coercing the defaulting government to accept a severely deflationary policy, and a tale foretold of increased poverty and unemployment would unfold. The incidence and the intensity of financial crises, especially affecting the developing and ex-Soviet countries, have both increased since the onset of financial liberalization (UNCTAD 1998).

One of the most telling illustrations of how financial liberalization and structural adjustment have affected numerous lands all across the world is what happened in Latin America from the 1980s to the early twenty-first century. Even in 1980, despite the tribulations of the 1930s and the doldrums of the 1960s, Argentina, Uruguay, Costa Rica, and Mexico were among the richer of the developing countries. The debt crisis starting in 1982 that over-whelmed Mexico, Brazil, Chile, Argentina, and several other counties of Latin America led to the adoption of structural-adjustment programs. The result was the lost decade of the 1980s: over 1950–1980 the income per capita of the region grew by 2.7 percent per year; in the 1980s despite a slowing of population growth, income per capita declined by 0.9 percent per year. By the end of the 1980s, most of the countries had carried out thoroughgoing economic reforms, including privatization of many state enterprises. After picking up a little over the period, from 1990 to 1997, when the growth rate of income per head was 2.0 percent per year, that figure again plunged and per capita income declined by 0.3 percent per year over the following six years (Ocampo 2004, table 1). One of the worst cases of econocide under neoliberal economic reform is that of Argentina. The country was richer than Italy before World War I, when Italians went every year to work in Argentina (Bagchi 1982, chapter 3). In the latest bout of income decline, according to World Bank data, the GDP, which was $236.5 billion in 1993, fell to $102.0 billion in 2002, and the ratio of those below the national poverty level shot up to 56 percent.[2] Argentina experienced this disaster after using all the weapons of the neoliberal armory. From 2002 it refused to accept the IMF nostrum, defaulted on its record external debt of more than $100 billion and, defying the predictions of doomsters, its economy has grown at the rate of 8 percent per annum in 2003 and 2004 (Rohter 2004). Argentina's performance has shown up the economic weakness of the neoliberal order, which I discuss in some detail later. But it will also I hope stiffen the resistance of other countries against the prescriptions of the neoliberal quacks.

The cases of Latin America and Argentina have been replicated in many other countries. Sub-Saharan Africa and most of the ex-Soviet countries embracing neoliberal reforms have been among the worst sufferers. While there is talk of a new financial architecture to prevent financial crisis, it has become quite clear that with unregulated movements of capital there is no way for nations with weaker economies to prevent the triple contagion of debt crisis, banking crisis, and currency crisis (Kaminsky, Reinhart, Carmen, and Vegh 2003).

When there are no restrictions on mergers and acquisitions and there is a free market for purchase and sale of firms, a firm that can command larger resources than another can take it over even if the targeted firm is well managed and profitable. Thus financial liberalization becomes a powerful force for the ruin of smaller firms and the growth of the larger ones.

Financial deregulation can also open up new opportunities and heighten incentives for fraud as was shown in the revelations surrounding the series of bankruptcies of multibillion-dollar firms and fraudulent accounting practices in the United States, starting with Enron in 2000, and continuing with Global Crossing and WorldCom (Krugman 2002).[3] Fraudulent practices were also discovered in the operations of investment bankers, mutual funds, and insurance companies. In all these areas, ordinary holders of shares, mutual fund securities, or insurance policies are at the mercy of brokers or advisors. In a situation of high risk and uncertainty, there is ample scope for collusion between the brokers and the concerned firms at the cost of the principal. Where mammon has been elevated to the position of supreme god, it is hardly surprising that brokers, advisors, and accountants seize opportunities to make easy money through fraud. After the introduction of economic liberalization in the 1990s, countries such as India, Poland, and Russia were repeatedly rocked by financial scandals, often involving the top bureaucrats and politicians.

With the arrival of electronic banking and fund transfers across borders, it has become far easier to launder illicit gains in political corruption and peddling of drugs and arms (Ignatius 2000). The embedding of corruption in this systematic fashion under the neoliberal order poses further grave problems for the building of a sane and prosperous democratic society.

The TRIPs clauses of the WTO have allowed big corporations to deny researchers access to scientific knowledge such as the decoding of particular parts of a genome sequence on the grounds that they had patented them. Protesting against this practice, Sir John Sulston, a pioneer in the decoding of the human genome for which he was awarded the Nobel Prize, described it as an attribute of "corporate feudalism" (Sulston 2001). Under this patent regime, even natural objects can be patented and people who have been using herbs occurring in nature for medicinal and nutritional purposes for thousands of years can be deprived of their use (Shiva 2001).

In the name of property rights, companies are acquiring the power to deny whole communities access to life-supporting drinking and irrigation water, as happened in the Cochabamba province of Bolivia until the people rose up to upset the designs of capital and its client politicians. As the state retreats from vital areas such as social security, including health care and pensions, and increasingly surrenders its power to tax the rich, most transactions are mediated through the financial sector. Fiscally beleaguered states are then bonded to transnational banks and their watchdogs, namely, the IMF and the World Bank, and citizens in all countries become helpless clients and often bonded servants of financial institutions.

TRIBULATIONS OF DEMOCRACY
UNDER THE NEOLIBERAL ORDER

Bourgeois democracy was born in the fight of the bourgeoisie against feudal lords. But from the very beginning the bourgeoisie have been engaged in a rearguard action to suppress the aspirations of the workers and peasants who helped them fight the feudal order. This happened in the English civil war of the 1640s, at the conclusion of which the Cromwellian dictatorship was established; in the course of the French Revolution of 1789, when the sansculottes were suppressed and Napoleon was allowed to destroy the republic; in 1848, both in Germany and France, the capitalists helped reestablish monarchical power. The antidemocratic tendency of the later bourgeoisie was demonstrated in the way the center-right politicians facilitated the Nazi destruction of democracy in Germany.

Democracy came much nearer achieving its goals in the twentieth century in contexts in which workers could successfully fight for better wages, security, and working conditions, as happened in the Scandinavian countries, and more incompletely in Britain and the United States from the 1930s, and in continental European countries after World War II. As I have noted earlier, the fear of communism and of the Soviet Union played an important part in persuading the ruling class to heed democratic demands. Beating back workers' power was one of the chief goals of the Thatcher regime in the United Kingdom and the Reagan regime in the United States. The victory of the Labour Party in the 1990s has done little to roll back the neoliberal policies that lie at the root of the worsening of the conditions of the laboring poor in Britain. On the other hand, deliberate attempts have been made to incorporate the workers of the advanced capitalist countries in the imperialist project by portraying the workers of the developing countries rather than footloose capital as their enemies (Fletcher 2003).

Increase in income inequality and increasing concentration of economic power have gone hand in hand with the weakening of democracy. In the United States, voters had long ceased to have any real choice between the two major parties, the Democratic and the Republican, because they espoused essentially similar policies in both domestic and foreign affairs (Hightower 2000). A critical issue is rising inequality in societies across the globe. The Congressional Budget Office in the U.S., for example, released a report in 2001 showing that while the real income of the top 1 percent of the U.S. population increased by 142 percent between 1979 and 1999, the real income of the bottom 20 percent of income earners actually declined. Since that time, this trend has accelerated. While many African Americans made it into the middle class and some even grew rich and powerful (e.g., Colin Powell and Condoleezza Rice in the Bush administration), African Americans were heavily overrepresented among the poor, the unemployed, and incarcerated. The United States has the largest proportion of the civilian population in jail in peacetime among all countries of the world, and that proportion has been rising (Stern 1998). African Americans, followed by Hispanics, bear the brunt of the imprisonment. Still, the poor and especially African Americans among them regarded the Democrats as less inimical to their interests because of their defense of some of the rights of organized workers and their more caring stance regarding health care and old age pensions. The Republican Party's victory margin in the 2000 election, in which the Democratic candidate obtained a larger number of votes, rested in part on the ability to suppress the votes of African Americans using both legal and illegal measures in Florida and elsewhere. After the attacks on the World Trade Center on 11 September 2001, the U.S. government passed the Patriot Act and created the department of Homeland Security, both of which significantly restricted the civil rights not only of resident foreigners but of dissident U.S. citizens as well (Chang 2002; Stein 2003). With an agenda of permanent war (the war on terror) at home and abroad, American democracy faces stern challenges indeed.

Not only in the United States but also in many other formally democratic counties such as Italy and India the democratic process has been repeatedly subverted by the power of money and oligarchy-controlled media, often in association with the most backward-looking worldviews, such as Christian fundamentalism or Hindu fundamentalism, racism, or casteism. The power of money has catapulted into power parties and leaders that have subverted the foundations of formal democracy and have consistently denied substantive democracy to the majority of the people.

Putnam (1993) built his theory of the importance of civic virtue in the proper flow of the democratic process by claiming that a high level of civic virtue obtained in northern Italy, in contrast with the feebleness of such virtue in southern Italy. Yet in that land, Silvio Berlusconi, who has made himself the richest Italian with an estimated fortune of $10 billion (Stille 2003), is trying to build a patrimonial state by using his wealth and his grip over 90 percent of the TV and other media audiences to trample democratic values and existing laws (Ginsborg 2003). Berlusconi became prime minister of Italy in 1994, but his parliamentary support collapsed after a few months. Between 1994 and 2001 he further increased his wealth, and in 2001 he became prime minister with a much larger majority in the parliament. During this period, he has manipulated the legal system to protect himself and his companies against the ongoing suits accusing him and his officials (many of whom are also members of parliament) of bribery, corruption, and diversion of public money to their own pockets. He has already had laws passed giving immunity to ministers during the time they hold office.[4] It is of a piece with his general worldview and his dictatorial ambitions that, chiming in with the initial reaction of the U.S. president, he called for a crusade against the (Muslim) terrorists after the 9/11 attacks against the World Trade Center and the Pentagon.

In India the Hindu fundamentalist and chauvinist parties led by the Bharatiya Janata Party (BJP) and Shiv Sena fanned anti-Muslim sentiments, destroyed a sixteenth-century mosque (the Babri Masjid), claiming that it is the birthplace of a Hindu god, Ram, and deliberately provoked riots between Hindus and Muslims on a large scale in 1992–1993. A BJP-led coalition captured power in the Central government in 1999. On 26 February 2002, the BJP used the police in Gujarat to carry out a hideous carnage against innocent Muslims following trumped-up charges of a Muslim plot: the estimated death toll is 2,000 (Concerned Citizens Tribunal 2002; Varadarajan 2002). Thousands of others lost all they had and were forced to take shelter in refugee camps.

We turn finally to post-Soviet Russia, whose neoliberal advisors envisaged a free-market economy and a functioning democracy after the fall of communist dictatorship and the collapse of the Soviet Union. However, the new leaders led by Boris Yeltsin proved adept at stripping public resources for their own benefit. Russia went into a severe economic crisis from which it is recovering only recently. The economic crisis was also associated with a health crisis. Between 1988 and 1994, the expectation of life at birth for males fell from around 65 years to 57.4 and that for females fell from 74.4 years to 71.3 (Andreev, Scherbov, and Willekens 1998). Health crises, connected with recession and shrinking job opportunities, also affected other ex-Soviet republics, such as Estonia and Lithuania (Hawkes 2000). The two elections in which Vladimir Putin has been chosen as Russian president have been widely regarded as less than a model of exercise of free choice. Abolition of state controls over productive assets as such establishes neither free markets nor the rule of law. In all the instances cited here, the power of money and a divisive ideology have played a part in depriving ordinary people of their real political freedom in choosing their mode of governance.

NOTES

1. Despite the neoclassical conceptualization of finance as a prime example of "a theory that emphatically fails empirically yet is generally considered to yield important insights" (Buiter 2003, F587), it continues to be the workhorse of courses on finance.

2. http://web.worldbank.org/ar.

3. The U.S. revelations also finished off the idea that only countries like South Korea or Indonesia are characterized by crony capitalism, it being discovered that the fraudulent business executives had extensive links with members of the Bush administration, including the Bushes themselves and, in some cases, with members of the earlier Clinton administration (Palast 2002; Phillips 2004).

4. Even the conservative newspaper *Economist* felt constrained to point out the falsification of evidence and the distortion of the legal process and send an open letter to Berlusconi to reply to its charges (*Economist*, 2 August 2003, pp. 9–10, 22–25).

24

Contradictions, Challenges, and Resistance

ANTINOMIES WITHIN THE CAPITALIST ORDER

One of the defining characteristics of capitalism has been a contradiction between its universalist claims (being unlike feudalism, ancient slavery, or caste-based systems in this respect) and the delivery of substantive gains to only segments of the population, leaving others in privation. Similarly, government by law has meant laws biased in favor of property owners. But the promises became embedded in the memory of the deprived and supplied them with goals to fight for. I have sketched the story of the promise of democracy under the capitalist world order and the way that promise has been repeatedly betrayed in the heartland of capitalism and imperialism and in some of the lands that had embraced parliamentary democracy.

A similar story can be told about the promise of international legality. It was at the very dawn of emergence of capitalism that Hugo Grotius and other jurists laid the foundations of international law. But in the whole history of the European powers against other peoples, the non-Christians and non-European states were generally considered beyond the pale of international law. However, the scope of international law became broader at the very time that the advance of war technology made possible killing on a grander scale. Thus by the end of the nineteenth century, international conventions were framed to minimize civilian deaths in war (Selden 2003). But in successive conflicts, from World War I to the ongoing U.S. war against resistance in Iraq, the proportion of civilian to combatant casualties has risen. Respect for both domestic and international law reached a nadir in the U.S.-led Gulf War II: a war conducted in violation of all the Geneva Conventions and the UN charter. In the treatment of prisoners captured in the war against Afghanistan and kept incommunicado in U.S. military prisons in Guantánamo Bay and of Iraqi prisoners in Abu Ghraib and elsewhere, the U.S. administration has put itself outside both international law and domestic law by denying legally sanctioned trials to the detainees and providing immunity to the top brass, including Defense secretary Donald Rumsfeld, for the torture and killing of the Iraqi prisoners (Danner 2004). But the promise of legality keeps resurfacing not only in the form of protests by U.S. citizens and criticism, even by the normally conservative organ of capital, the *Economist*, but also by U.S. judges who have ruled the treatment of Guantánamo detainees indefensible in U.S. law (*Economist*, 13 November 2004, "Here's to you, Mr Robertson").

Let us look at another area in which contradictions have become too glaring for the comfort of seasoned defenders of financial liberalization. The repeated financial crises in the world have put pension funds of even the advanced capitalist economies in jeopardy. In some instances they were stolen by company executives who used them to bolster share prices of a sagging company, as in the case of Enron; in others they were put into booming bond and loan markets of Southeast and eastern Asia only to collapse with the Asian financial crisis of 1997–1998. Now, the worry is that with increasing expectations of life and escalating proportions of the numbers of old people to the numbers in working age groups, above all in Japan, but extending elsewhere, social security savings will be insufficient to pay benefits.

Neoliberal economic reforms promised better economic opportunities for everybody and higher economic growth in every country. We have seen that they have led to a higher degree of concentration of income (and wealth) while large groups of people have been bypassed by the benefits or find themselves absolutely and relatively impoverished as millions are either unemployed or engaged in extremely low-paid occupations—the opposite of what the International Labour Office (ILO 1999) has characterized as decent work. The beginning of the twenty-first century has witnessed a collapse of the growth of employment worldwide, except in most countries of eastern Asia, and not only in the formal sectors but even in low-paid informal sectors (ILO 2003, 2004). This is especially true of the youth (that is, persons between the ages of fifteen and twenty-four according to the UN definition) who constitute 25 percent of the working-age population but account for 47 percent of the unemployed. Worldwide, there were 88 million unemployed youth in 2003 (ILO 2004). Moreover, women have been the first victims of spreading unemployment in many countries. In particular, in some Asian countries that had specialized in using female labor for export production, there has taken place a defeminization of labor as machines operated by men have displaced women (Ghosh 2003). Rates of unemployment have soared perhaps to levels as high as 36 percent in the Caribbean and Middle East and North Africa among young people between the ages of fifteen and twenty-five years (ILO 2003). Endemic unemployment and loss of livelihood breed new types of bondage in addition to traditional debt bondage or clientelist (or patronage politics) dependence. Unemployment is a fertile breeding ground for criminals, terrorists, and mercenaries, who find employment with the dictators of the Third World and as the enforcers of TNCs in countries like Colombia or as the counterinsurgency forces of the United States in Central America. At the end of the twentieth century, there has been a virtual collapse of growth of employment worldwide (ILO 2003, 2004). The spread of unemployment has meant that women have been the first to be retrenched. In most poor families, women are the final absorbers of shocks to family incomes and have to take on the burden of domestic provisioning by finding jobs that pay a pittance (Carr and Chen 2004). The consequent displacement or disintegration of their families and forced migration have led to increased trafficking of women.

The promise of peace at the end of the Cold War has been dashed not only by international wars but also by civil wars and insurgencies throughout the developing world, including the Balkans. According to one estimate, in continuing conflicts around the world, down to 2002 deaths reached 2.5 million in Congo, 2 million in Sudan, 13,000 in Israel and Palestine, 35,000 in Colombia, 35,000 in Kashmir, and 70,000 in Chechnya, controlled by Russia (Thussu and Freedman 2003, p. 2).

Precipitous environmental degradation on a global scale similarly threatens the future of humanity. Human beings have simultaneously used nature to improve their conditions of living and destroyed parts of it while doing so. A new scale of environmental degradation emerged with the discovery of new ways of using exhaustible resources and rapid urbanization that accompanied the growth of capitalism. In the North Atlantic seaboard, in Japan and other advanced capitalist countries, eventually better knowledge of sanitation and the use of resources to clean up the environment led to the arresting of some of the worst effects of urbanization on people's health (see part 2 of this book; Foster 1994; McNeill 2000). However, the poorer countries lack the resources and often the responsiveness of a participatory democracy to clean up the environment, so that their air and water become ever more polluted. On the other hand, the unregulated use of nonrenewable energy and mineral resources of the world lead to ever-higher levels of emission of greenhouse gases, depletion of the ozone layer, and the fast erosion of biodiversity. The promise that was held out by the environmental movement of the 1960s and 1970s has been belied by the refusal of the United States to sign international treaties that would curb the pollution by penalizing enterprises responsible for the problem (Prestowitz 2003, chapter 5). The WTO regime is likely to aggravate the situation because it removes virtually all social controls on the destruction of forests and water resources by capital. Finally, the possibility of use of nuclear weapons by the superpower, terrorists, or other warring states and, with that, the threat of destruction of the habitat of human beings (and sentient life) have to be taken very seriously.

CHALLENGES AND INTRAIMPERIALIST CONFLICTS

The United States has long been the strongest military power in the world and now is a power that no other combination of countries can challenge for military supremacy. But its supremacy in the economic field faces continual challenges. First, there is severe competition in most fields of manufacture using advanced technology from Japan and the more developed countries of the European Union. The United States has run up huge deficits in its current account since the latter half of the 1990s. Its current account deficit for the twelve months ending in 13 November 2004 came to a staggering $571.9 billion (*Economist*, 13 November 2004). The government, far from acting to control this deficit by reining in its own expenditure, under George W. Bush's presidency has expanded the budget deficit to 4.7 percent of GDP. The expenses of Gulf War II, and of pacifying Iraq, together with the Bush tax cuts will keep the budget deficit high. So far, other nations, notably China and Japan, have been willing to cover U.S. external deficits by buying treasury bonds and investing in U.S. business. Much of Japan's and Germany's huge surpluses, which amounted to $169.0 billion and $90.2 billion, respectively, for the latest twelve months (according to the *Economist*, 13 November 2004), and the foreign exchange holdings of eastern Asian countries with substantial surpluses on their external account also go to finance the U.S. profligacy. However, the dollar has been losing against the euro and the yen for the last three years. This is, of course, a mixed blessing for the European Union and Japan, because a cheaper dollar will confer a competitive advantage on U.S. exports. However, the tendency of the U.S. government to ride roughshod over other people's property rights when the latter are regarded as opponents has probably shaken the faith of other countries, particularly those not firmly aligned with U.S. interests in the security of their property in U.S. custody.

The United States also faces economic challenges from China and other dynamic economies of eastern Asia. China has become the production and investment dynamo of the global economy, whereas the United States has become the top consumer in the world (*Economist* 2004a). Other options of cooperation are being explored, for example, among Russia, China, and India, but thus far these do not significantly challenge the predominance of U.S. interests in the region. Collaboration in economic and political matters between Brazil, South Africa, and India, three of the dynamic democracies of the south, and between China and Latin America, where ambitious new resource and construction agreements were signed in November 2004, are also in progress.

Problems are created for a developing country if it tries simply to adapt to the game of rigged competition that neoliberal reforms have imposed on all players, but particularly on the poorer countries. Even regimes engaged in antisystemic struggles against the capitalist world order got caught up in the meshes of that order while struggling against it. As I have noted, the suppression of free speech within their societies and the fear that appeals for help to the capitalist powers would only endanger the state security without bringing real relief probably aggravated the famines in the Soviet Union in the 1930s and in China over 1958–1961. In the Soviet bloc, the drive toward industrialization at any cost led to huge ecological disasters such as the silting up of the Aral Sea and the smoke-filled cities of Poland (Foster 1994; McNeill 2000).

The problems of adapting to the international system are well illustrated by the recent history of China, which has remained the fastest growing economy from the 1990s to the present. While this growth has undoubtedly improved the income and living conditions of most people, it has created major ecological problems in the form of urban congestion, energy shortage, and pollution of water (Smil 2003). Growth has also been purchased at the price of a leap in income inequality (Khan and Riskin 2001). The degree of income inequality now matches or exceeds those observed in many developing countries such as India or Malaysia and exceeds that in most rich countries. China's urban areas do vastly better than rural areas; coastal regions better than interior provinces. The increase in inequality has adversely affected society-wide improvements in education and health care. However, the adoption of the policy of directing investments into the interior provinces appears to have checked the growth of inequality in China after 1995 (Khan and Riskin 2004).

The gains, moreover, have been purchased at the price of worsening of conditions of women by some standards. For example, China's one-child family policy had the unintended effect of creating large-scale abortion and infanticide of female fetuses and newborns in rural areas, with the result that gender ratios become ever more skewed against females (Agnihotri 2000; Park and Cho 1995). Nor is this phenomenon limited to China. In Taiwan, South Korea, and China, the ratio of the number of births of boys to that of girls exceeds 112 (as against the normal ratio of 106 boys to 100 girls among the newborn), and the disparity has increased substantially since 1980, that is, the high-growth period of these regions (Park and Cho 1995). In India also the sex ratio has continued to deteriorate, especially in the richer states and urban areas dominated by high-caste Hindus, who utilize new technologies for sex-selection and female feticide (Agnihotri 2003).

RESISTANCE AND ITS PARAMETERS

Numerous challenges continue to confront global capital. Cuba continues to defy American power in the face of protracted sanctions and open threats of armed attacks. The Zapatistas of Mexico have been agitating for more than a decade for the restoration of the rights and freedom of the native people, in solidarity with other Mexicans battered by decades of corrupt, capital-friendly governments and their policies. From Brazil to Ecuador and Venezuela, people have voted to throw out governments that acted as the collaborators and policemen of transnational capital and the U.S. government. Protests have erupted against the WTO and the International Monetary Fund–World Bank duo from Seattle, New York, and Washington, DC, in the United States to Quebec in Canada, Genoa in Italy, and Cancun in Mexico. They have produced martyrs such as the Korean farmers' leader in Cancun and the young victim of police brutality in Genoa. The U.S.-British attacks on Afghanistan and Iraq in 2002–2003 evoked some of the most massive anti-war demonstrations since World War II. In the European, Asian, and World Social Forums held in Porto Alegre, Florence, Hyderabad, and Mumbai, organized by dissenters of many hues, hundreds of thousands joined hands (for an analysis of the ongoing resistance movements around the world, see Amin and Houtart 2002).

As capitalism and imperialism have entered into every cell of the body politic, activists have come to realize that the fight against imperialism has to embrace all aspects of life, including the ideological formations, the state apparatus, and civil society as well (Bagchi 2003). With increasing numbers of people rendered insecure through unemployment and financial crises, with rising inequality and declining welfare and educational systems in many societies, neoliberalism opens new opportunities for resistance.

One of the major health disasters in poor countries, the spread of HIV/AIDS, has been aggravated by the neoliberal order of which WTO is a critical component. Antiretrovials necessary to prevent HIV from developing into full-blown AIDS are prohibitively expensive for most patients in Sub-Saharan Africa and other poor countries, where AIDS is taking the shape of a pandemic. Drugs and private health care systems have become too expensive for the poor even in the United States. The struggle against these aspects of the system could unite the poor of all countries.

Democratic movements can learn from experiments in participatory government that have been conducted in far-flung locales. At Porto Alegre in Brazil or in the states of Kerala and West Bengal people believing in the possibility of socially responsible democratic alternatives have experimented with decentralized, participatory modes of governance. Contradictions and challenges to the neoliberal, U.S.-dominated imperialist order are multiplying as the twenty-first century begins its turbulent course. Take, as the first of the many areas in which they are manifesting themselves, that of economic performance. It was surmised that with full financial deregulation the market value of companies rather than productive investment would determine the profits of shareholders and wealth of company managers; hence the rates of investment and saving would decline, because managers would have less interest in planning for long-term productivity growth and would watch stock valuations as the barometer of their own future prospects. This is borne out fully by the record of U.S. saving. The ratio of household saving to disposable income had gone down virtually to zero in 2001 and has since then inched up to about a quarter of what it used to be in the early 1980s (BIS 2004, chapter 2). The overall U.S. rate of saving as a percentage of GDP in 2003 was 13.4 percent, down 3.2 percent from 2002. By contrast, the rate of saving in the main economies of eastern and southern Asia was 34.6 percent, up 2.3 percent from 2002. It must be noted that most of these countries have resisted full financial liberalization so far. The current account balance of the United States as a percentage of GDP was −4.9 percent in that year as against +4.0 percent of the major Asian economies (BIS 2004, table 2.8). The global economy has picked up in 2003–2004, and it is driven by productive investment in eastern Asia, led by China and consumer expenditure in the United States, largely driven by inflated share and property values (*Economist* 2004a). Meanwhile, the U.S. current account deficits have reached a level that requires $1.9 billion of loans per day extended by the rest of the world to keep it going.

A very large part of the U.S. deficit is due to the enormous and accelerating military expenditure of the Bush administration. Japan has now emerged as the second highest spender on military budget in the world and the country is fast militarizing itself and thereby violating its own constitution (McCormack 2004b). It is also emerging as a frontline ally of the United States: not only are U.S. forces posted on Japanese soil but Japan has also committed troops for Gulf War II and kept them there as part of the occupation forces. The bond that binds the two allies is not only a fear of China but also the desire to keep a firm hold of the fossil energy resources of the world.

Japan is utterly dependent on foreign oil and gas supplies. If the United States is converting its army and the mercenaries it recruits as the protection force for oil wells and pipelines (Klare 2004), how can the Japanese refuse its contribution to that effort? Moreover, as U.S. corporations such as General Electric, General Dynamics, Halliburton, or Bechtel are making billions out of military contracts and wars in Afghanistan and Iraq and their postwar reconstruction, why should Japan's military contractors such as Mitsubishi Heavy Industries and Ishikawajima Heavy Industries be left behind? (*Economist* 2004b). The military-industrial complex goes on expanding as the neoliberal-military order reaches new heights of arrogance. There is a global imbalance between the growth of labor force and the creation of productive employment: the permanent reserve-army of labor cannot find employment in growth poles because, while capital is freely mobile, there are severe restrictions on the movement of labor. The neoliberal-military order seeks to keep this imbalance from explosive resolution by using force because it cannot persuade the majority of the world that it is working for their good.

As the costs of empire escalate and the power of corporate capital in core countries grows, neoliberalism has increasingly resorted to divesting the state of functions that Adam Smith thought could never be in the private domain. These include military and security operations both at home and abroad. Prison services are privatized and private firms profit from them. Military functions are contracted out to private firms, and in the name of security and war against terrorism, the executive branch of the government removes its own accountability and the accountability of the firms to the legislature or the electorate (Johnson 2004; Pieterse 2004). The deception and the disinformation about the weapons of mass destruction in the possession of Saddam Hussein (*Economist* 2003a, 2003b) are all of a piece with this attempt on the part of the White House and Whitehall to put themselves above not only international law but the laws of their own nations.

The rapid evolution of the neoliberal order into a neoliberal imperial order is characterized by the double-speak of freedom and democracy mouthed and practiced by the U.S. administration as well as by the adoption of U.S. unilateralism in solving political and trade issues on the international plane. As I noted above, the WTO regime was instituted primarily in the interest of big corporations. However, the United States has not only repeatedly flouted the WTO clauses related to the misuse of antidumping legislation and subsidies but has also negated the flexibilities allowed in the WTO agreement to developing countries with respect to GATS (general agreement on trade in services) and TRIPs by entering into bilateral trade and aid agreements with them. Under various threats, the United States has removed those flexibilities (such as nonenforcement of the patent regime) from the reach of those poor countries.

The challenges to the controllers of the neoliberal order are mounting in the military field as well. In 2001 China entered into defensive alliances with Russia and most countries of central Asia (SIPRI 2004, chapter 6). It has also engaged in negotiations with the Association of Southeast Asian Nations (ASEAN) on security matters. With its manufacturing prowess leading China to become the chief trading partner of many Asian countries, its credibility as a challenger to the superpower will increase. Whether these developments will curb the aggressive moves of the United States and Britain or will egg them on to further atrocities is not something anybody can predict.

The Industrial Revolution was based on new ways of exploiting exhaustible resources of the earth, in particular fossil fuels. But the use of fossil fuels has contributed to the rapid degradation of the environment, some of the effects of which I have analyzed in earlier chapters, especially in part 2. The capitalist mode of exploitation has also led to enormous imbalances in costs and benefits, supplies, and use of these resources. For example, according to one estimate, over 1950–2000, the G8 countries (including Russia), with only 13.6 percent of the global population (World Bank 2004), were responsible for 40.81 percent of the cumulative carbon dioxide emissions of the world, and their yearly emissions still continue to contribute a similar percentage. On the other hand, the major part of fossil fuel reserves of the world is located in the poorer countries (WRI 2004).

The U.S. neoconservatives, backed by the administration, have announced that the United States should enforce its will on the rest of the world and international laws are there only for other states. This doctrine is a sign of U.S. weakness in the economic field: the United States can no longer pay for the energy resources it needs for the kind of military-centered, environmentally destructive path of profit accumulation it is pursuing, and hence militarism has become a means of grabbing resources without paying a proper price, increasing the profits of crony companies and generating employment in defense industries. The United States has not really come out victorious in Iraq and Afghanistan: it has to maintain permanent occupation forces to control the resistance of people who have been deprived of their livelihood and liberty. In western Asia, North Africa, and Latin America, the neoliberal order is creating new badlands through wanton deforestation and environmental destruction and giving rise to unemployment on an unprecedented scale. The only means available to the militarist mind-set of the controllers of that order is naked force. Recently they are targeting oil-rich and resistant Iran for a military takeover. But the United States was defeated or stalemated in every Asian war that it undertook since World War II: Korea, Indochina, Afghanistan, Iraq. Will the story be different in Iran? And will the U.S.-led imperialists be capable of dealing with challengers from Beijing to Porto Alegre when the U.S. economic prowess is visibly declining?

The march of capitalism since the sixteenth century across the world led to momentous changes, redistributing economic resources and power from the eastern regions of Eurasia to the western promontory of Europe, and thence to North America. It also led to the breakup of old empires and creation of new nation-states. Ideals of new ways of reorganizing society and polity inspired the French and the Bolshevik Revolutions. Both of them inspired new movements, but the results often ended in new forms of tyranny. But the ideals of liberty and equality survived these assaults. The twentieth century witnessed the end of formal colonial rule and a surge of movements to usher in socialism. But human achievement with respect to substantive freedom such as better education, health care, and social security often went together with restrictions on freedom of speech and political and civil liberty, as in Russia and China. On the other hand, capitalism often denied substantive freedom to citizens even under formal democracy, the leading example of this cleavage being India. Moreover, in many countries a formally democratic apparatus was reduced to a façade of crony rule as people were denied real choice. The protection of even substantive freedom becomes endangered under existing socialism by the lack of freedom of choice. But under capitalism both substantive and procedural freedom can become casualties if the ruling classes feel really threatened by the power of the workers and peasants and resort to total suppression of freedom of the ordinary people, as happened most tragically in Nazi Germany and as has routinely happened in the developing countries of Africa, Asia, and Latin America. In the developing countries, such suppression was actively aided by the imperialist powers led by the United States, Britain, and France. The resulting conflicts led to enormous numbers of deaths in wars and famines, as recorded here.

The story of the grim twentieth century and its continuation into the twenty-first can be told as a series of Kurosawa's *Rashomon* tales. How will the grimness be dispelled? Does humankind have the choice between only regimes that will be formally democratic but imperialist in their actual operations and regimes that start with the promise of equality and suppress internal democracy as a way of meeting the challenges of the incumbent imperialists? Will the promise of freedom celebrated throughout history and formulated as a condition of being fully human by the theorists of the European Enlightenment, by Marx and Engels, by Rabindranath Tagore, or by Albert Einstein never be realized for all human beings? Can this spaceship earth be rescued as a habitable planet for sentient life including humankind from the consequences of unchecked denudation of forests, the demonic gouging out of the nonrenewable fossil fuels and metals from the entrails of the planet—activities that are driven by the greed and the competitiveness of the capitalist order and its putative challengers in the geopolitical system? In this book I have tried to sketch both the achievements and the destruction caused by the capitalist-imperialist order. The achievements lie in scientific progress, the vast widening of the world of knowledge, and the beckoning of the potential for every human being to live a free life. But the inequality built into the very structure of capitalism has led to the repeated destruction of that potential throughout history. The twentieth century and its young successor have witnessed new horrors in the shape of deliberate killing of tens of millions of people, the premature deaths of hundreds of millions, and the condemning of perhaps three to four billion people to a subhuman existence because of their lack of access to the basic necessities that make a human life worth living. But ours is not an accountant's balance sheet. It is also a plea to all lovers of freedom to struggle against the neoliberal order presided over by an increasingly arrogant U.S. administration that threatens the life and freedom of people in most counties, including the United States. But that fight has to be conducted against the logic of armed competitiveness itself, because otherwise the world itself may be destroyed by a thermonuclear Armageddon or may be divided up into competing tyrannies with unfree human beings teetering on the brink of destruction.

The hope against that possibility lies in the struggles of peoples empowered with ideals of liberty and equality, knowledge flowing from every corner of the earth, and the emergence of new regions of development that do not depend on the logic of armed, competitive capitalism. In a world in which technology offers the possibility of sustainable development in harmony with nature, all the people can then enjoy a healthy and long life in freedom and prosperity.

References

Abbreviations used are the following:

AAAG = Annals of the Association of American Geographers
AHR = American Historical Review
CJE = Cambridge Journal of Economics
CUP = Cambridge University Press
EEH = Explorations in Economic History
EHR = Economic History Review
EJ = Economic Journal
EPW = Economic and Political Weekly
HUP = Harvard University Press
IESHR = Indian Economic and Social History Review
JAS = Journal of Asian Studies
JEH = Journal of Economic History
LIC = Late Imperial China
MAS = Modern Asian Studies
MR = Monthly Review
NYRB = New York Review of Books
OUP = Oxford University Press
P&P = Past and Present
PDR = Population and Development Review
PS = Population Studies
PUP = Princeton University Press

Acharya, P. 1989. *Banglar Deshaja Shikshadhara* (in Bangla). Calcutta: Anustup.

Achcar, G. 2002. *The Clash of Barbarisms: September 11 and the Making of the New World Disorder*. New York: Monthly Review Press.

Adam, W. 1835–38/1941. *Reports on the State of Education in Bengal (1835&1838);* reprinted and ed. Anathnath Basu. Calcutta: University of Calcutta.

Adelman, J., and Aron, S. 1999. From Borderlands to Borders: Empires, Nation-States, and the Peoples in between in North American History. *AHR* 104(3): 815–41.

Adorno, T., and Horkheimer, M. 1944/1979. *Dialectic of Enlightenment*, transl. J. Cumming from the German. London: Verso.

Agnihotri, S. 2000. *Sex Ratio Patterns in the Indian Population: A Fresh Exploration*. New Delhi: Sage.

———. 2003. Survival of the Girl Child: Tunnelling out of the Chakravyuha. *EPW* 38(41): 4351–60.

Ahmad, A. 1992. *In Theory: Classes, Nations, Literatures*. London: Verso.

Ahuja, R. 1999. The Origins of Colonial Labour Policy in Late Eighteenth-Century Madras. *International Review of Social History* 44(2): 159–96.

Alam, M. 1986. *The Crisis of Empire in Mughal North India: Awadh and the Punjab 1707–1748*. London: OUP.

———. 1991. Eastern India in the Early Eighteenth-Century "Crisis": Some Evidence from Bihar. *IESHR* 28(1): 43–72.

Alam, M., and Subrahmanyam, S., eds. 1998a. *The Mughal State 1526–1750*. Delhi: OUP.

———. 1998b. Introduction. In Alam and Subrahmanyam 1998a, 1–71.

Alavi, Seema, ed. 2002a. *The Eighteenth Century in India*. London: OUP.

———. 2002b. Introduction. In Alavi 2002, 1–56.

Ali, Tariq. 2002. *The Clash of Fundamentalisms: Crusades, Jihads and Modernity*. New Delhi: Rupa.

Allen, G. C. 1965. The Industrialization of the Far East. In Habakkuk and Postan 1965, part 2, pp. 873–923.

Allen, R. C. 1982. The Efficiency and Distributional Consequences of Eighteenth Century Enclosures. *EJ* 92 (December): 937–43.

———. 1991. Labour Productivity and Farm Size in English Agriculture before Mechanization: Reply to Clark. *EEH* 28:478–92.

———. 1992. *Enclosure and the Yeoman: The Agricultural Development of the South Midlands 1450–1850*. London: Clarendon.

———. 1994. Agriculture during the Industrial Revolution. In Floud and McCloskey 1994a, 96–122.

Allen, T. W. 1994. *The Invention of the White Race, Vol. 1, Racial Oppression and Social Control*. London: Verso.

Ally, Russell. 2001. Gold, the Pound Sterling and the Witwatersrand, 1886–1914. In McGuire, Bertola, and Reeves 2001, 97–122.

Ames, E., and Rosenberg, N. 1968/1970. The Enfield Arsenal in Theory and History. *EJ*; reprinted in Saul 1970, 99–119.

Amin, S. 1999. History Conceived as an Eternal Cycle. *Review* 22(3): 291–326.

Amin, S., and Houtart, F., eds. 2002. *Mondialisation des resistances*. Paris: L'Harmattan.

Anderson, M. R. 1993. Work Construed: Ideological Origins of Labour Law in British India to 1918. In Robb 1993.

Anderson, P. 1974. *Lineages of the Absolutist State*. London: New Left Books.

Andreev, E., Scherbov, S., and Willekens, F. 1998. Population of Russia: What Can We Expect in the Future? *World Development* 26(11): 1939–56.

Appiah, K. A., and H. L. Gates, Jr., eds. 1999. *Africana: The Encyclopaedia of African and African American Experience*. New York: Basic Civitas Books.

Arasaratnam, Sinnappah. 1994. *Maritime India in the Seventeenth Century*. London: OUP.

Arendt, H. 1958. *The Human Condition*. Garden City, NY: Doubleday.

Aristotle. 1915/1975. *Ethica Nicomachea*, transl. W. D. Ross and rev. J. O. Urmson. In *The works of Aristotle*, vol. 9, ed. W. D. Ross. London: OUP.

Aristotle. 1988. *The Politics*, transl. B. Jowett, rev. J. A. Barnes, and ed. S. Everson. London: CUP.

Armstrong, P., Glyn, A., and Harrison, J. 1984. *Capitalism since World War II: The Making and Breakup of the Great Boom*. London: Fontana.

Armstrong, W. A. 1981. The Trend of Mortality in Carlisle between the 1780s and the 1840s: A Demographic Contribution to the Standard of Living Debate. *EHR*, 2nd ser., 34:94–114.

Arnold, D., ed. 1989. *Imperial Medicine and Indigenous Societies*. London: OUP.

———. 1993. *Colonizing the Body: State Medicine and Epidemic Disease in Nineteenth-Century India*. London: OUP.

Arnold, D., and Guha, R., eds. 1995. *Nature, Culture, Imperialism: Essays on the Environmental History of South Asia*. London: OUP.

Arrighi, G. 1983. *The Geometry of Imperialism*. London: Verso.

———. 1999. The World According to Andre Gunder Frank. *Review* 22(3): 327–54.

Arrighi, G., Hamashita, T., and Selden, M. 2003. *The Resurgence of East Asia, 500, 150 and 50 Year Perspectives*. London: Routledge.

Arrighi, G., Hui, Po-keung, Hung, Ho-Fung, and Selden, M. 2002. Historical Capitalism, East and West. In Arrighi, Hamashita, and Selden 2003, 259–333.

Atiyah, P. S. 1979. *The Rise and Fall of Freedom of Contract*. London: Clarendon Press.

Atkinson, A. B., Rainwater, L., and Smeeding, T. J. 1995. *Income Distribution in the OECD Countries*. Paris: OECD.

———. 1999. *Is Rising Income Inequality Inevitable? A Critique of the Trans-Atlantic Consensus*. Helsinki: UNU/WIDER Annual Lectures 3.

Atkinson, F. J. 1902. A Statistical Review of the Income and Wealth of British India. *Journal of the Royal Statistical Society* 65 (part 2): 209–59.

Bacon, Francis. 1627/1986. *The Great Instauration and New Atlantis*, ed. J. Weinberger, revised edition with translation of *Instauration Magna*. Arlington Heights, IL: Harlan Davidson.

Bagchi, A. K. 1972a. *Private Investment in India 1900–1939*. London: CUP.

———. 1972b. Some International Foundations of Capitalist Growth and Underdevelopment. *EPW* 7:31–33.

———. 1973a. An Estimate of the Gross Domestic Material Product of Bengal from Colebrooke's Data. *Nineteenth Century Studies* (Calcutta), no. 3:398–412.

———. 1973b. Foreign Capital and Economic Development in India. In Gough and Sharma 1973, 43–76.

———. 1976a. De-industrialization in India in the Nineteenth Century: Some Theoretical Implications. *Journal of Development Studies* 12(2): 135–64.

———. 1976b. Reflections on Patterns of Regional Growth in India during the Period of British Rule. *Bengal Past and Present* 95 (part 1): 247–89.

———. 1978. A Record of Colonial Exploitation in Indonesia. *Indian Historical Review* 4(2): 418–27.

———. 1979. The Great Depression and the Third World: With Special Reference to India. *Social Science Information* 18(2): 197–218. Reprinted in *India and the World Economy 1850–1950*, ed. G. Balachandran. London: OUP, 2003.

———. 1981. Daniel Thorner's India. *EPW* 16(13): 572–77.

———. 1982. *The Political Economy of Underdevelopment*. London: CUP.

———. 1986. Towards a Correct Reading of Lenin's Theory of Imperialism. In Patnaik 1986, 27–55.

———. 1987a. *The Evolution of the State Bank of India: The Roots, 1806–1876, Parts I and II*. London: OUP.

———. 1987b. Introduction. In *Political Economy: Studies in the Surplus Approach* 3(2) (Special issue on East Asian Development).

———. 1989a. *The Presidency Banks and the Indian Economy 1876–1914*. London: OUP.

———. 1992. Land Tax, Property Rights and Peasant Insecurity in Colonial India. *Journal of Peasant Studies* 20(1): 1–49.

———, ed. 1995. *Democracy and Development*. London: Macmillan.

———. 1996a. Markets, Market Failures, and Transformation of Authority, Property and Bondage in Colonial India. In Stein and Subrahmanyam 1996.

———. 1996b. Colonialism in Classical Political Economy: Analysis, Epistemological Broadening and Mystification. *Studies in History*, n.s., 12(1): 105–36.

———. 1997a. Contested Hegemonies and *Laissez Faire*: Controversies over the Monetary Standard in India at the High Noon of the British Empire. *Review* 20(1): 19–76.

———. 1997b. *The Evolution of the State Bank of India*. Vol. 2, *The Era of the Presidency Banks 1876–1920*. New Delhi: Sage.

———. 1998. The Growth Miracle and its Unravelling in East and Southeast Asia. *EPW* 33(18): 1025–42.

———. 1999. Dualism and Dialectics in the Historiography of Labour. *Comparative Studies of South Asia, Africa and the Middle East* 19(1): 106–21.

———. 2000. The Past and the Future of the Developmental State. *Journal of World-Systems Research* 6(2): 398–442. http://csf.colorado.edu/jwsr.

———. 2002a. Nationalism and Human Development. In Patel, Bagchi, and Raj, 327–42.

———. 2002b. The Other Side of Foreign Investment by Imperial Powers: Transfer of Surplus from Colonies. *EPW* 37(23): 2229–38.

———. 2003. The Parameters of Resistance. *MR* 55(3): 136–43.

Bagchi, Barnita. 2004. *Pliable Pupils and Sufficient Self-Directors: Narratives of Female Education by Five British Women Writers.* New Delhi: Tulika.

Bagchi, Jasodhara. 1990. Representing Nationalism: Ideology of Motherhood in Colonial Bengal. *EPW* 25(42–43), WS 65–71.

———. 1991. Shakespeare in Loin Cloths: English Literature and the Early Nationalist Consciousness in Bengal. In Joshi 1991, 146–59.

Bagchi, Tista. 1999. Generic Sentences, Social Kinds, and Stereotypes. In Bhargava, Bagchi, and Sudrashan 1999, 308–22.

Bairoch, P. 1981. The Main Trends in National Income Disparities since the Industrial Revolution. In Bairoch and Levy-Leboyer 1981.

———. 1988. *Cities and Economic Development: From the Dawn of History to the Present,* transl. C. Braider from the French. Chicago: University of Chicago Press.

———. 1993. *Economics and World History: Myths and paradoxes.* London: Harvester Wheatsheaf.

Bairoch, P., and Levy-Leboyer, M. ed. 1981. *Disparities in Industrial Development Since the Industrial Revolution,.* London: Macmillan.

Baker, C. J. 1984. *An Indian Rural Economy 1880–1955: The Tamilnad Countryside.* London: Clarendon Press.

Baker, D. 1991. State Policy, the Market Economy and Tribal Decline; the Central Provinces, 1861–1920. *IESHR* 28(4): 341–70.

Balazs, E. 1964. *Chinese Civilization and Bureaucracy,* transl. H. M. Wright and ed. A. F. Wright from the French. New Haven, CT: Yale University Press.

Banerjea, P. N. 1928. *Indian Finance in the Days of the Company.* London: Macmillan.

Banerjee, A., and Iyer, Lakshmi. 2002. *History, Institutions and Economic Performance in India: The Legacy of Colonial Land Tenure Systems in India* (mimeo.). Cambridge, MA: Department of Economics, MIT.

Banerjee, D. 1990. An Appraisal of the Profitability of the Indo-British Commodity Trade during 1871–1887. *Journal of Development Studies* 26(2): 243–59.

———. 1999. *Colonialism in Action: Trade, Development and Dependence in Late Colonial India.* Hyderabad, India: Orient Longman.

Banerji, A. K. 1982. *Aspects of Indo-British Economic Relations 1858–1898.* Bombay: OUP.

Bannerji, Himani. 2000. *The Dark Side of the Nation: Essays on Multiculturalism, Nationalism and Racism.* Toronto: Canadian Scholar's Press.

Barber, W. J. 1975. *British Economic Thought and India 1600–1858: A Study in the History of Development Economics.* London: OUP.

Baring, E. (Lord Cromer). 1908. *Modern Egypt.* 2 vols. London: Macmillan.

Barnes, J. ed. 1995. *The Cambridge Companion to Aristotle.* London: OUP.

Barrett, W. 1990. World Bullion Flows, 1450–1800. In Tracy, 224–54.

Bartlett, R. 1994. *The Making of Europe: Conquest, Colonization and Cultural Change 950–1350.* Harmondsworth: Penguin.

Batista i Roca, J. M. 1971. The Hispanic Kingdoms and the Catholic Kings. In Potter 1971, 316–42.

Bauman, Z. 1989. *Modernity and the Holocaust*. Cambridge: Polity.

Bayly, C. A. 1999. *Empire and Information: Intelligence Gathering and Social Communication in India, 1780–1870*. London: CUP.

BBC. 2001. Rabbi Calls for Annihilation of Arabs, *BBC Online*, Tuesday, 10 April.

Beardsley, E. H. 1987. *A History of Neglect: Health Care for Blacks and Mill-Workers in the Twentieth-Century South*. Knoxville: University of Tennessee Press.

Beckett, J. C. 1981. *The Making of Modern Ireland, 1603–1923*. London: Faber.

Behrendt, S. 1999. Transatlantic Slave Trade. In Appiah and Gates 1999, 1865–77.

Beller, E. A. 1970. The Thirty Years War. In Cooper 1970a, 306–58.

Berghahn, V. R. 1987. *Modern Germany: Society, Economy and Politics in the Twentieth Century*. London: CUP.

Bernal, M. 1987. *Black Athena: The Afroasiatic Roots of Classical Civilization*. Vol. 1. New Brunswick, NJ: Rutgers University Press.

Bhargava, R., Bagchi, A. K., and Sudrashan, R. eds. 1999. *Multiculturalism, Liberalism and Democracy*. London: OUP.

Bhattacharya, D. 1967. *Population of India 1751–1961* (mimeo.). Calcutta: Indian Statistical Institute.

Bhattacharya, N. 1995. Pastoralists in a Colonial World. In Arnold and Guha 1995, 49–85.

———, ed. 1998. *Forests, Fields and Pastures*. Special issue of *Studies in History*, 14(2).

Bhattacharya, Sanjoy. 2001. Re-devising Jennerian Vaccines? European Technologies, Indian Innovation and the Control of Smallpox in South Asia 1850–1950. In Pati and Harrison 2001.

BIS. 2004. *Annual Report 2004*. Basle: Bank for International Settlements.

Black, J. 1990. *The Rise of the European Powers 1679–1793*. London: Edward Arnold.

Blackbourn, R. 1984. The Discreet Charm of the Bourgeoisie: Reappraising German History in the Nineteenth Century. In Blackbourn and Eley 1984, 159–92.

Blackbourn, R., and Eley, G. 1984. *The Peculiarities of German History: Bourgeois Society and Politics in Nineteenth-Century Germany*. London: OUP.

Blackburn, R. 1988. *The Overthrow of Colonial Slavery 1776–1848*. London: Verso.

———. 1997. *The Making of New World Slavery: From the Baroque to the Modern*. London: Verso.

Blaut, J. M. 1993. *The Colonizer's Model of the World: Geographical Diffusionism and Eurocentric History*. London: Guildford Press.

Bloch, M. 1965. *Feudal Society*. 2 vols., transl. L. A. Manyon from the French. London: Routledge & Kegan Paul.

Blum, J. 1961. *Lord and Peasant in Russia from the Ninth to the Nineteenth Century*. Princeton, NJ: PUP.

Blum, W. 2002. *Rogue State: A Guide to the World's Only Superpower*. Monroe, ME: Common Courage Press.

Bodenhorn, H. 1999. A Troublesome Caste: Height and Nutrition of Antebellum Virginia's Rural Free Blacks. *JEH* 59(4): 972–96.

Bogin, B. 1999. *Patterns of Human Growth*. 2nd edition. London: CUP.

Bose, N. S. 1981. *Racism, Equality and Indian Nationalism*. Calcutta: Firma K L Mukhpadhyay.

Boxer, C. R. 1973a. *The Portuguese Seaborne Empire 1415–1825*. Harmondsworth: Penguin.

——. 1973b. *The Dutch Seaborne Empire 1600–1800*. Harmondsworth: Penguin.

Bramall, C. 1997. Living Standards in Pre-War Japan and Maoist China. *CJE* 21(5): 551–70.

Braudel, F. 1973. *Capitalism and Material Life, 1400–1800*. London: Collins.

——. 1982. *Civilization and Capitalism, 15th–18th Century*. Vol. 2, *The Wheels of Commerce*, transl. S. Reynolds from the French. London: Collins.

——. 1984. *Civilization and Capitalism, 15th –18th Century*. Vol. 3, *The Perspective of the World*, transl. S. Reynolds from the French. London: Collins.

Bray, Francesca. 1984. Agriculture, being *Part II: Agriculture* of Joseph Needham: *Science and Civilization in China*. Vol. 6, *Biology and Biological Technology*. London: CUP.

Breitman, R. 1997. A Nazi Crusade? *Simon Wiesanthal Centre Annual*. Vol. 7. http://www.mot.lc.wiesanthal.com/resources/books/annual7/chapter10.html.

Brennan, L., McDonald, J., and Shlomowitz, R. 1994. Trends in the Economic Well-Being of South Indians under British Rule: The Anthropometric Evidence. *EEH* 31:225–60.

Brenner, R., and Isett, C. 2002. England's Divergence from China's Yangzi Delta: Property Relations, Microeconomics, and Patterns of Development. *JAS* 61(2): 609–62.

Brewer, J. 1989. *The Sinews of Power: War, Money and the English State, 1688–1783*. London: Unwin Hyman.

Brewer, J., and Porter, R., eds. 1993. *Consumption and the World of Goods*. London: Routledge.

Brewer, J., and Staves, Susan, eds. 1996. *Early Modern Conceptions of Property*. London: Routledge.

Brink, Andre. 1991. *An Act of Terror: A Novel*. London: Secker & Warburg.

Britannica. 1887. Sweden, Part 2, History, by J. Sl. *Encyclopaedia Britannica*. 9th ed. Vol. 22. London: Adam and Charles Black, 744–53.

——. 1902a. Brazil: Geography and Statistics, by Rockhill, W. W., and Renwick, I. P. A., *Encyclopaedia Britannica*. 10th ed. Vol. 26. London: Adam and Charles Black, 348–52.

——. 1902b. Egypt. *Encyclopaedia Britannica*. 10th ed. Vol. 27. London: Adam and Charles Black, 686–719.

Brokaw, Cynthia J. 1996. Commercial Publishing in Late Imperial China: The Zou and Ma Family Businesses. *LIC* 17(1): 49–92.

Bromley, J. S., ed. 1970. *The New Cambridge Modern History*. Vol. 6, *The Rise of Great Britain and Russia 1688–1715/25*. London: CUP.

Brook, T. 1996. Edifying Knowledge: The Building of School Libraries in Ming China. *LIC* 17(1), June, 93–119.

Brown, D. 1970. *Bury My Heart at Wounded Knee: An Indian History of the American West*. New York: Holt, Rinehart, and Winston.

———. 1994. *The American West*. New York: Charles Scribner's.

Bryant, R. L. 1994. Shifting the Cultivator: The Politics of Teak Regeneration in Colonial Burma. *MAS* 28(2): 225–40.

Buiter, W. H. 2003. James Tobin: An Appreciation of His Contribution to Economics. *Economic Journal* 113: F565–631.

Bukharin, N. 1917/1972. *Imperialism and World Economy*, translated from the Russian. London: Merlin Press.

Burckhardt, J. 1860/1950. *The Civilization of the Renaissance in Italy: An Essay*, transl. S. D. C. Middlemore from the German. London: Phaidon Press.

Burke, E. 1760–1765/1988. Tracts on the Popery Laws. In Burke 1881/1988, 1–69.

———. 1881/1988. *Irish Affairs*, ed. Matthew Arnold; reprinted with a new introduction by Conor Cruise O'Brien. London: Cresset Library.

Burnett, J. 1966. *Plenty and Want: A Social History of Diet in England from 1815 to the Present*. London: Thomas Nelson.

Burnette, Joyce. 1997. An Investigation of the Female-Male Wage Gap during the Industrial Revolution in Britain. *EHR* 50(2): 257–81.

Burrow, J. W. 1991. Henry Maine and Mid-Victorian Ideas of Progress. In A. Diamond 1991, 55–69.

Burton, Antoinette. 1994. *Burdens of History: British Feminists, Indian Women, and Imperial Culture, 1865–1915*. Chapel Hill: University of North Carolina Press.

Cain, P. J., and Hopkins, A. G. 1986. Gentlemanly Capitalism and British Expansion Overseas, I, The Old Colonial System, 1688–1850. *EHR*, 2nd ser., 39(4): 501–25.

———. 1987. Gentlemanly Capitalism and British Expansion Overseas, II, New Imperialism, 1850–1945. *EHR*, 2nd ser., 40(1): 1–26.

Caldwell, J. C. 2002. Review of Maddison 2001. *PDR* 28(3): 559–61.

Caldwell, J. C., and Schindlmayr, T. 2002. Historical Population Estimates: Unravelling the Consensus. *PDR* 28(2): 183–204.

Calvocoressi, P., and Wint, G. 1974. *Total War: Causes and Courses of the Second World War*. Harmondsworth: Penguin.

Campbell, R. H. 1985. *Scotland since 1707: The Rise of an Industrial Society*. Edinburgh: John Donald.

Carroll, Lewis (C. L. Dodgson). 1872/1965. *Through the Looking Glass*; reprinted in *The Works of Lewis Carroll*. London: Feltham, Hamlyn.

Carli, G. 1994. Significant Episodes in the Evolution of the International Monetary System. In Kenen, Papadia, and Saccomani 1994.

Carr, Marilyn, and Chen, Martha. 2004. Globalization, Social Exclusion and Gender. *International Labour Review* 143(1–2): 129–60.

Carsten, F. L., ed. 1961a. *The New Cambridge Modern History*. Vol. 5, *The Ascendancy of France: 1648–1688*. London: CUP.

———. 1961b. The Empire after the Thirty Years War. In Carsten 1961a, 430–57.

Castiglione, B. 1528/1976. *The Book of the Courtier*, transl. G. Bull. Harmondsworth: Penguin.

CEI. 1976. *Changing Economy in Indonesia*. Vol. 2, *Public Finance 1816–1939*, initiated by W. M. F. Mansvelt and re-edited by P. Creutzberg. Amsterdam: Royal Tropical Institute.

———. 1979. *Changing Economy in Indonesia*. Vol. 5, *National Income*, initiated by W. M. F. Mansvelt and re-edited by P. Creutzberg. Amsterdam: Royal Tropical Institute.

———. 1987. *Changing Economy of Indonesia*, ed. by Boomgaard, P. Vol. 7, *Balance of Payments 1822–1939*, by W. L. Korthals-Altes. Amsterdam: Royal Tropical Institute.

Chakrabarty, D. 1974. The Colonial Context of the Bengal Renaissance: A Note on Early Railway Thinking in India. *IESHR* 11(1).

Chakravarti, R. 1998. The Creation and Expansion of Settlements and Management of Hydraulic Resources in Ancient India. In Grove, Damodaran, and Sangwan 1998, 87–105.

Chanda, Anuradha. 1998. Sylheti-Nagri: A Vehicle for Popular Culture. In Rahim and Schwarz 1998, 407–17.

Chandler, A. D., Jr. 1977. *The Visible Hand: The Managerial Revolution in American Business*. Cambridge, MA: HUP.

Chandra, S. 1982. Standard of Living: Mughal India. In Raychaudhuri and Habib 1982, 458–71.

Chang, Nancy. 2002. *Silencing Political Dissent*. New York: Seven Stories Press.

Chapman, S. D. 1972. *The Cotton Industry in the Industrial Revolution*. London: Macmillan.

Chartier, R. 1996. Gutenberg Revisited from the East. *LIC* 17(1): 1–9.

Chattopadhyay, R. 1975. De-Industrialization in India Reconsidered. *EPW* 10(12): 523–31.

Chaudhuri, K. N. 1978. *The Trading World of Asia and the East India Company 1660–1760*. London: CUP.

Chaudhuri, Supriya. 1996. Eating People is Wrong: Cannibalism and Renaissance Culture. In Supriya and Sukanta Chaudhuri 1996, 63–86.

Chaudhuri, Supriya, and Chaudhuri, Sukanta, ed. 1996. *Writing Over: Medieval to Renaissance*. Delhi: Allied Publishers.

Chaudhury, Sushil. 1995a. *From Prosperity to Decline: Eighteenth Century Bengal*. New Delhi: Manohar.

———. 1995b. International Trade in Bengal Silk and the Comparative Role of Asians and Europeans, circa 1700–1757. *MAS* 29(2): 373–86.

Chesnaux, J. 1973. *Peasant Revolts in China 1840–1949*. London: Thames and Hudson.

Chesnaux, J., Bastid, M., and Bergère, M.-C. 1976. *China from the Opium Wars to the 1911 Revolution*, transl. Anne Destenay from the French. New York: Pantheon Books.

Chesnaux, J., Barbier, F., and Bergère, M.-C. 1977. *From the 1911 Revolution to Liberation*, transl. P. Auster and L. Davis from the French. New York: Pantheon Books.

Chi'h Ch'ao-ting. 1936. *Key Economic Areas in Chinese History, as Revealed by in the Development of Public Works for Water-Control*. London: George Allen & Unwin.

Chia, Lucille. 1996. The Development of the Jianyang Book Trade, Song–Yuan. *LIC* 17(1): 10–48.

Chomsky, N. 1968. *Language and Mind*. New York: Harcourt, Brace and World.
———. 1998. *Class Warfare*. London: OUP.
Cipolla, C. ed. 1974. *The Fontana Economic History of Europe: Sixteenth and Seventeenth Centuries*. London: Collins/Fontana.
Clark, Alice W. 1989. Mortality, Fertility, and the Status of Women in India, 1881–1931. In Dyson 1989, 119–49.
Clark, Anna. 1995. *The Struggle for the Breeches: Gender and the Making of the British Working Class*. Berkeley: University of California Press.
Clark, G. N. 1947. *The Seventeenth Century*, 2nd edition. London: Clarendon.
———. 1961. The Social Foundations of States. In Carsten 1961a, 176–97.
Clifton, J. A. 1977. Competition and the Evolution of the Capitalist Mode of Production. *CJE* 1(2): 137–52.
Clingingsmith, David, and Williamson, Jeffrey G. 2004. *India's De-Industrialization under British Rule: New Ideas, New Evidence*. NBER Working Paper 10586. Cambridge, MA: National Bureau of Economic Research.
Cohen, P. A. 1997. *History in Three Keys: The Boxers as Event, Experience and Myth*. New York: Columbia University Press.
Cohn, B. S. 1983. Representing Authority in Victorian Britain. In Hobsbawm and Ranger 1983, 165–210.
Cole, G. D. H., and Postgate, Raymond. 1961. *The British Common People 1746–1946*. London: Methuen.
Colebrooke, H. T., and Lambert, A. 1795. *Remarks on the Present State of Husbandry and Commerce in Bengal*, Calcutta.
Coleman, D. C. 1961. Economic Problems and Policies. In Carsten 1961a, 19–46.
———, ed. 1969. *Revisions in Mercantilism*. London: Methuen.
Coleman, D. C., and Schofield, R. S., eds. 1986. *The State of Population Theory*. Oxford: Blackwell.
Concerned Citizens Tribunal. 2002. *Crime against Humanity: An Inquiry into the Gujarat Carnage*, Vols. 1 and 2. Mumbai: Citizens for Justice and Peace.
Conrad, L. I., Neave, M., Nutton, V., Porter, R., and Wear, A. 1995. *The Western Medical Tradition 800 BC to 1800 AD*. London: CUP.
Cook, N. D. 1998. *Born to Die: Disease and New World Conquest, 1492–1650*. London: CUP.
Cook, S. F., and W. Borah. 1971. *Essays in Population History*. Vol. 1. Berkeley: University of California Press.
Cooper, J. P., ed. 1970a. *The New Cambridge Modern History*. Vol. 4, *The Decline of Spain and the Thirty Years War 1609–48/59*. London: CUP.
Cooper, J. P. 1970b. General Introduction. In Cooper 1970a, 1–66.
Coox, Alvin D. 1988. The Pacific War. In Duus 1988, 315–82.
Corsini, C. A., and Viazzo, P. P. 1997. *The Decline of Infant and Child Mortality: The European Experience 1750–1990*. The Hague: Kluwer Law International for UNICEF.
Cornell, Laurel L. 1996. Infanticide in Early Modern Japan? Demography, Culture and Population Growth. *JAS* 55(1): 22–50.

Costa, Dora L., and Steckel, R. H. 1997. Long-Term Trends in Health, Welfare, and Economic Growth in the United States. In Steckel and Floud 1997, 47–90.

Crafts, N. F. R., and Toniolo, G., eds. 1996. *Economic Growth in Europe since 1945*. London: CUP.

Craig, G. A. 1981. *Germany 1866–1945*. London: OUP.

Craig, W. 1979. *The Fall of Japan*. Harmondsworth: Penguin.

Craton, M. 1982. *Testing the Chains: Resistance to Slavery in the British West Indies*. Ithaca, NY: Cornell University Press.

———. 1987. What and Who to Whom and What: The Significance of Slave Resistance. In Solow and Engerman 1987, 259–82.

———. 1996. Property and Propriety: Land Tenure and Slave Property in the Creation of a British West Indian Plantocracy, 1612–1740. In Brewer and Staves 1996, 497–529.

Crawcour, E. Sidney. 1997. Economic Change in the Nineteenth Century. In Yamamura 1997, 1–49.

Cressy, D. 1980. *Literacy and Social Order: Reading and Writing in Tudor and Stuart England*. London: CUP.

Crosby, A. W. 1986. *Ecological Imperialism: The Biological Expansion of Europe, 900–1900*. London: CUP.

CSO. 1993. *Selected Socio-Economic Statistics for India 1992*. New Delhi: Central Statistical Organisation, Department of Statistics, Government of India.

Cumings, B. 1990. *The Origins of the Korean War: II, The Roaring of the Cataract, 1947–1950*. London: PUP.

———. 2004. Consequences of the "Forgotten War," Korea: Forgotten Nuclear Threats. *Le Monde Diplomatique*, December.

Cunnigham, A., and Grell, O. P. 2000. *The Four Horsemen of the Apocalypse: Religion, War, Famine and Death in Reformation Europe*. London: CUP.

Curtin, P. D. 1969. *The Atlantic Slave Trade: A Census*. Madison: University of Wisconsin Press.

———, ed. 1971. *Imperialism: Selected Documents*. London: Macmillan.

Danner, M. 2004. Abu Ghraib: The Hidden Story. *NYRB* 51(50): 44–50.

D'Agata, A. 1998. Competition. In Kurz and Salvadori 1998, 174–79.

Dasgupta, P. 1993. *An Inquiry into Well-being and Destitution*. London: OUP.

Davidson, B. 1961. *Black Mother: The Years of the African Slave Trade*. Boston: Little, Brown.

Davis, K. 1951. *The Population of India and Pakistan*. Princeton, NJ: PUP.

Davis, L. E. , and Huttenback, R. A. 1986. *Mammon and the Pursuit of Empire: The Political Economy of British Imperialism, 1860–1912*. London: CUP.

Davis, M. 2001. *Late Victorian Holocausts; El Niño Famines and the Making of the Third World*. London: Verso.

Davis, Natalie Zemon. 1975. Printing and the People. In *Society and Culture in Early Modern France*, ed. N Z. Davis. 1975. Stanford, CA: Stanford University Press.

Davis, R. 1973. *The Rise of the Atlantic Economies*. London: Weidenfeld & Nicolson.

Deaton, A. 2004. *Health in an Age of Globalization*. NBER Working Paper W10669, August.

Defoe, D. 1724–1726/1971. *A Tour through the Whole Island of Great Britain*, 3 vols., London; abridged and ed. Pat Rogers. Harmondsworth: Penguin.

Denevan, W. M., ed. 1976a. *The Native Populations of the Americas in 1492*. Madison: University of Wisconsin Press.

———. 1976b. Epilogue. In Denevan 1976a.

Deprez, P. 1979. The Low Countries. In W. R. Lee 1979, 236–83.

Desjarlais, R., Eisenberg, L., Good, B., and Kleinman, A. 1995. *World Mental Health: Problems and Priorities in Low-Income Countries*. London: OUP.

Devereux, S. 2000. *Famine in the Twentieth Century*. IDS Working Paper 105, Brighton, Institute of Development Studies.

De Vries, J. 1976. *The Economy of Europe in an Age of Crisis, 1600–1750*. London: CUP.

———. 1993. Between Purchasing Power and the World of Goods. In Brewer and Porter 1993, 85–132.

De Vries, J., and Van der Woude, A. 1997. *The First Modern Economy: Success, Failure, and Perseverance of the Dutch Economy, 1500–1815*. London: CUP.

Deyell, J. 1983/1994. The China Connection: Problems of Silver Supply in Medieval Bengal. In *Precious Metals in the Later Medieval and Early Modern Worlds*, ed. J. F. Richards; reprinted in Subrahmanyam 1994, 112–36.

Diamond, A., ed. 1991. *The Victorian Achievement of Sir Henry Maine*. London: CUP.

Diamond, J. 1992. *The Rise and Fall of the Third Chimpanzee*. New York: Vintage.

———. 1998. *Guns, Germs and Steel: A Short History of Everybody for the Last 13,000 Years*. New York: Vintage.

Dickason, Olive Patricia. 1992. *Canada's First Nations: A History of First Nations from Earliest Times*. Toronto: McClelland and Stewart.

Dickens, T. H. 1857. *A Letter to the Rt. Hon. Vernon Smith, M.P., Upon the Professed Judicial Reform in India*. London (India Office Library Tract).

Dickson, P. G. M., and Sperling, J. 1970. War Finance, 1689–1714. In Bromley 1970, 284–315.

Digby, S. 1971/2001. The Problem of the Military Ascendancy of the Delhi Sultanate. In Gommans and Kolff, 311–20.

Dimitrov, G. 1935. *The Fascist Offensive and the Tasks of the Communist International in the Struggle of the Working Class against Fascism: Main Report Delivered at the Seventh World Congress of the Communist International*, delivered on 2 August 1935 (reproduced in Marxists CD Archive).

Dobb, M. H. 1946. *Studies on the Development of Capitalism*. London: Routledge & Kegan Paul.

Dore, R. P. 1959. *Land Reform in Japan*. London: OUP.

———. 1965/1984. *Education in Tokugawa Japan*. 2nd edition. London: Athlone Press.

Doyle, W. 1992. *The Old European Order 1660–1800*, 2nd edition. London: OUP.

Drabble, J. H. 2000. *An Economic History of Malaysia*. Basingstoke, UK: Macmillan.

Drèze, J., and Sen, A., eds. 1990a. *The Political Economy of Hunger*, vol. 1, *Entitlement and Well-Being*. London: Clarendon Press.

———. 1990b. *The Political Economy of Hunger*, vol. 2, *Famine Prevention*. London: Clarendon Press.

———. 1991. *The Political Economy of Hunger*, vol. 3, *Endemic Hunger*. London: Clarendon Press.

Du Boff, R. B., and Herman, E. S. 2001. Mergers, Concentration, and the Erosion of Democracy. *MR* 53(1): 14–29.

Du Bois, W. E. B. 1935/1992. *Black Reconstruction in America 1860–1880*, Harcourt Brace, ca. 1935; reprinted with an introduction by D. L. Lewis. New York: The Free Press.

Dumont, L. 1970. *Homo Hierarchicus: The Caste System and Its Implications*. Chicago: University of Chicago Press.

Dunn, C. J. 1969. *Everyday Life in Imperial Japan*. New York: Dorset Press.

Dunn, J. 1969. *The Political Thought of John Locke: A Historical Account of the Argument of the "Two Treatises of Government."* London: CUP.

Dunn, R. S. 1987. "Dreadful Idlers" in the Cane-Fields: The Slave Labour Pattern on a Jamaican Sugar Estate, 1762–1831. In Solow and Engerman 1987, 163–90.

Dunning, J. H. 1964/1972. Capital Movements in the Twentieth Century. *Lloyds Bank Review*; reprinted in Dunning, J.H. ed. *International Investment*. Harmondsworth: Penguin, 59–91.

Dupaquier, J. 1979. *La Population Francaise aux XVIe et XVIIIe Siècles*. Paris: Presse Universitaire des France.

Durand, J. D. 1967. The modern Expansion of World Population. *Proceedings of the American Philosophical Society* 111(3): 136–59.

———. 1977. Historical Estimates of World Population. *PDR* 3(3): 253–96.

Dutt, R. C. 1906/1960. *The Economic History of India*. Vol. 2, *In the Victorian Age 1837–1900*. Delhi: Publications Division, Ministry of Information and Broadcasting, Government of India.

Duus, Peter, ed. 1988a. *The Cambridge History of Japan*. Vol. 6. London: CUP.

———. 1988b. Introduction. In Duus 1988a, 1–52.

Dwyer, L., and Santikarma, D. 2004. "When the World Turned to Chaos": 1965 and Its Aftermath in Bali, Indonesia. In Gellately and Kiernan 2004, 289–306.

Dyson, T., ed. 1989. *India's Historical Demography: Studies in Famine, Disease and Society*. London: Curzon Press.

———. 1989a. Indian Historical Demography: Developments and Prospects. In Dyson 1989, 1–15.

Eaton, R. M. 1994. *The Rise of Islam and the Bengal Frontier 1204–1760*. London: OUP.

Economist. 2003a. Wielders of Mass Deception? (leader). *Economist*, 4 October, 13–14.

———. 2003b. Spies and Lies (letters). *Economist*, 18 October, p. 16.

———. 2004a. A Survey of the World Economy. *Economist*, 2 October, 3–24.

———. 2004b. Japan: Spend and Defend. *Economist*, 4 December, 28–29.

Edelstein, M. 1982. *Overseas Investment in the Age of High Imperialism: The United Kingdom, 1850–1914*. London: Methuen.

———. 1994. Foreign Investment and Accumulation, 1860–1914. In Floud and McCloskey 1994b, 173–96.

Edmonds, Robert Louis, ed. 1998. *Managing the Chinese Environment*. London: OUP.

Elias, N. 1939/1978. *The Civilizing Process*. Vol. 1, *The Development of Manners: Changes in the Code of Conduct and Feeling in Early Modern Times*, transl. E. Jephcott from the German. New York: Urizen Books.

———. 1939/1982. *The Civilizing Process*. Vol. 2, *State Formation and Civilization*, transl. E. Jephcott from the German. Oxford: Blackwell.

———. 1989/1996. *The Germans: Power Struggles and the Development of Habitus in the Nineteenth and Twentieth Centuries*, translated from the German by E. Dunning and S. Mennell. Cambridge: Polity.

Elliott, J. H. 1963a. *Imperial Spain 1469–1716*. London: Edward Arnold.

———. 1963b. *The Revolt of the Catalans: A Study in the Decline of Spain (1598–1640)*. London: CUP.

———. 1970. The Spanish Peninsula 1598–1648. In Cooper 1970a, 435–73.

Ellsberg, D. 2003. *Secrets: A Memoir of Vietnam and the Pentagon Papers*. London: Viking.

Elman, B. A., and Woodside, A., eds. 1994. *Education and Society in Late Imperial China, 1600–1900*. Berkeley: University of California Press.

Eltis, D. 1987. *Economic Growth and the Ending of the Transatlantic Slave Trade*. London: OUP.

Eltis, D., and Engerman, S. L. 1992. Was the Slave Trade Dominated by Men? *Journal of Interdisciplinary History* 23(2): 237–57.

Elvin, M. 1973. *The Pattern of the Chinese Past*. London: Eyre Methuen.

———. 2004. *The Retreat of the Elephants: An Environmental History of China*. Yale University Press.

Elvin, M., and Su Ninghu. 1998. Action at a Distance: The Influence of the Yellow River on Hangzhou Bay since A.D. 1000. In Elvin and Liu 1998, 344–407.

Elvin, M., and Liu Ts'ui-Jung, eds. 1998. *Sediments of Time: Environment and Society in Chinese History*. London: CUP.

Elyot, Sir Thomas. 1531/1966. *The Book Named the Governor*, reprinted with an introduction by S. E. Lehmberg. London: J. M. Dent.

Engels, F. 1845/1962. *The Condition of the Working Class in England*, translated from the German and reprinted in Marx and Engels 1962, 1–338.

Erdosy, G. 1998. Deforestation in Pre- and Protohistoric South Asia. In Grove, Damodaran, and Sangwan 1998, 51–69.

Eveleth, P. B., and Tanner, J. M. 1990. *Worldwide Variation in Human Growth*. 2nd edition. London: CUP.

Fairbank, J. K., Reischauer, E. O., and Craig, A. M. 1969. *East Asia: The Modern Transformation*. London: Allen & Unwin.

Famine. 2003. *Famine in Ethiopia and Kenya*. www.fhi.net/fhius/ethiopiafamine/famine.html.

Fanon, F. 1961/1967. *The Wretched of the Earth*, transl. C. Farrington from the French. Harmondsworth: Penguin.

Feaver, G. 1991. The Victorian Values of Sir Henry Maine. In Diamond 1991, 28–52.

Feinstein, C. H. 1998. Pessimism Perpetuated: Real Wages and the Standard of Living in Britain during the Industrial Revolution. *JEH* 58(3): 625–57.

Felix, D. 1956. Profit Inflation and Industrial Growth: The Historic Record and Contemporary Analogies. *Quarterly Journal of Economics* 71:441–63.

Field, A. J. 1981. The Problem with Neoclassical Institutional Economics: A Critique with Special Reference to the North/Thomas model of Pre-1500 Europe. *EEH* 18:174–98.

Fieldhouse, D. K., ed. 1967. *The Theory of Capitalist Imperialism*. London: Longmans, Green.

Finley, M. I. 1973/1985. *The Ancient Economy*. 2nd edition. London: Hogarth Press.

———. 1980. *Ancient Slavery and Modern Ideology*. London: Chatto & Windus.

Fisher, J. 2003. Eritrea's Growing Dependence on Aid. *BBC News*, 18 November.

Flagan, D. P., Ganshaft, J. L., and Harrison, P. L., ed. 1997.*Contemporary Intellectual Assessment: Theories, Tests and Issues*. New York: Guilford.

Fletcher, W., Jr. 2003. Can US Workers Embrace Anti-Imperialism? *MR* 55(3): 99–115.

Floud, R., and Harris, B. 1997. Health, Height, and Welfare: Britain 1700–1980. In Steckel and Floud 1997, 91–126.

Floud, R., and McCloskey, D., eds. 1994a. *The Economic History of Britain Since 1700*. Vol. 1, *1700–1860*. London: CUP.

———, eds. 1994b. *The Economic History of Britain Since 1700*. Vol. 2, *1860–1939*. London: CUP.

Fogel, R. W. 1991. The Conquest of High Mortality and Hunger in Europe and America: Timing and Mechanisms. In Higonnet, Landes, and Rosovsky 1991, 33–71.

———. 1992. Second Thoughts on the European Escape from Hunger: Famines, Chronic Malnutrition, and Mortality Rates. In Osmani 1992a, 243–86.

———. 1994. Economic Growth, Population Theory, and Physiology: The Bearing of Long-Term Processes on the Making of Economic Policy. *American Economic Review* 84(3): 369–95.

Folbre, N. 1994. *Who Pays for the Kids? Gender and the Structures of Constraint*. London: Routledge

Foreman-Peck, J. 1983. *A History of the World Economy: International Economic Relations since 1850*. London: Harvester Wheatsheaf.

Foster, J. B. 1994. *The Vulnerable Planet: A Short Economic History of the Environment*. New York: Monthly Review Press.

Foster, R. F. 1988. *Modern Ireland 1600–1972*. Harmondsworth: Penguin.

Foucault, M. 1977. *Discipline and Punish*, transl. A. Sheridan from the French. London: Allen Lane.

Francis, M. 1998. The "Civilizing" of Indigenous People in Nineteenth-Century Canada. *Journal of World History* 9(1): 51–88.

Frank, Andre Gunder. 1998. *ReOrient: Global Economy in the Asian Age*. Berkeley: University of California Press.

Freund, B. 1984. *The Making of Contemporary Africa: The Development of African Society since 1800*. Bloomington: Indiana University Press.

Fukazawa, H. 1982a. Agrarian Relations and Land Revenue: The Medieval Deccan and Maharashtra. In Raychaudhuri and Habib 1982, 249–60.

———. 1982b. Non-Agricultural Production: Maharashtra and the Deccan. In Raychaudhuri and Habib 1982, 308–15.

——. 1982c. Standard of Living: Maharashtra and the Deccan. In Raychaudhuri and Habib 1982, 471–77.

Fukazawa, H. 1991. *Medieval Deccan: Peasants, Social Systems and States, Sixteenth to Eighteenth Centuries.* Delhi: OUP.

Furet, F., and Ozouf, J. 1982. *Reading and Writing: Literacy in France from Calvin to Jules Ferry*, translated from the French. London: CUP.

Furnivall, J. S. 1939. *Netherlands India.* London: CUP.

Furtado, C. 1963. *The Economic Growth of Brazil: A Survey from Colonial to Modern Times.* Berkeley: University of California Press.

Gadgil, M., and Guha, R. 1992. *This Fissured Land: An Ecological History of India.* Delhi: OUP.

Gawthrop, R., and Straus, G. 1984. Protestantism and Literacy in Early Modern Germany. *P&P*, no. 104:31–55.

Gay, P. 1969. *The Enlightenment.* Vol. 2, *The Science of Freedom.* New York: Knopf.

Gellately, R., and Kiernan, B., eds. 2003. *The Spectre of Genocide: Mass Murder in Historical Perspective.* London: CUP.

Gerbi, Antonio. 1955/1973. *The Dispute of the New World: The History of a Polemic, 1750–1900*, translated from the Italian by J. Moyle. Pittsburgh: Pittsburgh University Press.

Ghosh, Jayati. 2003. Changes in the World of Work. *Indian Journal of Labour Economics* 46(4): 503–14.

Gilboy, E. 1936. The Cost of Living and Real Wages in Eighteenth-Century England. *Review of Economics and Statistics* 18:134–43.

Ginsborg, P. 2003. The Patrimonial Ambitions of Silvio B. *New Left Review*, n.s., no. 21 (May–June): 21–64.

Ginsburg, C. 1980. *The Cheese and the Worms: The Cosmos of a Sixteenth-Century Miller.* transl. John and Anne Tedeschi from the Italian. London: Routledge & Kegan Paul.

Glamann, K. 1974. European Trade 1500–1750. In Cipolla 1974, 427–526.

GoGwilt, C. 1993. *The Invention of the West: Joseph Conrad and the Double-Mapping of Europe and Empire.* Stanford, CA: Stanford University Press.

Goldfield, M. 2004. *The Decline of Organised Labour in the United States and the Impact of Globalisation* (paper presented at the Conference on Globalisation and Labour: State, Market and Organisation, Institute of Development Studies Kolkata, 2–4 December).

Goldstone, J. A. 1986. The Demographic Revolution in England: A Re-examination. *PS* 40:5–33.

——. 1998. The Problem of the "Early Modern" World. *Journal of the Economic and Social History of the Orient* 41(3): 249–84.

Gommans, Jos J. L. 1999. *The Rise of the Indo-Afghan Empire, c. 1710–1780.* Delhi: OUP.

——. 1995/2001. Indian Warfare and Afghan Innovation During the Eighteenth Century. *Studies in History* 11(2); reprinted in Gommans and Kolff 2001, 365–86.

Gommans, Jos J. L., and Kolff, D. H. A., eds. 2001. *Warfare and Weaponry in South Asia 1000–1800.* Delhi: OUP.

——. 2001b. Introduction. In Gommans and Kolff 2001, 1–42.

Goody, J., ed. 1968. *Literacy in Traditional Societies*. Cambridge: CUP.

Gopalan, C. 1992. Undernutrition: Measurement and Implications. In Osmani 1992a, 17–48.

——. 1995. Towards Food and Nutrition Security. *EPW* 30(52): A134–A141.

Gordon, Alec. 2004. Colonial Surplus and Foreign-Owned Investment in South-East Asia. *EPW* 39(4): 371–78.

Goubert, P. 1970. *Louis XIV and Twenty Million Frenchmen*, translated from the French. London: Allen Lane.

——. 1991. *The Course of French History*, translated from the French. London: Routledge.

Goudsblom, Johan, Jones, Erin, and Mennell, Stephen. 1996. *The Course of Human History: Economic Growth, Social Process and Civilization*. Armonk, NY: M. E. Sharpe.

Gough, K., and Sharma, H. P. ed. 1973. *Imperialism and Revolution in South Asia*. New York: Monthly Review Press.

Gould, S. J. 1981. *The Mismeasure of Man*. London and New York: Norton.

Gow, Ian. 1993. Civilian Control of the Military in Postwar Japan. In Matthews and Matsuyama 1993, 50–68.

Gowan, P. 2003. US Hegemony Today. *MR* 55(3): 30–50.

Graff, H. J. 1979/1987. Literacy, Education, and Fertility, Past and Present: A Critical Review. PDR. Vol. 5; reprinted in Graff 1987, 100–32.

——. 1981/1987. Reflections on the History of Literacy: Overview, Critique and Proposals. *Humanities in Society*. Vol. 4; reprinted in Graff 1987, 15–43.

——. 1986/1987. The History of Literacy: Toward the Third Generation. *Interchange*. Vol. 17; reprinted in Graff 1987, 241–55.

——. 1987. *The Labyrinths of Literacy: Reflections on Literacy, Past and Present*, London, Falmer Press.

Graham, R. 1968. *Britain and the Onset of Modernization in Brazil, 1850–1914*. London: CUP.

Grantham, J. 1989. Jean Meuvret and the Problem of Subsistence in Early Modern France [Review of J. Meuvret: *La problème des subsistences à l'epoque Louis XIV*, Paris, Mouton, 1977]. *JEH* 49(1): 184–200.

Gray, Jack. 1988. *Rebellions and Revolutions: China from the 1800s to 1980s*. London: OUP.

Green, M. D. 1996. The Expansion of European Colonization to the Mississippi Valley, 1780–1880. In Trigger and Washburn 1996, 461–538.

Green, W. A. 1984. The West Indies and Indentured Labour Migration—The Jamaican Experience. In Saunders 1984, 1–41.

Greenberg, M. 1969. *British Trade and the Opening of China 1800–42*. London: CUP.

Greenfeld, L. 1992. *Nationalism: Five Roads to Modernity*. Cambridge, MA: HUP.

Greenough, P. R. 1982. *Prosperity and Misery in Modern Bengal: The Famine of 1943–44*. London: OUP.

Grove, R. H. 1995. *Green Imperialism: Colonial Expansion, Tropical Island Edens and the Origins of Environmentalism, 1600–1860*. London. OUP.

Grove, R. H., Damodaran, Vinita, and Sangwan, S., eds. 1998. *Nature and the Orient: Essays on the Environmental History of South and Southeast Asia*. London: OUP.

Grover, B. R. 1966/1994. An Integrated Pattern of Commercial Life in the Rural Society of North India during the Seventeenth and Eighteenth Centuries. *Indian Historical Records Commission*; reprinted in Subrahmanyam 1994a, 219–55.

Guha, S., 1993. Nutrition, Sanitation, Hygiene, and the Likelihood of Death: The British Army in India, ca. 1870–1920. *PS* 47:385–401.

———. 1994. The Importance of Social Intervention in England's Mortality Decline: The Evidence Reviewed. *Social History of Medicine* 7(1): 89–113.

———. 2001. *Health and Population in South Asia: From Earliest Times to the Present*. New Delhi: Permanent Black.

Gump, J. 1998. The Imperialism of Cultural Assimilation: Sir George Grey's Encounter with the Maori and the Xhosa, 1845–1868. *Journal of World History* 9(1), Spring: 89–106.

Gunn, G. 2003. *The First Globalization: The Eurasian Exchange, 1500–1800*. Lanham, MD: Rowman & Littlefield.

Gupta, Bishnupriya. 1997. Collusion in the Indian Tea Industry in the Great Depression: An Analysis of Panel Data. *EEH* 134(2), April, 155–73.

———. 2001. The International Tea Cartel during the Great Depression, 1929–1933. *JEH* 61(1): 144–59.

Guz, Deborah. 1989. Population Dynamics of Famine in Nineteenth Century Punjab, 1896–97 and 1899–1900. In Dyson 1989, 261–84.

Habakkuk, H. J. 1940. English Land Ownership, 1680–1700. *EHR* 10:2–17.

Habakkuk, H. J., and Postan, M. M., eds. 1965. *The Cambridge Economic History of Europe*, vol. 6, parts 1 and 2. London: CUP.

Habib, I. 1963/1999. *The Agrarian System of Mughal India 1556–1707*. 2nd edition. Bombay: Asia Publishing OUP.

———. 1975/1995. Colonialization of the Indian Economy 1757–1900. *Social Scientist*, March; reprinted in Habib 1995, 296–335.

———. 1982a. Population. In Raychaudhuri and Habib 1982, 163–71.

———. 1982b. The Systems of Agricultural Production: Mughal India. In Raychaudhuri and Habib 1982, 214–25.

———. 1982c. Agrarian Relations and Land Revenue: North India. In Raychaudhuri and Habib 1982, 235–49.

———. 1985. Studying a Colonial Economy without Perceiving Colonialism. *MAS* 19(3): 355–81.

———. 1987. A System of Trimetallism in the Age of the "Price Revolution": Effects of the Silver Influx on the Mughal Monetary System (with an appendix by John S. Deyell). In Richards 1987, 137–70.

———. 1995. *Essays in Indian History*. New Delhi: Tulika.

———. 2002. The Eighteenth Century in Indian Economic History. In Marshall 2002, 100–19.

Haider, N. 1996. Precious Metal Flows and Currency Circulation in the Mughal Empire. *Journal of the Economic and Social History of the Orient*. Vol. 39, 298–364.

Hale, J. R. 1971. International Relations in the West: Diplomacy and War. In Potter 1971, 259–91.

———. 1985. *War and Society in Renaissance Europe, 1450–1620*. London: Fontana.

Hall, A. R., ed. 1968. *The Export of Capital from Britain 1870–1914*. London: Methuen.

Hambly, G. R. G. 1982. Towns and Cities. In Raychaudhuri and Habib 1982, 432–51.

Hamilton, E. J. 1929. American Treasure and the Rise of Capitalism. *Economica*.

Hanley, Susan B. 1983. A High Standard of Living in Nineteenth-Century Japan; Fact or Fantasy? *JEH* 43(1).

———. 1997. *Everyday Things in Premodern Japan: The Hidden Legacy of Material Culture*. Berkeley: University of California Press.

Hanley, Susan B., and Wolff, A. P., eds. 1985. *Family and Population in East Asian History*. Stanford, CA: Stanford University Press.

Hanley, Susan B., and Yamamura, K. 1977. *Economic and Demographic Change in Pre-industrial Japan*. Princeton, NJ: PUP.

Hardiman, D. 1998. Well Irrigation in Gujarat: Systems of Use, Hierarchies of Control. *EPW* 33 (20 June): 1533–44.

Harnetty, P. 1977. Crop Trends in the Central Provinces of India, 1861–1921. *MAS* 11(3): 341–78.

Harries, Meirion, and Harries, Susie. 1991. *Soldiers of the Sun: The Rise and Fall of the Imperial Japanese Army*. New York: Random House.

Hastings, Adrian. 1997. *The Construction of Nationhood: Ethnicity, Religion and Nationalism*. London: CUP.

Hatton, R. M. 1957. Scandinavia and the Baltic. In Lindsay 1957, 339–64.

———. 1970. Charles XII and the Great Northern War. In Bromley 1970, 648–80.

Hatton, T. J., and Williamson, J. G. 1994. What Drove the Mass Immigration of the Nineteenth Century? *PDR* 20(3): 533–59.

Hauser, William B. 1974. *Economic Institutional Change in Tokugawa Japan: Ōsaka and the Kinai Cotton Trade*. London: CUP.

Hawkes, N. 2000. Where People Die of a Broken Heart: Eastern Europe Has a Surprising Decline in Life Expectancy. *The Statesman* (Calcutta), 2 July.

Hayami, Akira. 1985. Rural Migration and Fertility in Tokugawa Japan: The Village of Nishijo, 1773–1868. In Hanley and Wolff 1985, 110–32.

———. 2001. *The Historical Demography of Pre-Modern Japan*. Tokyo: University of Tokyo Press.

Hayami, Akira, and Kurosu, Satomi. 2001. Regional Diversity in Demographic and Preindustrial Japan. *Journal of Japanese Studies* 27(2): 295–321.

Hays, Mary. 1798/1994. *Appeal to the Men of Great Britain in Behalf of Women*. London: Joseph Johnson; reprinted in Roberts and Mizuta 1994.

HDR. 1999. *Human Development Report 1999*. New York: OUP for the United Nations Development Program.

Heijdra, Martin J. 1994. The Socio-economic Development of Ming Rural China (1368–1644). PhD thesis, Princeton University.

Helms, J. E. 1997. The Triple Quandary of Race, Culture, and Social Class in Standardized Cognitive Ability Testing. In Flagan, Ganshaft, and Harrison 1997, 517–32.

Henry, L. 1987/1989. Men's and Women's Mortality in the Past. Transl. Nita Lery from the article in *Annales de Demographie Historique*. In *Population* vol. 44, English selection no. 1:177–202.

Herman, E., and Chomsky, N. 1988. *Manufacturing Consent: The Political Economy of Mass Media*. New York: Pantheon.

Herman, E., and McChesney, R. W. 1997. *The Global Media: The New Missionaries of Corporate Capitalism*. New York: Cassell.

Herrnstein, R. J., and Murray, C. 1994. *The Bell Curve: Intelligence and Class Structure in American Life*. New York: The Free Press.

Hershlag, Z. Y. 1964. *An Introduction to the Modern Economic History of the Middle East*. Leiden: E. J. Brill.

Heston, A. 1983. National Income. In Kumar and Desai 1983, 376–462.

Hightower, J. 2000. *If the Gods Had Meant Us to Vote, They Would Have Given Us Candidates*. New York: HarperCollins.

Higonnet, P., Landes, D., and Rosovsky, H., ed. 1991. *Favourites of Fortune: Technology, Growth, and Economic Development in the Industrial Revolution*. Cambridge, MA: HUP.

Hilferding, Rudolf. 1910/1981. *Finance Capital: A Study of the Latest Phase of Capitalist Development*. Transl. Morris Watnick and Sam Gordon from the German and ed. Tom Bottomore. London: Routledge & Kegan Paul.

Hill, C. 1955. *The English Revolution: An Essay*. 3rd edition. London: Lawrence & Wishart.

———. 1975. *The World Turned Upside Down: Radical Ideas during the English Revolution*. Harmondsworth: Penguin.

Hill, H. 1996. *The Indonesian Economy since 1966: Southeast Asia's Emerging Giant*. London: CUP.

Hill, K. 1998. Life Expectancy. *Encyclopaedia Americana*. Vol. 17. Danbury, CN: Grolier, 426–27.

Himmelfarb, G. 1984. *The Idea of Poverty: England in the Early Industrial Age*. London: Faber & Faber.

Hippocrates. 1924. Influences of Atmosphere, Water and Situation. In *Greek Historical Thought: From Homer to the Age of Heraclitus*, transl. and ed. A. Toynbee. London: Beacon Press, chapter 16.

Hirschman, A. 1977. *The Passions and the Interests: Political Arguments for Capitalism before Its Triumph*. Princeton, NJ: PUP.

———. 1982. Rival Interpretations of Market Society: Civilizing, Destructive or Feeble? *Journal of Economic Literature* 20(4): 1463–84.

Hirschman, C., Preston, S., and Loi, Vu Manh. 1995. Vietnamese Casualties in the American War: A New Estimate. *PDR* 21(4): 783–812.

Ho, Ping-Ti. 1959. *Studies on the Population of China, 1368–1953*. Cambridge, MA: HUP.

———. 1962. *The Ladder of Success in Imperial China: Aspects of Social Mobility, 1368–1911*. New York: Columbia University Press.

———. 1975. *The Cradle of the East: An Enquiry into the Indigenous Origins of Techniques and Ideas of Neolithic and Early Historic China, 5000–1000 B.C.* Chicago: University of Chicago Press.

Hobsbawm, E. J. 1954. The Crisis of the Seventeenth Century. *P&P*, V and VI.

———. 1957. The British Standard of Living, 1790–1850. *EHR*, 2nd ser., 10(1).

———. 1962. *The Age of Revolution*. London: Weidenfeld & Nicholson.

———. 1968. *Industry and Empire: An Economic History of Britain since 1750*. London: Weidenfeld & Nicolson.

———. 1990. *Nations and Nationalism Since 1750*. London: CUP.

———. 1992. *The Age of Empire 1875–1914*. Calcutta: Rupa.

———. 1995. *Age of Extremes: The Short Twentieth Century 1914–1991*. New Delhi: Viking.

Hobsbawm, E. J., and Hartwell, R. M. 1963. The Standard of Living during the Industrial Revolution: A Discussion. *EHR*, 2nd ser., 16(1).

Hobsbawm, E. J., and Ranger, T., ed. 1983. *The Invention of Tradition*. London: CUP.

Hobson, J. A. 1902/1938. *Imperialism: A Study*. 3rd edition. London: Allen & Unwin.

Hollingsworth, T. H. 1957. A Demographic Study of the British Ducal Families. *PS* 11(1).

Houdaille, J. 1977. La mortalité (hors combat) des militaires Francais a la fin du XVIIe et au debut du XIXe siècle. *Population*, 32e année, numero special, 481–97.

Houston, R. A. 1988. *Literacy in Early Modern Europe: Culture and Education 1500–1800*. London: Longman.

Hoyt, Edwin P. 1987. *Japan's War? The Great Pacific Conflict 1853–1952*. London: Hutchinson.

Huck, P. 1995. Infant Mortality and Living Standards of English Workers during the Industrial Revolution. *JEH* 55(3): 528–50.

Hufton, O. H. 1974. *The Poor of Eighteenth-century France, 1750–1789*. London: Clarendon.

Hume, D. 1752/1987. *Essays, Moral, Political and Literary, Part II*. Reprinted in *D. Hume: Essays Moral, Political, and Literary*, ed. E. F. Miller. Indianapolis, IN: Liberty Classics, 253–529.

Hung, Ho-Fung. 2001. Imperial China and the Capitalist Europe in the Eighteenth-Century Global Economy. *Review* 34(4): 473–513.

Hunter, Janet. 2000. The Roots of Divergence? Some Comments on Japan in the "Axial Age," 1750–1850. *Itinerario* 24(3/4): 75–88.

Hutchinson, D. S. 1995. Ethics. In Barnes 1995, 195–232.

Hymer, S., and Rowthorn, R. 1970. Multinational Corporations and International Oligopoly. In Kindleberger 1970, 57–91.

Ignatius, D. 2000. The Global Economy Is Tailor-Made for Money Laundering. *International Herald Tribune* (Paris), 1 June.

ILO. 1999. *Decent Work*. Geneva: International Labour Office.

———. 2003. *Global Employment Report 2002*. Geneva: International Labour Office.

———. 2004. *Global Employment Trends for Youth*. Geneva: International Labour Office.

Imhof, A. E. 1979. An Approach to Historical Demography in Germany. *Social History* 4(2): 345–66.

Imlah, A. 1958. *Economic Elements in the Pax Britannica: Studies in British Foreign Trade in the Nineteenth Century*. Cambridge, MA: HUP.

Inikori, J. E. 2002. *Africans and the Industrial Revolution in England*. London: CUP.

Inikori, J. E., and Engerman, S. L., eds. 1992a. *The Atlantic Slave Trade: Effects on Economies, Societies, and Peoples in Africa, the Americas, and Europe*. Durham: Duke University Press.

———. 1992b. Introduction: Gainers and Losers in the Atlantic Slave Trade. In Inikori and Engerman 1992, 1–21.

Israel, J. I. 1989. *Dutch Primacy in World Trade 1585–1740*. London: Clarendon.

———. 1995. *The Dutch Republic: Its Rise, Greatness, and Fall 1477–1806*. London: Clarendon.

James, C. L. R. 1989. *The Black Jacobins: Toussaint L'Ouverture and the San Domingo Revolution*. London: W. H. Allen.

Jannetta, Ann Bowman. 2001. Public Health and the Diffusion of Vaccination in Japan. In Liu, Lee, Reher, Saito, and Wang Feng 2001, 292–301.

Japan Statistical Yearbook. 2002. *Japan Statistical Yearbook 2002*. Tokyo: Statistics Bureau, Ministry of Public Management, Home Affairs, Ports and Telecommunications. www.stat.go.jp/english/data/nenkan/1431–02.htm.

Jayawardena, Kumari. 1995. *The White Woman's Other Burden: Western Women and South Asia during British Rule*. London: Routledge.

Jenks, L. H. 1927/1963. *The Migration of British Capital to 1875;* reprinted, Nelson.

Jog, N. G. 1969. *The Saga of Scindia*. Bombay: Scindia Steam Navigation Co.

———, ed. 1977. *Narottam Morarjee: The Architect of Modern Indian Shipping*. Bombay: Scindia Steam Navigation Co.

Johansson, E. 1977. The History of Literacy in Sweden. . . . *Educational Reports, Umea*, no. 12.

John, A. M. 1988. Plantation Slave Mortality in Trinidad. *PS* 42(2): 161–82.]

Johnson, Chalmers. 2004. *The Sorrows of Empire: Militarism, Secrecy and the End of the Republic*. New York: Metropolitan Books.

Johnson, D., Nathan, A. S., and Rawski, E. S., eds. 1985. *Popular Culture in Late Imperial China*. Berkeley: University of California Press.

Johnson, P. and Nicholas, S. 1997. Health and Welfare of Women in the United Kingdom, 1785–1820. In Steckel and Floud 1997, 201–50.

Jones, E. L. 1981/1987. *The European Miracle: Environments, Economies and Geopolitics in the History of Europe and Asia*. 2nd edition. London: CUP.

———. 1996. Recurrent Transitions to Intensive Growth. In Goudsblom, Jones, and Mennell 1996, 83–99.

Jones, Gary. 2003. A Million Iraqi Kids Would Die in Conflict. *The Mirror* (London), 29 February.

Jones, Vincent C. 1996. Emergence to World Power, 1898–1902. In *American Military History*. Vol. 1, 1775–1902, ed. Maurice Matloff, 319–42.

Joshi, Svati, ed. 1991. *Rethinking English: Essays in Literature, Language, History*. New Delhi: Trianka.

Justman, M., and Gradstein, M. 1999. The Industrial Revolution, Political Transition, and the Subsequent Decline in Inequality in 19-th Century Britain. *EEH* 36(1): 109–27.

Kahn, A. E. 1946. *Great Britain in the World Economy*. New York: Columbia University Press.

Kaminsky, Graciela L., Reinhart, Carmen M., and Vegh, C. A. 2003. *Journal of Economic Perspectives* 17(4): 51–74.

Kasza, Gregory J. 2002. War and Welfare Policy in Japan. *JAS* 61(2): 417–35.

Kenen, P. B., Papadia, F., and Saccomani, F., ed. 1994. *The International Monetary System*. London: CUP.

Kennedy, P. 1989. *The Rise and Fall of the Great Powers*. New York: Vintage Books.

Keynes, J. M. 1909/1971. Recent Economic Events in India. EJ, March; reprinted in *The Collected Writings of John Maynard Keynes*. Vol. 11, *Economic Articles and Correspondence: Academic*, ed. D. Moggridge. London: Macmillan, 1–22.

———. 1930. *A Treatise on Money*, vols. 1 and 2. London: Macmillan.

———. 1936. *The General Theory of Employment, Interest and Money*. London: Macmillan.

Khan, A. R., and Riskin, C. 2001. *Inequality and Poverty in China in the Age of Globalization*. London: OUP.

———. 2004. China's Household Income and Its Distribution, 1995 and 2002. Unpublished ms. Department of Economics, University of California, Riverside.

Kirby, A. 2003. West "Risks Another Ethiopia Famine." *BBC News*, 11 December.

Klare, M. T. 2004. *Transforming the American Military into a Global Oil Protection Service*. www. tomdispatch.com/index.htm (accessed 27 November 2004).

Kindleberger, C. P. 1970. *The International Corporation: A Symposium*.Cambridge, MA: MIT Press.

Ko, Dorothy. 1994. *Teachers of the Inner Chambers: Women and Culture in Seventeenth-Century China*. Stanford, CA: Stanford University Press.

Koenigsberger, H. G. 1968. Western Europe and the Power of Spain. In Wernham 1968, 234–318.

Komlos, J. 1987. The Height and Weight of West Point Cadets: Dietary Change in Ante-Bellum America. *JEH* 47(4): 897–927.

———, ed. 1994. *Stature, Living Standards, and Economic Development: Essays in Anthropometric History*. Chicago: University of Chicago Press.

Kosambi, D. D. 1962. *Myth and Reality: Studies in the Formation of Indian Culture*. Bombay: Popular Prakashan.

———. 1970. *The Culture and Civilisation of Ancient India*. Delhi: Vikas.

Kriedte, P., Medick, H., and Schlumbohm, J. 1981. *Industrialization before Industrialization*. London: CUP.

Kriner, Stephanie. 2000. Ethiopia's Famine Threat Increases. 17 April. http://www .disasterrelief.org/Disasters/000414Ethiopia.

Krishnaji, N. 1981. On Measuring the Incidence of Undernutrition: A Note on Sukhatme's Procedure. *EPW* 16(22): 989–92.

Krishnamurty, J. 1983. The Occupational Structure. In Kumar and Desai 1983, 533–50.

Krishnamurty, Sunanda. 1987. Real Wages of Agricultural Labourers in the Bombay Deccan, 1874–1922. *IESHR* 24(2).

Krugman, Paul. 2002. Flavors of fraud. *New York Times*, 28 June.

Kuczynski, Jurgen. 1965. Condition of workers (1880–1950). In Singh 1965, 609–37.

Kulchyski, P., ed. 1994. *Unjust Relations: Aboriginal Rights in Canadian Courts.* London: OUP.

Kumar, B. G. 1990. Ethiopian Famines 1973–1985. In Drèze and Sen 1990a, 173–216.

Kumar, Dharma. 1985. Private Property in Asia? The Case of Medieval South India. *Comparative Studies of Society and History* 27:340–66.

Kumar, Dharma, and Desai, M., eds. 1983. *The Cambridge Economic History of India.* Vol. 2, *ca. 1757–ca. 1970.* London: CUP.

Kunitz, S. J. 1986. Mortality since Malthus. In Coleman and Schofield 1986, 279–302.

Kurz, H., and Salvadori, N., eds. 1998. *The Elgar Companion to Classical Economics A–K.* Cheltenham, U.K.: Edward Elgar.

Kuznets, S. 1960/1965. Present Underdeveloped Countries and Past Growth Patterns. In *Economic Growth: Rationale, Problems and Cases*, ed. E. Nelson. Austin: University of Texas Press; reprinted in Kuznets 1965, 176–93.

———. 1965. *Economic Growth and Structure: Selected Essays.* New York: Norton.

Ladejinsky, Wolf. 1947/1977. Farm Tenancy in Japan, June 1947, *Report No. 79*, Tokyo, Supreme Commander for the Allied Powers (SCAP), General Headquarters, Natural Resources Section; reprinted in Louis J. Walinsky (ed.): *The Selected Papers of Wolf Ladejinsky: Agrarian Reform as Unfinished Business.* London: OUP, 68–93.

Lahiri-Choudhury, D. K. , ed. 1999a. *The Great Indian Elephant Book: An Anthology of Writings on Elephants in the Raj.* New Delhi: OUP.

———. 1999b. Introduction. In Lahiri-Choudhury 1999, xi–xxxv.

Landes, D. S. 1998. *The Wealth and Poverty of Nations: Why Some Are so Rich and Some so Poor.* London: Little, Brown.

Lane, F. C. 1958. The Consequences of Organized Violence. *JEH* 18(4): 401–17.

Langford, P. 1989. *A Polite and Commercial People: England 1727–1783.* London: OUP.

Laqueur, T. 1974. Debate: Literacy and Social Mobility in the Industrial Revolution in England. *P&P* 64: 96–107.

Lardinois, R. 1989. Deserted Villages and Depopulation in Rural Tamil Nadu ca. 1820–ca. 1830. In Dyson 1989, 16–48.

Lavely, W., and Wong, R. Bin. 1998. Revising the Malthusian Narrative: The Comparative Study of Population Dynamics in Late Imperial China. *JAS* 57(3): 714–48.

Lecky, W. E. H. 1912. *A History of Ireland in the Eighteenth Century.* Vol. 1. London: Longmans, Green.

Lee, J. 1999. Trade and Economy in Preindustrial East Asia, ca. 1500–ca. 1800: East Asia in the Age of Global Integration. *JAS* 58(1): 2–26.

Lee, J., Campbell, C., and Tan, G. 1999. Infanticide and Family Planning in Late Imperial China: The Price and Population History of Rural Liaoning, 1774–1873. In Rawski and Li 1999, 145–76.

Lee, J., Campbell, C., and Wang Feng. 2002. Positive Checks or Chinese Checks? *JAS* 61(2): 591–607.

Lee, J., and Wang Feng. 1999. *One Quarter of Humanity: Malthusian Mythology and*

Chinese Realities. Cambridge, MA: HUP.

Lee, R. 1979. Germany. In W. R. Lee 1979, 144–95.

Lee, W. R., ed. 1979. *European Demography and Economic Growth*. New York: St. Martin's.

Legum, C., ed. 1969. *Africa Handbook*. Harmondsworth: Penguin.

Lele, J. K. 1989. Revolution and the Utopian Core of Tradition: Some Thoughts on Elitism in Social Movements. In Lele and Singh 1989, 17–29.

Lele, J. K., and Singh, R. 1989. *Language and Society: Steps Towards an Integrated Theory*. Leiden: E. J. Brill.

Lenin, V. I. 1917/1964. *Imperialism, the Highest Stage of Capitalism: A Popular Outline*. In *Collected Works*, V. I. Lenin. Vol. 22. Moscow: Progress Publishers, 185–304.

Lenman, B. 1977. *An Economic History of Modern Scotland 1660–1975*. London: Batsford.

Le Roy Ladurie, E. 1996. *The Ancien Regime: A History of France 1610–1774*. Oxford: Blackwell.

Leung, Angela Ki Che. 1987. Organized Medicine in Ming-Ch'ing China: State and Private Medical Institutions in the Lower Yangtze Region. *LIC* 8(1): 134–66.

Li Bozhong. 1986. *The Development of Agriculture and Industry in Jiangnan, 1644–1850: Trends and Prospects*. Hangzhou, China: Zhenjiang.

———. 1998a. *Agricultural Development in Jiangnan, 1620–1850*. London: Macmillan.

———. 1998b. The Production of Wet-Field Rice in Jiangnan during the Ming and Qing Dynasties. In Elvin and Liu 1998, 447–84.

Liddell Hart, B. H. 1973. *History of the Second World War*. London: Pan Books.

Lindeborg, Ruth H. 1994. The "Asiatic" and the Boundaries of Victorian Englishness. *Victorian Studies* 37(3): 381–404.

Lindert, P. H. 1994. Unequal Living Standards. In Floud and McCloskey 1994b, 357–86.

Lindsay, J. O., ed. 1957. *The New Cambridge Modern History*. Vol. 7, *The Old Regime 1713–63*. London: CUP.

Linebaugh, P., and M. Rediker. 2000. *The Many-Headed Hydra: Sailors, Slaves, Commoners, and the Hidden History of the Revolutionary Atlantic*. London: Verso.

Liu, Ts'ui-jung, Lee, James, Reher, David Sven, Saito, Osamu, and Feng Wang, eds. 2001. *Asian Population History*. London: OUP.

Livi-Bacci, M. 1991. *Population and Nutrition: An Essay on European Demographic History*. London: CUP.

Lockwood, W. W. 1968. *The Economic Development of Japan*, expanded edition. Princeton, NJ: PUP.

Long, E. 1774. *The History of Jamaica*. 3 vols., London.

Lough, J. 1961. France under Louis XIV. In Carsten 1961a, 222–47.

Lovejoy, P. E. 1983. *Transformations in Slavery: A History of Slavery in Africa*. London: CUP.

Lovejoy, P. E., and Hogendorn, J. S. 1993. *Slow Death for Slavery: The Course of Abolition in Northern Nigeria, 1897–1936*. London: CUP.

Lovell, W. G. 1992. "Heavy Shadows and Black Night": Disease and Depopulation in Colonial Spanish America. *AAAG* 82(3): 426–43.

Lugard, F. D. 1929. *The Dual Mandate in British Tropical Africa*. 4th edition. London: William Blackwood & Sons.

Lunn, P. 1991. Nutrition, Immunity, and Infection. In Schofield, Reher, and Bideau 1991, 131–45.

Luxemburg, Rosa. 1913/1951. *The Accumulation of Capital*, translated from the German. London: Routledge & Kegan Paul.

Lynn, J. A. 1993. How War Fed War: The Tax of Violence and Contributions during the *Grand Siecle*. *Journal of Modern History* 65:286–310.

Macaulay, T. B. 1835. *Minute (on Education) recorded on 2 February 1835*, excerpted in Curtin 1971, 179–91.

Maddison, A. 1989. Dutch income in and from Indonesia 1700–1938. *MAS* 23(4): 645–70.

———. 1991. *Dynamic Forces in Capitalist Development*. London: OUP.

———. 1995. *Monitoring the World Economy 1820–1992*. Paris: OECD.

———. 1998. *Chinese Economic Performance in the Long Run*. Paris: OECD.

———. 2001. *The World Economy: A Millennial Perspective*. Paris: OECD.

Maharatna, A. 1996. *The Demography of Famines: An Indian Historical Perspective*. London: OUP.

Maine, H. S. 1861. *Ancient Law: Its Connection with the Early History of Society and Its Relation to Modern Ideas*. London: John Murray.

———. 1871. *Village Communities in the East and West*. London: John Murray.

Majumdar, R. C., Raychaudhuri, H. C., and Datta, K. K. 1978. *An Advanced History of India*. London: Macmillan.

Malcolmson, R. W. 1981. *Land and Labour in England, 1700–1780*. London: Hutchinson.

Manchester, A. K. 1933 *British Pre-eminence in Brazil*. Chapel Hill: University of North Carolina Press.

Mann, Julia de Lacy. 1971. *The Cloth Industry in the West of England: From 1640 to 1880*. London: OUP.

Mann, M. 1998. Ecological Change in North India: Deforestation and Agrarian Distress in the Ganga-Yamuna Doab 1800–1850. In Grove, Damodaran, and Sangwan 1998, 396–420.

Mann, Susan. 1997. *Precious Records: Women in China's Long Eighteenth Century*. Stanford, CA: Stanford University Press.

Manning, P. 1990. *Slavery and African Life: Occidental, Oriental, and African Slave Trades*. London: CUP.

Marglin, S. A., and Schor, Juliet, eds. 1990. *The Golden Age of Capitalism: Reinterpreting the Postwar Experience*. London: Clarendon Press.

Margo, R. A. 1990. *Race and Schooling in the South, 1880–1950: An Economic History*. Chicago: University of Chicago Press.

Marks, Robert B. 1998. *Tigers, Rice, Silk and Silt: Environment and Economy in Late Imperial South China*. London: CUP.

Marshall, P. J., ed. 2002. *The Eighteenth Century in Indian History: Evolution or Rev-*

olution? London: OUP.

Marsot, A. L. A. 1984. *Egypt in the Reign of Muhammad Ali.* London: CUP.

Marx, A. W. 1998. *Making Race and Nation: A Comparison of the United States, South Africa, and Brazil.* London: CUP.

Marx, K. 1849/1969. *Wage Labour and Capital,* first published in German in the Neue Rheinische Zeitung, April 5–8 and 11; translated from the German and reprinted with an introduction by F. Engels. In Marx and Engels 1969, 142–74.

———. 1857. The Indian Revolt. *New York Daily Tribune,* 16 September, reprinted in Marx and Engels, ca. 1961, 130–34.

———. 1857–1858/1973. *Grundrisse: Foundations of the critique of political economy (Rough draft),* translated from the German and with an introduction by M. Nicolaus. Harmondsworth: Penguin.

———. 1862. Marx to Engels, 2 August. In Marx and Engels, ca. 1957, 157–61.

———. 1867/1886. *Capital,* vol. 1, translated from the German by S. Moore and E. Aveling; reprinted, Moscow: Foreign Languages Publishing House, ca. 1955.

———. 1894/1966. *Capital.* Vol. 3, ed. Engels; translated from the German. Moscow: Progress Publishers.

———. 1971. *Theories of Surplus Value,* part 3, translated from the German by J. Cohen and S. W. Ryazanskaya. Moscow: Progress Publishers.

Marx, K., and Engels, F. 1845–46/1976. *The German Ideology,* translated from the German; Moscow, Progress Publishers.

———. ca. 1957. *Selected Correspondence.* Moscow: Foreign Languages Publishing House.

———. ca. 1961. *Marx and Engels on Colonialism.* Moscow: Foreign Languages Publishing House.

———. 1969. *Marx-Engels Selected Works,* vol. 1. Moscow: Progress Publishers.

Massey, D. S. 1988. Economic Development and International Migration in Comparative Perspective. *PDR* 14(3): 383–413.

Masuy-Stroobant, G. 1997. Infant Health and Infant Mortality in Europe: Lessons from the Past and Challenges for the Future. In Corsini and Viazzo 1997, 1–34.

Mathias, P. 1969. *The First Industrial Nation: An Economic History of Britain since 1700–1914.* London: Methuen.

Mathias, P., and Postan, M. M., eds. 1978. *The Cambridge Economic History of Europe.* Vol. 7, *The Industrial Economies,* parts 1 and 2. London: CUP.

Matthews, Ron, and Matsuyama, Keisuke, ed. 1993. *Japan's Military Renaissance?* London: Macmillan.

Mauro, F., and Parker, G. 1980. Spain. In Wilson and Parker 1980, 37–62.

Mavunduse, Diana. 2003. *Fear Looming of '84-like Famine in Ethiopia,* 4 April. http://gbgm-umc.org/umcor/03/ethiopiafamine.stm.

Mayer, A. J. 1967. *Politics and Diplomacy of Peace-Making: Containment and Counterrevolution at Versailles, 1918–1919.* New York: Knopf.

———. 1988. *Why Did the Heavens Not Darken? The "Final Solution" in History.* New York: Pantheon.

———. 2003. Iraq, Preventive War, "Old Europe." *MR* 54(10): 17–21.

Mazumdar, Sucheta. 1998. *Sugar and Society in China: Peasants, Technology and the World Market*. Cambridge, MA: HUP for Harvard University Asia Centre.

McBride, D. 1989. *Integrating the City of Medicine: Blacks in Philadelphia Health Care, 1910–1965*. Philadelphia: Temple University Press.

McCormack, G. 2004a. Reflections on Modern Japanese History in the Context of the Concept of Genocide. In Gellately and Kiernan 2004, 265–86.

———. 2004b. Remilitarizing Japan. *New Left Review* 29 September–October, 29–45.

McEvedy, C., and Jones, R. 1978. *Atlas of World Population History*. Harmondsworth: Penguin.

McGuire, J., Bertola, P., and Reeves, P., eds. 2001. *Evolution of the World Economy, Precious Metals and India*. London: OUP.

McKendrick, N. 1982. Commercialization and the Economy. In McKendrick, Brewer, and Plumb 1982.

McKendrick, N., Brewer, J., and Plumb, J. H., ed. 1982.*The Birth of a Consumer Society: The Commercialization of Eighteenth-Century England*. London: Europa Publications.

McKeown. T. 1976. *The Modern Rise of Population*. London: Edward Arnold.

McManners, J. 1970. Religion and the Relations of Church and State. In Bromley 1970, 119–54.

McNally, D. 2002. *Another World Is Possible*. Winnipeg, Canada: Arbeiter Ring.

McNeill, J. R. 2000. *An Environmental History of the Twentieth-Century World: Something New under the Sun*. New York: Norton.

McNeill, W. H. 1983. *The Pursuit of Power: Technology, Armed Force, and Society Since A.D. 1000*. Oxford: Blackwell.

McPherson, Kenneth. 1993. *The Indian Ocean: A History of People and the Sea*. London: OUP.

McWilliams, W. C., and Piotrowski, H. 1997. *The World Since 1945: A History of International Relations*. London: Lynne Riener Publishers.

Menzies, N. K. 1992. Strategic Space: Exclusion and Inclusion in Wildland Policies in Late Imperial China. *MAS* 26(4): 719–33.

———. 1996. Forestry. In *Science and Civilization in China*. Vol. 6, Part III, *Agroindustries and Forestry*, ed. Joseph Needham. London: CUP, 541–689.

Merchant, C. 2002. *The Columbia Guide to American Environmental History*. New York: Columbia University Press.

Merrifield, A. 1999. Class Formation, Capital Accumulation, and the Downsizing of America. *Monthly Review* 51(5): 36–49.

Milanovic, B. 2002. True World Income Distribution, 1988 and 1993: First Calculations Based on Household Surveys Alone. *EJ* 112:51–92.

Mill, James. 1817/1858. *The History of British India*, 5th edition with Notes and Continuation by Horace Hayman Wilson, 10 vols. London: James Madden, Piper, Stephenson and Spence.

———. 1831. *Minutes of Evidence before the Select Committee on the Affairs of the East India Company*, UK Parliamentary Papers, 1831. Vol. 5 (testimony of James Mill on 4, 9, 11, 19, 23, and 25 August 1831).

———. 1831–1832a. *Minutes of Evidence before the Select Committee on the Affairs of the East India Company*, UK Parl. Papers, 1831–32. Vol. 9 (testimony of James Mill on 16 and 21 February 1832).

———. 1831–1832b. Observations on the Land Revenue of India, *UK Parl. Papers*, 1831–32. Vol. 11, appendix 7.

Mill, J. S. 1836/1875. Civilization. *London and Westminster Review*, April; reprinted in Mill 1875, vol. 1, 160–205.

———. 1848/1857. *Principles of Political Economy with Some of their Applications to Social Philosophy*, in two volumes. London: John W. Parker & Son.

Milton, J. R. 1994. Locke's Life and Times. In *The Cambridge Companion to Locke*, ed. V. Chappell. London: CUP.

Milward, A. S., Brennan, G., and Romero, F. 1992. *The European Rescue of the Nation-State*. London: Routledge.

Mintz, S. W. 1985. *Sweetness and Power*. New York: Viking.

Mirsky, J. 2003. Wartime Lies. *NYRB*, L(15), 9 October, 42–47.

Mitch, D. 1993. The Role of Human Capital in the First Industrial Revolution. In Mokyr 1993, 267–307.

Mitchell, B. R. 1998a. *International Historical Statistics: Europe 1750–1993*. 4th edition. London: Macmillan.

———. 1998b. *International Historical Statistics: The Americas*. 4th edition. London: Macmillan.

Mitchell, B. R., and Deane, P. 1976. *Abstract of British Historical Statistics*. London: CUP.

Mokyr, J. ed. 1985. *The Economics of the British Industrial Revolution*. London: Hutchinson.

———. 1988. Is There Still Life in the Pessimistic Case? Consumption during the Industrial Revolution, 1790–1850. *JEH* 48(1): 69–52.

———, ed. 1993. *The British Industrial Revolution: An Economic Perspective*. Boulder, Colo.: Westview Press.

Mokyr, J., and Ó Grada, C. 1994. The Heights of the British, 1800–1815: Evidence from Recruits to the East India Company's Army. In Komlos, 1994.

———. 1996. Height and Health in the United Kingdom 1815–1860: Evidence from the East India Company Army. *EEH* 33(2): 141–68.

Molloy, J. S. 1999. *A National Crime: The Canadian Government and the Residential School System, 1879 to 1986*. Winnipeg, Manitoba: University of Manitoba Press.

Moodie, Susan. 1852/1989. *Roughing It in the Bush; or, Life in Canada*; reprinted, Toronto: McClleland & Stewart.

Moosvi, S. 1987. *The Economy of the Mughal Empire: A Statistical Study*. London: OUP.

———. 1993. *Man and Nature in Mughal India*, Indian History Congress, Symposia Papers 5, Delhi.

———. 2000. The Indian Economic Experience: 1600–1900: A Quantitative Study. In Panikkar, Byres, and Patnaik 2000, 328–58.

Moreland, W. H. 1920. *India at the Death of Akbar*. London: Macmillan.

Morishima, M. 1982. *Why Has Japan "Succeeded"? Western Technology and the*

Japanese Ethos. London: CUP.

Moriya, Katsuhisa. 1990. Urban Networks and Information Networks. In Nakane and Ōishi 1990, 97–123.

Morris, Cynthia Taft. 1992. Politics, Development, and Society in Five Land-Rich Countries in the Latter Nineteenth Century. *Research in Economic History*, vol. 14: 1–68.

Mosk, Carl. 2000. Inequality, Ideology, Autarky, and Structural Change: The Biological Standard of Living in Japan between the Two World Wars. *The Japanese Economy* 28(2): 39–75.

Mote, Frederick W. 1999. *Imperial China 900–1800.* Cambridge, MA: HUP.

Mousnier, R. 1970a. The Exponents and Critics of Absolutism. In Cooper 1970a, 104–31.

———. 1970b. French Institutions and Society1610–61. In Cooper 1970a, 474–502.

MR Editors. 2002. US Military Bases and Empire. *MR* 53(10): 1–14.

Mukherjee, Radhakamal. 1939. *The Economic History of India: 1600–1800.* London: Longmans, Green.

Myrdal, G. 1968. *Asian Drama.* New York: Pantheon.

Nakamura, Satoru. 1990. The Development of Rural Industry. In Nakane and Ōishi 1990, 81–96.

Nakane, Chie, and Ōishi, Shinzaburō, eds. 1990. *Tokugawa Japan: The Social and Economic Antecedents of Modern Japan.* Tokyo: University of Tokyo Press.

Neal, L. 1990. *The Rise of Financial Capitalism: International Capital Markets in the Age of Reason.* London: CUP.

Needham, J., et al. 1954. *Science and Civilisation in China.* Vol. 1. London: CUP.

Needham, J., and Wang Ling. 1956. *Science and Civilisation in China.* Vol. 2. London: CUP.

Nef, J. U. 1943. The Industrial Revolution Reconsidered. *JEH* III(1): 1–31.

Nicholas, S., and Oxley, D. 1993. The Living Standards of Women during the Industrial Revolution. *EHR* 46(4): 723–49.

———. 1996. Living Standards of Women in England and Wales, 1785–1815: New Evidence from Newgate Prison Records. *EHR* 49(3): 591–99.

Norman, E. H. 1940. *Japan's Emergence as a Modern Society: Political and Economic Problems of the Meiji Period.* New York: Institute of Pacific Relations.

North, D. C. 1989. Institutions and Economic Growth: An Historical Introduction. *World Development* 17(9): 1319–32

———. 1990. *Institutions, Institutional Change and Economic Performance.* London: CUP.

North, D. C., and Thomas, R. P. 1973. *The Rise of the Western World: A New Economic History.* London: CUP.

North, D. C., and Weingast, B. R. 1989. Constitutions and Commitment: Evolution of Institutions Governing Public Choice in Seventeenth Century England. *JEH* 49(4): 803–32.

Northrup, D. 1995. *Indentured Labour in the Age of Imperialism, 1834–1922.* London: CUP.

Nozick, R. 1974. *Anarchy, State and Utopia.* New York: Basic Books.

Nurkse, R. 1961. *Patterns of Trade and Development.* Oxford: Blackwell.

Nussbaum, Martha C. 1997. *Cultivating Humanity: A Classical Defence of Reform in Liberal Education*. Cambridge, MA: HUP.

———. 2000. *Women and Human Development: The Capabilities Approach*. Cambridge, London: CUP.

Nussbaum, Martha C., and Sen, A., eds. 1993. *The Quality of Life*. London: Clarendon.

O'Brien, Jean M. 1997. *Dispossession by Degrees: Indian Land and Identity in Natick, Massachusetts, 1650–1790*. London: CUP.

O'Brien, P. K. 1988a. The Costs and Benefits of British Imperialism 1846–1914. *P&P*, no. 120 (August): 163–200.

———. 1988b. The Political Economy of British Taxation, 1660–1815. *EHR* 41(1): 1–32.

———. 1999. Imperialism and the Rise and Decline of the British Economy, 1688–1989. *New Left Review*, no. 238:48–80.

———. 2000. The Reconstruction, Rehabilitation and Reconfiguration of the British Industrial Revolution as a Conjuncture in Global History. *Itinerario* 24(3/4): 117–34.

O'Brien, P. K., and Keyder, C. 1978. *Economic Growth in Britain and France: Two Paths to the Twentieth Century*. London: Allen & Unwin.

Ocampo, J. A. 2004. Latin America's Growth and Equity: Frustrations during Structural Reforms. *Journal of Economic Perspectives* 18(2): 67–88.

Offer, A. 1993. The British Empire 1870–1914: A Waste of Money. *EHR* 46:215–38.

Ó Grada, C. 1994. *Ireland: A New Economic History 1780–1939*. London: OUP.

Ohkawa, K., and Rosovsky, H. 1973. *Japanese Growth: Trend Acceleration in the Twentieth Century*. Stanford, CA: Stanford University Press.

Ōishi, Shinzaburō. 1990. The Bakuhan System. In Nakane and Ōishi 1990, 11–36.

Oliver, R., and Atmore, A. 1981. *Africa since 1800*. London: CUP.

O'Rourke, K. H. 2000. Tariffs and Growth in the Late Nineteenth Century. *EJ* 110 (April): 456–83.

Osborne, Anne. 1998. Highlands and Lowlands: Economic and Ecological Interactions in the Lower Yangzi Region under the Qing. In Elvin and Liu 1998, 203–35.

Osmani, S. R., ed. 1992a. *Nutrition and Poverty*. London: Clarendon Press.

———. 1992b. On Some Controversies in the Measurement of Undernutrition. In Osmani 1992a, 121–62.

Ostroot, Natalie M. 1997. L'estimation de la mortalité urbaine sous l'ancien régime, Aix-en-Provence et Toulouse en 1695. *Population*, 52e année, no. 1:63–76.

Pagden, A. 1986. *The Fall of Natural Man: The American Indian and the Origins of Comparative Ethnology*. London: CUP.

Palast, G. 2002. *The Best Democracy Money Can Buy*. London: Pluto Press.

Pandian, M. S. S. 1998. Hunting and Colonialism in the Nineteenth-Century Nilgiri Hills of South India. In Grove, Damodaran, and Sangwan 1998, 273–96.

Pandit, Y. S. 1937. *India's Balance of Indebtedness 1898–1913*. London: Allen & Unwin.

Panikkar, K. N., Byres, T. J., and Patnaik, Utsa, eds. 2000. *The Making of History: Essays presented to Irfan Habib*. New Delhi: Tulika.

Park, Chai Bin, and Cho, Nam-Hoon. 1995. Consequence of Son Preference in a

Low-Fertility Society: Imbalance of the Sex Ratio at Birth in Korea. *PDR* 21(1): 59–84.

Parker, G. 1988. *The Military Revolution: Military Innovation and the Rise of the West, 1500–1800*. London: CUP.

———. 1992. Success and Failure during the First Century of the Reformation. *P&P*, no. 136:43–82.

———, ed. 1993. *The Cambridge Illustrated History of Warfare: The Triumph of the West*. London: CUP.

———, ed. 1997. *The Thirty Years' War*. London: Routledge.

Parker, G., and Smith, L. M., eds. 1978a. *The General Crisis of the Seventeenth Century*. London: Routledge & Kegan Paul.

Parker, G., and Smith, L. M. 1978b. Introduction. In Parker and Smith 1978a, 1–25.

Parry, J. H. 1973. *The Spanish Seaborne Empire*. Harmondsworth: Penguin.

Parthasarathi, P. 1998. Rethinking Wages and Competitiveness in the Eighteenth-Century Britain and South India. *P&P*, no. 158:79–109.

Patel, S., Bagchi, J., and Raj, Krishna, eds. 2002: *Thinking Social Science in India: Essays in Honour of Alice Thorner*. New Delhi: Sage.

Pati, Biswamoy, and Harrison, Mark, eds. 2001. *Health, Medicine and Empire: Perspectives on Colonial India*. Hyderabad: Orient Longman.

Patnaik, P., ed. 1986. *Lenin and Imperialism*. Hyderabad, India: Orient Longman.

Patnaik, Utsa. 2002. On Famine and Measuring "Famine Deaths." In Patel, Bagchi, and Raj 2002, 46–68.

Patnaik, U. and Dingwaney, M., eds. 1985. *Chains of Servitude: Bondage and Slavery in India*, New Delhi: Sangam Books.

Payne, P. 1992. Assessing Under-Nutrition: The Need for a Re-Conceptualization. In Osmani 1992a, 49–96.

Pearson, M. N. 1987. *The Portuguese in India*. London: CUP.

———. 2001. Asia and the World Precious Metal Flows in the Early Modern Period. In McGuire, Bertola, and Reeves 2001, 21–58.

Pelletier, F., Legare, J., and Bourbeau, R. 1997. Mortality in Quebec during the Nineteenth Century: From the State to the Cities. *PS* 47(1): 93–103.

Perlin, F. 1978. Of White Whale and Countrymen in the Eighteenth Century Maratha Deccan: Extended Class Relations, Rights, and the Problem of Rural Autonomy under the Old Regime. *Journal of Peasant Studies* 5(2): 172–237.

———. 1987. Money-Use in Late Pre-Colonial India and the International Trade in Currency Media. In Richards 1987, 232–373.

Phelps Brown, E. H., and Hopkins, Sheila V.. 1981. *A Perspective of Wages and Prices*. London: Methuen.

Phillips, K. 2004. *American Dynasty: Aristocracy, Fortune and the Politics of Deceit in the House of Bush*. New York: Viking.

Pieterse, J. N. 2004. Neoliberal Empire. *Theory, Culture and Society* 21(3): 119–40.

Platt, D. C. M. 1985. Canada and Argentina: The First Preference of the British Investor, 1904–14. *The Journal of Imperial and Commonwealth History* 13(3): 77–92.

Plumb, J. H. 1964. The Prince and the State. In Plumb et al. 1964, 31–55.

Plumb, J. H., et al. 1964. *The Penguin Book of the Renaissance*. Harmondsworth: Penguin.

Pollard, S. J. 1985. Capital Exports, 1870–1914: Harmful or Beneficial? *EHR*, 2nd ser., 38(4): 489–514.

Pomeranz, K. 2000a. *The Great Divergence: China, Europe and the Making of the Modern World Economy*. Princeton, NJ: PUP.

———. 2000b. Re-Thinking the Late Imperial Chinese Economy: Development, Disaggregation and Decline, circa 1730–1930. *Itinerario* 24(3/4): 29–74.

Porter, R. 1990. *English Society in the Eighteenth Century*. Rev. ed. Harmondsworth: Penguin.

———. 1995. The Eighteenth Century. In Conrad, Neave, Nutton, Porter, and Wear 1995, 363–69.

Portes, A., and Hoffman, K. 2003. Latin American Class Structures: Their Composition and Change during the Neoliberal Era. *Latin American Research Review* 38(1): 41–82.

Posner, R. 1973. *Economic Analysis of Law*. 2nd edition. Boston, MA: Little Brown.

Postma, J. 1990. *The Dutch in the Atlantic Slave Trade, 1600–1815*. London: CUP.

Potter, G. R., ed. 1971. *The New Cambridge Modern History*. Vol. 1, *The Renaissance, 1493–1520*. London: CUP.

Pounds, N. J. G. 1985. *An Historical Geography of Europe 1800–1914*. London: CUP.

Prakash, Om. 1998. *European Commercial Enterprise in Pre-Colonial India*. London: CUP.

Prashad, V. 2002. *War against the Planet: The Fifth Afghan War, Imperialism, and Other Assorted Fundamentalisms*. New Delhi: LeftWord.

Prem, H. J. 1992. Spanish Colonization and Indian Property in Central Mexico. *AAAG* 82(30): 444–59.

Pressnell, L. S. 1956. *Country Banking in the Industrial Revolution*. London: OUP.

Prestowitz, C. 2003. *Rogue Nation: American Unilateralism and the Failure of Good Intentions*. New York: Basic Books.

Price, R. 1987. *A Social History of Nineteenth-Century France*. London: Hutchinson.

Procacci, G. 1973. *History of the Italian People*, transl. A. Paul from the French. Harmondsworth: Penguin.

Putnam, R. 1993. *Making Democracy Work: Civic Traditions in Modern Italy*. Princeton: PUP.

Q&A Ethiopia. 2002. *Q&A: Why Is Ethiopia Facing Another Famine?* 11 November. http://news.bbc.co.uk/hi/africa.

Radcliffe, Mary Anne. 1799/1994. *The Female Advocate; or an Attempt to Recover the Rights of Women from Male Usurpation*. Vernor and Hood; reprinted in Roberts and Mizuta 1994.

Raff, D. 1988. *A History of Germany from the Medieval Empire to the Present*, transl. from B. Little the German. Oxford: Berg

Raghavaiyangar, S. S. 1893. *Memorandum on the Progress of the Madras Presidency during the Last Forty Years of British Administration*. Madras: Government Press.

Rahim, E., and Schwarz, H. 1998. *Contributions to Bengal Studies: An Interdiscipli-*

nary and International Approach. Dhaka: Pustaka

Ramabai, Pandita. 2000. *Pandita Ramabai through Her Own Words: Selected Works*, ed. and transl. Meera Kosambi. London: OUP.

Raman, Sita Anantha. 1996. *Getting Girls to School: Social Reform in the Tamil Districts 1870–1930*. Calcutta: Stree.

Rangarajan, M. 1996. *Fencing the Forest: Conservation and Ecological Change in India's Central Provinces 1860–1914*. London: OUP.

———. 2001. *India's Wildlife History*. New Delhi: Permanent Black.

Rawski, E. S. 1979. *Education and Popular Literacy in Ch'ing China*. Ann Arbor: University of Michigan Press.

———. 1985. Economic and Social Foundations of Late Imperial China. In Johnson, Nathan, and Rawski 1985, 3–33.

Rawski, T. G., and Li, Lillian M., eds. 1999. *Chinese History in Economic Perspective*. Berkeley: University of California Press.

Raychaudhuri, T. 1982a. Non-Agricultural Production: Mughal India. In Raychaudhuri and Habib 1982, 261–307.

———. 1982b. Inland Trade. In Raychaudhuri and Habib 1982, 325–59.

Raychaudhuri, T., and Habib, I., eds. 1982. *The Cambridge Economic History of India*. Vol. 1, *ca. 1200–ca. 1750*. London: CUP.

Razzell, P. 1993. The Growth of Population in Eighteenth Century England: A Critical Reappraisal. *JEH* 53(4): 757–63.

Read, R. D., and Legum, C. 1969. Ethiopia. In Legum 1969, 105–16.

Rediker, M. 1987. *Between the Devil and the Deep Blue Sea: Merchant Seamen, Pirates, and the Anglo-American Maritime World, 1700–50*. London: CUP.

Reynolds, H. 1992. *The Law of the Land*. Harmondsworth: Penguin.

Rhodes, R. 1986. *The Making of the Atomic Bomb*. London: Simon & Schuster.

Rich, E. E. 1971. Expansion as a Concern of All Europe. In Potter 1971, 445–69.

Richards, J. F., ed. 1987. *The Imperial Monetary System of Mughal India*. London: OUP.

———. 1990. The Seventeenth-Century Crisis in South Asia. *MAS* 24(4): 625–38.

———. 1997. Early Modern India and World History. *Journal of World History* 8(2): 197–210.

Richardson, D. 1989. Slave Exports from West and West-Central Africa, 1700–1810: New Estimates of Volume and Distribution. *Journal of African History* 30: 1–22.

Rippy, J. F. 1959. *British Investments in Latin America 1822–1949*. Minneapolis: University of Minnesota Press.

Robb, P. ed. 1993. *Dalit Movements and the Meanings of Labour in India*. London: OUP

Roberts, M. 1970. Sweden and the Baltic 1611–54. In Cooper 1970a, 385–410.

Roberts, M. M., and Mizuta, T., eds. 1994. *The Radicals: Revolutionary Women*. London: Routledge.

Roediger, D. R. 1991. *The Wages of Whiteness: Race and the Making of the American Working Class*. London: Verso.

Roehl, R. 1976. French Industrialization: A Reconsideration. *EEH* 13(3): 233–81.

Rohter, L. 2004. Argentina's Economic Rally Defies Forecasts. *New York Times*, 26

December.

Rose, J. C. 1989. Biological Consequences of Segregation and Deprivation: A Post-Slavery Population from South-west Arkansas. *JEH* 49(2): 351–60.

Rosen, J. 1961. Scandinavia and the Baltic. In Carsten 1961a, 519–42.

Rostow, W. W. 1975. *How It All Began: The Origins of the Modern Economy.* London: Methuen.

Rousseau, Jean Jacques. 1755/1984. *A Discourse on Inequality*, transl. M. Cranston from the French. Harmondsworth: Penguin.

Rowe, William T. 1984. *Hankow: Commerce and Society in a Chinese City, 1796–1889.* Stanford, CA: Stanford University Press.

RUPE. 2002. *Behind the Invasion of Iraq.* Mumbai: Research Unit for Political Economy; reprinted. New York: Monthly Review Press, 2003.

Sabel, C., and Zeitlin, J. 1985. Historical Alternatives to Mass Production: Politics, Markets and Technology in Nineteenth-Century Industrialization. *P&P*, no. 108:133–76.

Said, E. W. 1978. *Orientalism.* New York: Random House.

———. 1993. *Culture and Imperialism.* New York: Knopf.

Saldanha, Indra Munshi. 1998. Colonial Forest Regulations and Collective Resistance: Nineteenth-Century Thana District. In Grove, Damodaran, and Sangwan 1998, 708–34.

Salisbury, N. 1996. Native People and European Settlers in Eastern North America, 1600–1783. In Trigger and Washburn 1996, 399–460.

Sánchez-Albornoz, N. 1974. *The Population of Latin America: A History.* Berkeley: University of California Press.

Sandberg, L. G. 1979. The Case of the Impoverished Sophisticate: Human Capital and Swedish Economic Growth before World War I. *JEH* 39(1): 225–41.

Sandberg, L. G., and Steckel, R. H. 1997. Was Industrialization Hazardous to Your health? Not in Sweden. In Steckel and Floud 1997, 127–60.

Sanderson, M. 1968. Social Change and Elementary Education in Industrial Lancashire, 1780–1840, *Northern History* 3: 131–54.

———. 1972. Literacy and Social Mobility in the Industrial Revolution in England. *P&P*, no. 56:75–104.

Sangari, Kumkum. 1991. Relating histories: Definitions of Literacy, Literature, Gender in Nineteenth Century Calcutta and England. In Joshi 1991, 32–123.

Sarkar, T. 1985. Bondage in the Colonial Text. In Patnaik and Dingwaney 1985, 97–126.

Sasaki, Y. 1985. Urban Migration and Fertility in Tokugawa Japan: The City of Takayama, 1773–1871. In Hanley and Wolff 1985, 133–53.

Sat?, T. 1990. Tokugawa Villages and Agriculture. In Nakane and ?ishi 1990, 37–80.

Sauer, C. O. 1935. *Aboriginal Population of North-western Mexico.* Ibero-Americana, no. 10. Berkeley: University of California Press.

———. 1939. *Man and Nature: America before the Days of the White Man.* New York: Charles Scribner's.

Saul, S. B. 1960. *Studies in British Overseas Trade, 1870–1914.* Liverpool: Liverpool University Press.

———. 1969. *The Myth of the Great Depression, 1873–1896.* London: Macmillan.

——. ed. 1970. *Technological Change: The United States and Britain in the Nineteenth Century*. London: Methuen.

Saunders, K., ed. 1984. *Indentured Labour in the British Empire*. London: Croom Helm.

Schama, S. 1987. *The Embarrassment of Riches: An Interpretation of Dutch Culture in the Golden Age*. London: Fontana.

Schofield, R. S. 1968. The Measurement of Literacy in Pre-Industrial England. In Goody 1968, 311–25.

——. 1973. Dimensions of Illiteracy, 1750–1950. *EEH* 10:437–54.

——. 1994. British Population Change, 1700–1830. In Floud and McCloskey 1994a, 60–95.

Schofield, R., and Reher, D. 1991. The Decline of Mortality in Europe. In Schofield, Reher, and Bideau 1991, 1–17.

Schofield, R., Reher, D., and Bideau, A., eds. 1991. *The Decline of Mortality in Europe*. London: Clarendon Press.

Schumpeter, J. A. 1911/1934. *The Theory of Economic Development*, transl. R. Opie from the German. Cambridge, MA: HUP.

——. 1943/1950. *Capitalism, Socialism and Democracy*. 3rd edition. London: George Allen & Unwin.

Seccombe, W. 1983. Marxism and Demography. *New Left Review*, no. 137:22–47.

Seed, P. 1993. Conquest of the Americas. In Parker 1993, 132–45.

Selden, Mark. 2003. The United States and Japan in Twentieth-Century Wars. In Selden and So 2003, chapter 2.

Selden, Mark, and So, Alvin, eds. 2003. *War and State Terrorism: The United States, Japan and the Asia-Pacific in the Long Twentieth Century*. Lanham, MD: Rowman & Littlefield.

Semmel, B. 1993. *The Liberal Ideal and the Demons of Empire: Theories of Imperialism from Adam Smith to Lenin*. Baltimore: Johns Hopkins University Press.

Sen, A. K. 1981. *Poverty and Famines: An Essay on Entitlement and Deprivation*. London: OUP.

——. 1999. *Development as Freedom*. New York: Knopf.

Senghaas, D. 1985. *The European Experience: A Historical Critique of Development Theory*. Dover, UK: Berg Publishers.

Sengupta, N. 1980. The Indigenous Agrarian Organization of South Bihar. *IESHR* 17(2): 157–89.

Shammas, Carole. 1993. Changes in English and Anglo-American Consumption from 1550 to 1800. In Brewer and Porter 1993, 177–205.

Sheel, A. 1992. Long-Term Demographic Trends in South Bihar: Gaya and Shahabad Districts, 1811–1921. *IESHR* 29(3): 323–42.

Sheridan, R. B. 1965. The Wealth of Jamaica in the Nineteenth Century. *EHR*, 2nd ser. Vol. 18.

Shiller, R. J. 2000. *Irrational Exuberance*. Princeton: PUP.

Shiva, Vandana. 2001. *Patents: Myths and Reality*. New Delhi: Penguin India.

Shlomowitz, R., and Brennan, L. 1990. Mortality and Migrant Labour in Assam.

IESHR 27(1): 85–110.

———. 1992. Mortality and Indian Labour in Malaya. *IESHR* 29(1): 57–76.

Simmons, Colin. 1985. "De-industrialization," Industrialization and the Indian Economy, ca. 1850–1947. *MAS* 19(3): 593–622.

Simms, Katharine. 1989. *The Norman Invasion and the Gaelic Recovery*. In *The Oxford Illustrated History of Ireland*, ed. R. F. Foster. London: OUP, 53–103.

Simon, M. 1968. The Pattern of New British Portfolio Foreign Investment, 1865–1914. In *The Export of Capital from Britain 1870–1914*, ed. A. R. Hall. London: Methuen.

Singh, Chetan. 1995. Forests, Pastoralism and Agrarian Society in Mughal India. In Arnold and Guha 1995, 21–48.

Singer, C., Holmyard, E. J., et al. eds. 1956. *A History of Technology: The Mediterranean Civilizations and the Middle Ages, c.700 B. C. to c. A. D. 1500.* . Vol. II. London: OUP.

Singh, Jyotsna G. 1996. *Colonial Narratives/Cultural Dialogues: "Discoveries" of India in the Language of Colonialism*. London: Routledge.

Singh, V. B., ed. 1965. *Economic History of India 1857–1956*. New Delhi: Allied.

Sinha, Mrinalini. 1995. *Colonial Masculinity: The "Manly Englishman" and the "Effeminate Bengali" in the Late Nineteenth Century*. Manchester: Manchester University Press.

SIPRI. 2003. *SIPRI Yearbook 2002*. Stockholm: Stockholm International Peace Research Institute.

———. 2004. *SIPRI Yearbook 2003*. Stockholm: Stockholm International Peace Research Institute.

Sivasubramonian, S. 2000. *The National Income of India of India in the Twentieth Century*. London: OUP.

Skinner, G. W. 1971. Chinese Peasants and the Closed Community: An Open and Shut Case. *Comparative Studies in Society and History* 13(3): 270–81.

———, ed. 1977. *The City in Late Imperial China*. Stanford, CA: Stanford University Press.

Skinner, Q. 1978a. *The Foundations of Modern Political Thought: The Renaissance*. Vol. 1. London: CUP.

———. 1978b. *The Foundations of Modern Political Thought: The Age of Reformation*. Vol. 2. London: CUP.

Smedley, Agnes. 1972. *The Great Road: Life and Times of Chu Te*. New York: Monthly Review Press.

Smil, V. 1994. How Many People Can the Earth Feed? *PDR* 20(2): 255–92.

———. 2003. *China's Past, China's Future: Energy, Food, Environment*. Armonk, NY: M. E. Sharpe.

Smith, A. 1791/1910. *An Inquiry into the Nature and Causes of the Wealth of Nations*. 6th ed. reprinted and ed. E. R. A. Seligman in 2 vols. London: J. M. Dent.

Smith, M. G. 1954. Slavery and Emancipation in Two Societies. *Social and Economic Studies. Vol.* 3, 239–80.

Smith, T. C. 1959. *The Agrarian Origins of Modern Japan*. Stanford, CA: Stanford

University Press.

Soderberg, J. 1987. Real Wage Trends in Urban Europe, 1730–1850: Stockholm in a Comparative Perspective. *Social History* 12(2): 155–76.

Solow, Barbara L., and Engerman, S. L., eds. 1987. *British Capitalism and Caribbean Slavery: The Legacy of Eric Williams.* London: CUP.

Soltow, L., and Van Zanden, W. L. 1998. *Income and Wealth Inequality in the Netherlands 16th–20th Century.* Amsterdam: Het Spinhuis.

Sommestad, Lena. 1998. Human Reproduction and the Rise of Welfare States: The United States and Sweden. *Scandinavian Economic History Review* 46(2): 97–116.

Sparks, A. 1991. *The Mind of South Africa: The Story of the Rise and Fall of Apartheid.* London: Mandarin.

Spence, J. D. 1981. *The Gate of Heavenly Peace: The Chinese and Their Revolution, 1895–1980.* New York: Viking.

———. 1999. *The Search for Modern China.* 2nd edition. New York: W. W. Norton.

Spooner, F. C. 1968. The Economy of Europe 1559–1609. In Wernham 1968, 14–43.

Stackelberg, R. 1999. *Hitler's Germany: Origins, Interpretations, Legacies.* London: Routledge.

Steckel, R. H. 1995. Stature and the Standard of Living. *Journal of Economic Literature* 33:1903–40.

———. 1999. *Industrialization and Health in Historical Perspective.* Historical Paper no. 118, August. Cambridge, MA: National Bureau of Economic Research.

———. 2001. *Health and Nutrition in the Pre-industrial Era: Insights from a Millennium of Average Heights in Northern Europe.* NBER Working Paper no. W 8542, October. Cambridge, MA: National Bureau of Economic Research.

Steckel, R. H., and Floud, R., eds. 1997. *Health and Welfare during Industrialization.* Chicago: University of Chicago Press.

Steensgaard, N. 1978. The Seventeenth-Century Crisis. In Parker and Smith 1978a, 26–56.

Stein, Burton. 1982. Towns and Cities: The Far South. In Raychaudhuri and Habib 1982, 452–57.

Stein, B., and Subrahmanyam, S., ed. 1996. *Institutions and Economic Change in South Asia.* London: OUP.

Stein, Eleanor. 2003. The Construction of an Enemy. *MR* 55(3): 125–29.

Stern, Vivien. 1998. *A Sin against the Future: Imprisonment in the World.* Boston: Northeastern University Press.

Steuart, J. 1767/1966. *An Inquiry into the Principles of Political Economy*; abridged and ed. A. S. Skinner, in 2 vols. London: Oliver & Boyd.

Stiglitz, J. E. 2002. *Globalization and Its Discontents.* London: Allen Lane.

Stille, A. 2003. Italy: The Family Business. *NYRB*, L(15), 9 October, 23–25.

Stocking, Jr., G. W. 1987. *Victorian Anthropology.* New York: The Free Press.

Stone, L., and Stone, J. C. Fawtier. 1984. *An Open Elite? England, Fifteen Forty to Eighteen Eighty.* London: OUP.

Subrahmanyam, S. 1991/1994. Precious Metal Flows and Prices in Western and

Southern Asia, 1500–1750: Some Comparative and Conjunctural Aspects. *Studies in History*; reprinted in Subrahmanyam 1994a, 186–218.

——, ed. 1994a. *Money and the Market in India 1100–1700*. Delhi: OUP.

——. 1994b. Introduction. In Subrahmanyam 1994a, 1–56.

——. 1997. *The Career and Legend of Vasco Da Gama*. London: CUP.

Sugarman, D., and Warrington, R. 1996. Land Law, Citizenship, and the Invention of "Englishness": The Strange World of the Equity of Redemption. In Brewer and Staves 1996, 111–43.

Sugihara, Kaoru. 1996. *The European Miracle and the East Asian Miracle—Towards a New Global Economic History.* rru.worldbank.org/psdforum/documents/sugihara .pdf.

——. 2004. *The State and the Industrious Revolution in Tokugawa Japan.* Working Paper No. 02/04, Graduate School of Economics, Osaka University, February.

Sukhatme, P. V. 1978. Assessment of Adequacy of Diets at Different Income Levels. *EPW* 13(31–33), Special number, August, 1373–84.

Sulston, J. 2001. Genome for the People. Summary of Sulston's Chatham Lecture, Trinity College, Oxford, as reported in *The Statesman* (Calcutta), 29 October.

Sutherland, G. 1990. Education. In Thompson 1990. Vol. 3, pp. 119–69.

Symonds, R. 1986. *Oxford and Empire: The Last Lost Cause?* London: OUP.

Szreter, S. 1988. The Importance of Social Intervention in Britain's Mortality Decline ca. 1850–1914: A Re-Interpretation of the Role of Public Health. *Social History of Medicine* 1(1): 1–37.

——. 1994. Mortality in England in the Eighteenth and Nineteenth Centuries: A Reply to Sumit Guha. *Social History of Medicine* 7:269–82.

——. 1996. *Fertility, Class and Gender in Britain 1860–1940*. London: CUP.

——. 1997. Economic Growth, Disruption, Deprivation, Disease and Death: On the Politics of Public Health for Development. *PDR* 23:693–778.

Szreter, S., and Mooney, G. 1998. Urbanization, Mortality, and the Standard of Living Debate: New Estimates of the Expectation of Life at Birth in Nineteenth-Century British Cities. *EHR* 51(1): 84–117.

Tagore, R. N. 1901/1941. *Naibedya* (in Bangla); reprinted in *Rabindra–Rachanabali* (Collected Works of Rabindranath Tagore). Vol. 8. Calcutta: Visva-Bharati, 3–75.

——. 1914/1994. *One Hundred Poems of Kabir*, transl. Rabindranath Tagore, London; reprinted in Tagore 1994, 487–540.

——. 1994a. *The English Writings of Rabindranath Tagore*. Vol. 1, *Poems*, ed. by S. K. Das. New Delhi: Sahitya Akademi.

——. 1994b. *The English Writings of Rabindranath Tagore*. Vol. 2, *Plays, Stories, Essays*, ed. by S. K. Das. New Delhi: Sahitya Akademi.

Tanner, J. M. 1981. *A History of the Study of Human Growth*. London: CUP.

——. 1998. A Brief History of the Study of Human Growth. In Ulijaszek, Johnston, and Preece 1998, 1–8.

Taylor, A. J. P. 1954. *The Struggle for Mastery in Europe 1848–1918*. London: Clarendon Press.

TePaske, J. J., and Klein, H. S. 1981. The Seventeenth-Century Crisis in New Spain:

Myth or Reality? *P&P*, no. 90:116–35.

Thomas, B. 1954. *Migration and Economic Growth*. London: CUP.

———. 1968. Migration and International Investment. In Hall 1968, 45–54

Thomas, P. J. 1926. *Mercantilism and East India Trade*. London: Macmillan.

Thompson, Dorothy. 1984. *The Chartists: Popular Politics in the Industrial Revolution*. New York: Pantheon Books.

Thompson, E. P. 1967/1991. Time, Work-Discipline, and Industrial Capitalism. *P&P*, no. 38. Reprinted in Thompson 1991, 352–403.

———. 1977. *Whigs and Hunters: The Origins of the Black Act*, revised edition. Harmondsworth: Penguin.

———. 1991. *Customs in Common*. London: Merlin Press.

Thompson, F. M. L. 1990. *The Cambridge Social History of Britain 1750–1950*, vols. 1–3. London: CUP.

Thussu, D. K., and Freedman, D. 2003. *War and the Media: Reporting Conflict 24/7*. New Delhi: Sage.

Tilly, Louise A., and Scott, Joan W. 1978. *Women, Work and Family*. New York: Holt, Rinehart & Winston.

Tinker, H. 1974. *A New System of Slavery: The Export of Indian Labour Overseas 1830–1920*. London: OUP.

Tocqueville, A. de. 1848/1964. *Democracy in America*. Vol. 1, 12th edition; English translation reprinted and ed. P. Bradley. Bombay: Popular Prakashan.

———. 1856/1988. *The Ancien Regime*, translated from the French by J. Bonner. London: J. M. Dent.

Tracy, J. D. ed. 1990. *The Rise of Merchant Empires*. London: CUP.

Traill, Catherine Parr. 1836/1989. *The Backwoods of Canada: Being Letters from an Emigrant Officer, Illustrative of the Domestic Economy of British America*; reprinted. Toronto: McCleland & Stewart.

Trigger, B. G., and Washburn, W. E., eds. 1996. *The Cambridge History of the Native Peoples of the Americas: North America*, part 1. Vol. 1. London: CUP.

Tsuru, S. 1993. *Japan's Capitalism: Creative Defeat and Beyond*. London: CUP.

Tucker, J. 1774. *Four Tracts on Political and Commercial Subjects*, second edition. Gloucester and London.

Ulijaszek, S. J., Johnston, F. E., and Preece, M. A., eds. 1998. *The Cambridge Encyclopaedia of Growth and Development*. London: CUP.

UNCTAD. 1997. *Trade and Development Report 1997*. Geneva: United Nations Conference on Trade and Development.

———. 1998. *Trade and Development Report 1998*. Geneva: United Nations Conference on Trade and Development.

———. 1999. *The Least Developed Counties 1999 Report*. New York: United Nations.

———. 2002a. *The Least Developed Counties Report 2002: Escaping the Poverty Trap*. New York: United Nations.

———. 2002b. *World Investment Report 2002*. New York: United Nations.

———. 2003. *Trade and Development Report 2003*. Geneva: United Nations Conference on Trade and Development.

UNDP. 1999. *Human Development Report 1999*. New York: OUP for the United Nations Development Program.

UNICEF. 2003. *The State of the World's Children 2003*. New York: UNICEF.

Valencia, R. A., and Suzuki, L. A., eds. 2001. *Intelligence Testing and Minority Students: Foundations, Performance Factors, and Assessment Issues*. Thousand Oaks, CA: Sage.

Vallin, J. 1991. Mortality in Europe from 1720 to 1914: Long-Term Trends and Changes in Patterns by Age and Sex. In Schofield, Reher, and Bideau 1991, 38–67.

Van de Valle, E. 1979. France. In W. R. Lee 1979, 123–43.

Van der Linden, M. 1997. Marx and Engels, Dutch Marxism and the "Modern Capitalist Nation of the Seventeenth Century." *Science and Society* 61(2) Summer: 161–92.

Van Zanden, J. L. 1993. *The Rise and Decline of Holland's Economy: Merchant Capitalism and the Labour Market*. Manchester: Manchester University Press.

———. 1994. *The Transformation of European Agriculture in the Nineteenth Century: The Case of the Netherlands*. Amsterdam: VU Uitgeverij.

———. 1997. Do We Need a Theory of Merchant Capital? *Review* 20(2): 255–67.

———. 1998. Did Holland's Golden Age Breed Inequality? In Soltow and Van Zanden 1998, chapter 3.

———. 2003. *The Different Faces of Dutch Colonialism and Patterns of Economic Development in Java, 1800–1913*. www.iisg.nl/research/jvz.colonialism.pdf (accessed 1 December 2003).

Varadarajan, S, ed. 2002. *Gujarat: The Making of a Tragedy*. New Delhi: Penguin India.

Vatuk, S. 2002. Older Women, Past and Present, in an Indian Muslim Family. In Patel, Bagchi, and Raj 2002, 247–63.

Vilar, P. 1956. Problems of the Formation of Capitalism. *P&P*, no. 10:15–38.

Vincent, D. 1989. *Literacy and Popular Culture: England 1750–1914*. London: CUP.

———. 2003. Literacy. *Victorian Studies* 45(3): 405–32.

Viner, J. 1948/1969. Power versus Plenty as Objectives of Foreign Policy in the Seventeenth and Eighteenth Centuries. *World Politics*. Vol. 1; reprinted in Coleman 1969, 61–91.

Visaria, L., and Visaria, P. 1983. Population (1757–1947). In Kumar and Desai 1983, 463–532.

Vitoria, Francisco de. 1991. *Political Writings*, ed. A. Pagden and J. Lawrence. London: CUP.

Vlastos, Stephen. 1986. *Peasant Protests and Uprisings in Tokugawa Japan*. Berkeley: University of California Press.

Wade, P. 1999. Blacks and Indians in Latin America. In Appiah and Gates 1999, 1127–32.

Wakefield, E. G. 1849. *A View of the Art of Colonization*. London: J. W. Parker.

Wakeman, F. 1985. *The Great Enterprise: The Manchu Reconstruction of Imperial Order in Seventeenth-Century China*. 2 vols. Berkeley: University of California Press.

Walker, Brett L. 1999. The Early Modern Japanese State and Ainu Vaccinations. Redefining the Body Politic. *P&P*, no. 163:121–60.

———. 2001. Commercial Growth and Environmental Change in Early Modern

Japan: Hachinhohe's Wild Boar Famine of 1749. *JAS* 60(2): 329–51.

Wallerstein, I. 1974. *The Modern World-System*. Vol. 1, *Capitalist Agriculture and the Origins of the European World-Economy in the Sixteenth Century*. New York: Academic Press.

———. 1980. *The Modern World-System*. Vol. 2, *Mercantilism and the Consolidation of the European World-Economy 1600–1750*. New York: Academic Press.

———. 1995. *Historical Capitalism with Capitalist Civilization*. London: Verso.

———. 1999. Frank Proves the European Miracle. *Review* 22(3): 355–91.

Ward, J. R. 1978. The Profitability of Sugar Planting in the British West Indies. *EHR* 3:197–213.

Washbrook, D. 1981. Law, State and Agrarian Society in Colonial India. *MAS* 15(3): 649–721.

———. 1997. From Comparative Sociology to Global History: Britain and India in the Pre-History of Modernity. *Journal of the Economic and Social History of the Orient* 40(4): 410–43.

Watanabe, S. 1987. On Socio-Institutional Conditions of Japan's Modernization. *Political Economy, Studies in the Surplus Approach* 3(2): 181–200.

Watson, I. B. 1980. Fortifications and the "Idea" of Force in Early English East India Company Relations with India. *P&P*, no. 88 (August): 70–87.

Weatherill, Lorna. 1988. *Consumer Behaviour and Material Culture in Britain 1660–1760*. London: Routledge.

———. 1993. The Meaning of Consumer Behaviour in Late Seventeenth- and Early Eighteenth-Century England. In Brewer and Porter 1993, 206–27.

Weber, E. 1976. *Peasants into Frenchmen: The Modernization of Rural France, 1870–1914*. Stanford, CA: Stanford University Press.

Weir, D. R. 1997. Economic Welfare and Physical Well-Being in France, 1750–1990. In Steckel and Floud 1997, 161–200.

Wernham, R. B., ed. 1968. *The New Cambridge Modern History*. Vol. 3, *The Counter-Reformation and Price Revolution*. London: CUP.

West, E. G. 1978/1985. Literacy and the Industrial Revolution. *HER* 31:369–83; reprinted in Mokyr 1985, 227–40.

Whitcombe, E. 1972. *Agrarian Conditions of Northern India*. Vol. 1. Berkeley: University of California Press.

———. 1995. The Environmental Costs of Irrigation in British India: Waterlogging, Salinity and Malaria. In Arnold and Guha 1995, 237–59.

White, Matthew. 2004. Statistics of Deaths in War. http://users.erols.com/mwhite28/warstat1.htm (accessed 12 October 2004).

Wilkins, Mira. 1970. *The Emergence of Multinational Enterprise: American Enterprise Abroad from the Colonial Era to 1914*. London: HUP.

———. 1974. *The Maturing of Multinational Enterprise: American Business Abroad from 1914 to 1970*. London: HUP.

Will, Pierre-Etienne. 1990. *Bureaucracy and Famine in Eighteenth Century China*, transl. E. Foster from the French. Stanford, CA: Stanford University Press.

Will, Pierre-Etienne, and Wong, R. Bin. 1981. *Nourish the People: The State Civilian*

Granary System in China, 1650–1850. Ann Arbor: University of Michigan Press.

Williams, E. N. 1972. *The Ancien Regime in Europe: Government and Society in the Major States 1648–1789.* Harmondsworth: Penguin.

Williams, T. H. 1981. *The History of American Wars: From 1745 to 1918.* New York: Knopf.

Williams, Naomi, and Galley, Chris. 1995. Urban-Rural Differentials in Infant Mortality in Victorian England. *PS* 49:401–20.

Williamson, J. G. 1989. The Constraints on Industrialization: Some Lessons from the First Industrial Revolution. In Williamson and Panchamukhi 1989, 85–105.

Williamson, J. G., and Panchamukhi, V. R., eds. 1989. *The Balance between Industry and Agriculture in Economic Development.* London: Macmillan.

Wilson, C. 1939. The Economic Decline of the Netherlands. *EHR,* IX (2), 111–27.

———. 1965. *England's Apprenticeship 1607–1763.* London: Longmans.

Wilson, C., and Parker, G., eds. 1980. *An Introduction to the Sources of European Economic History, 1500–1800.* London: Methuen.

Wilson, T. W. , and Grim, C. E. 1992. The Possible Relationship between the Trans-Atlantic Slave Trade and Hypertension in Blacks Today. In Inikori and Engerman 1992, 339–60.

Winegarden, C. R., and Murray, J. E. 1998. The Contributions of Early Health-Insurance Programs to Mortality Declines in Pre-World War I Europe: Evidence from Fixed-Effects Models. *EEH* 35(4): 431–46.

Wittfogel, K. A. 1957. *Oriental Despotism: A Comparative Study of Total Power.* New Haven, CT: Yale University Press.

Wolf, E. R. 1982. *Europe and the People without History.* Berkeley, CA: University of California Press.

Wolfe, M., ed. 1972. *The Economic Causes of Imperialism.* London: John Wiley.

Wong, R. Bin. 1997. *China Transformed: Historical Change and the Limits of European Experience.* Ithaca and London: Cornell University Press.

———. 2002. The Search for European Differences and Domination in the Early Modern World: A View from Asia. *AHR* 107(2): 447–69.

Woodruff, W. 1966. *Impact of Western Man: A Study of Europe's Role in the World Economy, 1750–1960.* London: Macmillan.

Woods, R. I., Watterson, P. A., and Woodward, J. H. 1988. The Causes of Rapid Infant Mortality Decline in England and Wales, 1861–1921, Part I. *PS* 42(3): 343–66.

World Bank. 2004. *World Development Report 2005.* Oxford: OUP for the World Bank.

WRI. 2004. *Climate Analysis Indicators Tool, Version 2.0.* Washington, DC: World Resources Institute. http://cait.wri.org.

Wrightson, K. 1982. *English Society 1580–1680.* London: Hutchinson.

Wrigley, E. A., and Schofield, R. S. 1981/1989. *The Population History of England 1541–1871,* 2nd edition. London: CUP.

Wu, Harry X. 2002. How Fast Has Chinese Industry Grown? Measuring Real Output of Chinese Industry, 1949–97. *Review of Industry and Wealth,* series 48, no. 2.

Xinzu, Gao, Shimin, Wu, Yunggong, Hu, and Ruizen Cha. 1962/1996. *Japanese Im-*

perialism and the Massacre in Nanjing; translated from the Chinese by Robert Gray, Vancouver, Canada. www.cnd.org/njmassacre/njm-trans (accessed 12 October 2004).

Yamamura, K. 1985. Samurai Income and Demographic Change: The Genealogies of Tokugawa Bannermen. In Hanley and Wolff 1985, 62–80.

——. ed. 1997. *The Economic Emergence of Modern Japan*. London: CUP.

Yasuba, Y. 1986. Standard of Living in Japan before Industrialization: From What Level Did Japan Begin? A Comment. *JEH* 46(1): 217–24.

Yates, M. D. 2001. The "New" Economy and the Labour Movement. *MR* 52(11): 29–42.

Yolton, J. W. 1985. *Locke: An Introduction*. Oxford: Blackwell.

Zhao, Zhongwei. 1997a. Long-Term Mortality Patterns in Chinese History: Evidence from a Recorded Clan Population. *PS* 51(2): 117–27.

——. 1997b. Deliberate Birth Control under a High Fertility Regime: Reproductive Behavior in China before 1870. *PDR* 23(4): 727–67.

Zimmermann, W. 2002. *First Great Triumph: How Five Americans Made Their Country a World Power*. New York: Farrar, Straus, & Giroux.

Index

Adam, W., 156
Adorno, Theodor, 40
Adrian IV (pope), 209
Afghanistan, xix, 253, 294–95, 332
Africa, xii, 11, 60, 255, 268–69, 289;
    European scramble for, 213–14; Sub-
    Saharan, 18, 305–6. *See also* slave
    trade, Sudan, transatlantic
African Americans: differential in living
    standards with whites, 118, 204–7,
    306, 323–24; U.S. policy towards,
    204–5. *See also* Du Bois, W. E. B.
Africans, 10, 198–200
Alcock, Rutherford, 189
Alexander VI (pope), 209
Ali, Muhammad, 246
Allen, R. C., 108
Allende, Salvador, 274
Amerindians, 10, 41, 195–98, 211–12;
    in Canada and the United States,
    221–26
Anglo-Portuguese trade treaty, 260–61
anti-systemic struggles: in Ireland,
    277n5; for self-determination,
    272–73; for socialism, 272, 279,
    281–82
Arabo-Persian civilization (scholars,
    texts), 3, 22, 121

Arabs, 22–23, 282–83
Arafat, Yasser, 303n2
Aragon, 56–58
Aral Sea, 331
Arendt, Hanna, 3
Argentina: British investment in, 260;
    economic crisis in, 320–21
Aristotle, 3–5, 41, 121
arms race, 275, 276–77
Asia, xii, xv, 10, 11, 289. *See also* East
    Asia; *individual Asian countries*
Asian financial crisis, 328
Atkinson, F. J., 245
atomic bombs: deaths from, 291;
    dropped on Japan, 286, 291; U.S.
    threats during Korean War, 290n3
axial ages of capitalism, xvi–xvii, 174

Bacon, Francis, 39
Bagehot, Walter, 243, 253
Bairoch, P., 86
Banerjee, Debdas, 230
Banister, Judith, 160
Barcelona, 58–59
Beghahn, V. R., 280–81
Bengal, 146–48, 149–50, 152, 213, 230,
    240, 255
Berlusconi, Silvio, 324, 325n4

Bharatiya Janata Party (BJP), 324
bin Laden, Osama, xix, 294
biological well-being, xvi–xvii, 7–8; in
  Australia, Canada, and United States,
  110–11; contribution of colonies to
  European improvement, 85–86; in
  developing countries, 18, 305–7,
  315–18, 331; in England, 103–8;
  measurement, 13–15; in Sweden,
  109–10
Blackburn, R., 201
Blair, Tony, xx
Bodin, Jean, 56, 60
body mass index (BMI), 16–17, 20n5
Bombay, 240
Borah, W., 196
Bose, Jagadis Chandra, 48
Bray, Francesca, 137
Bright, John, 129
Brüning, Heinrich, 281
Burt, Cyril (IQ fraud), 302
Bush, George H. W., 295–96
Bush, George W., xx, 294, 330
Boxer Rebellion, 251–52; and sacking
  of Beijing, 252
Brazil: debt crisis in, 320; economic
  growth in, 313; famine in, 260–64
Brezhnev, Leonid, 294
Britain, xiii, xv, 25, 156, 209, 274–81.
  See also Industrial Revolution
Brzezinski, Zbigniew, 295
Buchenwald, 254

Canary Islands, 209
Cantillon, Richard, 56
Canudos (Brazil), 263
Cao Xueqin, 140–41
capitalism: and armed conflict, xii–xv,
  35–37; and centralization, xx–xxi,
  38; and conflicts with democracy and
  equality, xxi–xxii; and control of
  labor (including slavery), 41–43; and
  counterattack by, xix–xx; crony,
  325n3; environment, 176, 264,
  264n3; expansionary means and

consequences, 39–43, 71–72;
  gentlemanly, 45–46; golden age of,
  xviii–xix, 307
capitalism, ideologies of: civilizing
  mission, xx, 44–47, 48–49;
  Malthusianism, xx–xxi; nationalism,
  43–48; racism, xx; Social
  Darwinism, xx–xxi
capitalist competition: Defoe on, 35–36;
  Marx and Engels on, 38–39; Steuart
  on, 37; and support by states, xiv;
  Tocqueville on, 37
capitalist expansion and environment,
  176, 264, 264n3
Caribbean, xii, 160, 196
Carr-Saunders, A., 78
caste system in British India, 26
Castile, xiii, 56–60
Catalonia, 57–59; revolts against the
  Spanish king, 58, 59
Catholicism, 55, 58, 123–24. *See also*
  Protestantism
Central Intelligence Agency, U.S. (CIA),
  294
Charles V (Holy Roman emperor), xiii
Charles XI (of Sweden), 64–65
Charles XII (of Sweden), 66
Chattopadhyay, R., 153
Chaudhury, S., 147
Chi'h Ch'ao-ting, 136
child labor in England, 127, 128–29
Chile, 274, 289
China, xv, 135–45, 156, 158–62,
  331–32; administrative system since
  the Han dynasty, 136; and deaths in
  China-Japan war, 287; ever-normal
  granaries and food security, 141–42,
  161; famine, 161, 249–52; life
  expectancy, 138; literacy, 139–40;
  macro regions, 136; manufactures
  since ancient times, 136–37;
  population estimates, 161, 166n4;
  population growth, 138; population
  loss, 250; printing and dissemination
  of printed books in, 140;

technological innovations in, 136.
See also gender discrimination;
World War II

China, People's Republic of, and the
mass-education movement, 139

China under the Ming dynasty, 136–37,
140, 142

China under the Qing dynasty, 89,
136–38, 140, 143, 168, 190; and
crop diversification and agricultural
growth, 137–38, 143–44; and
education, 139–41; and female
infanticide, 138; and fertility
control, 138; and growth in
Jiangnan 137; and health and
hygiene, 144; and life expectancy,
138; and literacy, 139–40; and
manufactures, 135–36; and
silviculture, sericulture, and
environment, 160–61; and the
position of women, 140–41; and
roots of decay, 142–43

China under the Song dynasty: and
diffusion of printed books, 140

Christian, 22

Christianization, 209

Churchill, Winston, 291

civilizing mission, xvi, xx , 44–45,
69–71, 76n1; and Castiglione and
Della Casa on etiquette, 70; and
contradictions, 48–49; Elias on,
69–70, 221; and Elyot on etiquette,
45; and Locke on education, 70

civilizing mission and racialization,
209–28; and Amerindians, 221–25,
228n1; and Khoikhoi, 227; and
Maoris, 228; and San, 227; and
Tasmanians, 226–27; and Xhosas,
228

civilizing mission in Africa, 219–20

civilizing mission in India, 214–18

Clingingsmith, D. and J. G. Williamson,
153–54

Cold War, 289, 290n3, 291–92; war
deaths after end of, 329

Colebrooke, H. T., 152

colonialism, 9, 249–64

Columbus, Christopher, 195–96

communism, 272, 274, 281–82, 289,
292–93

Comte, Auguste, 262

Confucius, 3

Conselheiro, Antonio, 263

Cook, S., 196

"corporate feudalism," 322

Costa, Dora L., 110

Cressy, D., 122, 124–25

Cromer, Lord (Evelyn Baring), 218

Crystal Palace exhibition, 268

Counter-Reformation, 122–26, 132

Cuba, 83, 261, 268–69

culture industry, 40

Cuvier, Georges, 213

Darwin, Charles, 213

Dasgupta, P., 14–15

Davidson, Basil, 200

Davis, Kingsley, 77

Davis, Mike, 142

Davis, Natalie Zemon, 127

Davis, Ralph, 93

democracy: in Britain, Scandinavia, and
United States, 322–23; in India,
323–24; in Italy, 323–24, 325n4;
participatory, 333; in post-Soviet
Russia, 324–25; weakening of,
322–24; in Weimar, Germany,
280–82

Defoe, Daniel, 35–36, 39

de Gaulle, Charles, 285

deindustrialization, 152–53

Denevan, W. M., 198

development, axial ages of, xvi–xvii,
174

De Vries, Jan, 71–72, 93, 180, 95, 125

Dickens, Theodore, 217

Digby, William, 255

Diggers and Levelers, 5

Dimitrov, 277n6

Disraeli, Benjamin, 253

Drabble, J. H., 246
Dream of the Red Chamber, The (Cao
   Xueqin), 140–41
Dubois, Abbé, on Hindus, 46
Du Bois, W. E. B., on Black
   Reconstruction, 204–5
Dumont, Louis, 5
Dutch East India Company (VOC), 147
Dutt, R. C., 245, 255

East Asia: decline in IMRs, 313–14;
   and economic growth, 308–9,
   312–13; fertility decline, 309,
   313–14; historians of, xv, 180.
   See also land reforms, life
   expectancy
East India Company (English), 106,
   147
Egypt, xvi, 246–47, 272–73
Einstein, Albert, 336
Elizabeth I (of England), xiii
El Niño (ENSO), 250, 255, 262
Elvin, Mark, 160, 162
England. *See* Britain
environment, 7–9; and capitalism, 8–9;
   before colonialism, in China, India,
   158–60; under colonialism and
   imperialism, in China and India
   20n2, 162, 163–65; in contemporary
   China, 160, 332
environmental determinism, in
   Hippocrates, and in Jones, 29–31
Erdosy, G., 8, 162–63
Eurocentrism in history, xxiii, 10, 12,
   21–23, 28–31, 245; critique of,
   xiv–xv, 21–32, 69, 114–15, 173–77
Europe: famine, 61, 71–72, 79, 85;
   genocide by the Nazis, 282–84;
   literacy, 122–32; and merchant
   capitalism, 74–76; plague in, 79;
   slave trade, 198–99; social insurance
   and health improvement, 114;
   population growth, 78–79
European, Asian, and World Social
   Forums, 332

European Enlightenment, 47, 132,
   213–14
European feudalism, 54, 89
European miracle: misdated, xiii–iv, 24,
   114; and private property rights,
   24–26; wrongly conceived, xiv–xv,
   21–24; wrongly explained, xiii–xiv,
   28–32
European migration: scale of, 115–17;
   effects of, 116–18, 176–77, 228
European Union, 299

Fairbank, J. K., E. O. Reischauer, and
   A. M. Craig, 250
famines: in Brazil, 261–64; in China,
   161, 249–52; in Ethiopia and Eritrea,
   315–18; in Europe, 61, 71–72, 79,
   85; and globalization, 316; in India,
   77, 253–55; protocapitalist, colonial,
   anti-systemic, and globalization,
   315–16; in Tokugawa Japan, 188–89;
   during the twentieth century, 314–18;
   in the Ukraine, 315
Fanon, Frantz, 221
fascism, 273–75, 277n6, 287–88. *See
   also* Nazism
Ferdinand and Isabella (of Spain), 55
   See also indentured labor
financial liberalization, 319–21, 323,
   325n3, 328; and financial crisis, 320;
   and fraud (Enron, Global Crossing,
   and WorldCom), 321; and Latin
   America, 320–21
Fogel, R. W., 106
Foucault, Michel, xv
France, 60–63, 127–30, 273, 275–76,
   279–80, 284–86, 287; and its
   common people under Louis XIV,
   60–63; and elementary education,
   129–31
Franck, James, 291
Frank, A. G., 11
freedom: civil, under capitalism, 41; in
   imperial Sweden, 65–66; and literacy
   as constitutive and instrumental

aspect of, 123; suppressed by imperialists, 336

free markets, and capitalism, xi–xii, 24–26, 35–36; and human freedom, xii–xiii, 36–37, 41–42

Gawthrop, R., 131
gender discrimination: in employment, 328–29; in England, 46, 105; as a marker, xii–xiii; and nationalism in India, 47; and sex ratios in China, India, South Korea, Taiwan, 331–32
General Agreement on Trade in Services (GATS), 307
genocide: in China by the Japanese aggressors, 287; in Europe by the Nazis, 282–84; motives for, 288; Puma on, 198; in Spanish America, 195–98; in South Africa, 227–28; in Tasmania, 226–27; in the twentieth century, 284, 293, 295–97; in United States and Canada, 224–26
Germany, 63, 79, 81–82, 84, 275–76; and crumbling civilization, 283–84; elementary education in, 132, 280–84; and Nazi Germany, 281–84, 291n1; and Norbert Elias, 283; post–World War I, 280–81
Gilboy, Elizabeth, 108
Glass-Steagall Act, 319
globalization famines, 316. *See also* neoliberalism
gold standard, 254
Goldstone, J., 108
good life, conception of; Aristotle on, 4–5, 121; Kang Youwei on, 5–6; literacy and longevity as components of, 6–8; Marx and Engels on, 6; Tagore on, 5. *See also* human development
Gopalan, C., 14
Goschen, George, 243
Greco-Roman civilization, xiii, 22–23
Grey, George, 227
Grove, Richard, 160

Guanches, 209
Guantánamo Bay, prisoners in, 328
Guha, Sumit, 113–14
Gulf Wars I and II, xix, 295–97; and legality, 327–28, 330
Guomindang, 292
Gustavus Adolphus (of Sweden), 63–64
Gutenberg, 123
Gypsies, 286–87

Habib, Irfan, 146–47, 148
Hamilton, Earl, 56
Hanley, Susan, 192
Hayami, Akira, and, Satomi Kurosu, 187
Hays, Mary, 105
Hegel, G. W. F., 22–23
height and biological well-being, 13–15, 193, 306; in Canada, 110; in England, 105–7; in Meiji Japan, 191, 193; in the preindustrial phase of developed countries, 193; in the United States, 110
Henry VII (of England), 68
Henry VIII (of England), 68
Henry of Navarre (of France), 61
Henry the Navigator (of Portugal), 44
Heston, A., 245
Hindenburg, Paul von, 279, 281
Hindu College, 48
Hindus, 46, 332
history, perspectives on: centered on human development, xii, 10–11, 19; development in East Asia, 11; Eurocentric, 10, 12; Marxist, xi, 10; world-system, xi, 10; Hitler, Adolf, 277n6, 281–82
HIV/AIDS, 332–33
Hobsbawm, E. J., 81, 108, 276
Hobson, J. A., 255, 270
Ho Chi Minh, 292
Home Charges (paid by India to British), 240, 254
Ho Ping-Ti, 250
Hopkins, Sheila, 108

human development: Aristotle on, 4–5;
    under capitalism, xi–xii, xxi;
    concepts and components,
    3–8,12–19; East Asia, 313; in
    Europe, 13, 65–66, 78–86, 103–8,
    123–28; growth, 4; non-European
    contribution, 86, 111–19; non-
    European upturn, 111–19; slave
    trade, xi
Human Development Reports (United
    Nations), 7, 18
hundis, 149
Hussein, Saddam, xix, 295–96, 334
Hussites, 5

Ilbert, Courtenay, 217
Imlah, A. H., 240
imperialism: and corporativism, 274;
    and fascism, 273–74, 277n6;
    ideologies of, 273–75; and legality,
    327–28; and nationalism, 272; and
    racism, 274–75; theories of, by
    Hobson, Hilferding, Luxemburg,
    Lenin, and Bukharin, 270–71
income growth in major regions since
    World War II, 307–9
indentured labor: Indian, Chinese, and
    Japanese, 202–4; mortality of,
    203–4; white, 202
India, xv–xvi, 321; and democracy,
    323–24; and environment after
    colonialism 20n2, 162, 163–65; and
    environment before colonialism,
    158–60; life expectancy, 77, 253–55;
    literacy, 255; population growth,
    77–78; real wages, 146, 152–53
Indian Association for Cultivation of
    Science, 48
India under British rule: caste system,
    26; civilizing mission, 214–18;
    decline in biological well-being,
    154–55; deindustrialization, 152–53;
    economic retrogression, 152–57;
    educational retrogression of, 156–57;
    environment, 255–58; estimates of

    British investment in, by Keynes,
        and Pandit, 234–35; expansion, 152;
        famines and deaths in, 252–56;
        Home Charges paid to Britain, 240,
        254; land tax in, 155; life
        expectancy, 155–56, 260–61; literacy
        in, 156; medicine and prophylaxis,
        258–59; Permanent Settlement, 257
India under Mughal rule, 145–51;
    agricultural growth in,146;
    commercialization of, 146, 149–50;
    consumption pattern of, 146–47;
    copper, gold and silver coins in, 150;
    craft production and exports of,147;
    fiscal policy of,148–49; foreign trade
    of, 146–47; income growth in, 147,
    151; monetization of, 149–50;
    peasant revolts in, 150–51;
    population growth in, 145–46; real
    wages in, 146, 152–53; silver influx
    and price change, 151; textile exports
    of, 147; urbanization of, 151
indirect rule under colonialism, 219;
    Lugard on, 219
Indonesia, 274
industrialization, 189, 152, 331
Industrial Revolution, xv–xvii, 11,
    91–92, 180; and the environment,
    8–9; and living standard in England,
    81–82, 102–7; and social
    reproduction of labor, 98–99; and use
    of non-renewable energy, 162, 335
industrious revolution, 24, 180
inequality in incomes and wealth,
    18–19, 323; during the Dutch golden
    age, 96
infant mortality rates (IMRs): in
    Belgium, 84; in Costa Rica, 83; in
    Cuba, 83; in Denmark,83; in East
    Asia, 313; in England, 83, 87n3; in
    France, 83, 101; in Iraq, 296; in
    Meiji Japan, 192; in Prussia, 83; in
    South Korea, 83; in Sweden, 83, 66,
    109; in the United States, 83
informal empire, 246, 269

instrumental reason, 283–84
Inter caetera (papal bull authorizing
    Spanish rule over the New World),
    209–10
interimperialist conflicts, 267–72, 277n2
International Labour Office (ILO) and
    decent work, 328
International Monetary Fund (IMF),
    310, 312, 332
Iran, xix, 294–95
Iraq, xix, 295–96, 332
Ireland, 209, 277n
Ireton, Henry, 69
"irrational exuberance" (Shiller), 320
Islamic terrorism, bogey of, 297
Israel, 297, 303n, 329
Italian city-states, 54–55
Italy, 53, 55

Jamaica, 261
Jampert, Carl Friedrich, 13
Japan: exceptionalism, 179–80; famine,
    188–89; genocide by, 287
Japan after Meiji restoration:
    industrialization, 189–91; militarism,
    189–90, 267–68; standard of living,
    191–93, 306; World War II , 284–85,
    287–88
Japan under Tokugawa rule:
    commercialization, 180, 183–86;
    economy and society, 181–89; export
    of silver from, 231; population
    growth, 180, 187–88; standard of
    living, 181, 187–88
Jenks, L. H., 234
Jews, 282–84, 286–87
Jiangnan (China), growth in
    productivity, 137–38
jingoism, 277n4
Johnson, P., 105–6
Jones, E. L., xiii, 12, 141
Judeo-Christian, 3, 23

Kennedy, Paul, 276
Kerala, 333

Keynes, John Maynard, 56, 234, 319
Khedive Ismail, 246
Khomeini, Ayatolla Ruhollah, 294
Kim (Kipling), 218
Kim Il Sung, 289
Kipling, Rudyard, 218
Komlos, J., 110
Korea, 190, 289
Krishnamurty, J., 153
Kroeber, A., 78
Kurosawa, 336

labor reproduction, 114–15; Brazil,
    263–64; overseas migration, 115–16
Landes, D. S., xiii, 12
land reforms: in East Asia, 312–13; in
    post–World War II Japan, 193
Laqueur, T., 127
Latin America, xii, 11, 246, 255, 289,
    300, 306, 313, 331; debt crisis and
    lost decade in, 311–12, 320–21
Lavely, W. 138
least developed countries and their
    income, 317
Lenin, V. I., 270
Li, Bozhong, 137, 160–61
Liebknecht, Karl, 279
life expectancy, 18, 81–82; of African
    Americans, 205–6; in Belgium, 84;
    in China, 138; in East Asia, 313; in
    England, 83–84, 103–4, 107; in
    France, 84; in Germany, 84; in India,
    255, 260; of indentured labor, 204;
    of peers of Britain, 103; in post-
    Soviet Russia, 324–25; of slaves in
    Trinidad, 113; of the Wang clan, 138
Lingnan (China), 159
literacy: of African Americans, 205–7;
    and the British industrial revolution,
    125–27; in China,139–40; in
    England, 106, 124–25; estimates,
    123–28,131; in Europe,122–32; in
    France, 127–28 in India, 255;
    measured by Schofield, 124–25;
    view of Mandeville,122

Louis XIV (of France), 61–62, 127
Lunn, P., 16
Luxemburg, Rosa, 270, 279
Lyall, Alfred, 218
Lytton, Lord, 253, 262

Macaulay, T. B., 215–16
Maddison, A., 78, 245
Maine, H. S., 217
Malthusianism, xx–xxi, 108
Manning, Patrick, on loss of African
    lives in slave trade, 200
Marks, R. B., 160
Maroon War of Jamaica, 201–2
Marshall Plan, 309
Marx, Karl, 38, 56, 297; *The Theories of
    Surplus Value*, 39
Marx, Karl and Frederick Engels, 3,
    336; on capitalist competition and
    expansion, 38–39; *The Communist
    Manifesto*, 38
Marxist perspective on history, 10
masculinity and the gentleman ruler,
    45–48; Elyot on, 45; and the imperial
    Englishwoman's attitude, 47
Massey, D., 115–16
Mauritius, 160
Mazumdar, Sucheta, 86, 137
McKendrick, N., 24
McKeown, Thomas, 102
McWilliams, W. C. and H. Piotrowski,
    286–87
media and the manufacture of consent,
    40, 302
merchant capital: and demographic
    crisis in the Netherlands, 94–96; and
    Dutch domination, 91–93; and
    European economic growth, 74–76;
    and the problem of supply of labor,
    90–92; and slave revolts, 69
mergers and acquisitions, 321
Mexico, xii, 56, 305–6, 320, 332
military-industrial complex, 267–68
Mill, James, 22–23, 213, 214–15,
    220n2, 220n3, 220n4

Mill, J. S., 213, 214–15, 220n4
Mokyr, J., 104, 106
Monroe Doctrine, 269
Montagu, Lady Mary Wortley, 86
Montesquieu, Baron de (Charles),
    213–14
Moreland, W. H., 77
Mossadegh, Mohammed, 295
Mote, F. W., 141
Mukherjee, Ashutosh, 48
Mukherjee, R. K., 146, 152–53
Mussolini, Benito, 273

Nanjing Massacre, 287
Naoroji, Dadabhai, 245
Napoleon (Bonaparte), 322
Nasser, Gamal Abdel, 294
NATO. *See* North Atlantic Treaty
    Organization
Nazism, 273, 280–87. *See also* fascism
Needham, Joseph, 136
neoliberalism: and environment,
    329–30, 335; and military order,
    333–34; resistance against, 332–33,
    335; and unemployment, 328–29
Netherlands: merchant capital and
    Smithian growth in, 91–93;
    contribution of surplus extracted
    from Indonesia to its economic
    growth, 97–98, 117–18
New Atlantis (Bacon), 39
Nicholas, S., 105–6
Nietzsche, Friederich, 132
North, Douglass, xiii, 12
North Atlantic Treaty Organization
    (NATO), 294
Nurkse, Ragnar, 234, 271
nutrition and health, 13–17, 105–7,
    306

Ó Grada, C., 106
oil and imperialist wars, 293–96
Olivares, Duke of, 59
Operation Iraqi Freedom, xx
Opium War, 249

Organization for Economic Cooperation and Development (OECD), 18–19, 307

Organization of Petroleum Exporting Countries (OPEC), 300–301, 311

Orientalism, 5, 27, 213, 220n2

Osborne, Anne, 160–61

Oshio Heihachiro, 188

Ottoman Empire, 269

Oxley, D., 105

Palestine, 329, 303n

Pandit, Y. S., 234–35

Parker, G., 72

Pasteur, Louis, 109

Pearl Harbor, 284, 287

peasants under European feudalism, Qing China, and Mughal India, 89–90

pension funds, 313–14

permanent settlement in British India, 257

Peru, xii, 56

Peter the Great (of Russia), 66

Phelps Brown, E. H., 108

Philip II (of Spain), 56, 58–60

Pinochet, General, 274

plantations: indentured labor, 202–4; slave-run, 199–200

Plato, 21–22

Poland, 286, 321, 331

Pollard, S., 242

Pomeranz, K., 137, 11

Popper, Karl, 21

population growth: in Belgium, 84; in China, 78–79, 138, 161, 166n4; in England, 79–80, 102–3, 105, 108; in France, 80, 101; in Germany, 81; in India, 77–78; in the Netherlands (Dutch Republic), 80; in western Europe, 78–79

Porto Alegre, 332, 333

Portugal, 44, 210, 260–61

poverty: France, 101; Olwen Hufton on, 101

Powell, Colin, 323

Pringle, Thomas, 227

Promised Land, The (Wajda), 39–40

property rights, common, 24

property rights, land: in China, 89; in England, 89; in Europe, 24–25; in India, 89–90

property rights, private: destroyed in India by European colonizers, 24–25; in India, before the British, 24

Protestantism, 55, 58, 60–61, 63, 122–24, 132

Putin, Vladimir, 325

Putnam, Robert, 324

racism, xii, xx, 213, 274–75

Radcliffe, Mary Anne, 105

Raman, C. V., 48

Rashoman (Kurosawa), 336

Rawski, Evelyn S., 140

Razzell, P., 87n3, 138

Reagan, Ronald, 311–12,

real wages: in Britain, 104, 108; in India, 146, 152–53; in Sweden, 66, 109–10; in the Netherlands, 96

Reformation, 121–26

revolutions: Bolshevik, 272, 282, 336; French, xiv, 69, 322, 336

Rhee, Syngman, 289

Rice, Condoleezza, 323

Rowe, W., 137

Rousseau, Jean-Jacques, 5, 213

Russia, 66, 190, 253, 269, 275, 321

Said, E. W., 27, 220n2

Said, Muhammad, 246

Salazar, Antonio, 274

Sanderson, M., 127

Sarkar, Mahendralal, 48

Saudi Arabia: and Islamic fundamentalism, 293–94; and U.S. geopolitical interests, 293–97

Sauer, C. O., 196

Schofield, R. S., 83, 106, 108

Schumpeter, J. A.: on innovations under capitalism, 38–39; on need for a precapitalist ruling class for capitalism, 45–46

Sen, Amartya, 113, 121

Sena, 5

Sharp, Granville, 202

Sher Shah Sur, 148

silver inflow, 56–57; into China, 137, 142; effects on prices, in Europe, 56–58; into Mughal India, 151; into Spain, and effect on common people, 57

Simon, Matthew, 234, 271

Simpson, L., 196

slavery: abolition, 202; of Africans, 198–202; of Amerindians, 196; Aristotle invoked in justification, 41–42, 197; contribution to European profit and nutrition, 201; Las Casas and Sepúlveda on, 197, 211–12, 220n2; revolts against, 201–3

slave labor vs. free peasants, 160

slave trade, internal: in Brazil and the United States, 199–200; in Europe, 198–99

slave trade, transatlantic: abolition of, 199, 201–2; on loss of African lives, 200; and volume and fluctuations, 198–200

smallpox vaccination, 86, 192

Smith, Adam, 38. *See also* Smithian economic growth

Smith, M. G., 200

Smith, Thomas C., 181–86

Smithian economic growth, 74–76, 89–93, 136–38; in Qing China, Mughal India, and Tokugawa Japan, 160, 180

social Darwinism, xix–xx, 40

Social Democrats, 272–73, 308

social insurance and health improvement in Europe, 114

social reproduction and proletarianization of labor, 90–94,
94–96; Marx on, 97–98; Van Zanden on, 91, 97–98

South Africa, 274, 276

Soviet Union (bloc), xviii, 284–89, 291–92, 294–97, 305, 315, 322. See also ...

Spanish Inquisition, 68

Spanish rule, over the New World (*Inter caetera*), 209–10

Spencer, Herbert, 262

Stackelberg, R., 286

standard of living in Britain, 104–7. *See also* biological well-being; life expectancy; real wages

St. Domingue (Haiti), 69, 261

Steckel, R. H., 15, 110, 193

Stephen, James Fitzjames, 217–18

Steuart, Sir James, 36–37

Straus, G., 131

structural adjustment policies, 302, 312

Sub-Saharan Africa. *See* Africa

Sudan, 296–97

Sugihara, Kaoru, 180

Suharto, General, 274

Sulston, John, 322

surplus extracted from colonies by imperial counties: and Braudel on its mechanism, 233–34; from Egypt, 246–47; G. Sutherland on, 129; from India and Burma, 239–42, 245; from Indonesia, 243–45; from Malaya, 246

Tagore, Rabindranath, 3, 5, 255, 336

Tainos, 196

Taiping Rebellion, xv, 161–62, 249–50

Talibans, 294

Temple, Richard, 253–54, 262; and Temple wage, 254

Temple, William, 68

Thatcher, Margaret, 312

Third World, xvii, 292, 311

Thirty Years War, 63, 79

Thomas, B., 112

Thomas, R. P., xiii, 12

Thompson, E. P., xv
Tocqueville, Alexis de, 5, 37–38
Tordesillas, treaty of, 210
trade and warfare: Asia, 167–68,
     170–71; Europe, 168–73
trade-related intellectual property rights
     (TRIPS), 307, 321–22
transnational corporations (TNCs), xviii,
     xx, 298–99, 301, 321–22
Tukaram, 5

uneven development, 305–7, 314
unequal interdependence and
     improvement in European living
     standards, 115–18
United Nations Development Program
     (UNDP). See *Human Development
     Reports*
United States: budget and current
     account deficits, 330; leader of
     capitalism, xiii, 112–13; infant
     mortality rates, 83; military
     expenditure and bases, 299–300,
     333–34; neoconservatives in, 335;
     postwar boom, 309–10; slave trade,
     199–200. *See also* democracy;
     genocide; U.S. imperialism; U.S.
     inmigration; U.S.-Korean War; U.S.-
     Vietnam war; World War I
urbanization, xiii, 103–4, 127; in the
     Dutch Republic, 94–95, 109; and
     fertility in Tokugawa Japan, 187–88;
     and health, 329; and longevity in
     Belgium, 84; and longevity in
     England, 104; in Sweden, 109–10
U.S. economy, challenges, 330
U.S. hegemony, 298–303; challenges
     against, 335
U.S. imperialism: and China, 292; and
     the Cold War, 292–96; and
     communism, 293–94; and Israel,
     303n2; and the Middle East, 294–96;
     and occupation of Texas, Cuba,
     Hawaii, and the Philippines, 268–69,
     277n2, 298; and Vietnam, 292–93

U.S. inmigration, 300; global army
     base, 299; labor oppression, 302–3;
     media, 302; military expenditure,
     299; military prowess, 300;
     transnational corporations, 298–99,
     301
U.S.-Korean war, 289, 290n, 292
U.S.-Vietnam war, 292–93, 296–97;
     death toll, 293

Vallin, J., 85
Van der Woude, Ad, 95, 125
Van Zanden, J. L., 91
Vasco da Gama, 55, 218
VOC. *See* Dutch East India Company
Versailles Treaty, 269, 279
Vitoria, Francisco de, 210
Voltaire, 68

Wajda, Andrez, 39–40
Wallerstein, Immanuel, 195
wars: of *ancien regime*, Europe, 60–63,
     71–74, 79; and common people, in
     Hapsburg Spain, 56–59; of the
     Dutch, 66–67, 93; and European
     absolutist states, 55–66; between
     Italian city-states, 54–55; during
     European feudalism, 54; between
     France and the other European
     powers, 61–63; of imperial Sweden,
     65–66, 72; between Spain and other
     European powers, 55–60, 93; of
     Sweden as an imperial aspirant,
     63–66. *See also* World War I; World
     War II
wars and their finance: in *ancien
     regime*, Spain, 56–57; and Dutch
     financing of other monarchs' wars,
     96; in imperial Sweden, 64
Watanabe, S., 189
Watterson, P. A., 113
weapons of mass destruction, 334
West, E.G., 127
Whitney, Eli, 268
Wilberforce, William, 202

Wilhelm II (of Germany), 251
Willcox, W., 78
Williams, T. H., 277n2
Winstanley, Gerrard, 69
Wong, R. Bin, 137, 138, 143, 180
Woodruff, W., 234
Woods, R. I., 113
Woodward, J. H., 113
workers and their struggles, 104–6,
    280–82, 322–23; and state action,
    111–12
World Bank, 310, 332
World Trade Center (9/11), xix, 294,
    324
World Trade Organization (WTO), 302,
    303, 332, 334–35
World War I: death toll, 276; differential
    capacity of major combatants, 275;
    effect of German defeat, 279–80;
    military expenditures by major

powers, 275; the United States in,
    275–76
World War II: and the atom bomb, 291;
    China in, 285, 286–87;
    consequences, 292; death toll,
    286–87; economic growth
    differentials after, 307–21, 320–21;
    Germany in, 284–86; Japan in,
    284–85, 287–88; Soviet Union in,
    285–87
Wrigley, E. A., 83, 108
Wycliffe, John, 5

Xhosa, 3, 5, 227

Yasuba, Y., 192
Yeltsin, Boris, 324
Yosef, Rabbi Ovadia, 393n2

Zapatistas, 332

About the Author

Amiya Kumar Bagchi was educated at Presidency College, Calcutta, and Trinity College, Cambridge. He is currently Professor and Director, Institute of Development Studies, Kolkata. He has taught and researched at Presidency College (Calcutta), University of Cambridge, University of Bristol, Cornell University, Roskilde University (Denmark), Trent University (Canada), Centre for Studies in Social Sciences (Calcutta), and Maison des Sciences de L'Homme (Paris), and acted as consultant to the ILO and United Nations. His books include *Private Investment in India, 1900-1939* (1972); *The Political Economy of Underdevelopment* (1982); a four-volume history of the State Bank of India, India's oldest and largest bank; and *Capital and Labour Redefined* (2002). He has edited books on democracy and development, globalization and its problems, and India's industrial growth and organization. He regularly joins debates on economic and social policies in developing countries.